The Daycare Handbook

A Parents' Guide to Finding and Keeping Quality Daycare in Canada

The Daycare Handbook

A Parents' Guide to Finding and Keeping
Quality Daycare in Canada

by

Barbara Kaiser

and

Judy Sklar Rasminsky

LITTLE, BROWN & COMPANY (CANADA) LIMITED
BOSTON ◆ LONDON ◆ TORONTO

Canadian Cataloguing in Publication Data
Kaiser, Barbara
The daycare handbook

Includes bibliographical references and index.
ISBN 0-316-48216-1

1. Day care centers – Canada.   2. Family day care –
Canada.   3. School-age child care – Canada.
I. Rasminsky, Judy Sklar.   II. Title.

HV861.C3K34 1991   362.7'12'0971   C91-093653-6

Cover design: Adams + Assoc.
Interior design and typesetting: Pixel Graphics
Printed and bound in Canada by Gagné Printing.

Little, Brown & Company (Canada) Limited
146 Davenport Road, Toronto, Ontario Canada

For Sonya, Jessika, Abigail and Maita,
who made us realize how important good daycare is

CONTENTS

APPENDICES

ACKNOWLEDGEMENTS

A great many people helped make this book a reality—too many for us to thank everyone individually. The parents and staff of Garderie Narnia, now and in the past, head our list: their experiences—their problems, their solutions—are the foundation of everything we have written. Among these, Liane Beauchesne deserves special mention.

Early childhood educators, researchers and administrators at other places made an invaluable contribution by opening the doors of their daycare centers and family daycare homes and/or sharing their accumulated wisdom. Our thanks go to Jane Bertrand, Janet Davis, Maria de Wit, Elizabeth Dunn, Karen Glass, Astrid Hilgren, Johanne Husereau, Jackie Jackson, Margot Janzen, Maureen Landry, Janice May, Nabila Mohktar, Marilyn Neuman, Pam Perry, Avril Pike, Adele Rosen, Kelly Schmidt, Karen Thorpe, Ellen Unkrig Staton, Wally Weng-Garrety, Donna White and Jean Wise.

Zsolt Alapi, Lamya Amleh, Kathy Bloydel, Mary Buckland, Kevin Dunbar, Penny Glickman, Matthew Lennig, Lucille Moskalewski, Laura Petitto, Myra Sourkes, Manuel Vidal-Sanz, Maria Paz Villegas-Pérez,

Kitty and Russell Wilkins and Judy Zucker allowed us an intimate glimpse of the parent's point of view.

Several specialists gave generously of their time and expertise: Dr. Julio C. Soto on daycare health, David Singleton on child sexual abuse, Richard Lewin on financial matters and Paul Schrodt on parent boards of directors. If this book is accurate on these subjects, the credit goes to them—but we the authors are responsible for any mistakes.

Sandra Tooze, Sarah MacLachlan and Kim McArthur deftly steered the manuscript along on its journey onto Canadian book shelves; Anna Aguayo helped us think about anthropology; Beverly Chandler rooted out quotations; Ilana Aronoff worked wonders with photos which perhaps will see the light in some other book.

Frances Hanna believed in us from the very beginning and backed us to the very end; and Martha Friendly directed us to superb resources, gave us a guided tour of the national scene and made incisive and provocative comments on the text.

The loving support of Daniel and Zachary Sklar and Joan and Margot Kaiser kept our panic level in check.

And Martin Hallett and Michael Rasminsky took up the slack on the home front, all the while ensuring that we never lost a quote or a computer file. Their patience, encouragement and willingness to roll up their sleeves have, in the end, made all the difference.

PREFACE

We're not anyone's arbiters. The child in daycare is yours and yours alone. When you're deciding where he will spend most of his waking hours for the next few years, what's most important is that you act according to your own values and feel comfortable with yourself.

Nonetheless, we'd like to help you make the best possible choice.

The two of us, one a daycare director with more than 15 years of experience and the other a writer concerned with family issues, have been juggling work and child care for almost two decades. Over the years one of us has shepherded thousands of children and parents through daycare; and in the course of writing this book together we've talked with dozens more parents, daycare staff and daycare experts; visited daycare centers and family daycare homes; attended conferences; and read countless books and articles. All of this appears here in one form or another.

Two passionately held beliefs, one large and one small, drive this book.

The first is that there is a correlation between the availability of high-quality child care and parents' understanding of what they have a right to expect. Too many daycares that endanger the safety of children remain open because parents who don't know any better continue to leave their children there. When we know more about daycare, we can make better and clearer demands, and we will not continue to allow sub-standard care of our children to be licensed and operated.

The second belief is that a book that tells people how to do something must be relentlessly clear, specific and occasionally obvious. Dr. Spock's instruction for giving a baby a bath ("First, take off your wristwatch"), read by a petrified and thankful new mother over 20 years ago, is our model.

For the sake of that all-important clarity, we have called caregivers *she* and children *he*, and we have changed the names of children, parents and caregivers to protect their privacy.

Once upon a time....
FAIRY TALE

INTRODUCTION

Because we all went to school, we all know something about what schools should be like. Those years of pencils, books and teachers' cross-eyed looks give us confidence in our ability to select the right schools for our children.

But most of our generation didn't go to daycare. We have no experience or tradition of our own to fall back on, no standards or memories to measure against. How, then, can we possibly make decisions about daycare for our children?

Our parents (whose lack of familiarity with daycare encourages little voices to whisper in our ear, "If my mother didn't do it, can it really be right and good?") often offer more in the way of guilt than useful advice.

Our high schools didn't include child care in their moral and social development courses; the priest, minister or rabbi failed to mention the topic when he discussed the sacred institution of marriage; and the hospital omitted it from the syllabus for its childbirth classes.

For us as parents it is also tempting to pretend that the large threatening cloud of daycare isn't there. Perhaps if we ignore it, it will blow away—or at zero hour gently bestow the perfect daycare solution like a beautiful perfect snowflake.

Luck might be with us. Without thought, we might blunder into an acceptable solution at the last possible minute. But it is more likely that daycare chosen this way will be inadequate—and, because we know so little about what it should be like, we won't even realize it.

Finding good daycare

Finding good daycare is not a Saturday-afternoon excursion, like buying a crib. Daycare is confusing and complicated, and the stakes— the well-being of your child and your own equanimity—are very high.

But if you set your mind to it, finding the right daycare for your family is not an impossible task. It just takes thought, time, hard work and information.

When you begin, it will feel like a gargantuan, mind-boggling undertaking. You'll remember that ignorance is bliss and fervently wish you'd never gotten involved in the whole affair. But the longer you spend at it and the more you see, the less overwhelmed you will be. Suddenly everything will make sense, the choice will become clear, and you'll be very glad that you made the effort.

The facts of life

In Canada today daycare is a fact of life. The majority of women with school-aged children are employed, the majority of women with pre-school-aged children are employed, and the majority of women with children under three are employed.[1] Women often have careers before they have families, and they value themselves as wage earners and as members of the work force. They depend on and enjoy the income they generate, and they take maternity leave rather than abandoning their jobs when they give birth. Chances are, if you are reading this, that you are a working parent or planning to be one.

More and more parents head households on their own, taking the full responsibility for paying the rent, putting food on the table and raising their children.

When men and women went to work in former times, they counted on their numerous relatives to help with child care. But these days an extended family—especially one that lives in the vicinity and is available during working hours—is almost a curiosity.

That is, our families have shrunk, and no one among us, male or female, is at home to take care of the children. We have structured our lives so that we need daycare in order to function. Without it, we have to give up either our work or our children—which we simply are not prepared to do. We are really and truly stuck.

An old idea
We tend to regard daycare as a brand-new idea. But the truth of the matter is that it's been with us from the beginning.

Anthropologists speculate that primitive families left their infants in the care of aunts and sisters while the young mothers went off to gather nuts, fruits and berries;[2] and Margaret Mead describes how the older Samoan girls take care of their young relatives for long periods.[3]

In ancient and medieval societies, wet nurses breast-fed the infants of the wealthy, and upper-class Western families have had nannies and mammies for more than two centuries.

All of these arrangements are forms of daycare—the care of a child by someone other than his mother or father for an extended period of time inside or outside the child's home.

I am a parent and a worker; therefore I am a daycare consumer
When you have a job and a baby, no matter what your gender, you immediately metamorphose into a consumer of daycare services.

Research shows clearly that good daycare is good for children, and bad daycare is bad for them. You therefore want good daycare for your child, and that is what this book is about—high-quality daycare. When your child has high-quality daycare, you can go to work without worry, knowing that he is in a safe, healthy, loving, stimulating environment where he can continue to learn and develop into that wonderful, special person that he is.

The key to finding high-quality daycare is knowledge. Once you know what is good for your child, you will be able to recognize it, demand it and find it, even when there isn't enough to go around, as is presently the case in Canada.

This book will give you that knowledge. Because it is easy to be deceived by smiling directors and freshly painted buildings which resemble little red schoolhouses, we will describe high-quality care in scrupulous detail. We will advise you to notice the teacher's face, posture, tone of voice—and where she puts the Kleenex. We will tell you about daycare centers, sitters and nannies, family or private home daycare and school-age child care. We will tell you what the research and the regulations say, what parents, teachers and daycare directors say—and we will help you to discover what really matters to you. Then we will provide you with checklists and contingency plans.

Satisfaction not guaranteed

But even after your child is happily settled in the daycare of your choice, it is possible to get stuck. You want and need your daycare arrangement to work so that you can work; and, of course, if you never examine it closely, it may appear to function perfectly. It is always easier to turn a blind eye than to look trouble in the face. But daycares change, directors and caregivers move on, children grow. When we don't watch our children and don't pay attention to their surroundings, that is when they get hurt, physically and emotionally.

As John F. Kennedy once put it, "The price of liberty is eternal vigilance." Having a child in daycare means watching closely. We will tell you all about being a vigilant daycare parent. We will describe strategies for keeping in touch with your child's caregiver; we will explain health issues and daycare politics; we will help you to figure out when to switch daycares.

In that world out there, there is a lot of good daycare and a lot of bad daycare. Parents who want and demand good daycare will help to create more good daycare and will make good daycare better. If we refuse to settle for bad daycare, bad daycare will have to improve or lose its customers. Governments that write the regulations and hold the purse strings will have to sit up and take notice. Like any other product, daycare will respond to the voice of the consumer.

An informed parent is an empowered parent. When you know what you are doing, you will have and make choices that are good for you and for your child.

"Who are you?" said the caterpillar.
Alice replied, "I hardly know, Sir,
just at present—at least I know who I was
when I got up this morning, but I think I
must have been changed several times since then."
LEWIS CARROLL
ALICE'S ADVENTURES IN WONDERLAND

CHAPTER 1

How and When to Start Thinking about Daycare

How and when do you decide to go back to work? How and when do you start thinking about daycare? Who are you, and what are your needs as a parent?

Life doesn't necessarily follow orderly rules. Some pregnancies are planned, some aren't. Sometimes returning to work and arranging child care are part of the choice to have a child, sometimes they're crisis management. People start thinking about daycare at different times because the need for it arises at different times.

Regardless of the circumstances, the decision about who will care for your child while you are at work is one of the most important you will make in the first five years of your child's life. It's a decision that has the potential to affect your child in all kinds of ways—it can turn him into a rocket scientist or give him nightmares that recur until adolescence. The whole family will live with its consequences for years.

As a working parent you aren't around for approximately 2,300 hours per year during a crucial period in your child's psychological, physical and intellectual development. You have to rely on your caregiver, your child and your own ability to read between the lines to find out whether—and why—your child is happy or miserable. Even though you may be entrusting your child to someone else, you are the boss, the one with the responsibility for your child. And you are the one who'll live with the results, the one who'll have to pick up the pieces. No wonder the decision looms so large. If this is your first child and you're new at this game, it's doubly scary.

When you have doubts about your child's well-being, it's very hard to pay attention to your work and even harder to live with yourself. That's why you want to give yourself enough time to investigate child care options and make the best decision you can. And that's why we're here to help.

HOW TO START THINKING ABOUT DAYCARE

In most families the mother selects the child care. It is usually she who makes the preliminary phone calls and usually she who does the interviewing, visiting, thinking and worrying. (In fact, she is probably reading this book!)

But fathers can play an important role, too—in fact, having an actively involved father can mean all kinds of extraordinary things to a child. Research shows that if his father takes an active part in his care, he may enter school with a higher IQ and a better chance of success; he'll have a better self-image, a better sense of humor and better relationships with his peers.[1]

On some level—remembering his own family, perhaps—the new father may want the new mother to stay at home with the baby. Making a joint decision about daycare will help you both to deal with these issues. He, too, will benefit from having it be the best one you can make.

If you're a single parent making these tough choices all alone, having someone to bounce ideas off will help. A friend, a mother or a sister with a willing ear will make the load you're carrying a little lighter and create a strong bond between your child and someone close to you.

Philosophy is the key
Whatever care you choose for your child, it should reflect your philosophy—your values and your lifestyle. You must find an arrangement that pleases *you*—because if you are happy, your child will be happy,

too. When home and child care complement each other and work together, that is good for your child.[2]

Daycares have philosophies, and they are usually clearly articulated—an important part of what they tell you about themselves. They've had time to work out what they believe in, and they hire staff, create programs, arrange rooms, buy food and discipline children in ways that carry out their philosophy. If you ask a family daycare provider, a nanny or a babysitter about her philosophy, she may look at you askance and deny that philosophy is remotely connected with her work. But that simply isn't true—philosophy underlies everything *every* caregiver does.

Even your mother has a philosophy—and it may not coincide with yours.

Your philosophy is everywhere. It's in the way you walk your dog; it's in whether you save the best bite of cake for last or gobble it down first; it's in whether you make your bed as soon as you get up in the morning or before you go to bed (or not at all).

The choice of child care is, therefore, an extremely personal matter. You have to know yourself, your child and your expectations of the person your child will be. In a very real way, your daycare arrangement will be an extension of you. It will reflect your views as a parent, as a spouse, as a working or studying person.

Know thyself
So the first order of business is to know yourself. Who are you, and what's important to you?

In the next few pages we'll raise some issues for you to consider. You may not yet know your views about them as a parent, but you certainly know how you felt about them when you were a child. We are products of our own upbringing—who we are and what we feel are based on the way we were as children in our own families. Sometimes we rebel against it; sometimes we're delighted to follow in Mom's or Dad's footsteps.

We're not telling you *what* to think; we're telling you to *think about* what you think so that you can figure out what is most important to you and act accordingly. That is the best way to minimize guilt.

1. *Politics.* Canada's unique cultural mosaic presents parents with a thorny dilemma: how do you teach your child about his own identity and, at the same time, encourage him to take his place in

our broader Canadian society? Do you want your child to meet children of different races and religions who speak different languages or who come from different socio-economic classes? Do you want daycare to be the beginning of an old-boy network, a grooming ground for an elite university? Should all the families be like yours? Or should they all be different?

For some, the language of care is primary—whether their goal is a unilingual, bilingual or trilingual child.

Although it may be obscure to you at the moment, daycare has a politics of its own. When the cash comes out of your own pocket, the question of who should pick up the tab hits you where it hurts. What are your views on raising the low salaries of daycare workers when that will mean a fee hike for you? Who should receive tax receipts, tax credits, vouchers and subsidies? Should daycare be commercial or non-profit? Should parents, professionals or businessmen and women be in charge? What is the role of the school and the school board in daycare? How do you feel about government regulation and unions?

2. *Religion.* How important is religion in your life? What part did school play in your own religious education, and what part do you want daycare to play in your children's? Do you have strong non-denominational preferences? Some church groups and synagogues offer daycare with religious content; non-sectarian daycares often use a thematic approach to give children a taste of many religions— at Christmas Santa appears, not Jesus; at Passover matzoh is served for snack.

A babysitter or family caregiver may also impart her religious views to your child, if they are important in her life. Susan, who attributed a flower's beauty to the human effort that went into planting and tending it, was astonished to hear her daughter Jessie, age four, exclaim, "Thank you, God, for this flower." Her babysitter, Mary, obviously had a different world view that she had been sharing with her young charge.

3. *Group and family/individual rights.* Some people believe that a group, like a family, should be foremost in the lives of its members—that a family should eat dinner together regularly, take vacations together and celebrate its occasions together. Others believe that individual rights are more important and that a family (or any group) is there to support its individual members. In some

families a teenaged girl would be allowed to go out with her boy-friend on Christmas Eve, and in others she would be expected to stay at home to open the presents with the family.

In a daycare setting, too, the individual can be more or less important in the group, depending on the philosophy. After half a day at kindergarten, Rebecca simply didn't have the energy to join in group activities at daycare. Her teacher, sensitive to her needs, realized that she was as good as new once she'd spent 20 minutes with a book, so it became a ritual for her to curl up in a corner every day before she joined in the group hurly-burly.

4. *Genes/environment or nature/nurture.* This controversial question might be phrased, Do personality, talents and faults all come in the package when a human being is born, or is a baby a tabula rasa, or blank slate, whose characteristics can be determined by his upbringing? What role should adults and surroundings play in the rearing of children? How much control should you exert?

Your beliefs about this issue have an enormous bearing on the nature of the care you seek because the caregiver will be making daily decisions about how your children will explore and experience the world. If your child shows signs of being the next Wayne Gretzky, will you seek out a daycare with a skating program or put him in the more convenient one around the corner?

5. *Discipline.* Discipline broadly defines parenthood itself. As the fox says in *The Little Prince*, "If you tame me, then we shall need each other. To me, you will be unique in all the world. To you, I shall be unique in all the world." It means teaching the child self-control, not punishment. "Discipline is teaching, education, and when it is employed for child-rearing it should have the significance of education of character," says Selma Fraiberg in *The Magic Years*. When you're handling the discipline yourself, it's all right to make mistakes; you know that you'll have plenty of chances to correct them. When someone else is in charge in your absence, you would like your stand-in to act the way you would as much as possible. If you believe that rules should be enforced without exception, you need a caregiver or daycare that will enforce them, too—that will insist that your son sit in his high chair to eat, not follow him around with a spoonful of cereal. If you believe in teaching a child by means of positive reinforcement, watch for a caregiver who praises him for his efforts to put together a puzzle rather than

correcting him when he takes the wrong piece. Interestingly, with their institutionalized, formal structure, daycare centers can often provide more consistency in discipline than an individual.

6. *Structured/free form.* If you plan to put your infant on a feeding schedule (as opposed to feeding him on demand), if you're firm about putting the baby to bed and leaving him to cry himself to sleep (as opposed to holding or rocking him), you are probably a person who believes in structure. Jennifer is strict about meals and bedtimes and chose a structured daycare where the teacher teaches according to a set schedule—math at 10:30, story at 11, lunch at 11:30—and there is relatively little free play.

Nannies, babysitters and family caregivers can allow their days to be relatively unstructured, taking their shape from the needs of individual children. A caregiver at home can probably arrange her schedule around a child who wants to finish a painting. But as the number of children grows, such flexibility becomes unmanageable. To prevent chaos from taking over, daycare centers find structure absolutely indispensable.

But structure, which manifests itself in scheduled activities, adherence to routines and the amount of choice it allows the children, can be imposed to different degrees and in different ways. When lunchtime is over, is all the leftover food packed away in the lunch box for the child to take home, or is the dawdler given some special encouragement to finish his apple?

Having to follow the schedule can be a positive force. For example, a child who puts up a battle royal over donning his snowsuit may be permitted to stay inside at home, but at daycare he has no choice, and he may be the most reluctant to come back inside when outdoor playtime is over.

A word of caution: your child may make your philosophy an almost academic matter. Some babies are very erratic and refuse all attempts to regulate their habits; others put themselves rapidly onto schedules—without asking your permission. Whatever your baby's behavior patterns, he will no doubt force you to come along.

WHEN TO START THINKING ABOUT DAYCARE

When to go back to work and when to look for child care are much less philosophical questions than how to think about them—and much less within our control.

There are financial considerations, job considerations, the needs of older or younger siblings and—more often than we would like to think—life crises, like unexpected changes in marital status, loss of a job, job transfer, the sudden breakdown of a perfectly good child care arrangement or just plain, ordinary disorganization and lack of proper planning.

We can't tell you exactly when to go back to work or when to look for child care, but we can provide some guidelines, information and support to help you make the best choice for your family as well as to understand why you may be finding the entire process of returning to work so difficult. The goal is to help you get on with it and put guilt behind you.

As the director of a Montreal daycare center, Barbara receives dozens of phone calls every month from desperate parents searching for daycare. As unrealistic as Mary Poppins' Mr. Banks, who expected the prospective nannies to line up outside his door, these parents are almost invariably out of luck, especially in August, when the daycare year, like the school year, is about to begin. You can't decide to go back to work one day and find your child a place in a daycare center the next. You can't count on Mary Poppins to arrive on your doorstep with her umbrella and carpetbag, and a family daycare home probably isn't going to open across the street.

Deciding when to look for daycare is based on that reality. In Canada in 1989, there were approximately 1,275,000 children aged six and under with mothers in the labor force, but only about 225,000 of them had found licensed daycare spaces. Of the more than 300,000 children under 18 months, a meager 5.02 percent ended up in licensed centers.[3]

Because daycare is so expensive, there may never be enough spaces for Canadian children. And although infant care, the most expensive of all, is expanding steadily, it will no doubt remain scarce for years to come. So the bottom line is this: as a parent you'll have to scramble for space even if you're extremely well prepared. There are no guarantees.

There's no time like the present
If you are looking for child care for an infant under a year, you have no time to waste. Although you can make a more leisurely decision if your child won't be going to daycare until he's three, don't put off thinking about it until then. Many top-quality centers take applications

from pregnant women for children who will enter in two or three years.

Child care is a fact of pregnancy, if you can focus on it. Pregnancy is such a special time that we almost hesitate to spoil it by thinking about the real child—during pregnancy, a baby can be anyone you'd like him or her to be. With the first child in particular, it's hard to come to grips with the notion that you will soon have responsibility for another person. You don't know how you'll feel once the baby is born, and you certainly don't know how much time a baby will consume and how much work—and fun—it will be. But in Canada today, waiting until the reality of the baby has sunk in is a luxury you just can't afford. You have to make child care plans, and contingency plans, before the birth.

Now is the time to inform yourself about the child care that is available near your home and your work. Even if it's impossible to imagine actually having your child enrolled there, look at daycare centers, ask about family daycare and babysitters, find out who takes care of infants in the neighborhood, and put your name on lists right away. You'll want to check out as many possibilities as you can, because that's how you'll find what suits you best.

If you work at a university, hospital or company that has a daycare center associated with it, phone them as soon as you've told your partner you're pregnant—certainly before you call your parents. (McGill Community Family Center, attached to McGill University in Montreal, suggests parents apply as soon as their pregnancy is confirmed, appending a note from their doctor.) Even then, your baby's name may not reach the top of the list until he is eight, ten or 15 months old.

If you think you'll need financial help to pay your daycare fees, make your third phone call to your local child care office to find out how to put your name down for a subsidy. Depending on where you live, the waiting list there may be even longer than the list at the daycare. (We'll tell you more about how to do this in chapter 3.)

Planned or unplanned, the road is the same

It's no easy matter for a working couple to decide to have a baby. If it is in your nature to make plans and stick with them and if your pregnancy was planned, then you've probably already thought about when you'll go back to work. It's likely that you've even made the leap to thinking about who will take care of the baby—whether Grandma has offered to help or not. Your plans may go into the garbage when you hold that bundle in your arms, but at least you've thought about what to do.

But a large number of pregnancies are unplanned. If you didn't expect to be pregnant, and you haven't thought at all about child care, don't panic. Perhaps you don't have quite the same edge as a couple who've been mulling over these issues for months, but all is not lost. Talk to your partner or a friend and start putting yourself on lists. Whether you planned your pregnancy or not, the process to follow for finding care is identical. It's the thinking you have to catch up on.

How will you pay the piper?
When most people think about going back to work, one hard-core reality comes first: money. If your salary is paying the rent or the mortgage and keeping the family in shoes, then you have little choice— you'll go back to work as soon as possible.

The calculations can be difficult. When you have a baby, your expenses go up and your income goes down, at least temporarily. Even returning to work quickly carries a dollar cost—infant care is much more expensive than care for an older child. How long can you go without working? What is your income going to be? Even if your pregnancy is unplanned, you may have been saving. How much money are you able to set aside beforehand? How much are you in debt? What loans or credit-card bills are you paying off?

How much do you earn, and how much does your husband earn? Do you need both salaries to make ends meet, or does the second salary permit you to take a ski vacation or bank some portion of your income? With a change in lifestyle, could you manage on a single salary?

Maternity leave and benefits
Like most of us, you are probably hoping that maternity or adoption benefits will see you through your maternity leave. Don't count on it— maternity leave and benefits are not as simple as they seem. The rules are complicated, confusing and prone to change. It's imperative to investigate them thoroughly before you commit yourself to living on them.

If you've been working for a while for the same employer, you are probably eligible for guaranteed leave—meaning your job or a comparable one will be waiting for you when you go back to work. But that doesn't mean you'll be able to take the full leave after your baby is born. In some provinces you are permitted to take a mere fraction of your leave after the birth. And some categories of workers don't qualify for any leave whatsoever. Extended leave, even though it's without pay, remains a dream almost everywhere in the country.

Unlike leave, which falls under provincial jurisdiction, maternity benefits—that is, the money you actually receive—are regulated by the federal government. Under the Unemployment Insurance Act, some people may not qualify for benefits at all, and the rest will receive a percentage of their salary for a maximum of 15 weeks—which may or may not be the same length of time as their leave. In addition, under recent amendments to the act, either the mother or father can claim another ten weeks of parental benefits, bringing the total to 25 weeks.

The first step is to talk to your employer. He will know how much leave and how much money you are entitled to have. Ask him, in writing, for the full 25 weeks of leave that the federal government will pay for, and perhaps he will agree. While you're at it, find out if the company has any special child care provisions for its employees. Even if there's no work-place daycare center, they may have an information and counseling service to help you find a daycare near your home or work.

Talk to your union, too. Some Canadian women have negotiated fully paid maternity leave through collective bargaining, and fathers may receive some benefits as well.

To verify your leave time and eligibility, call your provincial Ministry of Labour (or Manpower or Employment), listed in the blue pages at the back of the telephone directory. Then check with your local Employment and Immigration Canada office—the same office that handles regular unemployment-insurance claims—listed under Government of Canada in the phone book. The line seems perpetually busy, but once you've gotten through, they will supply you with a pamphlet describing the benefits and with a form to fill out, which you must return with your employment record from your employer and a doctor's certificate stating that you are pregnant. You can file as soon as you leave your job—as many as ten weeks before the baby is due. Be sure to file within a week of the baby's birth—otherwise you may not collect all the money to which you are entitled.

Depending on your job and the state of your health while you are pregnant, you might be eligible for other government benefits like Workers' Compensation. Ask your obstetrician for advice.

Job considerations

The nature of your job is another key factor in deciding when to go back to work. If you take more than a minimal leave, will your job be at risk? If you're a salesperson, will a sign go up in the store window advertising for your replacement? Do you have a career to consider? If you're a lawyer who will lose her clients or a marketing executive who'll lose her place on the corporate ladder, then you, too, probably have to go straight back to work. Other careers, like teaching, may allow more flexibility.

Time can be a subject for negotiation with your boss. Some companies may allow you to arrange a gradual return—you may be able to come back part-time initially or to develop a work-sharing plan with another employee.

Working at home is another possibility. Doing a full-time job while looking after a baby full-time is virtually impossible. Part-time work is more realistic, but some jobs just don't fall into neat divisions. If you're not careful, you could end up doing the same work load "part-time" for less money.

To make this option succeed, you must have portable work and the approval of your employer. Then you need the temperament and self-discipline to resist the myriad distractions that home offers—not the least of which is your fascinating baby. Lastly, the cooperation of your offspring, a thoroughly unpredictable affair, is essential. If you have a baby who never sleeps, you may end up working from 10 P.M. to 3 A.M.

At any rate, talk to your boss. You won't get a letter in the mail that says, "We've noticed that you're pregnant, and we'd like to tell you about your options." It's up to you to figure them out—or create them—for yourself.

A little help from your friends

Another consideration in the decision to return to work is your partner. How flexible is his job, and what kind of a father is he? If his schedule permits it, will he volunteer to take care of the baby for part of the day? A participating father could enable you to work part-time without relying on an outside caregiver.

Unfortunately, this route isn't usually open to single parents. Even if you have an unusually cooperative roommate or family, you will probably need a full-time salary.

Which child is this?
Your decision to return to work will also be affected by the number of children in your family. With the first child, you don't know exactly what you'll want, and your plans must be based on assumptions— which the hard facts of parenthood may turn upside down.

With your second child you'll have more realistic grounds for planning. If you are eager to get back in touch with advances in your field, remember that you have the right to return to work even if you stayed home with your older child. You do not have to make the same choices every time.

Another peculiar question rears its head with the second child: Is it financially worthwhile to go back to work? Giving your entire paycheck to someone else for child care is so depressing that you may find yourself asking, "What exactly does my job mean to me, anyway?" Your partner may ask himself the same question. (We will treat the question of the second child in chapter 19.)

Breaking a pattern
Having a baby may present an opportunity to change a pattern. Is this a good time for you to switch jobs or go back to school? Such a move would give you more flexibility, and if you could afford it, it could extend your leave. Although going to school part-time can be tricky financially, many students manage it with grants and bursaries.

What if you've decided to embark on a new career? Which do you do first, look for a job or look for child care? How can you afford a babysitter or a daycare center when you have no income? If you find a job and your new boss asks you to start on Monday morning, what will you do with your child?

From the point of view of both you and the child, we believe it makes more sense to start with child care. Once you've found an arrangement that suits you, take the time you need to help your child adjust to his new situation. Then you can begin your job search with your mind at rest.

Life crises
It is altogether too easy to believe that if you take all the right steps,

everything will go as planned. But the truth of the matter is somewhat different. Life insists on filling itself with unforeseen circumstances.

Maybe you were a happy nuclear family with enough money to enable you to stay at home for the first five years of your child's life, but all of a sudden your husband leaves and you're a single parent who has to work.

Maybe your partner is laid off.

Maybe you are finding your mother-in-law, who was a wonderful babysitter in theory, altogether intolerable in practice.

Maybe your perfect family caregiver gives you two weeks' notice.

Maybe you have to start work next week, and you still don't have child care.

What should you do? Research shows that families in stress make poor child care choices.[4] When you can't make ends meet or your personal life is collapsing, it's hard to apply any energy to the child care problem, and you tend to settle for the first thing that comes along. Because high-quality care doesn't grow on trees, what you end up with isn't usually very good.

It's important to keep this fact in mind when crisis strikes. Find an interim solution, like a babysitter, and *remember that you can change it.* No answer is written in stone.

As improbable as it seems at the time, somehow people muddle through. In all likelihood you're better at managing than you think because you practice every day. You managed to pull through when you had an important early meeting and your alarm clock didn't wake you, and you were able to joke when the heel came off your shoe on your way to a job interview. Think about it. Somehow we find the light at the end of the tunnel, even when the tunnel is very long indeed.

You probably won't find a daycare space just when you need it, but high-quality daycare is worth waiting for. Even if the odds look hopeless, go through the exercise of putting your name on lists, looking at the possibilities and making a daycare choice that really pleases you. Keep pushing for what you want, and don't feel guilty if you're doing something else while you wait for the magic number to come up.

NONETHELESS

When you go back to work, whether it's a last-minute decision or it's been planned down to the last detail, everything can still fall apart.

You have to realize that:

It's going to be much harder than you think, whether you're a single mother, half of a happy couple or a member of an extended family; whether you're leaving your child with your mother, a nanny, a family caregiver or in a daycare center; whether you love your job or hate it; whether you love being at home with the baby or not.

Your own feelings will be different from what you foresee. You may be exhilarated and want to stay with the baby forever, despite anticipating that you would go back to work two weeks after the birth; you may be depressed and unable to muster the strength to work, although you know it would make you feel better; you may resent staying at home and feel you have to get out of the house, even though you'd planned to be home for a year.

It's going to be different at work from what you envisage. You will be a different person because you've gone through a major life change. You haven't been there for months and life has continued without you. You'll get distracted and find it hard to concentrate because you're thinking about what's going on at home. By 11 A.M., you'll be feeling the fatigue created by chronic lack of sleep. You'll feel under pressure because you have to leave work at 5:30 when you used to be able to stay until you'd finished what you had to do or to have a drink with your co-workers. You may have doubts about your competence.

It's going to be different when you get home. You may burst into tears when you open the door. Someone else will be seeing the baby take his first step, and you will be jealous and resentful. Yet you might be too exhausted even to cuddle him. Putting food on the table, doing the laundry and cleaning the house will be staggeringly difficult.

All of this is perfectly normal. But to cope with it you will need support. Share the agony with your partner or your mother or your friend. Seek out people who have survived the return to work, who'll offer to bring you dinner tomorrow night. Avoid those who say, "I told you so," even if they are your parents. Make your life as simple as possible—prepare simple suppers and limit obligations. This decision doesn't have to suit anyone but you.

The more you know about yourself, the options, the obstacles and the shortcuts that lie ahead, the better you'll be at handling all of this, and the better the choice of child care you will make.

When I was One,
I had just begun.
When I was Two,
I was nearly new.
A.A. MILNE

CHAPTER 2

What Is the Best Age to Start Daycare?

Now that you've thought about when to go back to work from your own point of view, consider the question from your child's perspective.

What is the ideal age for a child to start child care?

Because more than half of Canadian mothers of children under the age of three are going back to work,[1] this is a question of grave importance.

But let us state right now that it is probably unanswerable. The child development and child care communities have been wrestling with it for decades.

Some parents worry that sending a child to daycare will make their bond with their child less strong. Everyone agrees that attachment—forming a very close bond with another person—is extremely important to human development. Babies need close relationships in order to develop emotional security, which in turn enables them to reach out to others and to explore the world. What isn't clear is, first, whether that loving relationship has to be exclusively with the mother;

and second, what happens to the relationship if a mother (or primary caregiver) returns to work in the first year of her baby's life.[2]

In 1987, when the controversy over this issue got too hot for comfort, 16 leading American researchers convened an "infant day care summit meeting" to reach a consensus and reassure anxious parents and policymakers. After much discussion, they issued the following statement: "When parents have choices about selection and utilization of supplementary care for their infants and toddlers and have access to stable child care arrangements featuring skilled, sensitive, and motivated caregivers, there is every reason to believe that both children and families can thrive."[3]

So when the child care is of high quality, when it's stable and when parents have a choice about it, babies and toddlers can handle it, just as older children can.

So how do you decide when your child should start daycare?

Who is this person?
Your child's character will certainly enter into your thinking. Every child—infant, toddler or pre-schooler—is an individual, with his own distinct personality. He may be a happy, easy-going fellow, who smiles and adapts to virtually any circumstance. Or he may be a sensitive little flower, who wilts at any deviation from the norm and gives out smiles only with the most persistent coaxing.

His personality will certainly influence the type of care you choose—for your delicate flower, you will probably prefer an intimate setting to a rough-and-tumble daycare center—and it will probably influence your timing, too.

You may feel that your happy guy who can get along anywhere will be ready to start daycare any time. On the other hand, he may be just too much fun to leave. Your pathetic, vulnerable bundle of nerves may need you for longer because you're the only grownup who can get him to stop crying and relax—but you might also find it much too enervating to deal with him full-time. Dr. Constance Keefer of the Child Development Unit of Boston Children's Hospital found that mothers who had difficult, inconsolable, unpredictable babies went back to work earlier than they had anticipated, while the mothers of easy, rewarding babies delayed their return.[4] The baby's personality interfered with their plans!

How does he grow?

Besides character, your child's rate of development will be a factor in your decision about when he should begin daycare. Every baby grows at his own pace, and no child has read the book that tells him when he's supposed to reach each stage.

Strategy

Getting into the daycare of your choice is partly a matter of playing your cards right: strategy may override other considerations. With a nanny, a sitter or a family caregiver who provides care in her home, you can usually pick out a starting date for your child. But if a daycare center is your best or only choice, the timing is often out of your hands. If you apply to a center when you're pregnant, a space for your child may crop up when he's eight or 12 or 16 months old; and you'll have to accept that space when it appears, regardless of whether it suits your child at that moment—or risk waiting several months for the next one. In a daycare center, you'll increase the odds in your favor by applying for the daycare's youngest age group. Or you may decide to wait simply because Canada has many more daycare spaces and choices for pre-schoolers, two and a half to five years old. Your chances of starting when and where you like rise with the number of places available.

Some ages are easier

It is easier to begin daycare at some ages than at others. There are times when children feel utterly confident about sauntering out into the world and times when they can't stand strangers.

Don't let this talk about stranger and separation anxiety scare you. A child who has separation anxiety doesn't suffer forever after. He may hurt as you depart, but when a warm, loving and responsive caregiver steps in, he'll fare just fine, and he'll gradually increase his own coping skills. Visiting high-quality daycare centers and family daycare homes, we found that the children were happy once they'd had time to settle down.

If your child continues to be sad, a first-rate caregiver will consult with you. Realizing that you don't have many options, she will work with you to figure out how to make your child feel more at home. Joan, a single mother, felt torn in half when she finally got a space in an excellent Toronto daycare center: her 18-month-old daughter Stacey wouldn't stop crying there. For five weeks, Stacey wept non-stop. Joan had already discovered that no family daycare was available, and her friends and relatives couldn't look after her little girl either. If Joan removed Stacey from the daycare, she would have to quit her job. The staff understood her dilemma and spent many hours talking with her and trying to find an approach that would work with Stacey. As a result of their joint efforts, Stacey cried less and less and eventually actually began to enjoy herself.

If your situation doesn't allow you any flexibility in timing, don't worry. By going slowly and carefully, you can successfully introduce child care to your son or daughter at *any* age.

What follows are some very rough guidelines to ages and stages of development. They come with a stern warning: they may or may not apply to your child. But if nothing else, at least they will alert you to some difficulties your child may encounter at different periods and give you a headstart in helping him to deal with them.

Up to four months

Although Canadian women are entitled to 15 weeks of maternity benefits plus ten weeks of parental benefits, you may not qualify for them, your province or your employer may not allow you to use them all, you may need to take some time off before your baby arrives, or you may want to return to work sooner for financial or career reasons.

If you must go back to work while your infant is still very tiny, you will need courage and fortitude. The baby may not have settled into any kind of schedule. He may be colicky in the evenings and wake at night for feedings. Because he is still unpredictable, you'll probably feel much less in control than usual, and you'll be very tired to boot.

But at least your baby will not object when you leave. If a warm and attentive caregiver tunes into his needs and responds to them promptly, he'll be just fine.[5] And being in child care won't stop him from loving you and regarding you as the most important person in his life. Daycare expert Alison Clarke-Stewart sums up the research: "Children in daycare are indeed attached to their mothers and...this feeling is not replaced by their relationship with another caregiver."[6]

By the end of his fourth month, however, most of your baby's disorganization will resolve itself. He'll eat and sleep more regularly and stop his colicky fussing. You, too, will feel better. More competent and confident, you'll handle him less like a fragile piece of china and have more faith in his ability (and yours!) to survive the rough patches.

Because you'll know him better, you'll be able to judge if he's happy, and you'll have a clearer idea about what to show and tell another caregiver—and what to expect from her. For this reason, Harvard University child development expert T. Berry Brazelton urges mothers to stay home and get to know their babies for at least the first four months of their lives.[7]

Five to seven months

Starting at about five months, your baby comes to know what to expect of you and the rest of his family, to take pleasure in your company and to want to be around you—he knows these familiar faces take care of his needs. When he was smaller, he cried with hunger and pain. Now he's more sophisticated; he can tell you he's unhappy with an unfamiliar person who isn't you and doesn't know how to hold him in a comfortable position.

This feeling is called stranger anxiety. When a stranger (including Grandma, if she doesn't visit often) comes too close, your baby will hold on tight to you, even burst into tears. In his longing for you he may lodge a protest when you disappear into the bathroom or put him down for a nap. This is just the first of several periods of stranger anxiety that your baby will experience in the next few months—and sometimes it doesn't stop. From now until much later it will be hard to find a brilliantly easy moment to introduce a new caregiver.

The timing is doubly tricky because infants vary so enormously. Fiona's mother returned to work when she thought that Fiona could make a painless entrance to the daycare center at three and three-quarter months. But for a full week, to everyone's consternation she yelled vigorously whenever a teacher drew near. Quite clearly Fiona, despite her young age, already knew when her mother was there and quieted immediately for her.

To help locate the right moment, Brazelton suggests another formula—introducing the baby to child care just after he has learned important skills and before he starts acquiring new ones. In a period of consolidation, when he knows that he can do the things he sets his mind to doing, he'll be better able to handle the stress on his slender resources.

It's important to remember that a baby who recognizes his family is also beginning to recognize familiar objects and will soon recognize his new caregiver. Because it's easier to form a relationship with one new person at a time, it makes sense to have just one caregiver. Your baby can certainly get to know several caregivers, as he will have to do in a daycare center, but presumably this will take a little longer. To facilitate this attachment, daycare centers often assign a particular caregiver to each child, but the baby will probably latch on to a favorite in any case.

Eight to 11 months
Babies acquire a series of earthshaking skills at about eight months as they begin to feed themselves, to pull themselves upright, to sit and to crawl. Besides the unsettled feeling that customarily accompanies new moves, your baby gets a real shock this time: he discovers that he can physically separate from you. Knowing that he can move away both delights and frightens him thoroughly, bringing on another even stronger burst of stranger anxiety. The result is that he sometimes hangs on for dear life.[8]

This is a very hard time to enter child care. Even if you've managed to avoid stranger anxiety by installing your child with a wonderful caregiver when he was three months old, now he might suddenly dissolve when she appears. However, he'll settle down more quickly with her than he would with a stranger. (Again, this unhappiness should dissipate relatively soon.)

At this age children often cry and cling at the daycare door, says Kelly Schmidt, supervisor at Toronto's Queen Street Childcare Centre, operated by George Brown College. When they see the daycare and the center's staff, they may simply turn their heads away, like ostriches willing it all to disappear. But in a loving, caring environment, they are easy to calm and distract once their parents have left. After they've mastered sitting and crawling, Brazelton says, you should notice a change in their self-confidence that makes them more welcoming to a caregiver.[9]

12 to 17 months
A third spurt of stranger anxiety looms around the time a child begins to walk at about a year, and it, too, may continue for several months. Watching the one-year-olds enter daycare every morning, Ellen Unkrig, director of the Royal Victoria Hospital Day Care Centre in Montreal, decided to cancel some extra months of maternity leave in order to avoid this troublesome entry time for her son Patrick and settled him in painlessly at six months instead. Paradoxically, although a baby of

this age is increasingly independent, he wants and needs you more. He is just beginning to realize that you'll come back for him at the end of the day. He may even temporarily regress to an earlier stage of behavior.[10]

On the other hand, these new capabilities that caused so much trouble also enable your child to enjoy his environment. He can travel by himself to any toy he desires. He can let his caregiver know when he wants to eat, to play with another toy, to be somewhere else. He has much more control over his world.

18 to 30 months

During toddlerhood, one can see separation anxiety full-blown. At 18 months, children normally acquire the notion of "object permanence," meaning they realize that you continue to exist when you're not actually in the room with them. This simple idea carries with it some very powerful implications. Your baby can comfort himself with the thought that you will return, but the other side of the coin is that he realizes that it's possible to lose you. Later it even occurs to him that you might abandon him because he's been bad—because he didn't eat his breakfast or because he didn't want to buckle his car seat to come to daycare.[11]

Now he knows exactly what he wants—his mommy—and he doesn't care a fig who knows it. Furthermore, he refuses to be distracted, so it takes longer for his crying to subside. Kelly Schmidt recalls a two-year stint on the 7 A.M. shift in the toddler room where seven out of ten toddlers cried for five or ten minutes every morning without fail, no matter what games or activities were in progress.

But once a group of toddlers passes through that tumultuous beginning, daycare offers them plenty to enjoy—finger painting, sand and water play, dancing and especially lots of running and climbing. In a high-quality center or family daycare home, the children can have a good time getting into everything.

Adults still have the primary place in their lives. They provide a safe base from which a child can explore; they explain the world and give meaning to his experiences.[12] By talking and listening, adults help toddlers to develop vital communications skills.

Although they often play independently alongside one another, children this age can actually make friends,[13] and they are beginning to learn to live together. Sometimes they fight over the toys, but usually they're friendly, helping each other to explore their environment in more imaginative ways than they do with an adult.

Because toddlers can look out for their own interests to some degree by speaking up and saying no loudly and often, parents feel more secure about putting them in daycare. And when they're walking and running confidently, they may be more receptive to a caregiver again.

Two and a half to three and a half years

By two and a half, your child is willing to be away from you and from home. He can cope with your departure, which he realizes is only temporary. He is also ready to explore the world on his own and to play with other children.

Going to the neighborhood playground is a start, but it's important for a child to meet and play with the same children every day. Like adults, children build relationships over time. A daycare center, a family daycare home, a playgroup or a pre-school offers them a stable group of peers, a place to reap the joys of friendship.

Unlike formal education, daycare aims to provide the best possible conditions for building self-esteem: a firm enforcement of limits, blended with the acceptance of the need to develop autonomy. At two and a half, children usually feel comfortable within this framework. They are doers, experimenters and risk-takers, asking questions about their role in their world. A high-quality daycare environment, laden with people, activities and objects to explore, is a wonderful place to answer them. Two-and-a-halfs are ready to learn that different people function in different ways and have different expectations—and that acceptable behavior at home isn't necessarily acceptable elsewhere.

Physically adept, the two-and-a-half-year-old can walk, run and play without fear of falling; he can climb onto chairs and sit at tables. His fine motor control, combined with his increasing ability to concentrate, enables him to enjoy scribbling, doing puzzles and looking at books. Most children are toilet trained, another leap towards independence. Out of diapers, a child no longer feels like a baby. Instead he is a big boy, ready to spend time away from Mommy and Daddy and with his friends.

Most important of all, he can talk. He can tell his teachers and his playmates what he feels, what he wants and what he needs, communicating without crying or pushing. He can understand what others say to him, too. He can even accept rules if they are well explained and not too numerous. When Debbie sees her friend Stephanie in the daycare playroom, the educators have no difficulty persuading her to follow the rule that she stow her teddy bear in her cubby until naptime. She herself realizes that she can have much more fun if she has both hands free to build with blocks or climb on the climbing apparatus with her friend.

Though he's growing up, you can't expect your two-and-a-half-year-old to walk away from you a totally independent being. He will need to get used to daycare, especially if he's never been away from home or in a situation where there are lots of people. The transition to any caregiving situation requires plenty of tender loving care, sensitivity and patience. (See "Integrating Your Family into the Brave New World of Daycare," pages 221-235.)

Three and a half to five and a half years
Pre-schoolers are social animals, thriving on peer interaction. On weekends they actually miss their daycare center, playgroup or family care playmates and look forward to seeing them and to participating in daycare activities. At this age they take charge. They know when they want to arrive, whom they want to play with, what they want to do and when they want you to pick them up. ("Mommy, hurry up. I want to get there before circle. Then I can sit with Rachel.")

*"I have got to spin gold out of straw,
and I don't understand the business."*
"RUMPELSTILTSKIN"
GRIMM'S *FAIRY TALES*

CHAPTER 3

A Word about Money

In virtually every family with small children, the price of daycare is a constant preoccupation—and an inescapable reality. Somehow, no matter what it costs, the money must be found. How big will the bill be? Is it financially worthwhile to return to work? Will the government help at all?

Cost

Because creating high-quality care costs a lot, finding care you can afford seems a Herculean task. Daycare *is* expensive—in fact it's right up there with housing, food and taxes in the budgets of most young parents.

But it doesn't necessarily follow that more-expensive daycare is better than less-expensive daycare. When governments, universities, colleges, companies, churches, schools or school boards help out, very high-quality care may actually cost less than dismally bad care. You may also be eligible for government assistance to help pay the fees.

Your children are precious. Good-quality care for them now is important to what they will later become. The first five years form patterns for life. You want your child to be happy, secure and stimulated. Can any parent place a price tag on these ideals?

Daycare fees vary enormously from province to province, from type of care to type of care, from center to center, from family caregiver to family caregiver, from nanny to nanny, from sitter to sitter. We found care that cost 16 dollars a day and care that cost 50 dollars a day. You can no doubt find it both cheaper and dearer still.

The various levels of government, from the federal to the municipal, help to pay for child care in three different ways. The first is extremely important but invisible to most parents—governments support daycare centers and regulated daycare homes and agencies that meet certain criteria by paying for renovations, operating expenses, equipment, professional development and even salaries, depending on the province.

The other two methods concern parents directly: governments give tax relief, and they provide subsidies.

No GST

Child care is totally exempt from the federal Goods and Services Tax. Talk about tax relief! (On the other hand, daycares must pay GST on goods they purchase, without the possibility of reclaiming it. The result is to push fees upward.)

Tax deductions

Child care is an expense that can be deducted when you are calculating your income tax. But first you must meet certain conditions:

1. *No matter how much you pay, the maximum child care deduction is 4,000 dollars per child under the age of seven and 2,000 dollars per child seven to 14—or two-thirds of your income, whichever is lower.*
2. *You must have a receipt or proof of expenses.* You can declare child care expenses when you use any form of care—nanny, sitter, nursery or pre-school, family daycare, daycare center or school-age child care center. A daycare center, school-age center or regulated family caregiver will automatically issue receipts. With an unregulated caregiver, you can't make this assumption. Be sure to discuss receipts with her when you are making arrangements.

When you hire a nanny or sitter, you become an official employer who must register with your local Revenue Canada office. (You must also make contributions for medical and unemployment insurance, federal and/or provincial pension plans and Workers' Compensation.) Although you have supplied your employee's social insurance number, at the year's end you will need receipts. (You do not need to file them with your tax return, but you must keep them.) It is probably easiest to give your nanny or sitter a receipt book and get into the habit of exchanging check and receipt at every pay period.

3. *In a two-parent family, both parents must be working (or one parent must be studying full-time).* You are eligible even if one parent is working part-time, but you are not eligible if one parent is not working at all.

4. *The partner with the lower income is the one who must claim the deduction.* But when one parent is studying full-time, the working parent can claim the deduction even though he has the higher income.

   If you have remarried, the spouse with the lower income must claim it, even if he or she is not the parent of the child. In Quebec, where there is a provincial tax deduction as well, either partner can use it.

5. *A single working parent can, of course, claim his or her child care expenses.*

6. *When a couple is separated or divorced, only the custodial parent is eligible for the deduction.* If the non-custodial parent pays for child care as part of a child-support settlement, at tax time the cost of the child care becomes taxable revenue for the custodial parent, to whom the receipt will be issued.

   Revenue Canada's "Child Care Expenses Tax Guide" will help you to deal with all this.

Subsidies

Families can apply for government financial assistance to help pay their daycare fees. This is called a subsidy. The amount and the eligibility requirements vary widely from province to province, but subsidies normally work on a sliding scale.

The Yukon and all the provinces except Ontario use an income test, where they provide subsidies to families whose incomes fall below a certain level (which is different in each province).

Ontario and the Northwest Territories use a needs test. Families who apply will be asked about both their income and their living expenses—food, rent, debts, etc.

In some provinces parents apply through the daycare center or family daycare. In others they apply at the area or provincial child care office or at the department of income assistance.

Families in some places can use a subsidy at any licensed daycare center or regulated family daycare home; elsewhere they must wait for a "subsidized space" to open. Because there aren't nearly enough subsidies to go around, people seem to wait at least a year in many parts of Canada. You can find yourself accepted by the daycare of your choice while you go into hock waiting for your subsidy to come through.

There are no subsidies available for families using sitters or nannies.

If you think you will need a subsidy, get yourself on a waiting list as soon as you can. We'll tell you more about this in chapter 8, "How to Find a Daycare Center."

In the meantime, let's take a look at the child care choices arrayed out there on the Canadian landscape.

The child takes a nurse
The child takes a nurse
Heigh ho the derry-o
The child takes a nurse.
"THE FARMER IN THE DELL"

CHAPTER 4

One Alternative: Nannies and Sitters

What is the best kind of child care? Will you be happier with a sitter whose only concern is your child, a family daycare provider who cares for just a few children in her own home, or a daycare center where trained staff look after a larger group? How does a parent know which to choose?

There is no simple answer to this question. It depends on where you live, what your job demands, what your child is like, what you can afford. It also depends on luck—what's available when you need it.

On top of these more-or-less rational considerations, most of us come equipped with strong prejudices about the kind of care we prefer. We get them from our parents and our friends, and it usually takes a crisis—a divorce, a trusted sitter leaving—to set us thinking in a new direction. Honor these prejudices, by all means, but don't let them blind you completely.

We are going to describe several types of care arrangements in the next four chapters, and we suggest that you take a gander at at least a couple of them, just so that you know the alternatives that are available to you. You may surprise yourself. Looking back on years of child care, Carol, mother of two children aged 12 and nine, sums it up this way: "As I get older, I get much less sure of these issues, because I see children who went through completely different kinds of care, and they seem just fine."

Any type of care can be good—and any type can be awful. The kind you choose is far less important than its quality, because according to research, good daycare is good for children and bad daycare is bad for them, especially for children who are at a disadvantage to begin with.[1]

The first step, therefore, is to inform yourself so that you can recognize good care when you see it. (The goal of this book is to help you do that.) The second step is to go for it—to keep that image in the front of your mind and hang in there like a bulldog until you find the real thing.

NANNIES AND BABYSITTERS

A nanny or babysitter is many parents' number-one choice in child care.[2]

Not so long ago, when we talked about a nanny we meant a person trained in child care at a nanny college, usually in England, and who, like Mary Poppins, was capable in the extreme. The term babysitter, back then, was limited to the local teenager who watched the children when the parents went out for the evening and who may or may not have known anything whatsoever about child care. (In fact, having been babysitters ourselves, we may shudder to think of the care we provided while we talked on the phone and raided the fridge.)

Now, however, when so many Canadian mothers need proper, reliable child care in order to go to work or school, they hire a nanny or sitter to come into their home on a regular basis especially to take care of their child. She may be trained or untrained; she may or may not do some housework. If she lives in the home with the family, we call her a nanny; if she lives out with her own family or friends, we call her a sitter.

ADVANTAGES

What makes parents prefer a sitter or nanny?

One-on-one
First and foremost is the attraction we've just mentioned: the sitter or nanny is there for your child alone. She can give him all the attention

he needs and deserves. She can comfort him when he cries, play with him when he's awake, talk to him, listen to him and introduce him to all the wonders of the world. Linda puts it this way: "I preferred to have a person in charge of just my child. I didn't want a person in charge of three children who had to start deciding who was the most important."

For infants, who are not ready to benefit from peer contact and who must have someone who responds quickly and consistently to their needs in order to develop self-esteem and trust in the world around them, an exclusive caregiver seems ideal—provided that she's caring, loving, warm, reliable, etc., etc., etc.

The comforts of home

At home in his own environment, a small child is comfortable and safe. He has just one routine to learn, little disruption to deal with, a minimal amount of stress. He is the king of the castle.

This is also an excellent arrangement for a school-age child, who can touch base at home, have a snack and do his homework—or go out to play hockey, do gymnastics or hang out with friends.

No traveling

Having help at home is convenient, that's for sure. You don't have to get the kids up, fed, bundled into their snowsuits and carseats and unbundle them all over again when you reach the daycare center or family daycare home. The only person who needs to be ready is you; and you are also the only one making the return trip. With just one destination—work—you save a lot of time as well.

Made to measure

Another advantage of a sitter or nanny is that you can choose someone tailor-made for your child and your family—a grandmotherly type who'll smother your giggling baby with kisses, a strong and energetic type who'll challenge your athletic toddler, an artsy soul who'll spend hours patiently setting up materials for your budding artist, a gentle nurturer who'll let your timid guy go at his own pace while giving him lots of chances to come out of his shell.

Control

With a sitter or nanny, you can have more control over your child's day. Together you can plan for him to go out before the sun gets hot; you can leave your homemade vegetable soup for lunch; you can arrange for child and nanny to go to playgroup every Tuesday morning.

And because she isn't supervising three (or seven) other children and dealing with three (or seven) other sets of parents, the sitter or nanny has more time and opportunity to talk with you about your child, the nitty gritty, the rough spots, the highlights.

Flexible hours

For the parents with long or erratic hours or the parent whose job entails traveling, a sitter or nanny is a lifesaver. "Robert's hours are very irregular and unreliable," says Maureen, a physician, "and my days are often long. I didn't want to be boxed in by a daycare center that closes at six when I rarely finish at six." Watching her friends grow anxious when they couldn't leave work on time prompted her to opt for live-in help.

Nannies and sitters are also more likely to be available for evening and weekend work.

Flexible duties

Nannies and sitters offer a second kind of flexibility: they can often do some light housework, though your child must be their first priority. If you make it clear when you hire your nanny or sitter, you can ask her to look after the children's rooms and do their laundry, tidy the house, make a salad. Linda says, "When I come home at 5:30 and everyone is screaming at me, it's wonderful not to set the table. It's one less thing to do."

In sickness and in health

Because he sees relatively few people, a child who's cared for at home is exposed to relatively few germs, and, as a result, he gets sick much less often than a child attending a daycare center. Even when he becomes ill, the nanny or sitter—his own familiar, trusted caregiver—will minister to him. Knowing she will promptly inform them of any alarming development in the status of his health, parents can go off to work with easy minds.

Cost

Having a caregiver all to yourself is bound to be expensive. But as soon as you have more than one child, a sitter or nanny becomes an economical solution. Caroline, who works as a researcher at a large hospital, reckoned she would save almost 500 dollars a month by moving her two daughters from their work-place daycare center and hiring a live-in nanny instead.

DISADVANTAGES

Of course, there are drawbacks, too.

Cost

Most people immediately rule out sitters and nannies for the reason we just mentioned: no matter which way they slice it, they cannot fit it into their budget. A ten-hour day, five days a week, adds up quickly. And the government offers little help. Low-income families, who might qualify for aid in a daycare center or regulated family daycare home, can't get it if they use a sitter or nanny. Middle- and high-income earners get relief only by claiming the Child Care Tax Deduction.

In addition, when you hire a babysitter or nanny, you become an employer, with the same obligations as any other employer. You must make deductions on your sitter's or nanny's behalf for income tax, unemployment insurance, Canada Pension Plan (and in some provinces for health insurance and Workers' Compensation); and pay the employer's share as well. Besides costing money (about a hundred dollars a month, depending on your nanny's salary and the province you live in), making these payments involves keeping records, filling out forms and following federal and provincial rules and regulations, all of which takes the patience of Job. For help in dealing with the paperwork, contact Revenue Canada and your provincial department of labor or employment. Colleen Darragh's excellent book, *The Perfect Nanny* (Toronto: Window Editions, 1988), is also helpful in all matters connected with nannies and sitters.

Families who need only part-time care can beat the high cost by sharing a sitter or nanny, thereby increasing their chances of finding a well-qualified person. Rita, a psychologist working three days a week, and Joan, a nurse who works two days, got together to hire one full-time sitter for their two infants.

Out of control

The second—and extremely serious—objection to sitters and nannies is that when you leave home, no one is around to see what actually happens. Your sitter isn't licensed. No government official comes by to inspect her work. You are the sole supervisor, and you are not on the premises. You may think your sitter is taking your child to the playground, but if she stays home to watch the soaps instead, you may never know, especially if your child doesn't yet talk. Linda, who has had one superb sitter for many years, confesses, "I'm glad I don't have to do it again. It's a heart-wrenching, gut-wrenching feeling leaving your child at home with someone."

Out of control, the sequel

Here is another problem of nanny or sitter care: the fact that your child will love another person. Who's the mother, anyway? Though studies clearly show that children prefer their mothers to their caregivers, inevitably you will feel in competition with her. She may well be there when he takes his first step; and who knows, you fantasize, he might even like her better. Even after 18 months, Maureen confides that the worst part of having a nanny is, "I'm concerned that Aaron doesn't differentiate enough between me and her, that he doesn't know for sure that I'm the best."

It is a tribute to your bond with your child that he loves someone else, but it hurts nonetheless. Child development expert T. Berry Brazelton urges parents not to let these feelings come between them and the caregiver.[3]

An allied issue, of course, is who's really in charge? You must give your sitter or nanny the authority to deal with your child—that is, if you want her to stay for longer than ten minutes. No matter how well you select your caregiver, you may not always agree, yet you have to give her responsibility. Linda believes this is one reason her sitter has been so loyal: "You have to give up some control. You have to trust the person and give her some autonomy."

By now you are beginning to understand that having a sitter or nanny is not necessarily a picnic. One of the most important facts to remember about child care is that the emotions surrounding it run deep and strong: people are easily upset and behave irrationally. You'll have a very special relationship with your sitter or nanny. You are an employer. You have to give direction. She is working in your home, your territory, taking care of your child, the most precious being in the world to you. Making everyone happy, finding the right blend of feelings, takes thought, tact, trust and plain old-fashioned nerve. Forewarned is forearmed.

Isolation

The little world of one child with one nanny or sitter is perfect for a baby or toddler, but as your child grows, he will need more stimulation. He will need some contact with the outside world; he will need peers—

children on the block, playgroup, nursery school, daycare. You can counteract this isolation to some extent by steering your sitter or nanny to your local library, Y, resource or drop-in center, where she, too, will find friends and support. Ontario and British Columbia have made a special effort to develop these community services.

Equipment

No family could possibly supply, house or tolerate as much equipment as a daycare center. Your caregiver may borrow books and toys from the library, use the big slide in the park and play with water in the sink, but she just can't match what's available in a well-equipped center.

Love me or leave me

Sitters and nannies have one last flaw. You depend on them absolutely. When your sitter turns up late in the morning, you're late to work, too. When she's sick, you may not make it to work at all. Who knows—you could use up all your sick days covering for your caregiver.

Worse still, nannies and sitters leave. You can ask them to commit themselves for a year—or two years in the case of a nanny from overseas—but you will be lucky if they stay any longer. When you've searched high and low for exactly the right person and your child has grown really attached to her, her departure will be a grievous blow.

You, too, may feel it's time for a change. A caring, loving sitter who was perfect for your infant may lack the energy, spontaneity, even the patience for a toddler who's into everything. In a center he can move to the next group, but if the sitter can't deal with the child's growing needs, you may find yourself looking for a new one.

WHAT SORT OF PERSON SHOULD SHE BE?

If you think nanny or sitter care is for you, take some time now to figure out exactly what you're looking for.

Personal qualities

Every child needs a warm and responsive caregiver who loves and enjoys children and who respects him as an individual. (We will describe what to look for in detail in chapter 11, "How to Look at a Daycare Center." See pages 139-206.) You will be looking for these qualities first. But what else is important to your child and your family? Will your child love the stimulation of someone lively and loquacious, or would he flourish with a contemplative type who's a wonderful listener? Should she love to skate or play the guitar or cook up a storm? Is a sense of humor essential in your household? Should she be compulsively neat or tolerant of mess? Let your needs and values guide you.

Relative or stranger

Sometimes families can induce a relative to take care of the baby. Because she shares your culture, language and values, a grandmother (or sister or cousin) is a tempting possibility. She will certainly love your child as if he were her own, and she may even refuse to take much money, considering this a unique opportunity to develop a close relationship with her grandchild (or niece or cousin).

However, relative care can be a mine field. Caroline's mother-in-law took care of her infant daughter two days a week, and Caroline heaved a sigh of relief on the day her work-place daycare center finally opened. "With my mother-in-law, nothing's as good as it was 30 years ago, and because she was doing me a favor, I couldn't tell her what to do." This situation leads to built-up resentments and hurt feelings on both sides. Strangers are easier to direct and certainly easier to fire, if necessary—but you never know quite what you're getting. With relatives at least you're dealing with a known devil.

The live-in or live-out conundrum

A live-in nanny offers far more flexibility, a godsend for those who travel or work unusual hours. Living in a distant suburb, Pamela likes to beat the traffic by leaving for work at 6:30 A.M. With a nanny in the house, she can tiptoe out before her daughters get up and spend more time with them in the afternoon when they're awake. And the nanny is available to babysit occasionally at night.

But when the nanny lives in, all the human problems are intensified. To make the arrangement work, everyone must have space to maneuver and escape. No one in the household will relish standing in line for the bathroom first thing in the morning. Employment and Immigration Canada requires that a foreign nanny have a room of her own and a reasonably private bathroom. One that's all hers, her own phone and her own television will go a long way towards easing the household pressure.

Space is a necessary but not a sufficient condition for live-in help. Just as important is your willingness to give up some of your privacy and adapt to the presence of another person in your life. If you want your live-in to be happy, you have to treat her like a human being that you enjoy having around, not one whom you wish would retire to the basement. Geography can make a difference here. Maureen credits the location of her nanny's rooms—in the basement, far from her and Robert—with their ability to handle the loss of privacy. Caroline takes a different tack. With two small children, she says, she and her husband have no privacy anyway.

You may find it harder to establish a relationship with your child when the nanny is around all the time, and if you feel threatened and jealous, perhaps you're a candidate for live-out care instead. This is largely a matter of personality. Some people thrive in a social situation; others are driven up a wall.

Privacy is the number-one benefit of a live-out sitter. She will go home at night to her own life, leaving you blissfully free to wander around in your underwear. Her well-being won't be your responsibility for at least 14 hours. But bear the side effects in mind. You'll have less flexibility (could you find someone willing to come to your house at 6:30 A.M.?). Evening and weekend sitting will be harder to come by. She'll probably call in sick more often. And she'll cost more, too.

Foreign or domestic
Although there are some Canadian nanny-training courses, the Canadian nanny or sitter is a rare bird, hard to spot, harder to capture. But young women from other countries are pleased to take these jobs, often because they offer entry to Canada.

One way to find a nanny is to sponsor her—to bring her to Canada and employ and house her for two years so that she can obtain landed-immigrant status.

Be sure you have plenty of patience, flexibility and a tolerance for uncertainty in stock before you begin. Depending on where you find your nanny, it takes six months to two years to negotiate the bureaucratic maze. What if she hasn't arrived by the time you have to go back to work? You'll need either a sympathetic employer or a sturdy backup system.

A leap of faith is also required—because you won't meet your nanny until she arrives on your doorstep. The newcomer may have no friends or relatives to introduce her to Canadian life, and the onus clearly falls on you to be the cordial host and help her to get established—unless you want her to pack her bags and return to mother forthwith. In exchange you'll get tons of gratitude, an insight into her culture, and your child may learn some Tagalog or Chinese along the way. (For a full explanation of the nuts and bolts of selecting a foreign nanny, we again recommend *The Perfect Nanny* by Colleen Darragh.)

Illegal immigrants often seek jobs in child care because private arrangements between individuals are so difficult for the government to trace. But this is a dangerous road to travel. Because your sitter or nanny won't have had the immigrant's mandatory health exam, she may present a health risk to your child. And, of course, you cannot deduct her salary from your income tax. In addition, you may find yourself in hot water should the immigration authorities catch up with her.

Your language or another

Children are sponges where language is concerned. Your child will learn whatever language you speak to him, and if you want him to learn another, give him a sitter or nanny who speaks it.

However, if the nanny doesn't speak your language and you don't speak hers, that presents problems. How will she understand your directions? How will you know what your child did all day? How will she get help in an emergency?

Young or old

Sometimes your child will decide this issue without consulting you. Elizabeth began to walk at eight months. By the time Linda looked for a sitter, she realized she needed a runner—someone willing to run up and down the stairs, over to the park, into the Y.

Location can also be a decisive factor—a sitter who has to lug baby and stroller up three flights of stairs needs a certain strength and resilience.

In general, younger nannies and sitters are more energetic and adaptable. Because they're not set in their ways, and because you're older than they are, it is easier to tell them what to do. On the other hand, they may need more parenting and protection. Maureen asks her parents to stay in the house when she and her husband are away because her 19-year-old nanny is afraid to be alone. Or they may lead such an active social life that they're exhausted in the morning. They are also more apt to go off in search of the gold at the end of the rainbow and never come back.

An older sitter or nanny is a mature, stable presence in the house. What she lacks in stamina and strength she makes up for in authority and wisdom. But if these very qualities turn you into a child in her presence, watch out. You're better off with someone less daunting. "I wanted somebody experienced," says Maureen, "but I was very inexperienced, and I didn't want to be intimidated by somebody, which I thought was a real possibility."

Trained or untrained

Trained nannies and sitters are extremely scarce, but they possess some skills that an untrained person probably won't have: ways to enhance self-esteem, develop independence, stimulate cognitive, emotional, social and physical growth. They will probably know the basics of first aid and CPR. A trained nanny or sitter will regard herself as a professional with a commitment to her work—a strong indicator of good quality in child care. But she will certainly demand a higher salary, and there may be things she refuses to do—housework, for one.

An untrained nanny or sitter may be more flexible and more willing to tackle any task, and her years of experience will give her her own bag of tricks for dealing with children. On the other hand, she may also be likely to watch the afternoon soaps instead of making a second trip outside after your child's nap.

Housework or no housework

This subject evokes surprisingly strong feelings. Some parents insist that the sitter or nanny focus exclusively on the child. Others want her to do a bang-up job in the house. If your child is your first priority, you will probably want your caregiver to concentrate on taking care of your child. (A trained nanny or sitter will not do housework in any case.) But unless you have several small children, there will be quiet moments when a caregiver can straighten up the apartment and throw a load of laundry into the washer. If you were at home, you would do those chores yourself, and your child wouldn't suffer one iota. (Some people believe it's unnatural to spend all one's time caring for one child.)

At the very least, she should clean up after herself. You don't need to come home to wall-to-wall toys in the living room or a sinkful of dirty dishes. But you can't expect her to do any heavy work in your home unless you're prepared to let your child pay the price.

WHAT SORT OF JOB ARE YOU OFFERING?

Before you can go out in search of the winning candidate, you had better figure out exactly what you expect your nanny or sitter to do and what you can offer in return.

Job description

Think hard about what you want your sitter or nanny to do with your child. Map out his schedule—what time he sleeps and eats, when you go for walks and to the library or drop-in center, when you read a story, when he watches television. Will you want your nanny or sitter to keep a journal, wash toys, plan and prepare lunches, make bottles, tidy the sitting room, do the laundry? Will you expect her to babysit at night? How often? Will she need to drive in order to do the job? Is what you're asking realistic? Draw up a job description that clearly identifies your expectations.

House rules

This is an especially important exercise if your nanny will live in. Will you allow your nanny or sitter to smoke? Under what circumstances can she take your child to other people's homes or go to the corner store? Will you allow her to invite other children to visit in your home? What about having her own friends over? When can she use the telephone? When can she watch television? Once you have discussed these arrangements with her, it is best to put them in writing.

Salary and benefits

What salary will you pay your sitter or nanny? Do you know the going rate in your city? One way to find out is to phone agencies and community organizations like child care resource centers. The classified ads might also provide some clues. Ask friends and colleagues who have sitters and nannies. You need to give her at least the minimum wage—when we pay our child care workers decent money, we'll have better candidates attracted to the field. The more experience and training a candidate has, the more you will want to offer her.

Based on her salary, figure out what you and she will both have to pay for taxes, Canada Pension Plan, unemployment and health insurance and Workers' Compensation.

What else can you provide in the way of benefits? Federal Employment and Immigration and your provincial Ministry of Labour or Employment will tell you the regulations on wages, hours, overtime, statutory holidays, vacations and notice, and it's up to you to decide what else to give. Will she have the use of the family car? When will you review her salary?

HOW TO FIND A NANNY OR SITTER

How do you go about finding this very special individual? As usual, we advise you to start early—as soon as you learn you're pregnant.

Activate the network

Ask everyone you know to help—because the best way to find a nanny or sitter is probably through another nanny or sitter, or through her employer, which amounts to the same thing. She'll know if someone's sister is dying to leave Singapore or someone's niece is here on a visitor's visa from Trinidad and wants to stay. She'll know who in the neighborhood can't stand her present job another minute or whose children are going to school full-time next year. This news spreads rapidly at local drop-in centers, playgroups, libraries and playgrounds.

Check the local resources

Another source is community organizations—child care resource centers, well-baby clinics, public-health nurses on home visits, childbirth classes. Schools sometimes have registries of sitters and nannies. So do nanny schools and colleges that offer courses in early childhood education. Most of these sources don't vouch for the names they provide, however—you have to check them out yourself.

Agencies

Theoretically at least, an agency can be a lifesaver—a magician who waves a magic wand over your nanny's or sitter's ideal specifications and transforms them into a real live person in your nursery.

Agencies are experts. They know how to evaluate your needs and desires, how to screen candidates and evaluate references, how to deal with Employment and Immigration, how to dismantle the roadblock you and your nanny have built during weeks of not saying what was bothering you. The difficulty is in finding a good agency—one that actually does all this well.

Reputation is important. Consult your friends and friends of friends. If they've had good results, you're probably knocking at the right door.

When you call the agency, ask if it's licensed. In British Columbia, Ontario and Quebec, this is a requirement. Do they specialize in nannies from a particular place or with a particular kind of training? Do they find nannies or sitters who live out as well as those who live in? What is their payment and refund policy? Do they offer a guarantee or trial period? If the arrangement doesn't work out, will they find you a new nanny without an additional charge?

If you like the sound of the place, visit the office. Peruse two or three files to get a sense of their perspicacity in interviewing and screening their candidates, and go over agency fees and charges as well as the salary, accommodations and perks you can offer. Any agency worth its salt will ask you lots of questions about your requirements, too.

When résumés and photos from putative nannies appear, scrutinize them carefully. Even if the agency is checking references, consider making a phone call or two on your own. With a live-out sitter who's already in the country, you'll get a chance to interview her in person and speak to her references yourself. Eventually you'll have enough information—and courage—to make a decision, and, barring immigration holdups, the nanny or sitter will be on her way to you at last.

Advertising

Your local paper offers a less esoteric route to finding a sitter or nanny. To attract candidates who truly suit your needs, make your ad as clear as possible: specify whether you want the person to live in or out, if you demand housework, whether the person should already have a working visa and whether experience and references are required. Include, too, the number and ages of your children, the location of your home, your phone number and the time of day you'll be at home to deal with the replies.

When the ad appears, plan to hang out near the phone with a pad of paper, a pen and a list of pertinent questions to ask. A good telephone grilling will give you a short, solid list of candidates to interview in person.

1. *Ask for her name and phone number.* It will make it slightly less awkward to talk to a total stranger. It will also give you a fall-back list in the event you need one later.
2. *Go over the contents of the ad.* A surprising percentage of the people who answer ads seem to have noticed nothing but the telephone number. If you want to avoid the immigration hassle and she wants the job to secure her working papers, if you're looking for someone to build snow forts and cavort in the municipal swimming pool with two bouncy pre-schoolers and she wants to cuddle a newborn baby, you can end the conversation immediately.

3. *What sort of training have you had?* If you're looking for a trained nanny or sitter, ask her about that straight away. Where was she trained? How long was the course? Does she have a certificate? She may have attended a proper two-year nanny school in England or Canada or picked up the odd continuing education class in child development or early childhood education.

4. *What experience have you had?* In the end you will need to know about every job a sitter or nanny has had—how many children she looked after, how old they were, how long she stayed with the family, why she left. But for now you might just ask her these questions about her two most recent jobs.

   Asking about experience helps you to establish some important information about your caller. First, how stable is she? If she hasn't managed to stay with any of her employers for at least a year, you'll know she's a flibbertigibbet (or possibly incompetent) and dismiss her without further ado. The longer she has stayed with each family the better. You'll know she's willing to commit herself for a reasonable length of time.

   Second, if she's stayed in her jobs for a long time, that probably means she's done them well, or at least that her employers have been satisfied with her performance. Another way to measure this is to look at the age of the children in her care. How old were they when she left? If the youngest was entering first grade, you know that the family outgrew her. If the youngest was two or three, he probably went to pre-school or daycare, but you'll want to ask her, and her employer, about this later.

   Third, you'll know what age child she's actually taken care of. If all her charges were pre-schoolers, she may not even like babies very much. You will also know something about her experience in juggling the needs of several children of different ages.

5. *Are you in good health? When did you last have a physical exam? Would you be willing to have one for this job?* It is extremely important for your child to have a healthy caregiver. Provincial legislation requires teachers at daycare centers, regulated family daycare homes and schools to have regular checkups, and you have a right to demand the same. If the cost isn't covered by medicare, consider offering to pay for it yourself. (Canada requires immigrants to have a medical before entering the country.)

6. *Do you know first aid or CPR? If not, are you willing to take a course*

at my expense? Where your child's safety is concerned, it's best to leave nothing to chance.

7. *Do you smoke?* Every parent has read about the dangers of second-hand smoke, and most of us can imagine all too vividly what careless treatment of a cigarette can do to a child or a house. Tolerance on this subject is not a virtue.

8. *Do you drive?* If the job demands a driver, you need this information.

If you like the sound of her, give her a chance to vet you, too, and tell her a bit about yourselves and what the job entails—the ages and sexes of your children, the hours, pay and holidays, a brief rundown of what you expect her to do, where you live and how to get there.

You should have her name and phone number already, but to be on the safe side confirm them now and invite her to come for an interview. Ask her to bring either her social insurance number or her immigration papers, three references and a complete résumé of all the jobs she's ever held. If this is her first job, ask her for character references—from a teacher, for example. This request should present no difficulty. References are essential, and it is foolish to hire anyone without them. We will give you some hints about checking them out at the end of this section.

THE INTERVIEW

Unless you interview people regularly as part of your work, an interview seems quite terrifying. It's so totally artificial, yet so much seems to hang on it. A nanny or sitter will probably wear her dress-up coat and best boots to meet you, yet you want to know whether she's got warm, durable, waterproof ones so that she can spend hours making angels in the snow. Though she found a nanny she adores, Maureen looks back on the interview process with horror: "It's very obvious how uncertain it all is and how easily you can be conned. We were just very lucky."

There are many ways to conduct interviews. For ease of comparison, you can schedule a whole day of people at hourly intervals. Or you can see one or two a day over a longer period. (Not over too long a period, however. Someone else will quickly snap up an outstanding candidate.)

If your partner is taking an active part in the rearing of his child, if you're going to make this big decision together, he'll probably want to form his own opinions. This requires setting up the interviews so that he can be present—in the late afternoon or evening. You can see all the candidates together, you can see them sequentially, you can screen them alone and invite the best to meet him at a second interview.

A single parent may want a trusted friend or relative to sit in and act as a sounding board.

Or one person can do all the work solo.

You will expect your candidates to be punctual—reliability is not an optional characteristic in a caregiver.

What about your child?

Some people think it's important for the child to meet the candidates. But many children don't like strangers and will cling to Mommy in their presence, especially when confronted with an endless procession through the living room. Other children will engage with anyone, friend or foe. What you see in this situation probably has little to do with what you will see when you introduce your child to a real-life sitter or nanny you've carefully chosen.

When your child is on the scene, it's hard to have an adult conversation. He will surely try to reclaim you from this intruder, and you don't want to ignore him, but for his sake you must focus on the newcomer, not on him. One solution is to schedule your interviews when he's asleep or to arrange for him to be otherwise occupied—watching "Sesame Street," for instance, or playing with an older sibling, neighborhood teenager or Grandma. Don't turn yourself inside out to manage this, though—you can always collect a stack of his favorite toys (or pick up a couple of new ones). We'll tell you how to judge your caregiver's reaction to your child on page 49.

Now what will you discuss?

1. *Tell me about your work experience.* This is an obvious moment to ask for her references and the complete list of her jobs. You can refer to it as she talks. Ask her to describe each job—what the children were like, what they did together on a typical day, what she liked and didn't like about the job and why she left. If there are holes in her résumé—periods when she had no job—ask her about them.

2. *What kind of education did you have?* Some training in child

development or early childhood education indicates commitment and a desire to do her job well. If she's very young, you might ask her how strict her school was and what subjects she liked. Her answers will explain where she's coming from.

3. *Why did you go into child care?* The very best answer to this question is "I love children." If she fell into it because her family expected it or she couldn't do anything else, the quality of her work may leave something to be desired.

4. *How long do you plan to stay in this field?* Someone who's deliberately chosen child care as a career will plan to stay indefinitely. She may see herself returning to school to get a teaching credential or opening a family daycare or daycare center in the future. Studies show that caregivers who think of themselves as professionals give better care.

5. *How long will you be willing to stay in this job?* For the sake of both yourself and your child, you need at least a year's commitment.

6. *Are you married? Do you have children? How old are they and where do they go to school?* Caring for a child in someone's home is difficult, lonely work. These questions give you insight into this person's support system. What forces are at work in her life? Do you want your family and your child to be the primary focus of her energy? How well do her goals dovetail with yours? Linda liked the idea of a sitter with older children, someone who had an interest outside of her child and wouldn't depend on her for emotional sustenance. "I really didn't want somebody who had nobody else," she says.

   She also found that talking with a woman about her children illuminated her values. If her children were doing well in school and she had plans for their future, Linda concluded, "She must have done something right."

   On the other hand, a woman who doesn't know many people in your town—an immigrant, for example—will be more willing to live in your home. You can provide her with a secure base for starting a life of her own here.

   Talk to a single woman about her parents, siblings and friends. That, too, will reveal aspirations. How was she raised? Were her parents strict or lenient? Does she agree with the way she was brought up? What work do her friends do?

7. *What do you like to do in your spare time?* This is the same genre

of question. Does she have outside interests and friends? Are they compatible with yours? Will she curl up with a good book, ski every weekend, dance at clubs every night?

8. *How would you organize a day for my child? What kinds of activities do you like best?* Now you can discover something about the way she organizes her time, how much she lets the child influence or decide, how much time she will spend outside, what she'll plan for lunch and snack, how energetic she is and how realistic.

Hypothetical questions help you to test your candidate's knowledge and skill and explore her child-rearing philosophy. Do you agree with her approach? Of course you won't ask these questions if her English isn't up to answering them or you don't like her anyway.

9. *What would you do if my child didn't want to eat?*
10. *What would you do if my child refused to nap?*
11. *When and how do you believe a child should be toilet trained?*
12. *What would you do if my baby wouldn't stop crying?*
13. *What would you do if my child wanted to play in the mud?*

Do you like her?

If you think she's a strong contender, review the job description and your house rules with her. Leave lots of time for her to ask you some questions, too. They may show where her concerns and interests lie even more clearly than the questions you ask her.

If you want her to live in, give her a little tour of the house, including her room. If you should run into your child while you're walking around, by all means take advantage of the opportunity to get them together. Notice how she speaks to him. Does she appear sincerely interested? Does she remember his name? (If she is one of your top possibilities, she'll spend more time with him at the follow-up interview.)

Before she leaves, ask to see her social insurance number or her working papers, and tell her you'll get back to her as soon as you've checked her references.

The minute she goes out the door, jot down your impressions. Did you like her? One school of thought is that you can look at references and experience until you're blue in the face, but in the end making a successful choice boils down to your gut feeling, pure and simple. You must like her. Take seriously any reservations you have about her.

Did you trust her? Did she seem forthright and honest? Her references will help in this area.

Could you talk easily with her? Did you feel comfortable being around her? Did you have enough common ground to understand one another?

Would you feel able to give her direction without being intimidated? Would she accept it without feeling threatened? Says Linda, "You can't be afraid she's going to quit if you say, 'I don't like this; please don't do it any more.' She has to be flexible."

After you've completed all your interviews, sit down with your partner (or your sister or mother or best friend) and do a preliminary evaluation. Which candidates did you like best? What are the strengths and weak points of each? Anyone who still looks like a real possibility moves onto the next phase, checking references.

CHECKING REFERENCES

What an insanely delicate process this is! You are about to call a complete stranger to find out all you can about another complete stranger. You have no idea of whether her opinion is reliable. Yet the fate of your child hangs in the balance.

The candidate has chosen this person as a reference believing she will testify favorably on her behalf, and the reference may or may not want to tell you the truth, the whole truth, and nothing but the truth. She and her family have a relationship with her former employee which implies responsibility. Theoretically, she is more loyal to her than she is to you. She knows she can influence your decision, which in turn may seriously affect the sitter's life. Therefore, unless she is wholeheartedly enthusiastic, she may be somewhat cautious. She may not say anything negative, but she may leave things out or tiptoe stealthily around them.

You have two weapons against this state of affairs. The first is to declare at once that it's very important to you to choose the right person for your child and that your conversation will, of course, be completely confidential. The second weapon is your ears. Listen carefully not only to her words but also to her manner. Does she hesitate? Is she reserved or uncomfortable?

Here are the questions

1. *How did you happen to hire this person?* You may discover at this point that she is the candidate's aunt. On the other hand, she may have interviewed 30 women to find her or inherited her from a family she'd worked for for years. You will also learn something about the reference herself.
2. *How long did the person work for you?*
3. *How old were your children?*
4. *Why did she leave?* Do both parties present the same view of the circumstances? In your opinion is the reason acceptable?
5. *What kind of person is she? How would you describe her personality?* You have already formed your own impression. Besides telling you about the candidate, this will give you another clue about the reliability of the reference.
6. *Did she miss many days of work? Did she come on time? Was she often sick?*
7. *How reliable was she in other ways? Could you count on her to do what you asked?* You'll need to know a bit about what this employer wanted in order to evaluate the answer to this question. Did she take the children to the park as planned? Did they watch more television than was agreed? Did she feed them nutritious lunches and snacks? Was your home in order when you came in?
8. *Did she do any housework? How did she manage it?* If she didn't do all her chores, was she spending her time with the children?
9. *Did you come home to a happy child? Was your child happy to see her in the morning? How well did she know your child?* These issues are crucial, of course.
10. *Did you have any concerns about the way she dealt with your child?* If she thinks the sitter spoiled her child or didn't let him do enough for himself or criticized him too much or let him watch too much television or didn't read to him enough, hopefully you'll hear about it now. This is another question where you may get a glimpse of the reference's philosophy, and therefore of the value of her opinion.
11. *What are her strengths? What did you like best about her?*
12. *What are her weaknesses? What did you like least?* These questions sometimes elicit wonderfully clear and useful replies.
13. *Would you hire her again?* By this point in the conversation, she may be relaxed enough to give you an honest response.

THE SECOND INTERVIEW

With luck and perseverance, the references have shed some light on the subject, and your list has winnowed itself to two or three names. How will you make the final decision?

In general, it's a good idea to meet the leading candidates again. The more you see of them, the better the odds you'll make the right choice. You'l have the opportunity to clear up doubts or questions raised by the references and to introduce your partner if they haven't already met.

Introducing your child

If you haven't brought your children into the picture yet, now is the time. You'll be hiring one of these people; you really need to know how they relate to your child. (If they met briefly before, this is a chance for them to become better acquainted.)

Introduce your child the way you would to any friend who came to visit, making the encounter as relaxed and as natural as possible. If your child is old enough to understand, you could say something like, "This is Lillian. She might be taking care of you when I go back to work." That stack of favorite toys and books will come in handy.

Watch to see whether she approaches him aggressively or waits for him to make the first move. Does she smile and talk with him at his eye level and his stage of development? You'll see if she's afraid—Rita eliminated several potential sitters by plopping her three-month-old infant into their laps. Does she show interest in your child by asking him questions? Is her manner warm and natural, or is it forced? Does she play with him? Does she seem aware of what children his age like to do? If he wants to keep his distance, does she respect that desire? Ask her to watch the baby for a couple of minutes while you make some coffee. Is she relaxed? Does she pick him up and talk to him? How does she relate to him?

On the adult level, go over any issues that you still feel uncertain about, and once again review the salary, hours, holidays and sick-leave policy. Make sure she asks you any lingering questions, too. Tell her that if you offer her the job, there will be a probation period of two months, just to be on the safe side. That way either party can back out gracefully if necessary. Ask her if she will sign a contract and commit herself to staying a year.

Tell her you'll let her know your decision in the next day or so.

Biting the bullet

Grit your teeth, gather your notes together, and caucus until the matter, like tea leaves, sorts itself into a recognizable pattern. Then sleep on it. If it looks the same in the morning, phone and ask this wonderful person to come sign the contract before she turns into a pumpkin.

The contract

Contracts make people nervous. "Why do we have to write it down?" they ask. "We trust each other." Yes, but you'll trust each other more if everything is written down. You can't write a letter specifying days, hours, salary, time off, overtime, holidays, vacation, deductions, sick leave, probation, how long the contract will run and how it can be ended without having all these items very straight in your own mind. When you go over them carefully with your new employee, you'll both know exactly what to expect (and when and how much)—which is the best possible start toward making the relationship work smoothly.

You'll also want to append the job description and the house rules you drew up earlier. If she'll live in, be sure to include information about her room and board and the use of the car and the phone. Make two copies, one for each of you, and sign them both.

At the same time, give her a letter authorizing her to get medical care for your child in the event of an emergency. (See appendix E.)

A last word

Though the formalities are over, don't leave just yet. Plan to take a day or so off and come home early for a few days to show the sitter or nanny all the little tricks of your child, your house, your neighborhood. What sort of diapers, bottles and baby food do you use? How does the baby like to be held? What position will guarantee a burp? What toys does he like at the moment? Where are all the emergency phone numbers? How does the microwave work? Where is the park? And so on and so forth. You want her to feel secure so that she'll make your baby feel secure, too.

At six o'clock their Mummies and Daddies
will take them home to bed,
Because they're tired little teddy bears.
JOHN W. BRATTON
"THE TEDDY BEARS' PICNIC"

CHAPTER 5

Another Choice: Family or Home Daycare

Paradoxically, when your child goes to home-based daycare—or family daycare, as it is often called—he does not stay at home. Instead he goes out—to someone else's home. Although statistics in this field are hard to come by, a recent large study showed that home-based providers care for about 45 percent of Ontario's children who need daycare, from big cities to rural areas.[1]

Family daycare is as old as the extended family, when grandparents cared for their grandchildren, aunts and uncles for nieces and nephews, cousins for cousins, older siblings for younger ones. Most children experience family care by visiting Grandma or spending a night at Uncle Daniel's house.

These days, however, one's family doesn't often provide family daycare. Neighbors, friends or acquaintances may sometimes agree to look after a child for a working parent, but most Canadians bring their children to the homes of strangers.

In many cases it is the only form of care available to them: they can't afford a sitter or nanny, and there aren't enough daycare-center spaces to go around, especially for children under two years. As the mothers of younger and younger children join the work force, family daycare is all they can find. And many families prefer a homey setting, especially for infants and toddlers.

It looks deceptively simple. What could be easier than asking the neighbor who's staying home to look after her own kids to take care of yours?

You might be lucky. This solution could work.

On the other hand, it could be a complete disaster.

The truth is that there's a lot you need to know before you leave your baby in someone else's arms.

REGULATED AND UNREGULATED CARE

Family daycare comes in two basic flavors, regulated and unregulated.

Unregulated family daycare

The vast majority of care is unregulated, otherwise known as unlicensed, informal, independent or unregistered. All of these terms mean that no government body watches over it. The caregiver (or family daycare provider or daycare mother) is running a small business out of her own home. She has to follow the rules that any small-business person does—she must keep records, give receipts for money taken in, keep receipts for operating expenses, file a tax return and so on.[2]

She must also respect the provincial laws regarding the service that she is selling, which happens to be child care. Her province usually permits her to take care of no more than four or five children, including her own, under the age of six. Some provinces also restrict the number of babies—British Columbia and Ontario, for example, allow only two under the age of two.[3]

If she abides by the law, she is providing legal child care, even though she has no license. If, however, she breaks the law—by failing to declare her income, for example, or by caring for too many children or too many infants—she is giving illegal care.

But no one actually comes around to see whether or not she's following the law and whether the care she's providing is any good.

Regulated care

Very few people realize that family home daycare can also be regulated—known in different provinces as licensed, registered, agency-sponsored, sponsored, supervised, approved or (in the case of Ontario) private. This means that the province makes laws regulating approved or regulated homes just as it does for daycare centers. It can compel the caregiver to put hazardous products out of reach, install smoke detectors, submit to a medical exam and police check, serve nutritious meals and snacks, not use corporal punishment and the like.

Regulated family daycare is supposed to meet certain minimum standards. It will probably be safe, healthy and caring at the very least, and under the right conditions it can be even better than that.

The provinces regulate care in two different ways.

Manitoba, Saskatchewan, British Columbia, New Brunswick, Prince Edward Island, the Yukon and the Northwest Territories have chosen to license individual homes directly. Their provincial social service offices approve and take charge of inspecting and supervising the homes, though their visits may be few and far between.[4]

Ontario, Quebec, Alberta and Nova Scotia have a different approach to regulation. These provinces issue licenses to agencies, which in turn approve homes, enforce provincial laws and provide resources to caregivers. Because they are the most closely supervised, these homes (called supervised or agency-sponsored or sponsored daycare homes) usually provide the best family daycare, though an association of family caregivers who've banded together for mutual support and education can do the same job.

To quote the Task Force on Child Care, "Sponsored homes provided better child care environments for children, including more stimulation and more supervision, than did other homes, whether licensed or unlicensed."[5]

The license or regulation is important, but not as important as the supervision.

Subsidies

To help pay their fees, families who use regulated family care can apply for a subsidy from the government. But because there are so few available, plan to apply as soon as your province allows. You aren't eligible for a subsidy if your caregiver isn't regulated.

ADVANTAGES

What are the advantages of a family daycare home? What does it offer a child? How is it different from a sitter or nanny on the one hand and a daycare center on the other?

Substitute mommy

The allure of home care is obvious: it is like home.

For many people, family care is the closest you can get to staying at home taking care of your child yourself. If the real mommy isn't available, some prefer a real-mommy stand-in to love and care for their child instead.

Maureen Landry, coordinator of the Family Day Care Program at Ville Marie Social Service Centre in Montreal, observes, "There is so much anxiety in leaving a child that parents want to be sure that the caregiver will meet his emotional needs. They want to be sure that someone is really interested in him."

And, in fact, when a family daycare arrangement works well, this is its greatest advantage. Says Nicole, whose eight-month-old son Paul attends a regulated daycare home, "I like the fact that he's being spoiled. It gives me a good feeling to know that he is getting a lot of attention."

Ratio

Of course a child won't get very much individual attention if the daycare mom has too large a daycare family, and that is another primary attraction of family daycare—there are just a few children.

The small size of the group makes family daycare particularly appealing for infants, toddlers, children who are shy or withdrawn and children with special needs. The caregiver has a chance to establish a close relationship with a child who might get overlooked in a daycare center.

Because someone inspects a regulated family daycare, if you find a home with a small number of children, it will probably remain small.

Children of different ages

The province also regulates the ages of the children in a family daycare home. Two babies are plenty for one caregiver to handle, especially when there are other children around, and experts suggest that three toddlers and one caregiver are quite enough to form a complete group.[6]

Within a family daycare that mimics a real family, a child will find other children to imitate, play with and fight with. An only child can have an older one to learn from and a younger one to help. Siblings can be together to develop a relationship that center care might deny them.

The caregiver's family

Somehow a caregiver with children of her own—especially children that you like—gives a parent confidence in the caregiver's abilities. "That was important to me," says Mirna, whose 18-month-old daughter Evine started family daycare at four months. "When you have children of your own, you give more care, more attention, more love. You understand more, and you don't get nervous." Ville Marie's Maureen Landry agrees. "We find it's an asset when a caregiver has young children because she's in that mind set. She knows about activities and routines."

The caregiver's older children, who join the fun after school, are an extra added attraction. These exotic creatures often regard the little ones with delight, and the younger children return their affection with full force. Paul uttered his first words to his caregiver's 12-year-old daughter, a home daycare regular. Josh's mother regards her caregiver's older children, boys 12 and nine, and a girl, five, as definite assets: "They get along fabulously with Josh. It's like having older brothers and sisters, and it's so much more fun than just staying home with Mommy, which can get dull and boring. That was the main thing: I wanted him to be stimulated."

Family life

Although you can't count on it, family daycare also offers the possibility of having a man around the house, a real bonus for a child from a single-parent family. A dad who works shifts or evenings may pitch in and help. When Elizabeth walks Louis, a kindergartner, to school at 1 P.M., her husband John, a meteorologist at the airport, stays home with the rest of her brood, two pre-schoolers and two infants. The father of four teenagers, he takes it all in stride.

An unstructured day in familiar surroundings

The homey atmosphere of family daycare is another of its appeals. The child is more comfortable and less stressed in this familiar setting with its familiar activities. With no fixed schedule, he can do as he pleases and take the time he needs to finish what he starts. He can mold the environment to satisfy his needs, make an impression on it, take control. The pace seems especially suitable for children who will trot off to the structured world of junior or pre-kindergarten at age four and for older school-age children who yearn for freedom after a structured day at school.

Self-fulfillment

In the relaxed atmosphere where child and caregiver know each other very well, a child can feel free to be himself and to express himself, to discover his own likes and dislikes, to grow into his own person.

Similar values

A marvelous aspect of family daycare is the idea of finding a mother substitute who shares your values and child-rearing philosophy. A good match is good for everyone, especially your child. He will learn what you would like him to know, in the same manner that you would teach him.[7]

Nicole, a religious Catholic, gladly gave her caregiver permission to say a prayer with Paul every morning. Mirna, a young Arab engineer, was delighted to find Yasmin, an Egyptian caregiver, for four-month-old Evine. "I preferred the idea that she had the same culture and the same religion as I do."

Close relationship with the caregiver

In family daycare the child isn't the only one who can befriend the caregiver. The parent can, too.[8] Because she looks after your child from morning to night, she knows every detail of his day and what he's like as a person. Because the group is small, she has more time to talk. Because children dominate her world, she enjoys adult conversation.

The end of the day presents a natural opportunity to get caught up on events. After 15 minutes spent discussing their favorite topic, their child, parents go home much more in touch with both their offspring and the caregiver. This kind of parental participation is another hallmark of quality care.

It is particularly comforting in the beginning. Says Mirna, who simultaneously weaned Evine and enrolled her in family daycare, "The first few days I missed her so much that I called every five minutes. Yasmin calmed me down."

It's also helpful when a child is sick or teething or upset to know that you can pick up the phone and get a personal up-to-the-minute report. Nicole, whose older child attends a daycare center, considers this a real plus to family care. "I can always contact the caregiver and know how Paul is doing. At Trevor's daycare center it's harder to talk to the teachers."

More control
Because they're in close contact, parents may have more control. If they prefer their child to eat whole-wheat bread and no meat, if he has a sore throat and shouldn't play outside today, a flexible family caregiver can accommodate him more easily than a daycare center.

Location
Family daycares pop up virtually everywhere. A recent Ontario study found them in communities of any size, from large cities to rural districts of less than 10,000.[9] A family daycare in your own neighborhood allows your child to go to his local park, shops and YMCA and meet his friends the way he would at home. Having the daycare nearby is also extremely convenient for parents, whose travel time shrinks accordingly.

Health
A powerful argument in favor of family daycare is that it's healthier—children in family care are three to four times less likely to contract respiratory and intestinal illnesses than children in daycare centers.[10]

Another advantage for a parent who has a demanding boss, no family leave and no relatives to take over in a pinch is that family daycare providers are often willing to take care of a mildly ill child.[11]

Flexible and extended hours
If you're a nurse who works different shifts each week or a photographer whose hours vary with every assignment, you probably want to spend your off-hours with your child. Family daycare holds out the possibility of flexible care. A caregiver may be willing to take your child at 6 A.M. or keep him until 8 P.M.; she may be willing to look after him half days, or Mondays and Wednesdays, or change as your shift changes.

Cost
You may hear that one of the greatest advantages of family daycare is that it's cheaper than center care. This is sometimes true, and it's usually true for unregulated care, at least in some parts of the country. But alas and alack, depending on where you live, it is not necessarily

true for regulated care. Don't make any assumptions about cost without checking out the scene in your community.

On the other hand, family daycare is certainly less trouble, financially speaking, than hiring a nanny or sitter and paying contributions to unemployment, medicare, Workers' Compensation, and the like. With regulated family daycare, all you do is pay your money, collect your receipt and file your tax return.

Stability

Theoretically, family daycare is incredibly stable. Your child has the same caregiver all day; in fact, he can have the same caregiver from infancy through his elementary-school years. This long, close relationship with one person gives him a secure base for the future.

Custom-made

If you live in a province that has agency-sponsored care, you usually tell the agency exactly what you're looking for, and a trained, experienced person finds a caregiver to match your requirements. If you don't like the provider the agency comes up with, you can ask for another. Looking for either a nanny or a daycare center is a murderously difficult process by comparison.

DISADVANTAGES

Life being what it is, for every advantage there is a corresponding disadvantage. What are the drawbacks of family daycare?

Substitute mommy

Having a substitute mommy isn't all roses. Jean Wise, manager of the Day Care Finders Program at Family Day Care Services in Toronto, always warns parents, "No one will look after your child the way you would." It seems obvious, but let us remind you that people are not rational when it comes to child care.

Here is another problem. When push comes to shove, a substitute mommy may not be what you want at all. Social worker Adele Rosen, who's been matching up parents and caregivers at Montreal's Ville Marie Social Service Centre for six years, points out that finding a warm and loving caregiver may bring unexpected emotions—like the green monster, jealousy. Although it is a tribute to you as a parent when your child develops a close relationship with someone else, although it's wonderful to see him happy and well cared for, it's hard at the same time. It takes a certain maturity and a powerful dose of philosophical detachment for Penny, mother of 22-month-old Josh, to say, "It's like having two mommies."

With a substitute mommy, you also run the risk of losing your self-confidence as a parent. Advice and discussion are great, as long as there's give and take and you don't go away feeling you'll never be able to do it as well as she does.

And there is guilt, lots of guilt, because she is staying home looking after your child, and you aren't. Studies have found that parents who use family daycare tend to feel more guilty about leaving their children than parents who use center care.[12]

Ratio
There are two potential problems with the caregiver-to-child ratio in family daycare. The first is that the caregiver may ignore the provincial law and take too many children. In fact, we have heard about illegal family daycares with as many as 15 children. The second is that she may take more children than she or her space can comfortably handle, which amounts to the same thing. This is more likely with unregulated homes.

Children of different ages
In a small group of children of different ages, it's hard to get a fair share of the caregiver's attention. Babies can't wait for meals and naps, and they need the caregiver more. Even one baby can change everything. When Craig collected his three-year-old son Ethan from his family daycare on a beautiful sunny day, he was dismayed to learn that the children hadn't been outside. "The baby was fussy," the caregiver explained apologetically. Experts have suggested that a narrow age range of about two years works best.[13]

In an intimate setting, personalities intrude more, too. An aggressive child can change the group's chemistry completely.

Although it's very handy to have siblings together, it may be hard to find a caregiver who'll take them. She doesn't have space, or she specializes in children of a particular age. (See chapter 19, "The Second Child," for a full rundown on this subject.)

The caregiver's family
Unfortunately, being a mother does not automatically qualify a woman to be a family daycare provider. Many mothers can't cope with their

own children, let alone someone else's. Research shows that training (in family daycare, child development or early childhood education) works much better.[14]

As for the caregiver's own children, having other children come into their home is not a piece of cake. Though they're gaining playmates, they're paying a high price—they have to share their toys, their space and their mother. They're bound to be jealous and angry, and it takes clear thinking, sensitivity, tact and patience on the part of the caregiver to make them feel comfortable. And she has to do all this without favoring them! Needless to say, many providers have trouble walking this tightrope.

Family life

Some fathers (and other family members) resent having other people's children in the house, resent not having dinner ready when they come home from work or school. They can even be potential child abusers.

These risks, though small, are real, especially in unregulated care, where there is no investigation of police and youth-protection records, and no one demands a medical exam or home check.

There is more. "The biggest disadvantage of family daycare is that one is subject to what's going on in that family's life," says Maureen Landry. A provider can move, become pregnant, have a miscarriage, get a divorce. These events will inevitably affect her daycare children, no matter how well she handles them.

An unstructured day in familiar surroundings

Structure is one of the great issues of family daycare. With just one child, perhaps a caregiver could have a thoroughly spontaneous, unscheduled day. But the moment a second child enters the picture, the caregiver has to be organized—that is, if anyone is ever going outside again. At the very least, every caregiver needs to plan snacks, meals and naps. With two infants, Nicole's caregiver juggles meals and naps so that she can have time alone with each baby. Caregiver Yasmin knows her three toddlers will collapse into their sandwiches if she doesn't give them lunch by 11:30 A.M.

Although they recognize that a daycare mother can do lots of spontaneous teaching as she and the children move together from baking muffins to sorting socks, family daycare agencies encourage their caregivers to plan their hours with the children and do their housework later. The structure needn't be detailed or complex, but if the environment is to be rich and stimulating it ought to exist. In order to have an art activity, the caregiver has to get the materials ready and figure out a time to sit down with the children. When she has a baby in the group, she needs to calculate when he'll fall asleep so that he can nap in his stroller while she supervises the older kids in the park. If she's always in the kitchen fixing someone a snack, the time fritters itself away, and there's none left for intellectually and developmentally stimulating activities—or even for hugs.

Overcontrol

In a family daycare, the caregiver is on her own, responsible for absolutely everything. One way for her to get safely through the day is to demand good behavior from the children. When she leaves the room momentarily to put a very tired child to bed, she needs to know that the rest won't destroy one another or the house. If she knows the children well, and she has done a good job of planning activities and providing plenty of different toys, good behavior will follow logically. But a less skilled caregiver will end up using a lot of coercive measures—an angry voice, criticism, threats, "no!," punishment—and the children may be overcontrolled and afraid. This atmosphere is definitely not conducive to the growth of self-esteem.

Similar values

Family daycare providers, who earn less money and may have less education than their clients, are a conservative group who still sometimes believe that mothers who work outside the home are not doing their best for their children.[15] What values will a caregiver who thinks this way impart? Will she—probably without even realizing it— subtly undermine the mother and treat the child with pity? Will she understand the mother's point of view? How can a mother be up front with someone who disapproves of her?

Similar values are particularly important when it comes to discipline. "These issues often break down the relationship," says Maria de Wit, executive director of Toronto's Family Day Care Services, the largest family home daycare agency in the country. "There might be willingness on both sides to have a good arrangement, but if I believe my child has to eat everything on his plate and you don't, we're never going to see eye to eye."

Close relationship with the caregiver

The closeness you have with a family caregiver has a down side: it can become a kind of tyranny. The good relationship is so important that a parent doesn't dare to speak her mind. When Paul had a mild case of diarrhea, Nicole brought bananas and rice cereal for him to eat. Her caregiver brushed aside her concerns, saying, "Don't worry, he's just teething. I'll feed him his regular food, and if there's a problem I'll call you." Nicole didn't argue. Because she depends on the caregiver so heavily, she doesn't want to put the relationship at risk by disagreeing. She feels as if she's over a barrel.

Parents also sometimes find themselves the captive audience of a caregiver. The pleasant 15-minute conversation at the end of the day can turn into a marathon because it seems so rude to leave. Phone calls, too, can become addictive.

Location

Again, one has to be lucky. Sometimes you can find family daycare in your neighborhood, and sometimes you can't. Needless to say, regulated care is much harder to find than unregulated, and you have to be especially lucky to find sponsored care if you don't live in Alberta, Ontario, Quebec or Nova Scotia.

Even when the caregiver is next door, however, it's not as easy as having a sitter or nanny. Your child is not in his own home, and you still have to bundle him into boots and snowsuits and make extra stops on your itinerary morning and evening.

Health

Although your child will probably be healthier than he would be in a daycare center, family daycare doesn't let you off the hook completely as far as health is concerned. One day he will come down with a flu that turns him into a dishrag, and no caregiver, however amenable, will accept him. You will need a backup system, just as you will when your caregiver gets sick. Although she may carry on anyway, the hardiest soul sometimes succumbs.[16] Even agencies can't promise backup service.

Flexible and extended hours

Again, the problem is that these caregivers may be hard to find, especially in the regulated sector.[17] (In Ontario, only 4 percent offer extended hours.)[18] And a caregiver who accepts children under these circumstances may have to set some rules—like requiring you to arrive by 10:30 A.M. so that she can take the crew outside before lunch.

Cost

The cost of family care will depend on where you live and whether the care is regulated or not. Defying myth, it may not be cheap. In Toronto, where everything is expensive, agency-sponsored family daycare costs 23 dollars a day, but a first-class unregulated provider (who may have recently worked for an agency) can command a daily fee of 40 or 50 dollars.

With unregulated care you cannot get a subsidy, and many caregivers don't give tax receipts, which means that you don't get any money back at tax time.

Stability

Statistics tell a sad story. Caregiver turnover in family daycare is very high.[19] When your caregiver quits, the change will be hard on your child—he will miss her, and he will have to adjust to a whole new scene. (See chapter 20, "Switching Daycare," pages 306-325.) In some provinces, your agency will help find you a new caregiver, but in provinces without sponsoring agencies you're on your own, shuttling your child from sitter to sitter and taking time off work to search for someone you like.

There is also great turnover among the children in family daycare; and because the groups are so small and close-knit, the loss of one child or the arrival of another has an enormous impact. When Ethan's best friend left the family daycare, his caregiver replaced him with a baby. Ethan was devastated. He had lost not only his friend but also his peer contact, and having the baby there meant the caregiver was always busy. Because Paul was her only daycare child, Nicole's caregiver lavished attention on him. But six months later, when she had accepted four other children, Nicole felt that she was neglecting Paul. The group was the very opposite of stable: it seemed to be in constant flux.

Family daycare is unstable in another sense. As more and more mothers of babies go to work, home daycare is becoming geared to infant and toddler care, for which it is extremely well suited. But as the babies crowd in, the older children drift away. With the arrival of the baby, Ethan's parents realized that he had outgrown his family daycare, and they decided to send him to a daycare center instead. Many family daycare children go this route.

Choice and availability

Although a large proportion of Canadian families use family daycare, most of them don't actively choose their provider. In provinces with agency-sponsored care, the agencies usually pick out a caregiver for you, but they can rarely offer more than one because so few are available. In provinces without agencies, where you must do all your own legwork for both regulated and unregulated homes, people tend to settle for the first home they see. It's hard to invade someone else's privacy, even when it's important.[20]

It's not always a fair process, either. A daycare center will take a child as soon as his name reaches the top of their list, and they will keep him, pretty much for better or for worse, until he chooses to leave. But your family caregiver has the power to select, and reject, the children in her home. She may eject your child on the basis of something so simple as a tendency to projectile vomiting or as complex as not fitting in socially with the group. Like a landlord who wants to rent his apartment to his son, a caregiver can ask a child to leave in order to open a space for a friend or sibling. She can accept new children to suit her own interests, not yours (and not necessarily those of your child). To make ends meet, she may have to add a baby to the group, even though the older children may suffer.

Variability in quality

Perhaps the greatest problem with family daycare is that its quality varies enormously. The best embodies all the advantages we've mentioned—a warm, loving, responsive caregiver who, with the help of a family daycare association or a sponsoring agency, transforms her home not only into a comfortable and relaxed place for a child but also into an exciting learning environment.

The worst is unspeakably bad. Many homes are unsafe and unhealthy, and the care is basically custodial—the caregiver believes she is discharging her obligations if she feeds the children, changes their diapers and puts them down for a nap. They may spend the whole day inside watching television, never reading a book, painting a picture or singing a song.

Unregulated homes are particularly liable to these abuses. No one comes around to evaluate the care. No one knows how many children are there or what they do all day, and the children are far too young to speak up for themselves.

Regulated homes are approved before they first open, but because only a small proportion of them receive frequent or regular inspections, regulation isn't a guarantee of quality.

Except in Manitoba, it is mainly agency-sponsored homes that are supervised adequately enough to offer quality care.

HOW TO FIND FAMILY DAYCARE

The best way to decide whether you want regulated family home daycare is to go see it.

Working with an agency
If you live in a province where agencies are responsible for regulated family daycare, you are in luck. The job of finding a safe, healthy, stimulating family daycare home to suit your needs will be relatively easy.

The first step is to call your provincial child care office. (The number is listed in the blue pages of your telephone directory under the provincial ministry of social services, or you can find it in the appendix to this book.) They can give you a list of agencies that supervise the regulated homes near you. Because regulated family care is still a well-kept secret in many places, you may have to be quite persistent. Don't give up. Eventually you'll reach someone who has the information you need.

There are two kinds of agencies, non-profit and commercial. We prefer non-profit agencies—they supervise more frequently and comprehensively, and their homes therefore provide better care—but we suggest that you phone and register everywhere that makes sense from the point of view of geography. You never know how long you'll have to wait for a place, especially for an infant, and it's always better to have a choice. (For more information about non-profit versus profit daycare, see pages 98 to 100.)

Some agencies will hand you a list of family daycare homes with available spaces and send you out to brave the world alone. But most try to team you up with a home that's just right for you and your child. Eventually you'll have an interview with a specialist who will ask you about your daycare needs in great detail.

If you're very lucky, she may have a couple of possibilities for you to choose from. When she thinks she's found you a compatible provider, you, your partner, if possible, and the child care specialist will go to visit her home. (We'll give you some visiting pointers in the section coming up.) If you haven't asked for the moon and the agency is doing its matching job well, you'll probably like the provider very much, and, presto, you'll be all set. But if for any reason you don't click, of course you can request another. Eventually the right one will turn up.

Working without an agency

If you live in a province that licenses family daycare homes directly, you still need to phone your local child care office. They will tell you how to find a regulated family daycare in your district.

While you're on the phone, ask about regulations in your province. How many children is a regulated caregiver allowed to have in her home, both in total and by age group?

Looking for unregulated care is like searching for a needle in a haystack. You, too, must call the child care branch, this time to discover the legal number of children a provider can take without a license.

Then the real search begins.

Caregivers advertise in neighborhood newspapers—in fact, you may come across both regulated and unregulated caregivers in the classifieds—as well as posting notices on supermarket bulletin boards and listing themselves with community organizations and schools. Some provinces and cities actually have child care resource and information centers that help both parents and caregivers. But because the grapevine often fills family daycare spaces before any outsider knows about them, ask about child care arrangements whenever you see friends and family with children. You never know who'll come up with a hot tip.

MAKING TELEPHONE CALLS

Once you have a list of possible homes, what do you do? Get on the phone.

Here's what you'll need to ask

1. *Is your home regulated or licensed?* This remains a crucial question.

2. *Do you have a space for a child of (whatever age child yours is) for (whenever you will need daycare)?*

3. *How many children do you take care of, including your own, and how old are they?* High quality depends on a good caregiver-to-child ratio, so knowing the total number of children present every day is crucial. You want a caregiver who abides by the law, you want her to have enough time and energy to give your child lots of individual attention, and you want the age grouping to suit your child's needs.

4. *Do you have as many children as you want in your family daycare home right now?* A caregiver may have just one or two children when she starts out, but her aim may be to care for the legal maximum. When you've visiting a home, you want to know whether she will have the number you actually see plus one (your child) or two or three or four more. She can continue to add children at any time as long as she stays within the ratio requirements. The regulations set a maximum number and some age limits, but the real question is always how many children she can handle comfortably. It depends on the personalities of the children and the caregiver's skill—but you can't judge those on the phone!

5. *Where are you located?* If you don't have the caregiver's address or you don't know the neighborhood, find out her exact location and how to get there. Is it on your route to work? Is it convenient?

6. *What are your hours? Do you work full-time?* If you need flexible or extended hours, ask about that now. Even if you need part-time care, search for a caregiver who has children in her home all day every day. A recent study shows that full-time caregivers tend to be more professional and offer a better program.[21]

7. *Do you belong to a caregivers' association or support network?* As we mentioned earlier, caregivers who belong to an association provide better care, whether they're regulated or not. Associations, networks and agencies all assist the caregiver in planning activities and meals, act as a resource when problems arise with children or parents, provide toys, materials and equipment, help with tax returns and administration, inform her about drop-in centers, toy libraries and special events in her neighborhood, offer her first aid or child development courses, give her a shoulder to cry on.

8. *Do you have any training?* To reiterate, training in child develop-

ment, early childhood education or family daycare is a key component of quality care.[22]

9. *What are your fees? Do I pay when my child is sick or I'm on vacation?* Caregivers' policies on this point vary. Although it's obviously less expensive if you don't pay when your child doesn't attend, it means the caregiver doesn't have a secure financial base and may take on extra or part-time children to make up the difference. You should expect to pay for care when your child is sick, even if you have to pay a babysitter, too.

   As for vacations, the best arrangement is for everyone to take them simultaneously. Caregivers desperately need a break. You can figure out a convenient time over a coffee.

   A caregiver who doesn't hold firm on these points may not consider herself a professional, which may in turn indicate lower-quality care.

10. *Do you give tax receipts?* Without a receipt, you won't be able to deduct child care at tax time, which will, of course, hike up the cost of your daycare. And the provision of the tax receipt is also an index of quality care. According to a study by the Independent Child Caregivers Association in Ottawa, caregivers who give tax receipts are more likely to visit the library and drop-in and resource centers, more likely to have taken courses in their field, more likely to belong to a caregivers' association and more likely to be satisfied with their work.[23]

11. *Do you have liability insurance?* Because accidents can happen anywhere, this is an extremely important question. It will also tell you whether the caregiver takes her job seriously.

VISITING A FAMILY DAYCARE

If this conversation has made this caregiver sound like a real possibility for you, make an appointment to visit her.

Visiting a family daycare is a ticklish business.

How long should your visit last?
Maria de Wit counsels parents to stay at least half a day. "They say to me, 'I can't afford to,' and I say, 'You can't afford not to.'"

Should I bring my child?
Many people—including family daycare agencies—suggest that your

child accompany you on this first visit to the family caregiver. The caregiver herself is probably more interested in meeting your child than in meeting you, and if you don't bring him you run the risk of losing the place to a child-escorted rival.

Nonetheless, we don't recommend it. Of course you can bring an infant sleeping in a carrier, but an active wanderer, whose doings and whereabouts you'll have to monitor, should stay at home. You don't know the caregiver's rules or the hazards of the house, and this is not a recommended way to test them. Besides, you need to concentrate on the task at hand, not your child. You want to see how the caregiver deals with the children she has at present and then calculate whether she can handle yours as well.

Choosing daycare is a decision for grown-ups. If you like and trust the caregiver, then you can bring your child to meet her. Because you will have confidence in her, your child, who will inevitably take his cue from you, will, too. He will get along better if his parents feel committed to the arrangement. The real trial period is the first few weeks, when either you or the caregiver can change her mind.

Approaching the caregiver

First and foremost, this is someone's home, and you are a guest as well as a total stranger. Yet your goal is to get to know this person and her home well enough to trust her with the nearest and dearest person in your life, your child. How can one carry out this delicate mission effectively?

In a daycare center you can open cupboard doors to see whether there's bleach under the sink, but in a private home it even seems rude to ask, "Where do you keep the medicine?" Although we aren't going to suggest you snoop around in the closets, we do think you'll have to look at this environment very carefully, take your courage in your hands, and oh so politely ask a few slightly awkward questions.

But not just yet.

There are at least two extremely good reasons to treat this caregiver as nicely as possible. The first is that she has the power to reject you and your child if she doesn't like you. The second is that she may actually become your daycare provider, and you'd like to start your relationship off on the right foot. We suggest that you go slowly. Give her a little time and space to feel comfortable with you, and give yourself a chance to read her a bit. As you get to know each other, you'll figure out how to approach her.

When you first come in, you will meet not only the caregiver but also the children she cares for. To them, you will be a large stranger, intruding on their private territory, and they may seek refuge with their Rock of Gibraltar, the caregiver. This is perfectly normal behavior. Say hello, and then just let them be. In a while, when they're feeling more comfortable in your presence, they'll climb off the caregiver's lap and go about their business. Then you'll have a chance to see how they get along together and how they interact with the caregiver.

Unless her husband or an agency worker is around, the caregiver can't stop looking after the children while she talks to you. That is her primary responsibility, and she mustn't neglect it. You can't jump in and help either—because then how will you know how well she does her job? You, the keen observer, must sit back and watch.

What should you look at?

Although a family daycare isn't really a mini-daycare center, evaluating these two types of care isn't very different. Chapter 11, "How to Look at a Daycare Center," applies to choosing family care as well.

As you sit with the caregiver or follow her from room to room, notice the space. You can't expect her to turn her entire home into a play area, but she should have at least one room set up for the children. It should be totally safe and childproofed, with sturdy furniture, covers on electrical outlets and no breakable objects in reach. Toys and equipment should be on low shelves, accessible to the children. Are there enough toys to go around?

The layout is important, too. The caregiver should be able to change diapers and prepare meals while keeping an eye and ear on the children. It's almost impossible for her to be with them every second of the day, but the design of the space can minimize her time away. An intercom is a help, too.

The television shouldn't be on without a special reason: the caregiver is making lunch, or it's the end of a long rainy day. It goes without saying that the program should be educational. Are books and records or tapes in evidence? Are there art activities or eye-catching pictures on the walls?

Watch the caregiver as she changes diapers. Does she clean the changing area well between changes and/or use a separate changing mat for each child? Does she wash her hands thoroughly between children?

Does she also wash her hands well before she handles food?

Before you leave, ask to see all the rooms that the children use—where they sleep, where they eat, the bathroom (now you can ask where the medicine is!), the backyard. Do gates or closed doors keep them out of unchildproofed areas?

The caregiver herself

The caregiver is always the most important element in a daycare, and it is she you've really come to see. Is she warm and responsive? Does she squat at the children's level and look them in the eye? Is she listening and talking to the children all the time? Is her voice kind and gentle? Does she come quickly to the aid of a child in distress? Is she animated, brimming with energy and fully involved in being with them?

Does fruit salad for lunch mean a spontaneous lesson in colors or shapes or sizes? Is she a natural teacher who uses every mundane activity to encourage the children to explore and participate?

Do you approve of the way she handles problems, for example, if one child takes a toy away from another?

Do you like her?

Listen to the way she talks to you about the daycare children, and compare what she says to what you see. Does she seem to know them well? Does she talk about them with pride? Yasmin, describing 22-month-old Josh, said, "He's very smart, and I'm not just saying that because I'm his...." Though she caught herself at this point, she clearly regarded the little boy with enough pride and affection to be his mother.

Look at the children. How do they relate to the caregiver? Do they seem at ease and relaxed in her presence? Do they feel comfortable enough to crawl onto her lap? Do they ask her questions? Are the children smiling, chattering and giggling? Are they absorbed in their play?

Look at the caregiver's own children. Do you like the way they and their mother behave together? Do you like her children? Does she treat them the same way she treats the daycare children, or does she tend to take their side? How do the daycare children relate to them? When you go on your little tour, notice if the caregiver's children have their own space and toys. If they have some things they don't have to share, they'll probably share everything else, including their mother, more willingly.

How do the children get along together? How will your child fit in?

What is the age range? Remember that the experts recommend a span of just two years.[24] For an older child, 18 months and up, the makeup of the group is a particularly important consideration. (Two is company, and three never works.)

Ask some questions

When the opportunity arises, ask the caregiver a few questions. These are the important ones:

1. *Do you have a daily schedule? Can you tell me about a typical day?* As we mentioned, programming enhances the quality of the care. This doesn't mean the caregiver has to plan every minute, but she should have a routine, and she should be able to mention a few special activities.

   If she doesn't belong to a caregivers' group, the schedule should tell you about her contacts with the outside world. Does she regularly meet another caregiver in the park? Does she go to a playgroup every Tuesday morning? Has she created her own informal network?

2. *How often do the children go outside? Where do you take them?* Of course, the children should go out every day unless it's 30 degrees below zero or raining cats and dogs. If she has non-walkers, does she have a double stroller? If she drives, does she have car seats for everyone?

   Most of the time it's fun to play in the yard, go for a walk around the block, visit a nearby playground. It's hard, and possibly dangerous, for a family caregiver to go any farther afield without additional adult help. If there is an accident, she must manage several children all alone.

3. *Do you have an emergency procedure?* An accident can frighten everyone in a family daycare, but the caregiver has to maintain her cool. This means she should have some first aid background as well as a plan of how to proceed. Will she call 911? What if she isn't near a phone? What will she do with the injured child? What will she do with the others?

4. *What do you serve for meals and snacks? Do you have a menu?* The caregiver will no doubt serve the children something to eat while you're visiting, so disregard your mother's advice and keep your eyes on their plates. Does her idea of a healthy meal coincide

with yours? Agencies often work actively with their caregivers in this area, giving training in nutrition and menu planning. If you and the caregiver disagree about what's nutritious, a lunch box lunch may solve the problem. (Note, too, whether the caregiver demands that the children eat every last bite and whether she makes them sit still at the table until everyone has finished. Are your child-rearing philosophies in sync?)

5. *When do you do your housework? What chores do you do while the children are here?* Just as you wouldn't dust while you have guests, the caregiver will not do her normal round of housekeeping tasks while you're in the house. The only way to find out about this important issue is to ask. Of course, she should never do dangerous jobs like ironing while she's caring for the children, but she may do laundry or start dinner. It is the rare individual who can take care of small children and manage household chores at the same time, except during nap (if all the children happen to sleep simultaneously). In our opinion, the caregiver's job is to take care of the children, not her house, even though some agencies permit it. The more time caregivers spend doing housework, the less they spend interacting with the children.

6. *What is your policy about watching television?* No one can ignore this fact of modern life, but a person who looks after children must give hard thought to its use. According to one scale, a first-rate caregiver allows no television at all or joins the children in watching educational programs and follows up on them afterwards.

    But it is also all right to allow the children to watch an educational program on their own, as long as they can choose to do something else instead. Says Maureen Landry, "Putting the children in front of the TV at 11 A.M. when 'Sesame Street' is on is a way of making sure they're safe and entertained while the caregiver gets lunch ready."

    It's not acceptable for them to watch adult programs or for the caregiver to leave the set on for more than one show per day.[25] You no doubt have views on this subject. Do they match the caregiver's?

7. *What will you do if my child hits someone?* If the children and the caregiver haven't already enacted this scene before your very eyes, do ask about discipline. By law, a caregiver may not use corporal punishment, and she should have lots of tricks for helping children of different ages to learn self-control and to sort out their problems.

She could ask them to sit out quietly for a few minutes, tend to the victim before she deals with the perpetrator or offer an alternate toy. She could explain to younger children that it hurts; she could help older ones to talk things over. Do her methods agree with yours?

8. *What do you like about your work? Why do you do it?* "I love children" is the best possible response to this question. Someone who's really interested in children and is willing to spend the day helping them to learn and grow is going to be a better caregiver than someone who can't get any other job or someone who's merely seeking playmates for her own children. Agencies try to weed out these people, but if you're looking at unregulated care, you'll have to ferret out this very important piece of information yourself.

9. *How long do you plan to continue being a family daycare provider?* With so much turnover among caregivers, this question has immediate, practical implications—you need to know how long you can count on this caregiver. But it also tells you about her commitment and sense of herself as a professional. If she intends to stick with this career, she'll probably be more willing to invest her time, money and energy in outfitting her house and getting some training for herself.

REFERENCES

If you like what you've seen, be sure to ask the caregiver for references from two different sets of parents—one whose child is still with her and one who has recently left. Before giving out their numbers, she'll need their permission, so she may suggest they call you directly or ask you to phone back.

Speaking to these parents is essential—they are bound to know more about her than you can possibly find out in a visit or two. Occasionally the information is quite startling (one reference said, "I'm pretty sure she's stopped using drugs"), but that is a rare occurrence. You're more likely to stumble across a caregiver who left the children alone or who never took them outside in the winter. Some experts suggest that you check the caregiver's references before you visit. We prefer to form our own impressions and check afterwards.

When you talk to a reference, you're trying to learn several things at once. The most important is the one we just mentioned—that the family and the caregiver did not part ways because of the caregiver's incompetence. You hope to find that the child simply outgrew the situation or the family moved across the city.

You're also trying to gather more information. Ask how long their children have been there, whether the caregiver works best with a particular age group, what they do all day, how often they go out, how much time they spend watching television, what they eat, how she disciplines and what their own relationship with the caregiver is like. What do they like about their caregiver? What don't they like? What kind of a mood is their child in when they pick him up at the end of the day?

At the same time, you're trying to confirm your own impressions, a very difficult task because you know the other parent even less than you know the caregiver. To establish the reliability of your witness, ask about something you really care about, like, "How did you and the caregiver go about toilet training your child?" or "What does she do if she thinks your child isn't well?" That way you're more likely to discover whether you're on the same wavelength.

Talking to another parent serves one more purpose: it gives you a preview of your compatriots if you choose this caregiver. A family daycare is a little like an extended family. Your children will be intimates, and if you work similar hours you may get to know their parents well, too. It's nice if you like each other. And it's a real bonus to encounter a familiar person on the first day.

AND VISIT AGAIN

To double-check your impressions, Maria de Wit recommends making a second visit, this time unannounced. "Hold back a couple of questions so you can say, 'Oh, I forgot to ask you something.'"

Because you may not always pick up your child before other family members arrive home, de Wit offers another piece of advice: meet the whole family. From seeing them together, you'll know whether you want to expose your children to their influence.

Last but not least, don't rush. "If you have a gut feeling," she says, "if you are uncomfortable, don't put your child there. Keep looking." But the obverse is also true: if you feel good about it after you've checked the references, go with your feelings and sign up.

No matter whom you choose, you have to keep an eye on the situation. Having good family care means talking regularly with the caregiver and other parents, dropping in at key times (11 A.M. to 1 P.M. when the caregiver is preparing lunch and the children are eating and getting ready for their naps), making phone calls at all hours and listening for background noises (television, children crying), picking up your child at different times of the day and observing what they're doing.

Boys and Girls come out to play
And join your playfellows....
MOTHER GOOSE

CHAPTER 6

What about Nursery
or Pre-School?

Originally intended to provide enrichment for the children of the affluent, nursery or pre-schools have been a popular choice for middle-class families since the 1930s. Traditionally they have run a half-day program for three- to five-year-olds, emphasizing social experience, learning and creative expression under the watchful eyes of trained teachers.

More recently, as women of all economic classes joined the labor force, nursery and pre-schools took on a second function, sometimes without noticing: they began to supply child care. But only part-time, of course.

Such schools still exist, and—except for their operating hours— they're sometimes hard to distinguish from daycare centers. They generally fall under the same provincial legislation, and they offer a similar (if shorter) round of activities.

But there are some important differences that parents ought to know.

ADVANTAGES

What attracts families to nursery and pre-schools?

Part-time

If you think that your child is ready for some regular contact with his peers, but you believe that the daycare day is too long and too intense for him, then nursery or pre-school may be just the ticket for you. After two or three creative, stimulating hours with a stable group of companions, he can come home for lunch and a rest, spend some time with his siblings and bask in the one-on-one care of a relative, a sitter, a nanny or his own real-life mommy.

Nowadays parents who choose to stay at home are so rare that their children sometimes have trouble finding playmates—the other youngsters are all tucked away into daycare centers, family daycare homes or at home with their sitters and nannies. For these children, a good nursery or pre-school is ideal: a child can spend half his day with his friends and half with his mom or dad.

If you work part-time and can arrange your hours to coincide with the school's, then nursery or pre-school also makes good sense— perhaps more sense than a daycare center, which is geared to full-time care. It's no fun being one of a handful of children who leave every day at noon when almost everyone else stays until 5:30 or 6 P.M. A child feels left out. His friends, unable to count on him, find someone else to play with. Children who need part-time care deserve a consistent group of friends. They also deserve a program created for a half day— one that is more condensed and includes all the activities that a daycare center stretches over a full day. (If a daycare center schedules art in the afternoons, for example, a child who comes mornings only will never have a chance to do art.)

Health

Most pre-schools and nurseries don't admit infants or toddlers, and when they and their diapers fail to make an appearance, germs and disease tend to stay away, too.

Parents who work all day occasionally find themselves pressed to send sick children to child care—it's hard to arrange a reliable backup scheme, and their boss just doesn't understand their problem. But many families who use pre-schools have full-time help at home or one parent who isn't working, so it's easier for them to keep a child with a cough and a runny nose away from school. When there are fewer sick children present, the risk of illness drops for everyone.

Availability

Like daycare centers, nursery and pre-schools sometimes have waiting lists, but the process of getting in isn't usually so stressful. Most operate on a school calendar, and they recommend that you apply in January or February, just as soon as registration begins for the following September.

Quality

Because the pre-school day is very short, it avoids the rough patches in the child's day like lunch and nap, and transitions are fewer and easier to cope with. The children don't get so tired, and the program can be packed with activity—but, of course, that depends on the individual school.

Variety

No matter what your philosophy, you'll probably find a nursery or pre-school to match it. There are profit and non-profit pre-schools, Montessori and parent-cooperative pre-schools, French-immersion and fine-arts nursery schools. If you want your child to decide everything for himself, you'll find him a program that emphasizes independence. If your desire is to give his school career a boost, you may discover a program that will teach him pre-reading, writing, science and math. If you want him to get along with others, you'll send him to a school that emphasizes social skills.

DISADVANTAGES

Almost every item on the list that follows stems from the fact that nursery or pre-school is part-time and therefore not a viable daycare option on its own.

Part-time

If both you and your partner hold full-time jobs, you will need an auxiliary system to make pre-school work for you. A relative, sitter, nanny or family daycare provider who can take over until you arrive home in the evening is mandatory.

If you're the parent of an infant or toddler as well as a pre-school-age child, you may already have such a caregiver.

A part-time sitter (like a university student) who bridges the gap from noon to 6 P.M. is another possibility—but that leaves you with a different set of problems. What if your child is running a 102-degree fever? What about summer vacation, Christmas vacation and spring break? Will your sitter be available, or will you have to go back to square one and devise a whole new child care plan?

Inflexible

Nursery or pre-school starts at a certain time and ends at a certain time. You have to bring and collect your child at the designated hour, not at your own convenience. (Your child may be scheduled for either a morning or an afternoon session.) This implacable state of affairs implies that you have a means of transport (as well as a parent or parent-substitute) on tap. A nanny or sitter who can drive is a big help. Some pre-schools and nurseries can arrange busing or taxi service. And then there is the ubiquitous car pool. Are you prepared to drive and manage several children at once—and in the middle of the day at that?

It's useful if the pre-school is nearby. By the time you or your surrogate gets there and back, it's time to turn around and make the trip all over again—a particular inconvenience on a bitter February day or if the baby is asleep.

No babies allowed

Although the lower limits are loosening now, nursery and pre-schools don't ordinarily allow children who are under two and a half or three and who aren't toilet trained. Your infant or toddler will have to socialize some other way.

Cost

Since you will need at least one kind of supplemental care to make pre-school a functional daycare alternative, the cost is bound to be high. Even a family that is already using a sitter for a younger child will be adding a hefty item to its budget. Though prices vary widely according to the area where you live, the type of school and the number of hours your child attends, we've heard of pre-schools that cost almost as much as daycare centers, although they're providing just a half-day program.

Quality

Besides philosophical diversity, there is a vast range in the quality of pre-schools and nursery schools. Some, catering to the well-heeled in the community, sport buildings of their own with well-equipped classrooms and trained teachers. Others, which rent rooms in schools or church basements, don't have a space to call their own and struggle along with parent volunteers and too many untrained people working at minimum wage.

Every province regulates nursery and pre-schools in its own way, and in several places the standards may not be as high as they are for daycare centers. The group size may be larger, and each teacher may be responsible for more children—key areas when it comes to high-quality care.

In Quebec in particular, where at the moment nursery and pre-schools aren't required to meet any norms or standards (the only rule is that a child can't stay longer than four hours), parents must be wary. Of course, there are many fine pre-schools in the province, but if you need four to eight hours of care a day, a licensed daycare center or regulated family daycare home with required group sizes, staff-child ratios and trained staff is a far better (and legal) alternative.

Although a child will not spend as much time in any pre-school as he would in a daycare center, it remains extremely important for parents to investigate a school carefully before enrolling their child. In fact, you should evaluate a pre-school exactly the same way that you evaluate a daycare center. Chapter 11, "How to Look at a Daycare Center," will tell you all about recognizing a good one. Choose one with a license—then you'll have some hope that it's actually following the rules in your province. If you phone your provincial daycare authority (the number is in the appendix of this book), you can find out just what the regulations are.

Once your child has begun to attend, monitor the care closely. Drop in and observe, talk to the teachers often, and keep in touch with other parents. In pre-school, as in all other kinds of child care, the more attention parents pay to what is going on, the more likely it is that their child's needs will be met.

I've got a Special Person
At my day-care, where I'm in
Her name is Mrs. Something
But we mostly call her Lynn.

DENNIS LEE

ALLIGATOR PIE

CHAPTER 7

The Daycare Center Option

Though they had been around for immigrants and the poor since the 1850s, daycare centers made a dramatic reappearance on the Canadian scene during World War II. In the 1940s, for the first time, ordinary children went to daycare so that ordinary mothers could go out to work in Canadian factories. It was patriotic, and Canadian women got a titillating taste of the economic and social freedom that comes with a paycheck.

But demobilization brought home men who reclaimed the jobs, and with them came the resurgence of a persistent, old Victorian idea: that a woman's place is in the home.

Throughout the 50s most women stayed there, looking after their children; and the daycare centers became a mere shadow of their former selves, reverting to their earlier function as a welfare service for needy families. (Even in the 1960s, Head Start in the United States had this distinct flavor.)

In the last 20 years, however, all of that has changed forever. For women, working has become a matter of survival—in both economic and personal terms. And daycare is its necessary corollary.

Nannies and sitters in the child's own home—vestiges of an upper-class British system—already had a very respectable air. Family home daycare—personal, private, quiet arrangements with a family member, friend or neighbor—has likewise seemed relatively mild and unthreatening. But daycare centers, the formal grouping of children and teachers in a public place, have retained their stigma. "Why would you have your children in a daycare center?" wailed a whole generation of grandparents. "It's awful and dreadful and they pick up every disease."

Though some parents still hang on to these old stereotypes, by and large today's families are shaking them off with a vengeance. They see daycare centers as a necessary, useful and safe solution to the child care problem—full stop. Many parents also view daycare centers as wonderful places for their children to grow and learn, and, given the right circumstances, they wouldn't hesitate to use one if only they could get a space.[1]

ADVANTAGES

Why would parents choose a daycare center over a sitter, nanny or regulated family daycare home?

Reliability

Daycare centers are by far the most reliable form of care. Because babysitters, nannies and family caregivers are individuals working alone, with no organization to fall back on, they are bound to let you down from time to time. Like the rest of us, they sleep through their alarms, get the flu and encounter emergencies. They may also change their minds about what they're doing—Eileen's wonderful family daycare provider decided one day that she was getting too old to look after young children, and two weeks later she went out of business.

But a daycare center is always there. Your child's teacher may be sick, but that will not close the center. Aside from statutory holidays, most centers are open during regular hours, usually between 7 A.M. and 6 P.M. If they close at other times, for a week at Christmas, for instance, they will let you know when you sign up. There will be no surprises.

Stability

Stability is the sister of reliability. In most centers that serve full-time working parents, the same children come every day, anchoring your child in a calm, stable atmosphere with a regular group of friends. Next year when he's ready for the toddler group, the center will still have a toddler group. Most of his friends from this year will move with him from the infant room, so even though he'll have different caregivers he'll be in familiar company. You'll know the director and the teachers, and you'll know where to go and what to do if you have a problem.

Licensing

In order to operate, every daycare center must have a license. This means it is adhering to the minimum standards and regulations set out by the province or territory—standards and regulations that govern health, safety, staff, program, group size and so on. It also means that the province inspects the center occasionally. Licensing assures parents of a basic level of care—and peace of mind. (One study showed that parents who use daycare centers feel less guilty than parents who use other kinds of care.)[2]

Trained staff

Many daycare-center staff have been trained in early childhood education or child development. Trained teachers know how to help children in all aspects of their growth—physical, emotional, cognitive and social. They plan and carry out activities that are appropriate for each child's age and stage of development. Says Lola, the mother of two, "I don't know quite honestly how I could provide what the teachers do or have that kind of energy. I know that my children are really learning at the daycare center."

Trained teachers can also pick up auditory, visual and coordination problems that require the attention of a specialist. Annie, a bright three-year-old with an excellent vocabulary, mispronounced certain simple sounds. At her teacher's suggestion, her mother took her to a hearing specialist who referred her for speech therapy.

Equipment

Jungle gyms, tricycles, big wheels, sand boxes, water tables, enormous wooden blocks, dozens of puzzles, books and tapes are all standard fare in a daycare center. You and I could never afford their toys and equipment, even if we knew what to buy or how to use it.

Other people

In daycare centers, children meet other children—an experience that teaches them social skills (to negotiate, cooperate, share) and helps them to discover their own strengths and weaknesses. Those who are aggressive may learn self-control; those who are timid may learn to defend themselves. Because they're in a group, they will also learn self-help skills (like cleaning up after themselves and putting on their jackets without help), independence and decision making.

Parent participation

A good daycare center is an open book: any parent can always walk in and take a thorough look around. If you're prepared to spend the time, you can know pretty much everything your child will do there during the day, and you can always peek in and survey the scene for yourself. A high-quality daycare center encourages parents to do this—to observe the program and to talk about their child with his teachers.

Non-profit centers offer parents another way to participate: they can join parent committees or the center's board of directors and have a say in the way their daycare is run. Lola, who has helped raise—and spend—thousands of dollars for the wish list at her daughters' daycare center, says, "Having that level of control in the operation of the daycare is a real advantage."

A daycare in the work place allows a unique mode of participation: true accessibility. "It doesn't seem so much as if I'm leaving them because I can be there in two minutes," Lola says. You can pop down to nurse a baby, join your child for lunch, give him an inside view of your own work or take him to breakfast in the employees' cafeteria.

A community

Parents also have a chance to meet other parents—and become members of a real community. Everyone is going through the same dramas and traumas in juggling work and family, and the daycare center is a natural meeting ground for the formation of alliances and the exchange of information of all kinds—how to deal with the terrible twos, a great place to buy this year's snowsuit, a babysitter for days when your child is sick. This informal support network can be especially useful for single parents.

Cost

Though daycare-center fees vary from province to province and area to area, they are usually lower than a nanny's or sitter's wages—at least for one child. (Infant care is more expensive, but, depending on where you live, it's probably still less than having someone in your home full-time.)

Surprisingly, in some provinces daycare centers are cheaper than regulated family home care; and, believe it or not, they sometimes charge less than unregulated family daycare providers.[3] When you're weighing costs, don't rely on hearsay. Get the facts straight from the horse's mouth!

Families in licensed daycare centers can apply for a subsidy, and at tax time you will appreciate the child care tax deduction.

DISADVANTAGES

There is no silver lining without a cloud. Though daycare-center critics are less rabid than they used to be, they can still find plenty to howl about.

Availability

Canada simply doesn't have enough daycare-center spaces to serve its children under six. Infants and toddlers in particular are being shortchanged. (Many centers do not accept children until they're 18 months or two or three years old.) You must apply early (in pregnancy for an infant), but even then, waiting lists seem to stretch into infinity, especially if you need a subsidy. Though you can't count on getting a spot when you're ready to use it, the lists sometimes move in mysterious ways, and it's worthwhile taking the trouble to sign up at a good center—you may well end up in the money.

Hours

Daycare-center hours were created for people who work a nine-to-five day. For anyone else they present real problems. Those who start work early, finish late, work odd shifts or part-time will find precious little give in the schedule. Some daycare centers do enroll children on a part-time basis, but opening and closing hours are immutable, and if you're late in picking up your child the fines will make you a pauper.

The exception to this rule is a work-place daycare center designed to fit the hours of its employees. The new Labour Community Child Care Centre, run by the Canadian Auto Workers in Windsor, Ontario, keeps its doors open from 5:30 A.M. to 1 A.M. to meet the needs of auto-industry shiftworkers.

Cost

In a survey carried out for the Task Force on Child Care, 52 percent of the parents who preferred daycare centers for their pre-schoolers didn't use one because it was too expensive or they could not get a subsidy.[4] The sad fact is that many families simply cannot afford daycare centers, and a family who managed with one daycare-age child may well have to make different arrangements when the next one comes along, even if the center offers a sibling discount. It is middle-class families who most often find themselves in a financial bind: they make too much money to qualify for a subsidy, yet the full fee puts an unbearable strain on the pocketbook. Centers strive to keep their prices within reach, but high-quality care is expensive.

Health

Children who attend daycare centers are at greater risk of getting sick than children at home or in family daycare. (They are most vulnerable while they are building up immunities, in their first year of care.) In order to protect the other children and staff, a center should exclude sick children, but many centers, striving to help working parents, accept them without protest, even though their presence sometimes compromises care.

Parents are supposed to have backup for these occasions, but many—perhaps because they lack resources, perhaps because they don't understand the importance of it—never get around to figuring out a workable system for themselves. John and Rita decided to withdraw their nine-month-old daughter from the university daycare when they realized that they were the only ones who obeyed the rules. Although they conscientiously found a sitter so that they could keep their child home when she was sick, no one else did, and she caught a new bug every time she set foot in the door.

Traveling

Getting a sleepy child to daycare in the morning is probably not going to be the highlight of your day. Children move at their own pace and have their own priorities, and decking themselves out in the full regalia of snowsuit, boots, hat, scarf and mitts while it's still dark outside is usually not one of them. When you are late for work, this can be infuriating, and it takes real organization, time and patience on your part to make the transition to the daycare center a success.

The evening collection is apt to hold its own share of thrills, with everyone tired, hungry and wired with the mixed emotions of reunion. (But, of course, family daycare is no better in this department.)

Parent detachment

Although many centers theoretically encourage parents to participate, in fact it is very easy to drop off your child in the morning, scoop him up in the evening and never speak to a living soul about how he's doing. This is because of the daycare center's size and level of activity. The teachers will always have another child or parent to talk to, and although they will usually be happy to chat if you hang around or present yourself at an opportune moment, it takes effort on your part to make this happen. The same is true of daycare committees and boards of directors—you have to be prepared to expend time and energy, sometimes with frustrating, infuriating results.

Commercial daycare centers, operated for profit, rarely permit parents to influence policy, though they will allow them to speak with teachers on an individual basis.

Quality

Even with licensing and inspection, the quality of daycare centers varies enormously. Some are superb; some are frightening; most are merely mediocre. It is, therefore, extremely important to look around and evaluate carefully before making a decision.

For parents who don't know what the requirements are, perhaps the greatest concern is that their child won't get enough individual attention—that he'll be lost in the crowd, that the teacher won't have enough time for him. In bad daycare centers, where there are too few teachers for the number of children or the teachers aren't trained and competent, children *are* neglected, and the ones who cause the most trouble or cry the loudest monopolize the teacher's time. Obviously this is not the sort of center you want.

Another common fear is that daycare centers are too institutional—that the needs of the group override the needs of the individual, and there is too much structure and conformity and not enough quiet space, privacy, creativity or freedom. Once again, all of this can happen in a center that isn't giving high-quality care, but it shouldn't occur in a first-rate center.

GOOD QUALITY IS THE KEY

None of these daycare alternatives—nanny, sitter, family daycare, nursery school or daycare center—is inherently better than the others. Choose whichever type suits your child and your family best—but, above all, choose quality. To repeat the obvious, good daycare—in whatever form—is good for children. Bad daycare is bad for them.

In the next few chapters we will tell you all about finding and recognizing a daycare center or regulated family daycare home that will provide high-quality care for your child.

Bye, Baby Bunting,
Daddy's gone a-hunting....
TRADITIONAL SONG

CHAPTER 8

How to Find a Daycare Center

I. WHERE TO START

Now we come to the tricky part—actually finding a daycare center for your child. Where on earth do you start? Who knows about daycare centers? Is anybody in charge?

Who's in charge?

There are lots of ways to find out about daycare, and you'll probably use several of them: talking to friends, family and neighbors about places they've used and liked; looking in the Yellow Pages; contacting community information centers, churches, ethnic organizations, public health units and the personnel department where you work; scouring newspaper want ads and supermarket bulletin boards.

If you're the first among your friends to seek daycare, you may not be able to count on word of mouth to get you much data, but sometimes even rumors and theoretical discussions can give you ideas and clues. If your friends are using daycare, be sure to benefit from their experience. It's important to talk, even if you end up in heated arguments.

Although this informal, unofficial information is a good starting point, you need some official information, too. In Canada, daycare is a provincial responsibility, and legislators in every province and territory have created laws and regulations to ensure a minimum standard of quality. Daycare centers—unlike babysitters, nannies, family daycare homes and nursery and pre-schools in some provinces—must be licensed in order to operate. Through your provincial Ministry of Social Services or Social Affairs (the Ministry of Health in British Columbia), which issues licenses, you can get three crucial kinds of information: first, a list of licensed daycare centers in your area; second, a copy of the laws and regulations governing daycare in your province; and third, information about how to get a government subsidy if you need help paying your fees.

In some provinces, a single phone call will elicit a wealth of material, including maps and instructive booklets. In others, the first call may lead to a second, a third or a fourth (in decentralized Ontario, for example). The provincial office may refer you to an area or regional office, which may send you to a resource center or a social worker or a municipal office. In some provinces you'll have to call the government printer or publications office and pay a small fee for the daycare act and regulations.

To find a list of the names, addresses and phone numbers of these occasionally elusive government bodies, use the list in appendix A at the back of this book, or try the government blue pages of your telephone book.

Could these documents possibly be worth all this expense and bother? The answer is definitely yes. The list of licensed daycare centers is *essential*. Although a license doesn't guarantee high-quality daycare, it gives you a fighting chance. Some conditions can be created (or prevented) by licensing laws—like having proper fire exits and a reasonable amount of space for each child. Being familiar with the regulations means that when you go out to observe centers, you will know what to expect—and what to accept. The government's subsidy information should tell you roughly whether you will qualify for aid, which documents you'll need and where and how to apply.

A little while after you make your phone calls, a large manila envelope will arrive on your doorstep. You're going to be sorely tempted to cast aside the act and regulations, which look far too fat and dry, and instead leaf through the daycare list to see if there's a licensed center near you. Go ahead and look. But before you make a preliminary list of daycares to visit, there is serious work to be done.

What do the regulations say?

Gather your courage and read the provincial acts and regulations. Those boring pages are chock-full of amazing, vital information. Some are short, sweet and crystal clear; others are lengthy, verbose and thoroughly muddling. They set up boards or individuals to take charge of daycare in the province, create licensing requirements, outline conditions for obtaining subsidies and grants, and set standards to ensure the provision of child care that is "safe, of good quality, and appropriate to the needs of children," to quote Prince Edward Island's act.

Not every line is important. But some are very important indeed. To help you wade through the legalese and make sense of it all, here is a guide to daycare acts and regulations. Pages and pages deal with the physical setting, which must be safe and healthy. We will point out and explain some essential provisions in this area. But good-quality daycare does not just take care of children's minimal needs. If they are to grow into the competent, self-respecting people they have the right and potential to be, daycare must also enhance their emotional, social, intellectual and physical development. The regulations should address these issues by controlling group and center size, staff-child ratios, teacher training, programming and parent involvement.

The regulations tell you exactly what the acceptable bare minimum is in your province. Every daycare center is supposed to have *at least* what they demand, and no daycare center is ever supposed to go below that floor. When you are choosing a daycare center for your child, you need to know where that floor is, because the fact that something is written down does not automatically make it so. In fact, many daycare centers in Canada do not fulfill provincial requirements. By visiting daycares you'll see how the regulations work in real life.

ENVIRONMENT

Physical things are basic. It's hard for a child to do much of anything, including learning through play, unless he feels safe, healthy and free. That means the daycare environment must be absolutely hazard-free, healthy and uncrowded. Because physical aspects are usually measurable and observable, they lend themselves to regulation relatively easily. You can see at a glance how many toilets and sinks there are and whether the playground is fenced.

Physical space

Whether they're located in schools, office buildings, shopping malls, church basements, private houses, apartment buildings, condominiums or portable housing, daycare centers must all meet certain standards for their space. By this the regulations mean not just the size of the rooms but the area provided for each child.

Do you remember what it was like when you had to share a room with your sister—how often you fought and how hard it was to feel yourself when someone else was always there? Then you can appreciate the importance of space. Research backs this up. As one expert puts it, "As the number of children per square feet increases, so do aggressiveness, destructiveness, and unoccupied behavior." More space means more freedom to move around and better relationships among children and staff.[1]

The studies recommend about 3.5 square meters per child indoors (not including closets, corridors, bathrooms and kitchens) and 7 square meters outdoors—which most provincial regulations mandate. Many daycare centers do not provide a single centimeter more than the regulations require.

Of course, the design of the space is equally important. Regulations often call for the outdoor space to be fenced and adjacent to the center. Indoor space should be organized for both large- and small-group activities, as well as a bit of privacy. Materials and toys must be easily available to the children.

Several provinces require a separate space for infants. Because they don't really benefit from being around older children, infants fare better in groups by themselves where they don't get exposed to lots of germs. Toddlers should also have their own room; some research indicates that they suffer when they are with either older children or babies.[2]

Health and safety

A healthy, safe environment is equally essential.

Fire drills, fire-evacuation procedures, smoke detectors, fire extinguishers and regular fire-department inspections appear in one form or another in the regulations of virtually every province and territory. To facilitate a speedy exit in an emergency, some provinces require daycare centers to be on the first or second floor.

A telephone and a first aid kit are *de rigueur*, as is the posting of emergency phone numbers (fire, ambulance, police, hospital, poison center, doctor). First aid training for staff is also required. If you discover that your province doesn't require first aid training, be sure to ask about it when you visit centers.

Everywhere, dangerous cleaning supplies are supposed to be inaccessible to children.

Good ventilation, good lighting and comfortable temperatures— all a matter of common sense—are often a matter of law as well.

Furnishings and equipment are supposed to be "safe, well maintained, free from hazards, and suitable to the age and development level of children in care."[3] Cribs must have properly spaced bars and snug mattresses, and toys must be made of safe materials, with pieces that aren't too small.

Cleanliness is extremely important. Food areas should be well separated from diapering areas, and each must have its own adjacent sink. To minimize the spread of disease, each child must have his own cubbyhole or hook to hang his clothes on and his own individually labeled linens, cot or crib.

Most provinces prohibit smoking and the drinking of hot beverages in areas used by children.

Some provinces require both children and staff to have health certificates or proof of immunization. Sick children must be isolated, and communicable diseases must be reported. Medicines may be given to a child only when prescribed by a doctor and with the written consent of the parent.

Bathroom

Did you ever cross your legs in desperation when you were a child at school? At daycare centers the children often go to the bathroom in groups, and depending on the number of toilets, the line may be very long indeed! Several provinces regulate the number of toilets and sinks—one for every ten children is common. The towels should be disposable and the water not too hot.

Kitchen

Daycare kitchens, like restaurant kitchens, have to meet strict standards. The regulations often require a knowledgeable person to take charge of preparing both menus and food. Menus must be posted in advance, and meals and snacks, which are supposed to be both "nutritious and adequate," must follow the Canada Food Guide. The kitchen itself should be immaculate, and food handling and storage have to be in accord with local health regulations.

PEOPLE

People are the heart of the daycare center. Although it's impossible to mandate and enforce good teaching by law, it's not impossible to set out some conditions to encourage and nurture it.

Group size

Researchers have identified group size as one of the most important factors influencing the quality of daycare. "Smaller groups are consistently associated with better care, more socially active children, and higher gains on two developmental tests."[4] It stands to reason. With a smaller group, the teacher has more time to spend with each child, and she can create activities that encourage the development of independence, self-assertion, problem solving, cooperation and friendliness.

Beware. Not every province regulates group size. Some deal with the question by limiting the number of children in a room or the number in an age category. Some don't even mention it. Be sure to look for this information in the regulations. If your province doesn't control group size, use the standards recommended by both the Canadian Task Force on Child Care (whose excellent comprehensive report on child care in Canada came out in 1986) and the prestigious American organization, the National Association for the Education of Young Children (see below).

Staff-child ratio

The ratio of staff to children, so closely linked to group size, is also extremely important, especially for younger children. A teacher must have enough time to talk and listen to each child, to respond to questions, to hug and smile, to comfort a sad child and laugh with a happy one, to supervise, guide and encourage all kinds of play. She can't do these important tasks if she has too many children to take care of. When a teacher cares for more than four infants, studies have found, the children become apathetic and distressed. Older children also benefit from more contact with adults.[5]

The *Report of the Task Force on Child Care* recommends the following *maximum* ratios and group sizes:

Infants up to 18 months – ratio of 1:3 to 1:4; six to eight in a group
Toddlers 18 to 35 months – ratio of 1:3 to 1:5; six to ten in a group
Three-year-olds – ratio of 1:5 to 1:8; ten to 16 in a group
Four-year-olds – ratio of 1:8 to 1:10; 16 to 20 in a group
Five-year-olds – ratio of 1:10 to 1:12; 20 to 24 in a group[6]

Although every province regulates ratio, not every province's regulations match these acceptable limits. What ratio does your province demand for each age group?

Center size

Yet another aspect of the numbers game is the total number of children enrolled in the daycare center. One study found that when a center has more than 60 children, rules and routines become more prevalent and rigid, and the children have fewer chances to initiate and control their own activities. In general, in a big center it's hard for people to get to know each other. Some provinces set no maximum size for daycare centers, and others allow them to enroll 75 or 80 children. Of course it depends, too, on how a center is organized, but bear in mind that a large center may present problems.

Who are the teachers?

In the end, a daycare is only as good as its teachers. Teachers, being human, resist objective measurement, but one fact about them is clearly known: teachers who are trained in child development and/ or early childhood education are better. New research shows that teachers with special training and more formal education may be the best of all.[7] Trained teachers are absolutely essential to a daycare's ability to provide high-quality care.

Many provinces have instituted minimum educational qualifications for daycare directors and teachers, but others say that just some teachers need be qualified, and a few still don't demand any training at all. It is important to know the regulations in order to be certain that a center meets *at least* the minimum provincial standards, but you should be looking for one where all the staff members are trained. The more trained staff, the better.

PROGRAM

Activities

Studies show that children learn more when their day includes both structured and unstructured activities—some that they initiate, some that the teacher initiates.[8] In addition, experts see a balanced day—with indoor and outdoor play, quiet and active play, individual, small-group and large-group play—as an important element in a child's development.

Provincial regulations often share these concerns. Some provinces and territories require a written statement of the center's philosophy and a daily-program plan, available at any time to any parent. Some go so far as to specify the amount of time a child must spend outdoors, how often he should make his own choices about play and what he should do during nap (in Ontario, a child who isn't sleeping should be permitted quiet activity). Several provinces demand that caregivers hold infants when giving them a bottle.

Discipline

When it comes to discipline, the regulations draw a clear bottom line: "No physical, emotional or verbal abuse or denial of physical necessities" is permitted in several provinces. Others ban corporal punishment and isolation—a child must never be left alone. Positive guidance is preferred.

Parent involvement

Parental involvement in daycare is good for children, and a strong relationship benefits parents, too. Several provinces recognize the importance of parents by making their participation on boards of directors of non-profit centers a condition for obtaining licenses or grants.

MORE INFORMATION

The Childcare Resource and Research Unit at the University of Toronto publishes a series of one-page information sheets with succinct information about standards and services in each province. You can reach them at the Centre for Urban and Community Studies, 455 Spadina Avenue, Toronto, Ontario M5S 2G8, (416) 978-6895.

II. *WHAT ELSE MATTERS?*

When parents begin to think about daycare, they encounter a strange new language. It sounds so much like ordinary English that it's sometimes hard to recognize. But terms like *profit* and *non-profit*, *community, work place, lab school*, and *college* have important implications when they're applied to daycare.

At least two of these terms describe every daycare center in Canada. It is essential for parents to know what they mean.

PROFIT VERSUS NON-PROFIT

Let us begin with the question of profit versus non-profit, known in daycare parlance as "auspice."

Is a daycare center a business, operated for profit by a private owner or a company, or is it a non-profit organization, under the auspices of parents, a church, or a group like the YMCA?

Non-profit centers

Boards of directors, usually composed of parents, run non-profit daycare centers, sometimes with the help of staff or sponsoring agencies like universities, hospitals, community and church organizations. The board of directors has the ultimate responsibility for the daycare center, and the director or supervisor and staff are their employees. The board makes major decisions about hiring and firing, philosophy and policy, purchase of new equipment and renovations to the physical plant. Because the center is directly accountable to the parents, it is more likely to respond to their needs.[9]

In some provinces only non-profit centers qualify for government aid in the form of start-up, renovation and operating grants, and this help can make a big difference in a tight budget. The extra money from the government goes into improving the quality of the care and keeping parents' fees affordable.

In 1989 the National Child Care Staffing Study, a major survey of 227 child care centers in five metropolitan areas in the United States, found that non-profit centers provided better quality care than for-profit centers, even if they were government funded.[10] Non-profit centers rated consistently higher on teachers' education, specialized training and experience; on staff-child ratio; on the number of teachers in the classroom; on the amount of developmentally appropriate activity; and on the amount of appropriate caregiving. Non-profit centers paid higher wages and more benefits to their staff and spent a larger proportion of their budgets on their staff; and as a result, they experienced much less staff turnover than profit centers. All of this, the researchers concluded, directly affects the children: "Children attending lower-quality centers and centers with more staff turnover were less competent in language and social development.... Auspice [meaning whether the center was non-profit or profit] was the strongest predictor of quality."[11]

In a 1986 study for the House of Commons Special Committee on Child Care, daycare consultants rated about a thousand Canadian daycare centers in ten provinces and two territories and found that "non-profit care is likely to be higher in quality than for-profit care, and this superiority seems to hold up on virtually all measures."[12] Even the incidence of diarrhea and upper-respiratory infection is lower in non-profit centers, a public-health team found in a 1986–87 surveillance program of 33 Montreal daycare centers.[13]

Profit centers

"The business of young children is growth and development, and the business of corporations is making money. If you mix the two, can the needs of both be satisfied?" asks Alice Lake in *The Day Care Book*.[14] Many educators passionately believe that no one should make a profit at the expense of children.

A profit center is a daycare that is operated as a money-making enterprise. Its owner can be an individual with a single center (who may or may not run it himself), a proprietor who owns a small chain of two to seven or eight centers, or a corporation with a large chain.

In order to squeeze any profit from its budget, a profit center must cut costs. Because staff salaries are a center's biggest expense, they are the obvious place to start. Profit centers pay lower wages,[15] hire fewer and less-qualified staff and fail to replace teachers who are sick.[16] As a result, their staff turnover is very high.[17] Students who are completing a degree and not earning a salary are sometimes used to fulfill ratio requirements; and when provincial rules allow, they may accept children on a "drop-in" basis, assigning teachers even more youngsters to care for.[18]

The meals may not be as nutritious and appetizing as one would like.[19] In many cities commercial centers choose to locate in heavy-traffic areas or shopping malls, affording them a high profile with the public but little safe green space for the children to play.[20]

When the owner is a sort of absentee landlord who does not actually work full-time at the center but skims a salary off the top, these problems can be exacerbated. Either the owner must pay an extra person, or the center must function without a proper director. Sometimes the owner of several daycare centers plays checkers with the staff, switching them from center to center to fill holes or to troubleshoot—a disconcerting practice for both children and parents.

The owner makes the decisions at a for-profit daycare center. There is no parent board of directors, and parents really do not have any say in the running of the center. If they disagree with daycare policy, their only recourse is to withdraw their child. If the owner chooses, he can make his profit by selling his center to the highest bidder—leaving children, staff and parents to cope with a new owner and the possibility of very different conditions.

Under these circumstances high-quality child care becomes a difficult goal to achieve. Researchers for the House of Commons Special Committee on Child Care found that for-profit centers were less likely to meet government standards than non-profit centers,[21] a finding confirmed when the Toronto *Globe and Mail* reviewed 1,600 inspection reports of Ontario daycare centers in 1989.[22] A study of 431 Metro Toronto centers found that commercial daycares were also more likely to have complaints lodged against them, staff-child ratio violations and restrictions on their licenses.[23]

The Special Committee's daycare consultants rated 25 percent of small for-profit centers—a frightening number—as poor or very poor,[24] and the *Globe and Mail* found that 11 percent of profit centers lack basic toys or equipment.[25] According to the Special Committee's study, chain centers tend to provide exactly as much quality as the provincial floor demands—85 percent met minimum provincial standards (56 percent were "adequate"), but not a single one ranked as excellent (or as very poor). Small for-profit centers, on the other hand, varied widely in quality, from excellent to very poor. But just 32 percent were better than adequate.[26]

COMMUNITY VERSUS WORK-PLACE DAYCARE

Where do you want your daycare center to be—near your home or near your work? Which is better? Can you use a work-place daycare center if you don't work at a place that has one?

Community daycare

Although people don't yet select their housing according to the reputation of the daycare in the neighborhood, that day is probably not far off. Canadian families prefer daycare in their own neighborhood, surveys show.[27] If you're about to move, inquire about nearby daycare centers as you would about schools or public transportation. It will make your life much easier if you live near a good daycare.

Community daycare has all the advantages of a community. Located where you live, it connects your child with other children in the area and gives him the opportunity to make friends who will stick by him well into his school career. If the community is stable, the daycare population will be stable, too.

Encounters at the playground, swimming pool, skating rink, supermarket and eventually elementary school constantly reinforce friendships, giving children the sense that they belong. Because preschoolers don't go anywhere alone, a community daycare even helps make parents, both single and married, feel part of the community. As you watch your child dig in the sand alongside Lauren from the daycare center, you will meet Lauren's parents and find yourself looking for them when you go to the park. When the children get older and want to see one another on a weekend, it's very simple to arrange visits, which may include a cup of coffee for the adults. When they play with neighborhood friends, children aren't separated from their older brothers and sisters, who gather in the neighborhood park and library as well.

In Canada, where half the year is winter, having a daycare center near at hand is a considerable advantage. Even if he doesn't get carsick, traveling with a tired, hungry, cranky child bundled in a snowsuit in a traffic jam or in a crowded bus or subway can hardly be called "quality time." And during a snowstorm, it's a relief not to have him in the car.

Parents also like to have some time to themselves before and after work—in the morning to shift from family gear into work gear, and in the evening to wind down and compose themselves before picking up their child. Community daycare offers them this breathing space.

Work-place daycare

Work-place daycare has its fans, too, and you don't necessarily have to work in the work-place to use the center attached to it. A majority of employer-sponsored daycares are open to families living and working nearby.[28] Don't automatically eliminate a work-place daycare just because your employer doesn't sponsor one!

In 1964, Riverdale Hospital in Toronto became the first employer in Canada to establish a work-place daycare center. Not including university- and college-operated daycares, there are now about a hundred work-related child care programs—mainly in public organizations, mostly in Quebec and Ontario—providing 3 to 4 percent of the licensed group care in the country.[29]

For infants especially, work-place or on-site daycare can be a lifesaver. For one thing, employers, responding to the needs of their employees, are helping to make available more than their fair share of the infant and toddler care in daycare centers in Canada. If you are looking for a daycare-center place for a baby, you are more likely to find it if there is a work-place daycare center where you work.[30]

Secondly, on-site daycare makes the prospect of separating from an infant much less bleak for a mother. When you work nearby, you can continue to nurse your baby at lunch and on breaks. If he wakes up early, perhaps you can nip over and feed him. You can peek in and give him a hug; you can put him down for a nap if the timing is right.

In an emergency, or when a child is ill, you can go to him right away.

Although you still have to fight rush-hour traffic, work-place daycare reduces your travel time. You have just one place to go—you and your child go to work; you and your child go home.

Like community daycare, on-site daycare can create a community, a work-place support system. At McGill Community Family Center, where parents are required to feed their infants at lunchtime, friendship among families blossoms as they share the glories and agonies of parenthood. It's good for the soul to discover new friends who are going through exactly the same trials that you are. Networking at the center, you learn more about what's going on at work, too, and work becomes a healthier, happier place to be. A daycare center gives the employer a more human face by indicating his concern for his employees, and at the same time it gives the employees themselves a fuller existence by integrating their families into their working lives.

Work-place daycare centers face strong pressure to provide high-quality care. Being in a fishbowl—under surveillance at all times—they are very accountable. Employers want the daycare center associated with them to be an asset, not a liability. In fact, a survey of Canadian work-place daycare centers showed that many of them exceed the province's minimum staffing requirements, many pay their staff higher salaries than other daycare centers in their area, and many have a high-degree of parental involvement—all indicators of high-quality care.[31]

Even though the employer often contributes to the cost of running the center—usually by waiving or paying the rent, utilities and maintenance—the cost to the parents is about the same at work-place daycare as it is in community daycare.[32] The additional income goes to improve the quality of the care— buying more and better equipment, supplying healthier meals, renovating facilities and, above all, paying higher salaries and staff benefits, which makes for a better-trained, more stable work force.

Theoretically, one of the great advantages of work-place daycare would appear to be that it can accommodate the odd working hours and shifts that the employer demands. In fact, however, very few work-place daycares open very early in the morning, stay open very late at night or care for children overnight or on weekends. It just turns out to cost too much.[33] However, an employer that needs its employees over Christmas is not likely to close the work-place daycare over the holidays, as some community or school-based centers may do.

Employer-sponsored daycare has pitfalls, however. On weekends you may end up traveling halfway across the city so that your child can play with his best friend. And when he starts school, he may find himself the odd man out—the other children will know one another from being in community daycares, pre-schools, swimming, ballet and soccer together, and he will be a stranger. Not every parent is willing to give up some of his own very precious time with his child to counteract this effect, but those who are might consider enrolling him in Saturday activities at the local YMCA, library, playground and hockey rink, where he can make some neighborhood friends, too.

Although the daycare center is usually run by an independent parent board of directors, not by the employer, the parents on the board may experience a paralyzing conflict of interest. If you and your boss are both board members, you may not feel free to speak your mind, especially if you disagree with her. As a result, a member of management, although she means well, may wield an inordinate and inappropriate amount of power, a situation which could compromise the work of the daycare director and staff and, at the same time, the care of the children.

Perhaps the biggest drawback of employer-sponsored daycare is the dilemma you face if you hate your job. If your child will lose his place at the daycare center, you may not want to quit. This is awkward indeed; however, it is not inevitable. Because the majority of work-place daycare centers accept children from the community at large, your child may be allowed to remain even if you no longer work there. When you look at a work-place daycare center, find out about the policy for non-employees and former employees.

Although your work place may not have on-site daycare, employers may offer other solutions to the daycare problem. Through a professional consultant or in the organization's personnel office, a company may have an information, referral or counseling service to help you locate daycare. Sometimes the service is comprehensive and personal—a counselor helps to assess your needs, makes suggestions and tells you how to make a decision for yourself. At the other extreme, you may receive a computerized list from a data bank, but you don't know whether the places are actually available or how good the centers are. When you use a service like this, be sure to ask how much checking they do. With any of them, of course, you will make the choice in the end.[34]

An employer may reserve spaces in a daycare center either near the work place or in your own neighborhood. It may have flextime or, like the Prince Edward Island government, allow you to take the summer off.[35] As part of an agreement negotiated with the Canadian Union of Public Employees, the Metro Toronto YMCA gives its employees a small monthly cash payment to help defray the cost of high-quality care.[36]

University- and college-sponsored daycare centers
About a hundred universities and colleges in Canada operate a special kind of work-place daycare center to accommodate their own staff and student population who are also young parents and to provide a training ground for students in early childhood education.[37] Because they may serve as model teaching programs for students, university- and college-daycare centers are usually of very high quality—well funded and equipped by both government and university and well run and staffed by top-flight professionals. And they offer the same advantages that other work-place daycares do: membership in a com-

munity within a community and wonderfully easy access to your child, at about the same price as any other daycare.

With student teachers around to pitch in, the adult-child ratio of a university daycare can be extremely high. Students can also help to bring in fresh ideas and the latest approaches to early childhood education. With an open, receptive staff, this can lead to an exciting and dynamic learning environment.

But even these advantages can lose their glow unless they're handled well. Students are young and less skilled than the educators on staff, who are already professionals. They should be used to *augment* the required adult-child ratio, not to fulfill it. For the sake of the children, who need to see the same few caregivers regularly, there should be only one student per group per semester. Perhaps infants are an exception. Although it would be ideal for each baby to have his own permanent caregiver, loving students who stay for four or five months are still a very big help. The student teachers should be at the center at least three times a week.

Although student parents are full of ideas and enthusiasm, most of them have not yet had very much administrative experience, and a board of directors composed of very young and well-intentioned parents can, on occasion, give a daycare center a very rough ride— for instance, by causing a rapid turnover in directors. However, this problem can be solved if members of the university personnel office or education faculty sit on the board to lend a calming effect as well as useful experience, knowledge and consistency.

BEWARE OF THE RISKS

Now that you know the pros and cons of each kind of daycare, you will know where to look for what you want. You are far more likely to find high-quality care in a non-profit center, but there are no guarantees. A non-profit center can be poor, and a profit center, though very rarely excellent, can be acceptable. In some parts of the country, like Alberta, where non-profit centers are few and far between, you may not have the opportunity to choose a non-profit center anyway. High- and low-quality centers exist in both the private and the public sectors, in the community and in the work place. In the end you must inform yourself about high-quality daycare and then rely on your own powers of observation to choose the best center you possibly can, regardless of where it is or who runs it.

III. MAKING A SHORTLIST

The next step is much more fun. It's time to make a shortlist of daycare centers. Depending on where you live and work, this list may not be short at all—in fact, in the beginning it may well be as long as your arm. But you'll be astonished at how quickly it reduces itself when you try to match it with your family's needs.

To begin, go through your area's official list or directory, and, using a map, jot down the name, address and phone number of all the daycare centers near your home and your place of work. If you've collected the names of daycares from other sources, this is the time to check them out. Are they licensed? If so, add them, too.

HOW WILL YOU KNOW THE REAL POSSIBILITIES?

At the end of this chapter you'll find a questionnaire we've created for this express purpose. You'll need several copies—one for every daycare on your preliminary list. Since it's impossible to compare apples and oranges, you must ask every daycare center the same questions. If the official daycare list provides answers to some of the questions, note them in the appropriate space on the form. But be sure to ask the questions anyway. The information might have changed since the list was compiled, or the daycare director may alter the truth to suit her purposes. One director told us on the phone that her center was non-profit, although the provincial listing classed her center in the profit category. Maybe she meant that they weren't making much money, but that was no excuse for her reply.

To answer the rest of the questions, you'll have to make some phone calls. But first go through the questions and figure out which ones apply to you. Remember that you're after basic information.

Ask to speak to the director if possible—it's important for you to get a sense of what she's like. If she isn't there, find out when would be a good time to talk to her.

She may try to sign you up for a visit long before you've gotten through the whole list, so arm yourself with an excuse for not running straight over—you're just making preliminary phone calls, you're not ready to visit yet—and tell her that you want to ask her some questions first.

If the responses to your questions lead you to think that this center offers good care, ask for an application. In most cases there is no obligation or fee. It is best to apply right away, because a daycare that has a space on Tuesday may fill it by Wednesday. In order to be sure of getting a place, we suggest that you apply now to all the centers that sound like possible candidates.

HERE ARE THE QUESTIONS

We've explained the questions you should ask and repeated them on the questionnaire. Of course you should end the conversation whenever an answer rules out a daycare—if you need space for a baby and the center accepts only pre-schoolers, for example.

1. *Is this center licensed? Does the license have any restrictions?* In some provinces there are categories of licenses. A center with a full, clear license fulfills all the provincial requirements, but some centers receive licenses for a shorter period if they don't meet all the rules. When there is a history of serious violations, the license may be provisional or conditional.

2. *What age must a child be to attend the daycare?* Some centers accept infants; the vast majority enroll only older children. If you are looking for a center for a four- to 18-month-old, this question will probably eliminate a large number of choices right off the bat.

3. *What are the hours of operation?* Is the center open early enough in the morning for you to get to work on time, and will you be able to struggle through rush-hour traffic to pick up your child before the center closes at the end of the day? A warning here: charges for late pick up can be very steep indeed.

4. *Are there any places available for the date that you need daycare?* If you are beginning your search early enough—for infant and toddler care, when you are pregnant; for pre-schoolers, at least nine months to a year ahead—there may be room for your child. If you need care next week or even next month, your options on this score will be limited.

5. *Does the center have a waiting list?* If you do not need a space yet, or if the daycare has no space now but is accepting applicants for their waiting list, you have nothing to lose by adding your name, especially if this daycare has an excellent reputation. A list may sound much longer than it actually is. Often people put their names

down for several centers and then accept a place somewhere else, opening up a spot for you. Ask how long it usually takes to move to the top of the list.

6. *Are there any special criteria for entrance?* Most centers admit siblings of children who are currently enrolled first and all other applicants on a first-come, first-served basis. Some centers give priority to people who live in the neighborhood or who work for a particular company or organization. But even these daycares sometimes accept others when they aren't full. Ask employer-sponsored daycares if they accept applicants who aren't employees.

7. *Do you accept children on a part-time or drop-in basis?* Whether you're looking for part- or full-time care, it is important to ask this question. If you need a full-time space, it's better for your child if all the children come every day. No matter how good the daycare, part-timers take longer to adjust, diverting the caregivers' attention from the full-timers. Lots of coming and going makes it harder for them to feel secure and increases the incidence of sickness. At most established centers, full-time applicants take precedence.

If you're looking for part-time care, you might have a better chance at a brand-new daycare that is ready and willing to take part-timers to fill their places.

Avoid any center that accepts "drop ins"—that is, children who don't sign up but just appear when they need an hour or a day of care. The teacher-child ratio rules at these centers are different, and the extra children (who don't know the rules or the other children and who bring in new germs that raise the illness rate) lessen the quality of the care considerably.

8. *Is the center non-profit or profit?* This is an important question, as you have just seen. If it is a profit center, ask if the owner has more than one daycare and if he works full-time on the premises. This information will tell you whether or not he's on the spot to look after the children and staff at his center or if it's an entrepreneurial venture geared more toward making money than providing high-quality child care.

9. *How many children are in each group? What is the adult-child ratio? What is the total number of children in this center?* As you've just learned, numbers are very important to the quality of daycare. Any center that does not conform to the provincial regulations in these matters should be crossed off your list. If your

province doesn't regulate group or center size, eliminate the centers that don't meet the Task Force recommendations.

10. *How many teachers do you have? How many of them have a college or university degree in child development or early childhood education?* Training is an important indicator of quality. Whether or not training is required in your province, you should be looking for a center with trained personnel.

11. *What is the cost?* Cost for daycare varies widely across Canada, but in general fees are probably competitive within each city.

    Is there a reduction for two children? Some centers, aware that having two children in daycare can bankrupt a family, offer some relief for siblings.

    Are there any additional costs? Beside fees, you may have to pay for registration, diapers, meals or field trips—which call for a bundle of extra cash. This is more common in profit centers. It's best to know now what you're in for.

    Will I have to pay when I am on holiday? Just as daycare centers expect parents to pay for the days that their child misses because of illness, they expect parents to pay for every month of the year—even when they're on vacation and the child doesn't attend—in order to hold their place. Some daycares do, however, allow you to take two to eight weeks of holiday without payment.

12. *Are subsidies available and how do I get one? Will the subsidy cover my fees?* Families who will have trouble paying daycare fees may be eligible for government assistance. The rules about who qualifies are different in every province, but even after a family has qualified they may not receive help right away. Subsidies are in short supply virtually everywhere in Canada, with waiting periods of up to a year or two not unheard of. If you need aid, it is therefore extremely important to ask about subsidies in this preliminary phone call. In some provinces you apply through the daycare center; in others you must go through the regional or provincial daycare office or a municipal department. Some provinces have a voucher system, enabling you to use your subsidy wherever you wish; others don't.

    The amount of subsidy varies enormously, too. It may cover your fees or leave you with a substantial bill still to pay. If you are confused about what to do, ask the director.

13. *Is the center ever closed? When?* If you're a teacher who has

summers off or a salesperson whose busiest time is the Christmas season, this is vital information. Daycares based in schools often close for Christmas. Some daycares close for a week at the end of August to get ready for the new school year which begins in September; some daycares have a spring break.

14. *Does the center serve meals?* A center that serves meals will cost more than a center that doesn't, but for parents who prefer their child to have a hot meal in the middle of the day and for those who can't face the lunch box hassle, the additional charge is worthwhile. In some provinces hot meals are required.

    May my child bring his own food? If so, will the fee be the same? Parents of children who have special dietary needs or who are very picky eaters must find out if they can bring food from home and whether the fee will be the same.

15. *Do parents have an obligation to work in the daycare?* Some daycares expect parents to help out by doing odd chores on Saturday mornings; others have parent boards of directors that determine the policies of the center. Some activities are optional, some compulsory. Since you're a working or studying parent, married or single, with a limited amount of time, you want to be sure you can fulfill your commitment before you sign up. Saturday is probably your only day for cleaning the house and doing the shopping, and Sunday is precious time to spend with your child. You may not be willing to sacrifice any of this for the daycare center.

16. *How and when can I apply? Is there an application fee?* The sooner you apply, the sooner you'll get to the front of the line. Making an application to a center does not commit you to sending your child there, but it gives you the possibility of sending him. Some daycares will mail you an application form and recommend that you apply that day; others will insist that you visit the center and pick up an application in person. If a center has a good reputation, you may think you have no chance to get in, but don't fall into that trap. You may miss out on a wonderful opportunity.

    Most daycare centers don't have an application fee, but some do—not because it's difficult to process the application forms but because they want only serious applicants on their list. However, if you run into several centers that require a fee, it can become quite costly.

    If your baby is three months old, but you are considering daycare for when he is two, don't be embarrassed that you are thinking so far ahead. The need is so great and the number of places so limited that you are certainly doing the right thing.

WHEN YOU HANG UP

After you phone each daycare, make some notes for yourself. How did you feel about the conversation? Was the director warm and patient? Did she listen carefully to your questions and answer them seriously? Did she sound rushed and harassed? A director who gives you the impression that your questions are foolish, unnecessary and a waste of her time probably isn't someone you'll enjoy dealing with when your child attends her center. We all have bad days, so you can't automatically eliminate her daycare, but her impatience may indicate that your questions are making her squirm.

Of course, you must visit the centers to know if they're as good as they sound and which ones you prefer. Seeing is believing.

When you have phoned all the daycare centers on your preliminary list, you'll know which ones to visit. They will have recommended group sizes and ratios, qualified teachers and hours and conditions that meet your family's particular needs.

DAYCARE SHORTLIST

Daycare center: _____

Address: _____ Telephone: _____

_____

Director's name: _____

1. Is this center licensed? _____

   Does the license have any restrictions? _____

2. What age must a child be to attend the center? _____

3. What are the hours of operation? From_____ to _____

4. Are there any places available for (the date that you need daycare)? ___

   _____

5. Does the center have a waiting list?_____ How long does it take to move

   to the top? _____

6. Are there any special criteria for entrance? _____

   _____

   If the center is a work-place daycare, can non-employees apply?

   _____

7. Do you accept children on a part-time or drop-in basis? _____

8. Is the center profit or non-profit? _____

   If the center is for profit, does the owner own more than one daycare?

   _____ Is the owner on the premises full-time? _____

9. How many children are in each group?_____ What is the adult-child

   ratio? _____

   What is the total number of children in the center? _____

10. How many teachers do you have? _____

    How many have a college or university degree in child development or

    early childhood education? _____

11. What is the cost?_____ per _____

   Is there a reduction for two children? _____

   Are there any additional costs? _____

   Will I have to pay when I'm on holiday? _____

12. Are subsidies available, and how do I get one? _____

   _____

   Will the subsidy cover my daycare fees? _____

13. Is the center ever closed? _____ When? _____

14. Do you serve meals? _____ Can my child bring his own food? _____

   Will the fee be the same? _____

15. Do parents have an obligation to work in the daycare? _____

16. When and how can I apply? _____

   _____

   Is there an application fee? _____

Impressions of the director on the phone:

_____

_____

_____

_____

You've got to take your time
To do it right.
FRED ROGERS

CHAPTER 9

Making an Appointment to Visit

Observing a daycare center can give you a giant headache or a kick like champagne.

Of course you're worried that you won't find a daycare center that's good enough for your child, and, on top of that, you probably wonder if you'll recognize a good one when you see it. Those are natural concerns, and we will help you to deal with them in the next few chapters.

Making an appointment to visit a daycare center
Now that you've reduced the number of centers on your shortlist, you know which ones are theoretically possible. The next step is to visit the daycare centers and to see which is most desirable in practice.

Plan to visit every center you are seriously considering—three at the very least. To get an idea of the kind of center you prefer, try to include a large one and a small one on your list. Organize yourself so that you can spend a morning or a block of time—a minimum of two hours—at the daycare. Call each center and ask to make an appointment with the director to find out more about the daycare and to look around.

When should I go?

What is the best time to visit a daycare center? First of all, in order to make a valid comparison, you should plan to go to all the centers at about the same time of day. If you go in the morning, everyone and everything is clean and fresh, and you'll see the daycare at its best. If you go in the late afternoon, you'll see the daycare at its worst.

Try to avoid early morning (7 to 9 A.M.), when the children are arriving; early afternoon (1 to 3 P.M.), when the children are asleep (infants and toddlers may eat as early as 11 A.M. and be napping by noon); and late afternoon (5 to 6 P.M.), when parents are coming to pick them up. Although you'll see clearly how parents and staff get along and exchange information, and how skillfully the teachers help children make the transition between home and school, you won't see how the staff and children interact when the parents aren't around— and that's *crucial*.

Avoid Mondays, if possible. After the weekend, an exciting time totally unrelated to the rest of the week (and which, for the children of divorced or separated parents, often entails a change in household), children find adjusting to daycare on Mondays a little harder than on other days. Some children wish they could stay at home another day; others are hyper with the excitement of being back. If you can, try to choose another day.

How much time will I need?

It's important that you take your time, ask the questions you need to ask and watch enough of the children's day to have a good sense of what the daycare center is like. After your interview, which should last about half an hour, the director will take you for a short tour. It may be no more than ten minutes, but you should ask to stay longer to observe. (If the director refuses this request, remove this center from your list.) The longer you stay, the more you will see. It is all important.

Observe for as long as you feel comfortable or as long as it takes you to get a feeling of what the daycare is like. You may want to spend an hour with the infants and another hour with the pre-schoolers. If the children at the daycare range in age from six months to six years, you might be there for a whole morning. When you leave, be sure to thank the director and say goodbye. If you like the daycare, it would be appropriate to tell her.

Who should go?

Because this decision affects your child so directly and profoundly, you may be tempted to bring him along to see how he likes the center.

Don't.

This is not a decision for a child to make. He will be very scared, very nervous and very confused by seeing several daycare centers, and he'll have no idea of what to make of the whole affair. He might seem comfortable in one daycare and not in another, but it may be because they served macaroni for lunch. He cannot judge how he would feel over a sustained period of time.

When you have made your choice, you will bring your child to visit his daycare, and he'll know from your attitude—your commitment to the place and to making him feel good about being there—that he will be happy there.

If your partner wants to visit with you, and he can find the time to go without making you feel pressured to leave quickly or to make a decision before you're ready, by all means bring him. If he's at all reluctant, it's better not to drag him along. Do the looking yourself, and talk with him afterwards about what you've seen. Perhaps at the very end, when you've narrowed it down to a choice between two centers and you're considering a second visit, you might induce him to accompany you. But it's not essential. What is essential is that you discuss the alternatives and make a decision together.

If you're a single parent, you'll probably be visiting centers alone, which means no one will distract you from doing the job properly. But try to find someone—a friend or a relative—to discuss your impressions with when you get home. Having a sounding board helps to clarify your thoughts.

But my baby is weeping
For want of good keeping....
TRADITIONAL NURSERY SONG

CHAPTER 10

Interviewing the Director

In this interview the director's job is to fill the places in the daycare center; yours is to find the best possible daycare for your child. You have a right and a responsibility to ask her questions. You will not insult her in the least—she should be proud to tell you about her daycare.

Having an interview with a daycare director is not like seeking a prestigious job or entrance to a private school. Admission is *not* selective or competitive: it's on a first-come, first-served basis. The interview is an opportunity to exchange information, and you as a parent do not have to try to impress the director. It's more likely that she will try to impress you. If you don't like her, you don't have to bring your child to her center; but once you reach the top of her waiting list, she has to accept you. If her daycare is going to retain its credibility in the community, she must respect the center's admission policy.

WHO IS THE DIRECTOR?

Before you talk to the director, take a few minutes to assess the potential importance of this person in your life. Although she won't be your child's primary caregiver, she is ultimately responsible for the quality of the care he receives. She is the one who must ensure that it is consistent, reliable, warm, stimulating and appropriate. In the event of an emergency, she will probably be directly involved with your child. If you have a problem at the daycare center—with your child, your child's teacher or a family matter that affects your child—you will want to discuss it with the director. She will play many roles in her relationship with you and your child—mother, educator, caregiver, administrator and a shoulder to lean on. She should, therefore, be a person you like and trust. As you talk with her now, you will have to make a judgment about her character, as well as about the program she runs.

Daycare directors, like other people, come in many shapes, sizes and colors. Barbara, as director of Garderie Narnia in Montreal, could almost be mistaken for the janitor. She prefers to dress casually in jeans, sweatshirts and sandals so that she can be comfortable with the children. In the course of an ordinary day, she needs to stand, bend, sit on the floor and on tiny chairs, pick children up and hold them on her lap, all activities that are easier in pants and flat shoes. She likes to get to know each child as an individual so that he will know and trust her, too—important in an emergency where she may be the one who takes him to the hospital. Other directors dress more in the style of management, in skirts, stockings and high-heeled shoes. They may spend more time in the office or observing the children from a distance. The director's clothes provide clues about how she perceives her job and how available she is to the children.

You need to be impressed with her integrity and openness, two vital qualities in someone who is caring for your child, especially a child who does not yet talk. Most of us instantly size up new acquaintances without being aware of how we do it: we just know whether we like them or not. Put your own best instincts to work and notice whether the director makes eye contact, whether she uses language that you can understand or fills her speech with jargon and whether she makes an effort to talk to you as a parent instead of impressing you with her knowledge of early childhood education. Does she listen to your questions and concerns and respond to them carefully, or does she put on an old record that she's played many times before?

It is important that you feel that the director is dealing appropriately with the priorities of her job. Working with small children often means crisis management. Although you have scheduled an appointment with her, she cannot predict when a child will develop a fever or a staff member will require emergency assistance. If she temporarily abandons you because of a problem concerning a child, forgive the director. She is correct—the children are her top priority. And seeing her in action will give you the opportunity to evaluate the quality of her relationship with the children and her staff.

But you are important, too, and once she's dealt with the crisis she should have enough time to answer your questions and take you on a short tour. If she can't manage to fit you into her schedule now, when you're a potential customer, how will she ever find the time when your child attends her center? You must feel that you will have access to her when you need her.

You are here to assess the program as well as the director herself. There are some questions that you absolutely must ask her (we've called them "cold, hard facts") and many more that you could ask. First we will explain what you need to find out and why; then we will supply you with some questions. Do read the entire explanation before you go on to the questions, which are in a convenient checklist form at the end of the chapter. Not all the questions apply to every family. (For the sake of convenience, questions about infants and toddlers are at the end.) Sort through them and figure out which are most important to you, write in your provincial requirements for ratio, group and center size, and copy the pages, making a copy for each daycare center that you intend to visit. Fill in the answers as you talk with the director.

One word of caution: the director's job involves a lot of public-relations work. What she says and what actually happens in the daycare may be very different indeed—not necessarily better or worse, but definitely different. She may tell you that her daycare has a warm, nurturing environment, but if you don't see any children on teachers' laps or any adults in intimate conversation with a child or anyone smiling, what the director says doesn't matter one iota. The real answers to your questions will be found not in her office but in the rooms with the children. That is why you will tour the center when your interview is over.

COLD, HARD FACTS

If you have very little time and can ask just a few questions, these are the ones to ask:

License

First, you will want to see the daycare's operating permit. By law all daycares are required to display their license. Be sure that it is valid: check the expiration date and see whether it has any conditions attached to it. Look for the maximum number of children allowed—infants, toddlers and pre-schoolers. In Ontario daycares must also display a poster report of their last inspection. Check it out carefully.

Numbers

Even though the director gave you this information on the phone, ask her again how many children are permitted, how many are enrolled and how many teachers are in each group. When you go into the playrooms, you'll see whether these numbers are accurate.

When you ask about group size and ratio, you are asking a philosophical question as well as a numerical one. Does the daycare separate the children by age or mix different ages together? Does it put a small group with one teacher or form a larger group with two teachers? Do the teachers stay with the same children all day?

1. *Several ages together.* There are pros and cons to all these arrangements. Some studies have shown that pre-schoolers two or three years apart in age do very well in multi-aged groupings. Besides being socially competent, they are cooperative, persistent, flexible and knowledgeable.[1] But for learning specific skills, a developmentally appropriate group (where children are doing the same things and are usually about the same age) works better. A three-year-old won't get a proper chance to do a puzzle when he's playing with a five-year-old.

   Multi-aged groupings are not appropriate for infants and toddlers, who should be in groups of their own, separate from the older children and each other.

2. *A small group with one teacher.* A small group with one teacher has many advantages. In the intimacy of a small group, the children and the teacher have more opportunity to develop a one-on-one relationship. The children feel very secure—they know exactly where to turn when they have a problem, there is less noise and

distraction and there are fewer confusing choices to make. Studies show that children perform better on developmental tests when they are in small groups,[2] perhaps because they spend more time talking, cooperating, reflecting and working at elaborate activities.

But a small group of pre-schoolers with one teacher presents problems, too. If a child throws up, the teacher must help the sick one and cope with seven others at the same time. If the children go to the bathroom in a group but Rory needs to pee ten minutes later, she must decide whether to take the whole group again, to make Rory wait or to allow him to go alone. Does she sacrifice the needs of the individual to the needs of the group? It can be dangerous, too, in an emergency, if she has no backup. Watch for these situations when you are observing.

3. *A larger group with two teachers.* If the rooms are large enough, some daycare centers prefer to group two adults with a larger number of children, although it takes highly skilled teachers to work in a team. The children get to know that people are different—that they go to Eva for a tickle and a joke and to Helen for a hug. In a larger group, the children gain self-esteem by learning to rely on themselves and one another. Ian, who tied his shoe for the first time last week, can help Amelia this week. And there are more possibilities: more playmates, more activities and more opportunities to make decisions.

But in a larger group there are other problems. While one teacher is taking a child to the bathroom or handling an emergency, she leaves the other with a very large group of children until reinforcements arrive. Again, be sure to see how the daycare copes with these situations.

In a larger group, even with more than one teacher, there is more noise and more distraction, and the children may not get enough individual attention. If the teacher forgets to tell Jason how well he washed his hands and neglects to praise Jim for talking to Rachel instead of hitting her back, the children may develop the skill of getting attention by misbehaving. It is important to have teachers who constantly remind themselves to notice the quiet children, too. As you tour the center later, keep an eye out for this positive reinforcement. If you have a quiet or shy child, you might prefer a center with small groups.

Teacher qualifications

Qualified teachers give children better care. Daycare expert Alison Clarke-Stewart sums up the research this way: teachers with training are "more interactive, helpful, playful, positive, and affectionate... and the children are more involved, cooperative, persistent, and learn more."[3] This is really the only opportunity you'll have to ask about the training of the teachers (except in Ontario where this information is posted on the license).

Be sure to find out exactly how many teachers there are, both full- and part-time, and how many of them have a degree in early childhood education or child development from a college or university. The ideal is to find a center where every teacher has training.

Turnover

Research is clear on another point involving teachers: high staff turnover has a negative effect on children. You want to know exactly how long the staff members have been at the center. Of course, you'll ask about the teacher for your child's group, but eventually he'll have several different teachers, and you'll want to know about the stability of the center in general.

Because the salaries in daycare are so low, the turnover rate is very high—people burn out and move on. Every time someone leaves and a new person appears to take her place, the children experience distress. They miss the teacher they know and love; they have to get used to a stranger who does things differently. Turnover is hard on fellow staff, too. It takes time to learn how a place runs and time to become part of a smoothly functioning team. A recent large study showed that centers with more staff turnover offer poorer quality care.[4] A center where the staff have been there for years—five, seven, ten—is probably a gem. Avoid one where almost everyone is new.

Director's qualifications

While you're at it, ask the director about her own qualifications. A well-trained director will have more confidence and ability to select and lead a well-trained staff. The director ought to have a degree in early childhood education or child development and some background in administration and curriculum development. It is important for her to have taught for at least two or three years herself so that she can set realistic goals for both children and staff. If she has been at the center for a long time, she will have selected the staff; she'll know the children and parents well; she'll have an understanding of the center's needs and objectives; and she'll be able to respond more accurately to your questions. It takes six months to a year before a new director can really take hold of her job and have an impact. If the director has just started, you may want to ask how long the previous director was there and why she left. A center that is having trouble holding onto a director may have other serious problems.

Student teachers
Even daycares that aren't attached to a college or university often train student teachers. If there are a lot of them (a different student each day of the week, for example) and they stay for just a few weeks, the children can get very confused. You'll want to know how many come every week, how often they come and how long they stay. No group of children should have more than one student each term. Because they are not yet fully trained and because they are not always there, students cannot be used to meet provincial ratio requirements.

Holidays
Double check the holiday policy. When is the center closed? Do you pay for time you're away and your child does not attend?

Fees and subsidies
The last cold, hard fact involves money. If you will need assistance in paying your daycare fees, you will have asked the director about subsidies in your preliminary phone call. If you haven't yet followed up that query, find out when and where you must apply. In some provinces the wait for a subsidy may be even longer than the wait for daycare.

MORE QUESTIONS

The questions that follow are less important than the previous set, but it is definitely a good idea to ask those that apply to your family:

PHILOSOPHY

Every daycare should have a philosophy, and if you and your child are going to feel happy at this center, you should feel good about the philosophy the director describes.

Some daycares focus on intellectual development, others on social growth. The better centers focus on both, helping the whole child to discover himself as an individual and as a member of a group. A pre-schooler prepares for school by feeling good about himself and by learning how to ask questions and find answers. Learning is developmental, and a center's expectations, rules, and curriculum should respond to the children's growth. Beware of the director who says, "In the morning we do academics, and in the afternoon we have fun"— as if learning weren't fun.

Other centers might respond to the philosophy question by saying that they follow a Montessori or High Scope method, or that they utilize a thematic approach. If you don't understand the director's answer, ask her what she means.

Schedule

Every center should have a written schedule of activities. If the director doesn't offer it to you, ask for one. It will tell you what your child will be doing each day. When you look at it, consider these questions: Do children have both active and quiet free-play periods during the course of the day? Is there a circle time scheduled? Do they go outside at least once every day? Is there variety? Does the schedule look interesting?

Ask the director how much room the schedule leaves for individual moods—if a child can't sit down that day, can he do gym instead of science? Is there extra time to spend outside on a particularly beautiful day? Is there flexibility within the structure, or is it immutable?

Staff scheduling

To build a trusting relationship, an infant or toddler should be with the same caregiver (or the same two caregivers) during the day. Pre-schoolers also need the comfort of familiar teachers. But daycare staff cannot be expected to work more than eight hours. This means that in the course of a ten-hour day at the daycare center, a child will have two or three different caregivers—his regular teacher or teachers and one or two others who take over in the morning and evening, when fewer children are present.

This separation from the main caregiver may hit some children very hard. Be sure to ask how the shifts work, how the staff makes the transition from one caregiver to another and how many people will actually be looking after your child during the day.

For some children the entry to daycare sets the tone for the entire day. Because each child has his own way of getting settled in the morning, some centers assign the same staff person to greet the children on the early-morning shift every day. That way someone always knows whether a child needs to have two minutes on his own or to run to the window to wave goodbye to his mom; whether he needs a special friend, a hug or a simple, "Hello, Jamie." Having the same teacher there every day also makes it easier for parents to know whom to speak to when they have information to convey.

At the end of the day, the teacher doesn't play such a large role because the parent is returning, not leaving. But there should be a system for passing news from teachers to parents.

Where are the children?

Use of space can also be a philosophical question. In some centers, the children remain in the same room for most of the day (the four-year-olds in the four-year-old room, for example). In others, the rooms have special functions (the art room, the noisy, free-play room), and the children move from place to place. Variety is essential. If the children stay in the same room, the teachers should rearrange it periodically so that the children can have different activities, like active play and quiet play, during the course of the day.

Discipline

You no doubt want to know what forms of discipline the center uses. It goes without saying that corporal punishment, denial of necessities like food or use of the toilet and emotional and verbal abuse are totally unacceptable. Hopefully, the director will mention positive reinforcement and learning self-control when she talks about discipline.

The major tools are talk—teaching children strategies for dealing with conflict and unacceptable behavior—and "time-out," where a child sits quietly on the sidelines for a few minutes to regain control of himself. Involving parents may be another way for a daycare to handle a difficult behavior problem.

THE DAYCARE DAY

You've come to see the daycare day, but unless you stay from opening to closing you won't manage to see it all. You'll need to ask about those parts that you can't observe.

Meals and snacks

Although you asked on the phone about whether the daycare served meals and snacks, now is the time to get more detailed information. Every daycare should have a weekly menu that follows basic principles of nutrition. Ask for a copy, and if the children are eating as you make your tour, be sure to notice if they're following the menu. If your child is on a special diet, confirm that he will be able to bring food from home or that the center can accommodate his requirements.

Nap

A traumatic naptime can change a child's whole feeling about daycare. You'll want to know how long the nap period lasts and how dark the room is. There are many ways to help children sleep, some of which seem to be pure magic. Tried and tested ones are playing soft music, allowing the children to have their own cuddly objects in bed and having a teacher gently tuck them in and rub their backs. Children who no longer nap and those who are afraid of the dark need alternatives. If your child doesn't sleep, he should be allowed to read a book quietly. If the room is dark and reading is not allowed, this is not a place for your child.

Bathroom

You might want to watch how the children go to the bathroom, but in case you miss it, ask the director about toileting policy. If they go in a group, be sure that you understand the procedure and what will happen if your child needs to go at a different time. If they go individually as they need to, how are they supervised? Does the arrangement satisfy you?

Outside play and trips

When they play outside, some children crave organized activity, and others prefer to be left to their own devices. Both options should be available. Although a downtown center may not have access to much outdoor space, all daycares should use the community around them as much as possible to expand the children's horizons. Skiing, skating, swimming, library and playground expeditions are obvious choices, but treks to the local fire station or post office can be exciting and educational as well. If the children have gone to distant destinations like apple picking or sugaring off, ask if they've used a bus and whether it had seat belts.

HEALTH AND SAFETY

You probably won't see an accident or a sick child as you walk around the center, but they are certainly part of daycare life, no matter how assiduously one tries to avoid them. A director who tells you she never has accidents at her center isn't being honest. You want to be sure that a daycare has well thought out and well practiced procedures for dealing with virtually any eventuality.

Prevention
Simply because children are in groups at daycare, they get sick more often, and it is very important for the center to do everything in its power to prevent illness. They should have a health professional—pediatrician, nurse, public-health officer—whom they consult when a problem arises, and they should have a policy requiring that every child be immunized appropriately for his age before he starts at the center.

Most daycares require a health record or letter from the child's doctor listing immunizations and stating that the child is healthy and able to take part in the program. When a child attending the daycare contracts a contagious disease, the center should let you know immediately.

How often will your child be sick?
Despite these precautions, your child will be ill, and you'd like some idea of how often. Because each child is different, the director can't answer this question precisely, but at least she can give you a rough idea of what to anticipate. Swedish parents of one- to four-year-olds use an average of nine days of parental leave every year to look after a sick child.[5]

Exclusion
A daycare center is no place for a sick child. He needs to be at home to rest and receive extra tender loving care, and the other children and caregivers, who are extremely vulnerable to illness, do not need exposure to his germs. The daycare will, therefore, almost certainly request that you do not send your child when he is sick—if he threw up during the night, if he has a fever, if he is coughing uncontrollably.

If he becomes ill during the day, the center will phone you and ask you (or a relative or sitter) to collect him, often within a specified period of time. Some daycares even reserve the right to ask parents to withdraw their child if they do not collect him promptly, but others are very lenient, understanding that sometimes parents simply cannot leave work. When you consider the director's answer to this question, you'll have to weigh the demands of your job against the health of your child—no easy feat. The center should have a quiet, isolated spot for a sick child to rest and wait.

Medication

The child can probably return to daycare when he is no longer contagious, although some centers may require a doctor's letter. The parent can usually bring medication (which must be in the drugstore bottle, labeled with the physician's written instructions) to the daycare, where a staff member will administer it. Ask if there is a monitoring procedure—you don't want your child to get his medicine twice or not at all.

Backup care

You might take this opportunity to ask if the center can help you find backup care when your child is sick. Some centers maintain lists of caregivers.

Health problems

If your child has an allergy, asthma or another chronic health problem, be sure to mention it to the director and ask how she would handle it. Does she seem to take the problem seriously? It could be dangerous if the center does not understand its significance.

Accident policy

There should be at least one person at the center at all times who has up-to-date first aid training. Quebec, for example, requires everyone who has contact with the children to have a current first aid certificate.

When the children go outside, there should always be enough staff present to deal with an emergency, as well as with the children who aren't involved—a minimum of two teachers and a maximum ratio of 1:6 for children two and a half years and younger, and 1:8 for children older than two and a half. Teachers should take a first aid kit along, even on trips to the neighborhood playground; and the center should ask you to leave your child's medicare number and to sign a consent form so that the staff can take him directly to the hospital for treatment in an emergency. But, of course, they should phone you so that you can meet them there. Ask which hospital they use.

Fire drills

Other safety measures are equally important. Centers should hold fire drills at least once a month, at various times of the day, in order to accustom both staff and children to the procedure. A fire drill during nap can be quite frightening, but it is also absolutely necessary.

Pick-up procedure

Ask who is allowed to pick up your child from the center. Again, every daycare should have a procedure. You should supply a list of people who have your permission to collect your child, and if you deviate from the list, it should be standard practice for you to inform the daycare and for the daycare to request identification from a stranger. This is especially important for a divorced parent worrying that the former spouse will take the child out of turn.

PARENT INVOLVEMENT

Whatever your child's age, parent involvement in a daycare center indicates high-quality care.

Integration

When your child first goes to daycare, he will need you, and you will need to be with him. You should be welcome at the center during this stressful period. If a daycare will not permit you to stay for the first few days, strike it from your list. To quote T. Berry Brazelton, "If the [caregiver] doesn't want you and your [child] to take your own time in separating, you don't want to be there. It's a difficult transition for both mother and child, and mothers need to be sensitive to it. Otherwise they feel guilty...."[6]

Open-door policy

Are you welcome at the center? Even after your child is settled, you should be able to drop in any time. At some daycares, the director may insist that you make an appointment, offering a billion reasons: children find it difficult to separate, visiting disrupts the schedule, having a parent present makes it harder for the caregiver to build a relationship with the child.

None of these excuses is acceptable. You should be able to visit absolutely freely, and if you are not allowed, you should discard this center. The reason is simple: when a daycare restricts access, in effect it is saying, "You are not part of the team. You are handing your child over to us, and we are taking complete control of him." In such a situation you can easily lose your confidence as a parent and find it difficult to trust your instincts when you need them. It is also in this situation that child abuse can occur.

Contacting the teacher

Work shifts make the matter of talking with your child's caregiver a complicated affair. When you have a very young, non-verbal child at daycare, close daily contact is an absolute necessity, but it's important for pre-schoolers, too. If the teacher who supervises lunch or naptime goes home at 3 P.M., the center needs a system for letting parents know whether their child ate and slept and what the rest of his day was like. Find out if the daycare has a daily sheet, blackboard, bulletin board or communications book where both you and the teacher can record this important information. Ask, too, how you can get together with the teacher if there are problems.

Parent-teacher interviews

Some daycare centers hold formal parent-teacher interviews several times a year. Unlike report cards in school, these visits with the teacher are an opportunity for uninterrupted talk, a chance for parents and teachers to share individual progress and figure out how they can work together. The teacher might tell you how well Amy does puzzles and fine work with her fingers, and suggest that skating with her on the weekends might improve her skill in using her large muscles. You might want to tell the teacher that you and your husband are separated, and that Mondays are really rough with Timothy after he's spent the weekend with his father. The teacher can then give him more space and T.L.C. to help him make the transition from parent to parent.

Working for the daycare

Depending on the center, parents can get even more deeply involved. In private, for-profit centers, parents tend to have relatively little input. In non-profit centers, they can play a central role. Some centers require them to help with maintenance, classroom duties or fundraising. In others parent volunteers, acting as members of the board of directors, set daycare policy.

A reference

If you don't know anyone whose child attends this center, ask the director about talking to one of the parents. She can't hand over a phone number without asking permission, but she can get someone to call you. You might find out how this center relates to its parents—as well as any other inside information you'd like to know.

INFANTS

Schedules

When their needs are quickly and lovingly met, babies learn that the world is a safe place and come to trust other people as well as gaining a sense of their own worth. This means that they ought to eat, sleep and play when they need to, and not when an adult schedule says they must. Some provincial regulations actually stipulate that babies must sleep and eat according to their own needs and rhythms, but even without official rules, daycares should respect their infants by allowing them to function as individual human beings with their own needs and desires. Ask whether the infants are permitted to set their own schedules.

Outdoor time

Sometimes when infants regulate their own schedules, they sleep through the outdoor play time. If it is important to you that your child go outside every day, you might like him to be wakened especially for outdoor play. Would this daycare do that?

Breast-feeding

If you are breast-feeding, and if the daycare center is close to your work place, you may want to nurse your baby at lunchtime. Ask about the center's policy. Is the staff supportive? They should be willing to phone you when your child wakes up and try to keep him happy until you get there—without giving him a bottle.

Bottle-feeding

If you are bottle-feeding your infant, you'll need to know who supplies the bottles, you or the daycare center. If you bring your own each day, of course they should be clearly labeled and refrigerated. If the daycare prepares them, you'll want to ask how they wash and sterilize the bottles and nipples.

Pacifiers

Parents have the right to give their babies pacifiers or soothers if they wish, and the daycare should respect the parents' choice. Ask how this daycare feels about pacifiers. How do they keep them clean and prevent children from sharing them? A loving caregiver can gradually help a child to do without the pacifier as he copes better with his environment.

Crying babies

Even with a superb staff-infant ratio of 1:3, the caregivers will run into problems if all the babies start crying at once. The director or other staff should be available to help out in a pinch.

TODDLERS

Graduating

Daycares have different divisions between infants and toddlers. Sometimes a whole group will enter as young babies, stay in the infant room for 18 months and then move together into the toddler group as the toddlers become three-year-olds. Sometimes both infants and toddlers will be a variety of ages, and they will move individually from one group to the next according to their readiness and the availability of space. Either way takes some adjustment to a new room, new caregivers and new activities. But without the help of his friends, a child facing a new set of peers on his own will probably find the move harder. Some daycares allow children to visit their new room and move back and forth for a period to ease the transition.

Toilet training

Toilet training is a very important aspect of daycare for toddlers. Unless the child is ready, it can be an endless and frustrating battle. Parents and staff should evolve a plan together, and the daycare should respect the child's individual pace in order to make toilet training a positive experience. Regardless of the results, the staff should encourage and praise the child, never scold or shame him when he has an accident or fails to perform.

Bottles

If your toddler still likes a cuddle with his bottle, is the daycare willing? Good care dictates that children be held when they're having a bottle, but toddlers may refuse to be held. Does the daycare allow children to walk around with bottles all day or do they give them one at snack or lunch? May they take their bottle to nap? These troublesome questions may force you to deal with these issues at home, too. Do you agree with the daycare's attitude?

Pacifiers

Again, parents must make the decision about giving a child a pacifier, but as children get older they respond well to the caregiver's suggestion, "Let's put this aside while you play. You can have it at naptime." To keep pacifiers clean and out of the reach of other children, the center should have individual, labeled containers to store them in.

QUESTIONS FOR THE DIRECTOR

Here is a checklist of questions to ask the director. Choose the ones that are most important to you, mark them clearly, and ask the same questions at each daycare center. Then you can compare the answers.

All of these questions deserve a reply, and the director should respond to them in a way that you respect. To run a daycare center that provides high-quality care, the director should know more about child care issues and child development than you do. If she doesn't seem intelligent or up to date, or if she describes substandard conditions or a philosophy that clashes violently with yours, end your tour now.

You will notice that there is no scoring system. The process of sifting information and drawing conclusions from it is subjective and complex, and people make decisions in many different ways. A five- or ten-point scale works for some; but for those who rely on instinct, numbers mean nothing. We suspect that most people use a combination of head and heart. Use whatever tools work best for you, but do make notes of some kind, whether they are numbers, ticks or comments. Otherwise, you'll find it surprisingly difficult to remember which director said what. Be sure, too, to add your overall impressions as soon as you leave the center. Those notes will be invaluable at decision-making time.

DIRECTOR CHECKLIST

Name of daycare: _____

Address: _____

Date:_____ Time: _____

Cold, hard facts

1. May I please see the daycare center's license? _____

   (Is it up to date and without conditions?)_____

2. How many children can be registered here? _____

3. What is the total enrollment of the center? _____

4. How many children and how many teachers are there in each group?

_____

(Figure out the ratio. How does it compare with the recommended and provincial regulations? How does the group size compare?) _____

_____

5. How many full-time educators are there? _____

How many have a degree in early childhood education (E.C.E.) or child development? _____

How many part-time educators are there? _____

What are their qualifications? _____

6. How long has the staff been at the center? _____

How many of the present staff are new this year? _____

7. What are your qualifications? _____

How many years have you been director at this center? _____

8. Do you train students? _____

How many students come per week? _____

Are they counted in the adult-child ratio? _____

9. Does the center operate all year around? _____

Do I pay when I am on vacation? _____

10. What are the fees? _____

11. How do I go about getting a subsidy? _____

Philosophy

1. What is the daycare's philosophy? _____

2. Do the children follow a schedule? _____

Does each group follow its own schedule? _____

May I please have a copy of the schedule for my child's group? (If the schedule is posted in the center but she does not have a copy for you, ask her to make one for you to take with you when you observe the center.)

_____

3. How flexible is the schedule? _____

4. How many people will be looking after my child during the day? _____

Is the same teacher always on the early shift? _____

How do they inform one another about what is going on? _____

5. Are the children always in the same room? _____

6. What kind of discipline do you use? _____

The daycare day

1. Do you serve lunch? _____

May I have a copy of the weekly lunch and snack menu? _____

2. May my child bring food from home? _____

3. How will I know if he's eaten enough? _____

4. How long is nap? _____

How dark is the room? _____

Are children allowed to have cuddly objects? _____

How do caregivers get the children to go to sleep? _____

Are there alternatives for those who no longer nap? _____

5. Do the children go to the bathroom in a group? _____

What if my child needs to go at a different time? _____

If they go individually, how are they supervised? _____

6. What do the children do when they go outside? _____

Do the children play anywhere beside the daycare's playground? _____

7. Can you tell me about a couple of recent trips? _____

If they used a bus, did it have seat belts? _____

Health and safety policies

1. Does the daycare have a health professional that you can consult when necessary? _____

2. Is immunization compulsory? _____

3. What are the center's policies about fever, colds, diarrhea, chicken pox and strep throat? _____

4. Will my child be sick very often? What should I anticipate? _____

5. What will happen if my child becomes sick at daycare? _____
   Where will he stay until I can come to get him? _____
   How much time will I be allowed to pick him up? _____

6. Can my child return to the center while he is still taking medication? _____

7. Is there a monitoring procedure for giving medicine? _____

8. Can the daycare help me find backup care? _____

9. My child has a health problem (describe it to the director). How would you handle it at the center? _____

10. How many staff members have up-to-date first aid training? _____

11. When the children go outside, how big are the groups and what is the adult-child ratio? _____

12. Do the teachers take a first aid kit on outings? _____

13. What will happen in an emergency? What if a child throws up or falls and gets a deep cut on his chin, for example? _____

14. Which hospital do you use? _____

15. How often does the center conduct fire drills? _____

16. Who is allowed to collect my child from the daycare? _____
    What if someone comes for him who isn't on my list? _____

Parent involvement

1. How do you integrate new children, and may I stay for the first few days to be sure my child is comfortable at the center? _____
   _____

2. Can I drop in to see my child at any time? _____

3. How can I find out about my child's day? _____

Is there a written information system? _____

4. Does the center have regular parent-teacher conferences? _____

5. As a parent, will I have any obligations to work at the daycare center?

_____

6. Is there a parent board of directors or a parent committee? _____

What does it do and how often does it meet? _____

7. Could you please suggest a parent I might talk to whose child is currently

at the center? _____

Infants

1. Do infants eat, sleep and play on a schedule or on demand? _____

2. Do the infants go outside all year around? _____

What happens if my child sleeps through outdoor time? _____

Will you wake him if I request it? _____

3. How does the center feel about mothers coming to breast-feed? _____

_____

If my child wakes up early, will you let me know so that I can come to feed

him? _____

Will the staff refrain from giving him a bottle? _____

4. If I bring my own bottles, how are they stored? _____

If the daycare supplies them, how do you sterilize the bottles and nipples?

_____

5. Do you allow pacifiers and how do you handle them? _____

_____

6. What do you do when all the babies cry at once? _____

_____

Toddlers

1. When does a child move from the infant group to the toddler group? __

Are parents consulted? _____

Does the whole group move at once, or do some children move in the middle of the year? _____

How is that transition made? _____

2. How do you decide when toilet training should begin? _____

What do you do? _____

3. Are bottles allowed? _____

When are they given? _____

At meals? _____

At nap? _____

Anytime? _____

4. Are pacifiers allowed? _____

How are they handled? _____

The director herself (questions to answer yourself at the end of the interview)

1. What is the director wearing? _____

2. Does she seem honest and open? _____

3. Does she deal appropriately with the priorities of her job? (You can see this by the way she handles interruptions by a teacher, a child or a parent, either in person or on the phone.) _____

4. When she comes into contact with individual children, does she know their names, and do they know her? _____

5. Does she have enough time to spend with you? _____

Don't forget to write down your own feelings and comments:

__ _____

_____

_____

_____

But when Goldilocks...sat down in
the chair of the Little Wee Bear, that was
neither too hard, nor too soft, but just right.
"THE STORY OF THE THREE BEARS"

CHAPTER 11

How to Look at a Daycare Center

Talking to a director has a familiar ring about it. There isn't one among us who doesn't face another grown-up person—doctor, employer, teacher—across a desk from time to time. But when you leave the sanctuary of the director's office, you enter an alien world—one that belongs entirely to children.

The furniture is their size, but they don't seem to sit in it for long. Instead they play and move, sometimes in groups, sometimes alone, and so do the teachers. The walls are decorated with colorful paintings and collages; the tables hold fish and gerbils. Toys, games, art supplies, science materials and books fill the shelves. Sand, water and moving vehicles seem to have moved in from outside. When a daycare center is in full swing, it's a wonderful place to be, but for an outsider it can be totally confusing.

With so much going on at once, how do you know what to look at? How do you know if the caregiver is doing a good job? How do you know if the children are learning the right things? How do you know if it's safe for your child? Is what the director told you really true? How do you know if this is the right daycare for *your* child?

There is no doubt that it's hard to sort all of this out. Of course you will have a personal guide—usually the director—to take you on a whirlwind tour. But if the passage through this maze is going to be comprehensible, you really need to spend a little time just sitting and watching on your own. To help you to figure out what to look for, this chapter will provide you with some maps and guides.

Part I is a detailed explanation of an infant-toddler program for children up to 30 months of age. Part II is a detailed explanation of a program for pre-schoolers, two and a half to six years. Because there are many similarities in the needs of these age groups, you can read just the section that applies to your child—or you can read both. What's important is to read and think about it now, before you actually visit. Part III contains three checklists of questions to answer when you're actually observing the daycare: one for infants, one for toddlers and one for pre-schoolers. Again, do as many as you're inclined to.

I. *VISITING AN INFANT-TODDLER PROGRAM*

Nowhere are the stakes as high as in infant daycare.

It is perfectly normal for parents of infants to be extremely sensitive, anxious and concerned when they are about to hand over a tiny being who can't protest and can't look after himself. This unique individual, so new and so helpless, needs a very special kind of care to grow up into a trusting, secure person.

Parents of toddlers face a different but equally difficult challenge. Even though they're away from their children during most of the day, parents need to play their rightful role in all of the crucial events of this age—toilet training, bottle weaning and the development of autonomy, among others.

The first two and a half years of life are a period of enormously rapid growth, when social, cognitive, emotional and physical development are intimately intertwined; and very young children, who depend totally on adults, are especially vulnerable to stress. Children of this age need a program designed especially for them. Every aspect of it is extremely important—you the parent must be part of it; the numbers must be right; it must be safe and healthy; and the caregivers must be attentive, loving and knowledgeable. If a program doesn't fulfill these criteria, it isn't a suitable place for your child.

PARENT INVOLVEMENT

An infant-toddler program must take care of you as well as your child. As T. Berry Brazelton puts it, "Strengthening the family should be the major priority of any program directed to the care of infants from birth to two years."[1]

As you tour the center and see the teachers in action, think about how they make you feel. How important are the parents in this world?

There should be a regular system in place, a daily-record sheet, book or chart or bulletin board, for parents and staff to record daily occurrences—for you to write that Deborah slept badly last night because she was teething; that Jonathan didn't want to come today because Grandma is visiting. It should also contain practical information, like how much milk Ruthie drank at each feeding and what other food she ate, what her bowel movements were like and what hours she slept, as well as observations about her behavior—"Ruthie needed a lot of close contact. She seemed happy when held but didn't want to be left to her own devices. I think she's preparing to take a big step forward."

Read some of the comments. Are they open and supportive? There may be many days when you won't be able to talk to the person who looked after your child all day because your working hours don't match—she works for eight hours and your child is at the center for ten. Of course you'll talk to the staff who takes over when she goes home, but this book or chart is another important link with her.

As you walk around, notice other signs of the home connection. Are there photos of parents and siblings? Is there a parents' bulletin board crammed with articles about child development, notices of meetings, parent work schedules and information about clothes and equipment exchanges? Have children brought their own cuddly objects and blankets from home? Are there any nursing mothers or visiting fathers present?

NUMBERS

As Napoleon proclaims in George Orwell's *Animal Farm*, "All animals are equal but some animals are more equal than others." High-quality infant-toddler care is like that. All of its components are essential, but some are more essential than others: most notably, it cannot function well without a high teacher-to-child ratio and a small number of children per group.

Caregivers play the central role in an infant program. When they respond warmly and attentively to a baby's cues, they help him to develop trust in the world and feelings of competence that are essential for his self-esteem.[2] But caregivers have just two arms, two legs and one lap. If they are to provide consistent and individual care, there must be enough of them.

Ratio for infants

Ideally, an infant caregiver should have no more than three babies to look after. In Ontario, which requires a 3:10 ratio, every infant room should have one teacher for almost every three babies. But in other provinces, like Quebec, for example, which demands only one teacher for every five babies, it may be next to impossible to find a 1:3 ratio, and you may have to settle for 1:4. Keep in mind, however, that 1:4 is the bare minimum, and that a float should always be available—the director or a teacher who moves from room to room—to pitch in when there's an emergency or several babies are crying at once.

When you enter the daycare's infant section, count both adults and infants. Remember to include babies who are asleep in the sleep room. (If there are large-scale movements of children from room to room at your approach, that may be a sign that the daycare isn't observing the legal ratios. In a center where all the children come full-time, counting cubbies might help you to pin down the exact number registered.) What ratio of caregivers to babies does this group actually have?

Ratio for toddlers

Although toddlers spend their days letting us know how separate and independent they are, they also need continuing relationships with loving adults. Putting herself in a toddler's shoes, Kelly Schmidt, supervisor at Toronto's Queen Street Childcare Centre, operated by George Brown College as an early childhood education lab school, describes the toddler's perspective: "I need to know that you're going to help me, though I want to do it myself." While they struggle with conflicting feelings—independence and dependence, confidence and doubt, anger and love—they have to be able to rely on the adults around them for comfort, affection and guidance in expressing what they feel in acceptable ways.

But even an adult with the humor of Woody Allen and the patience of Mother Theresa cannot do her job well if she has too many toddlers to care for. The Task Force on Child Care finds an adult-child ratio of 1:3 to 1:5 acceptable for toddlers 18 to 35 months. For two-year-olds (24 to 36 months), it accepts 1:4 to 1:6. Again, count both adults and children, and if there are no part-timers, count the cubbies to account for those who are absent. The ratio that applies is the ratio required for the youngest child in the group. Does the ratio here conform to your province's minimum standard? How closely does it approach the recommended ratio?

Are the ratios for both infants and toddlers the same as the director said they would be? If not, ask why. Is the excuse legitimate?

Group size

Group size is important because it takes a long time for young children to establish relationships, and too many people can be frightening and stressful. A group of six babies with two adults is ideal, but infants can probably handle a group of eight or nine if the caregiver-infant ratio is 1:3.

If the daycare respects the recommended ratio, toddlers under two can manage a maximum of ten children (though fewer are better), and two-year-olds can deal with 12 children at the very most. How large is this group? Is it what the director indicated?

We consider these ratios and group sizes crucial to high-quality care. You'll want to find a daycare that comes as close to them as possible.

PHYSICAL SPACE

A room of one's own

To prevent the spread of germs, infants and toddlers need their own space, separate from the older children, who can't help carrying myriad bugs and viruses around with them. Furthermore, infants and toddlers need to be separated from one another most of the time, each age group with its own teachers, space, toys and equipment. If they're together, chances are that the teachers will end up spending too much of their time with the more demanding infants, leaving the toddlers on their own.

Within their own space, infants need separate areas for playing, eating, sleeping and diapering. (Toddlers can sleep in their playroom.)

Each section should be scrupulously clean, warm, light, spacious and uncluttered. Good ventilation keeps everyone healthy—when the children go outside, staff should open the windows, even in the winter. Daycares in new buildings with sealed windows may have a high sickness rate.

The furniture should be as sturdy as the pigs' brick house—able to hold its own against any number of small bodies using it as a counterweight. It should be constructed of different materials—some soft, like cushions (which as a bonus help to keep noise down), and some hard, like rocking chairs. Infants and toddlers love to be rocked, and a rocker is the perfect spot for a mother or caregiver to sit comfortably with a baby on her lap. In fact, a daycare can use several rockers, strategically placed where no one can crawl behind and crush small fingers.

Low tables provide a splendid surface to stand and work at with a friend.

Playpens

An infant room can probably use one playpen occasionally, especially if one child is much younger than the others. The caregivers will deposit him in it for safety's sake—so that no one will hurt him—while they are busy changing diapers and helping children at the other end of the room. It's also useful for a distressed child who finds the whole playroom space too vast and overwhelming. If he has some stimulating toys and can interact with the other children, he'll be fine in its enclosure for a few minutes. But if you see a child in a playpen crying, unattended, with nothing to play with, or if you see several playpens in a room, beware. This daycare center is not allowing children the freedom they need to explore on their own.

Things to look at

Because babies like bright colors and human faces, cheerful pictures of animals and faces should be displayed at their eye level. Mobiles are great fun, but they should be out of reach. Mirrors not only give infants a chance to learn about their bodies, but also show them that they are independent beings who can make things happen.[3] Shatterproof ones should be affixed where children can gaze at themselves as much as they like—next to the changing table, at floor level on the wall and where they can act as a reward for achieving a standing position.

Walls in the toddler room should feature the children's recent, signed artwork. Toddlers are old enough to begin exploring different media—fingerpaints, collage, scribbling. You should see many different materials being used, and each child's work should be unique.

When infants are learning to stand and walk, bare feet are a definite asset. Linoleum floors feel cold, but carpets are virtually impossible to keep clean. At home, kids live with tile, vinyl and wooden floors and weather the real-life bumps that accompany those surfaces. Provided they aren't drafty, we prefer linoleum or mats to the dirt inherent in rugs. Be sure the floor is clean, free of cracks and splinters and not highly polished (i.e., slippery).

Things to do

Toys must be washable and just the right size—too big to be swallowed but small enough to be easily chewed and grasped (at least 1 1/2 inches in diameter). They should also be light and unbreakable, with no splinters, small pieces or hard corners.

What's safe at home isn't necessarily safe in a daycare center—Tonka trucks can turn into lethal weapons when they develop metal fatigue. When a nine-month-old plays his favorite game of pulling everything off the shelf, no one in the line of fire should get hurt.

Look for a wide assortment of age-appropriate toys, ranging from the simple to the complex, some that children can manage alone, some that require assistance. For infants you should see rattles, balls, squeaky toys, teethers, nesting cups, shape sorters, beads that snap together and busy boards. Puzzles, pull toys, blocks, Duplo, shapes, balls, bean bags, threading beads, toy phones, musical instruments, Fisher-Price toys and dress-up clothes for imaginary play should be provided for toddlers. Washable vinyl, cloth and cardboard books filled with bright pictures of familiar objects are essential. So are sand and water play, important tactile experiences.

Infants and toddlers can't be expected to share, so there should be enough duplicate toys to go around—if three children love the shape sorter, there should be three shape sorters.

A daycare should never use a toy box, which can all too easily slam shut. Instead, the staff should arrange the toys by type in different areas of the room so that children learn to categorize and adults can supervise when necessary. When there are low, open shelves, children can make their own choices—which is important in making them feel like competent people with some control of their lives. Babies and toddlers need free play as much as pre-schoolers do.

One of a toddler's main tasks is learning how to move around in the world. He has the capability, the will and the energy to develop his large muscle skills, and the daycare must supply the space and the chance to try things out. Safe steps and low climbing equipment are a must. They should be surrounded by mats and low enough so that when a child falls down he can pick himself up and climb back on again. Barrels, boxes and tubes to crawl into and pull up on help develop large muscle skills. So do riding toys.

Although the center should have a lot of equipment, the amount that's accessible to the children at any one time should be controlled so that the profusion doesn't overstimulate or confuse them.

Noise

As you sit in the daycare, listen to the sound level. Each person has a different tolerance for noise, and too high a decibel level can turn a sensitive soul into a case for the loony bin. On the other hand, a daycare that's too quiet may mean that the staff is overcontrolling the children. Does the caregiver screech instead of talk? Is the noise the sound of contented children at play? Will your child be able to live happily with it?

The playroom should have areas where a child can be by himself and still be visible to the staff. Like big people, small people need a bit of privacy.

How would *you* feel about spending 50 hours a week in this atmosphere?

SAFETY

The first principle of safety is that a caregiver must *always* be present and paying attention to the children. That means she must be able to see every nook and cranny of the room, and she should never leave three little ones alone while she diapers a fourth in an adjoining bathroom.

Beyond that, an infant-toddler daycare should be the ultimate in babyproofing. In order for children to have the freedom to move toward interesting objects and to test the limits without being told no unless someone is in danger, all hazards must be removed—cleaning materials and medicines put away in locked cabinets and electrical outlets, heating grates, air conditioning vents, fireplaces and stairways covered or blocked off. The kitchen, too, should be gated off—as you know from your own experience, it is full of dangerous possibilities. Scissors, paint and glue should be out of reach. There should be no table edges or swinging doors to bang into, and countertops should be above toddlers' head level.

Ask to see the daycare center's first aid kit and emergency telephone numbers, which should be posted by the phone. You should also see a fire-exit plan and smoke alarms. (One daycare center puts all the babies into a crib on wheels to make a speedy exit.)

Some activities need more than safe space—they need a safe way of using them, too. How many children can use the slides and climbing equipment at once? How do the children go to the bathroom? How do they get outside? Rules and systems are essential as the babies grow into toddlers.

Of course you should never see a caregiver smoking or drinking hot tea or coffee.

The potential for disaster in the safety department is so great that if the daycare fails to meet any of these basic standards you should leave.

HEALTH AND HYGIENE

Playroom

Because babies and toddlers learn by putting things into their mouths, germs pass among them like lightning. Toys that have been in a child's mouth must be set aside for a bath in a bleach solution before they return to the shelves. You should see caregivers collecting toys and dropping them into an inaccessible plastic bucket or basket when a child puts them in his mouth. (The toys should be disinfected every day.)

As you watch the children at play, you may see several runny noses, acquired by contact with a hostile germ. Keeping the children healthy means dealing rapidly with each nose on an individual basis— the caregiver should use a clean tissue every time and wash her hands between blows. She can also begin to teach toddlers to cover their mouths when they cough or sneeze.

All of the children should appear well enough to participate. But because daycare children are so susceptible to sickness, if you visit several centers you may encounter at least one child who's sick enough to send home. Once the teacher has identified the problem, she should separate him from the others and allow him to rest on a couch or cot under supervision. (The director's office is the most likely spot.) You should not see a sick child asleep on a mat in the middle of the playroom floor.

If an extraordinary number of children (50 percent, for instance) is absent from the group, this may mean that this daycare doesn't handle health and hygiene as well as it should.

Diapering area and bathroom

Does the room look and smell clean and fresh—or does it reek of dirty diapers, unflushed toilets and unwashed floors and sinks?

This is an area that requires meticulous attention. Diarrhea, which passes all too readily from child to child, can make an infant very ill. A daycare center that cares for infants and toddlers must maintain an extremely high standard of cleanliness in order to protect its vulnerable little charges.

There are two essential rules.

The first is to keep food and diapers in separate realms. Staff should never prepare food where they change diapers, and no diapers should ever darken the door of the kitchen or food area.

The second rule is that the staff should wash their hands thoroughly and often—whenever they change a diaper, help a child use the toilet, wipe a nose, prepare food or feed a baby. Proper handwashing can reduce diarrhea by 50 percent,[4] and it cuts down respiratory illness, too.[5] To do the job properly, they should carefully scrub in hot running water using liquid soap and dry their hands and turn off the faucet with a paper towel.[6] A sink with running water should be adjacent to the diaper-changing area. (Listen for the sound of the running water when you know a caregiver is changing a diaper out of your sight!)

Diaper-changing tables, which are fraught with danger because of their height, should have a strap or belt and high sides. As you watch a caregiver change a diaper, notice whether she has everything she needs close at hand. She should never have to leave the baby—she just doesn't know when he'll decide to roll over.

If you see diaper rashes, you'll wonder if the caregivers are changing the babies often enough.

Again, to lower the risk of disease, caregivers should clean bottoms with disposable wipes and put dirty diapers in a lined, covered pail. Diaper-changing tables must be cleaned after each change by replacing disposable paper covering and by disinfecting with a bleach and water solution made fresh daily.

Bathrooms are especially important for toddlers because many of their first toilet experiences will take place here. The room should be inviting—quiet, either with small toilets or with ordinary-sized ones reachable by step stools. Kids seem to prefer home-like toilets, where the seat is a complete circle, not open at the front. Potties are extremely difficult to keep clean in a group setting and are therefore much less desirable. In a center that uses them, each child should have his own.

The toilets should be relatively secluded so that the teachers can supervise closely yet allow children to have their privacy if they wish. Not everyone wants an audience when he's learning.

When it comes to using the toilets, toddlers can't wait. There should be enough toilets (and enough caregivers) so that they won't have to stand in line.

Supervised by adults, toddlers should wash their own hands after they use the toilet, and the daycare can encourage them by having low sinks, soap dispensers and disposable paper towels that they can reach themselves.

Toilet accidents are an ordinary part of life in a toddler group. Watch to see whether the caregiver handles them gently and without humiliating the child. She should never threaten, punish or condemn him. She should clean up with disposable washcloths and put the soiled clothes directly into a double layer of sealed plastic bags for mom to collect and wash. (The caregiver shouldn't rinse anything herself.) Of course, when she's finished she should scrub her hands thoroughly.

SLEEPING AREA AND NAPTIME

An infant sleeping area is just that: a room filled with cribs, with perhaps one chair for a caregiver to sit in and rock a baby or supervise the whole angelically sleeping crew. But the caregiver's physical presence isn't actually required—as long as she can see the babies through a window or one-way glass and hear them when they wake, either with a special monitor or because she's close to the door.

To minimize the spread of germs, cribs should be at least three feet apart and arranged head to toe, and each child should sleep in his own crib with his own sheets, blanket and cuddly object. You'll know they're his if they're clearly labeled with his name. Of course the baby linen should be changed at least once a day and any time it's wet or soiled. In other words, you should see clean, dry sheets on every bed.

Provincial safety standards require close-fitting mattresses and bars spaced so that children can't get stuck in them. And for a speedy exit in case of fire, be sure each crib has an uncluttered aisle to the door.

Toddlers probably won't sleep in a special room but will use their playroom to rest instead. That means you won't see whether the cots are three feet apart unless you're there while the staff is rearranging the room for nap. But you can check to see whether each child has his own labeled cot and blanket—they are usually stacked in a cupboard or corridor, ready to be trundled out at noon hour.

Babies should sleep on their own schedules, according to their own body's needs. Grown-ups should not force them into an artificial, rigid routine designed for their convenience. It is unlikely that very small infants are heeding their own rhythms if you see them all asleep or all awake or all eating at the same time. When the babies follow the same schedule, the staff gets a few moments to wash toys and restock shelves—and to eat lunch. But when the babies are awake at different times, the caregivers can give them much needed one-on-one attention.

Toddlers and older babies are likely to end up on similar schedules, and their day should follow a relatively predictable course that meets their needs. If the kids are falling asleep in their spaghetti, it's not.

While you're near the sleep room, listen for the sound of crying. How long does the staff let a baby cry there? Though he may take a few minutes to settle down for his nap, when he wakes they should come to him promptly.

FOOD AREA

The kitchen, which should be at least as clean as yours at home, should be fully equipped, even for infants and toddlers who are still having bottles and baby food. It should have its own sink and a dishwasher that heats the water enough to sterilize the utensils. They need a refrigerator to keep bottles of milk, baby food and medicine; and they need a stove to heat bottles and food. Some may have a microwave.

Since you're here to look around, be nosy and open the fridge and cupboards to see how the foodstuffs are stored. Everything should be clean, and the food should be kept in closed boxes and plastic containers to keep bugs out.

The handwashing routine you encountered in the bathroom is equally important in the kitchen—before anyone touches food, both staff and children should scrub thoroughly.

Eating is a sociable, happy part of the day, one of the best times for your child to have a private conversation with his caregiver, to feel her warmth and regard for him. The minutiae of the daily routine—eating, dressing, diaper changing and toileting—offer countless opportunities for forming relationships, talking and learning. "It's all part of the program, not just something you have to do to get somewhere else," says Marilyn Neuman, director of the McGill Daycare Centres in Montreal. Does the staff make the most of these chances, or are they merely getting things done?

Bottles propped into infants' mouths are a crystal-clear signal for you to cross this daycare off your list. A good caregiver holds a baby when she gives him his bottle, and she should feed him when he's hungry, on his own schedule.

Although he may eat with a pal when he's old enough to sit up, the teacher should still be there to help and encourage him to explore his food and feed himself as much as possible. Finger foods are a must!

A first-class teacher sits and talks with the toddlers at mealtime, too. Children who are ready can use spoons, bowls and cups. Little children, experimenting with the law of gravity or determined to get your goat, often spill or throw food on the floor intentionally. How does the teacher respond? Does she set limits in a calm, good-natured way? Or does she lose her temper?

Don't forget to notice the food. It should look healthy. Has the daycare served the dishes that it lists on the menu? And is the menu posted? (Ask for a copy and give it a closer look when you get home.)

Watch to see whether the teachers disinfect the high-chair trays and tables when everyone's finished eating.

OUTDOORS

Even if the children aren't on their way in or out while you're visiting, be sure to notice the cloakroom. Because parents have to be at work at about the same time, they tend to arrive all at once, bringing with them their bundled-up baby plus stroller or backpack and diaper bag bulging with bottles, food and diapers. When they hit the warm inside air, they urgently need a place to divest their infant of the many layers of clothing he needs to survive the Canadian winter. To control traffic, there should be a separate infants' cloakroom, preferably with changing tables equipped with safety rails and built at a comfortable height for parents. Where is the storage area for snowsuits and equipment? Does each baby have his own labeled cubby or hook?

The minute he begins to walk, a toddler needs his own cloakroom space—a place to sit down and take off wet boots and snowsuit and a hook to hang clothes to dry. He may also keep his spare clothing and precious belongings there. His area or cubbyhole should be a place that he can identify—labeled with his name or a photograph.

To cut down on noise and to keep germs at bay, the cloakrooms should have doors or be well separated from the other rooms.

Every child should go out every day—fresh air and exercise are essential to health, even for babies. If you don't see the children go outside while you're observing a daycare, be sure to ask one of the teachers about it. Did they go earlier? Will they go later? If not, why not? Notice if there are multi-seated strollers around—evidence that the center is equipped to take the babies for a walk. A teacher in one daycare that we visited in February told us frankly that she hadn't taken the babies out since November.

The teacher should encourage the toddlers to dress themselves and make the task a pleasant one, even for the kids who have trouble, by turning it into a game. Then she should check to see that the full winter regalia is in place and secure. Watch how the group makes the trip outside—is there a system to ensure that they all arrive safely? In this transition, as in every other transition throughout the day (from toilet to snack, from playtime to lunch, from storytime to nap), getting there should be half the fun. Can the caregivers lure the children from one place to another without making them line up and march like soldiers?

Once they're mobile they should have their own fenced outdoor play space with safe low slides and climbing frames in good working order. The surface should be soft—grass or sand, not gravel or cement. A lot of space, a bit of sun and a smidgen of shade make outside play more fun. If you're visiting in the winter, notice what they're doing.

There should be some place for them to play and something to do when it's unsafe to use metal slides and climbing equipment. Again, children must understand and follow the rules of safe play, and staff must supervise very closely.

WHAT SHOULD THE TEACHERS BE LIKE?

Let's look at that question from a general perspective before we examine the teachers up close. Look first at what they're wearing. Work with infants and toddlers is bound to be messy. Are these caregivers prepared? Can they move around comfortably and easily in their clothes and shoes? Will they mind getting cherry yoghurt on their pants?

Next, notice their position in the room. If they are doing their job well, they should be hard to find—they'll scatter themselves among the children and talk with them at their own level. Groups of teachers chatting together, or teachers standing at the wall with their hands in their pockets, are not doing what they're supposed to do.

Now let's look more closely.

People often believe that anyone with a good heart and a strong back can look after a small child. That's a start, but it certainly isn't enough. According to Burton L. White, author of *The First Three Years of Life*, a first-rate infant or toddler caregiver is "warm, interested, experienced, knowledgeable, intelligent, verbal, patient, enthusiastic, and not overly protective."[7] She gets to know her children and responds to them as individuals with their own style, rhythm and preferences. She also knows how they grow and learn—the developmental stages they pass on their way through childhood—so that she can gear actions, speech, toys and activities to their constantly expanding interests and abilities.

Affect

The teacher must like, appreciate and enjoy the children. As we visited daycare centers, we saw too many teachers who were doing their jobs competently in every way but one: they seemed to take no pleasure in it. They were just going through the motions. A truly good caregiver loves being with children and is really engaged with them. She smiles, she makes funny faces, she listens, pays attention and responds to the person she's with. She has what the experts call "affect." The children should have affect as well—they should look happy or sad; they should have feelings about what's going on around them and about what they're doing themselves. Being busy is not the same as being involved, and being happy is more than not crying. If you want your child to care about things, he must be with people who care, who have feelings and aren't automatons.

You have to look actively for affect, to sensitize yourself to it. If you find a daycare where all the teachers and children have affect, you have almost certainly found a winner. The opposite is also true: unstimulated, spaced-out babies or toddlers sitting by themselves with nothing to do for more than a few moments are real cause for concern.

Look for lots of one-on-one, face-to-face interaction. Whenever a caregiver is changing a diaper, dressing or feeding a baby, the teacher should smile, look into the baby's eyes, talk to him, gently answer and repeat his attempts to communicate.

The teacher should squat or sit at the toddler's level and let him begin conversations, even if he can't say much yet. When she waits patiently for his comments, labels objects and amplifies his remarks, she helps to extend his vocabulary. She should answer his questions promptly and ask him questions as well.

Relaxed physical contact is very important, too. Does the caregiver often hold the baby and carry him around, perhaps in a Snugli? When he cries, she should come at once to soothe and comfort him—and to feed him if he is hungry. She should respond quickly, too, when toddlers are in distress or crying. Children should not be left unattended. If one of them is having a rough time, a caregiver should be helping him through it. As the caregiver meets their needs, infants and toddlers learn that they can count on her—and by extension they come to trust others.

Independence

It's extremely important for a child to direct his own play—it makes him feel competent, which in turn builds his self-esteem. Offering encouragement, ideas and praise a good caregiver provides equipment and choices but allows the baby to be in charge. "It takes a special teacher not to butt in all the time," says Marilyn Neuman. "If a child is content and able to play on his own for five or ten minutes, the teacher should allow him the dignity to do that."

Children learn through play. The seven-month-old who's struggling to grab the rattle that's just beyond his reach is developing eye-hand coordination and the physical ability to move forward. When someone takes the toy away, he's getting a lesson in object permanence—that what's out of sight isn't necessarily gone forever. A good caregiver plays peek-a-boo with the babies, offers them stimulating toys and gives them different perspectives by changing their position throughout the day. They play on the floor, sit on laps, swing, rock, move around under their own steam and go outside. Because talk is crucial to language development, she also chats, sings and reads books with the children whenever an opportunity presents itself.

A toddler doing a puzzle is working on problem-solving and eye-hand coordination, learning about shapes and figuring out that things have to go the right way in order to fit—an important pre-reading skill. In the group, he is developing social skills like sharing, verbal communication and understanding concepts like cause and effect (if you hit me, I'll hit you back). He is expressing his feelings and enhancing his creativity. Toddler play is parallel play. The children are aware of each other and make contact—if Catherine sees Robert building a block tower, she may try it later herself. They feel a sense of community; they know they're not in the room alone.

Watch to see if the teacher supports the toddler as he acquires new skills and preferences. Does she successfully negotiate the thin line between allowing him to grapple with problems on the one hand and not becoming too frustrated on the other? When he's excited by what he's doing, a toddler will repeat and practice an action for what seems an eternity. Does the teacher praise his efforts?

Along with letting him make his own play choices, a good caregiver will let a child take responsibility for himself instead of moving him unilaterally from one place to another. Toddlers love to help and clean up and are capable of quite extraordinary independent exploits when given half a chance. Among other things, they can certainly get themselves to the toilet if there's one in the playroom.

Toddlers thrive on individual or small-group play with the teacher, including reading and acting out stories. They even have structured activities, but they don't look the same as they do when older children have them. Everyone plays in the sand box together; everyone walks around the room banging or blowing on a musical instrument; everyone paints on a white sheet; but not everyone has to participate. A toddler group needs one structured activity in the morning and one in the afternoon to give some variety to the day and to introduce the children to new experiences. The teacher should supervise closely but she shouldn't make so many rules and limits that it takes away the children's pleasure—they should definitely be enjoying themselves. There should be opportunities for social growth (like sharing and courteous behavior) and opportunities for cognitive growth (like learning to manipulate objects like a funnel or a paint brush or seeing the difference between wet and dry). The teacher shouldn't expect any particular result—it's the process of exploration and manipulation that's important, not the product.

How can you tell if the teacher has control of the group? You may not be able to tell until you hit a daycare where she doesn't. Then you'll see children running around, screaming, unwilling to cooperate and generally doing things that are potentially dangerous to their own safety and well-being. Where the teacher has control, the children are involved in what they're doing, they're visible to at least one educator at all times, and their activities seem appropriate for the space (if they're running, they're in the gym).

Discipline

Infants and toddlers learn to say no because they hear a lot of "no!" as they explore the world around them. A high-quality daycare center is an environment with very few prohibitions and accompanying admonitions. Its safe, child-oriented space lets infants and toddlers get to know one another and learn about social behavior as they begin to share and take turns.

The key to a happy playtime is to have enough equipment to go around and enough staff to anticipate what's going to happen and to head off conflict and violence. Teachers use different behavior-management techniques, but they should always be positive, never critical or destructive of the child. You shouldn't hear anyone saying no. Positive reinforcement—praising a child when he's done something well—is very important. From the very beginning, a good caregiver will explain, "Ouch, that hurts," when a baby hits someone or pulls his hair, and she will immediately redirect him to another activity. As he acquires more language, she will explain more: "He's not done. You can have it when he's done." But she should follow up with a hug and the reassurance that she still loves him, letting him know that it was his action, not himself, that made her angry.

Punishment is not appropriate for this age group. They simply don't understand enough of what's going on. If you see a child in a corner being punished, that's a bad sign.

Each child comes into the daycare carrying his own little life with him, and each child requires a unique approach. When a child loses control, how does his behavior affect the rest of the group? Is the teacher calm and patient? Rather than yelling at a child from across the room, she should approach him quietly and lovingly and try to help him to understand why his behavior is not acceptable. Close contact, body language and facial expression are all important. Does she use these tools to her advantage? She must give the child the confidence and sense of well-being he needs to return to the activity or to start a new one. Does she find positive ways to direct his attention?

With both infants and toddlers, the teacher should model caring, helping and sharing—even toddlers can come to the aid of a friend in distress. When she saw Sonya crying, 18-month-old Tam brought "Yazzi," her favorite orange blanket, to comfort her.

II. *VISITING A PRE-SCHOOL-AGE DAYCARE PROGRAM*

Sometimes it feels as if babies grow up almost instantaneously. By the time they are two and a half, they begin to have a command of language, use their memories, control their bodies and understand that others have feelings. They need lots of chances to exercise their newly discovered independence and build their competence. Even so, pre-school children continue to need love, warmth, patience, guidance and support, just as they did when they were infants.

Which daycare program will best provide for the complex needs of your growing child? Again, the best way to tell is to take a deluxe tour, guided by the checklist at the end of this chapter. Aside from the time you spend with the director, plan to stay about an hour with the pre-schoolers. Concentrate on making the most of whatever time you have. If you're there early in the morning, watch how the teachers greet the children entering the center. If you're there while they go outside, notice how they get ready and what they do in the playground.

As you move from room to room, you'll need a copy of the daycare center's daily schedule (available from the director) which tells you what the children are doing and when. You will want to refer to it along the way. The center should be following the schedule, but with small children flexibility is required, too. If you happen upon a deviation, ask the director about it. If you find the children outside instead of inside on an unusually warm, sunny day, consider this lapse a plus. But if they're engaged in noisy free play when they're supposed to be doing an art activity, that's a distinct minus. An absent art teacher shouldn't prevent the director from filling the gap with another organized activity, like music. If she hasn't, it probably means that this daycare has no staff member who can improvise an organized activity at the last minute.

What follows is an explanation of what to look for in a high-quality daycare program for pre-schoolers. First of all, you need to know that you will be welcome and that the environment will be a safe and healthy place for your child. Then you will be ready to observe the staff, the core of the daycare experience. They must offer top-quality caregiving for your child. After you've assured yourself that they are professionals who are doing a good job, it becomes worthwhile to examine the physical space and ambience, the schedule and activities.

You will probably find, as we did, that good things come in bunches. In a high-quality center, everything will be childproofed and spic and span, and the teachers and program will be delightful. In a poor-quality center, on the other hand, you'll find dustballs in the corners, children who slip out of the classroom and down the stairs unnoticed and no one going outside.

PARENT INVOLVEMENT

No matter what the age of the child, his parents need to know what's going on in his daycare, and his daycare needs to know a bit of what's going on at home. Everyone has to make an effort to meld the separate pieces of a child's life into a whole. You and your child's caregivers must talk about your child.

How do parents and caregivers communicate at this center? Because of shift changes, his teacher might not be around when you come to collect him in the evening. That means the daycare has to have another method of letting you know how long he slept, whether he ate his fish fingers and if Jimmy refused to play with him today. Every daycare should have some written system for conveying this information to parents and for receiving it from them as well. If Bettina needs a dose of antibiotics before lunch or if an older sister is collecting Darren tonight, that information should be in the daycare's daily sheets, book or ledger. Ask if you can read a few pages. Are the comments open and positive?

A bulletin board also gives insight into the center's relationship with its parents. You might see minutes of a daycare board meeting, articles about child rearing and nutrition and information about community resources.

Notice, too, whether parents hang around and come for lunch. They should always be welcome.

A good daycare is not just a place where your child spends 50 hours a week. It is a community, where children and parents form relationships with teachers and with one another, people in their neighborhood or work place who are having the same experience. For the center to be a place where networks develop, it must be welcoming. When you walk in, you should feel that you've entered a user-friendly environment.

NUMBERS

Counting is a simple act, but as we've learned, it reveals crucial information. The adult-child ratio is vital to high-quality daycare. How many children are in this room? How many adults are supervising them? Ask how old the children are. Are provincial requirements being observed?

Keep in mind that the regulations set *minimums*—a good daycare should have more staff than the rules demand. According to the Task Force on Child Care, one caregiver should look after just three to five two-year olds; between five and eight three-year-olds; eight to ten four-year-olds; or eight to 12 five-year-olds.

Group size is crucial, too. In smaller groups the children receive more individual attention and, as a result, flourish in virtually every area of their development. The Task Force suggests a maximum acceptable group size of six to ten for twos; ten to 16 for threes; 16 to 20 for fours; and 16 to 24 for fives. In our opinion, however, group size should never exceed 16, and one teacher should never be responsible for more than eight children.

The size of the center's rooms may determine the size of its groups. A daycare with small rooms will have eight three-year-olds and one teacher in a room. A daycare in a school building with larger rooms is more likely to group 16 three-year-olds with two teachers.

If a teacher is working alone with a small group, everything—bathroom, clean clothes, water to drink and to clean up—must be accessible so that she does not have to leave the children alone to look after individual needs.

The ratio and group size apply to all rooms at every time of the day. Perhaps the only exception is at naptime, when one teacher can supervise a larger number of children—provided other teachers are immediately available. In an emergency—or even for that predictable event, a trip to the toilet—the teacher must be able to get help without abandoning the other children in her charge.

Different activities require different ratios and group sizes. A cooking activity with several stages—measuring, mixing, baking—might require more supervision than a circle activity where everyone sings familiar songs together.

When you are looking at group size, consider the ambience of the daycare. Are the children smiling? If they seem happy and busy, they probably are. Then consider your own child. How sociable and how rambunctious is he? How well does he concentrate? How well does he follow directions? Will the challenge of a large group help him to bloom, or will he get lost in the crowd? Does he need the safety and security of a small group, or will he quickly get bored? Like Goldilocks, he needs one that is just the right size for him.

SAFETY

Safety is absolutely basic. No parent wants to leave his child in a place that is unsafe. Sometimes we take chances—we run across streets or we drive to the supermarket without a seatbelt—but when we leave our children in the care of others, there is no risk worth taking. Every item on this list should check out positively; the center you choose should be thoroughly childproofed.

Indoors
Wander around the room. Lysol and cleaning equipment should be in the original labeled containers in a locked cabinet. Medicines, too, should be locked up. Electrical outlets, heating grates, air conditioning vents, fireplaces, stairways and kitchens should be blocked off.

Ask to see the first aid kit, and note whether emergency telephone numbers—fire, police, hospital, doctor, poison control, ambulance—are prominently posted by the phone.

Daycare centers are often located on the ground floor to make it easier for the children to leave the premises in case of a fire or emergency, but there should be an emergency fire-exit plan in every room. There should also be smoke alarms, sprinkler systems and emergency lights.

It is harder to get a handle on equipment safety. Nothing in the daycare environment should be dangerous for a child—glass objects, metal trucks, sharp edges, splinters and rusty nails should all be outlawed. Furniture and climbing apparatus should be sturdy, solid and in good repair and countertops and table edges well rounded. Paint, glue and markers should be non-toxic and well out of reach, along with scissors and other sharp implements.

However, even a very safe space is only as safe as its supervision. Every section of the room should be visible to a staff member at all times. How can she supervise what she can't see? And, of course, she should supervise closely—teachers really need eyes in the backs of their heads.

Large wooden blocks, wonderful toys that belong in every daycare, become lethal objects when they fall from a hand-built skyscraper or whiz across a room. Daycares, like cities in earthquake zones, need building codes—as well as safety rules regulating how many children are allowed to use the apparatus, which direction traffic moves in, and so on. Pre-schoolers are old enough to understand and heed the safety laws.

If by chance you're at the daycare when the staff is readying the room for nap, notice whether there are clear aisles to the door between the cots. The children must be able to exit quickly in an emergency.

No one should ever be smoking or drinking hot tea or coffee in an area where there are children.

Outdoors
When you came in, you may have seen the outside play space. Be sure to look at it closely before you leave the center. Whether it is on the ground or the roof, every daycare needs an attractive and well-kept outdoor area enclosed by a fence that children can't climb over, under or through. To be safe, the space must be large enough for children to run freely without getting in one another's way, and it should have

some sun and some shade. The surface should be soft grass, sand, wood or rubber indoor-outdoor tile, not unforgiving gravel or concrete. (Sand should be covered at night to protect it from meandering animals.) Bikes, swings and climbing apparatus must be safe and in good repair.

If this center leaves you in doubt about any of these matters, you should not consider sending your child to it.

HEALTH AND HYGIENE

Because small children are so vulnerable to illness, a daycare center must make every effort to control the spread of germs. For a start, the rooms should look and smell clean. At 10:30 A.M. you can expect to find sand and toys on the floor, but the question is, what is underneath them? If the floor is mopped every day, you won't feel sticky juice underfoot or glimpse dustballs gathering in the corner.

Playroom
Wall-to-wall carpet looks great, but it takes just one child to pee and one to throw up to make it a perfect mess. Because a daily shampoo is out of the question, area rugs and linoleum are much easier to keep clean. (In Quebec, wall-to-wall carpets are illegal.)

Every day, even in winter, the staff should open the windows for a while to change the air and disperse the accumulated germs. This is easiest to do when the children are outside but should even be done on indoor days. (In a study of six Montreal daycare centers, those that didn't open their windows increased the risk of illness for both children and staff.)[8]

Have a look at the dress-up corner. Worn by dozens of children, the wardrobe there takes a daily beating and should take the plunge into someone's washing machine every week—the clothes needn't be ironed, but they should be clean. Sadly, hats pass head lice, so they don't belong in the dress-up box at all.

It's hard to tell how dirty the dolls are, but if they don't look clean they must be very dirty indeed.

The awareness of hygiene in the daycare is very important, too. The teacher should model and teach good health habits. She should remind the children to cover their mouths when they cough or sneeze; and when she is wiping noses herself, she should throw the Kleenex away after each wipe and immediately wash her hands thoroughly.

She should discourage children from putting toys into their mouths, but if Patrick eats a toy banana, she ought to deposit it in a special container to wash later in a bleach solution—not return it to the housekeeping corner for Caroline to munch, too.

All the children who are present should be healthy enough to play and enjoy themselves, but if someone falls sick during the day, the daycare should have a comfortable, warm, quiet place where he can be isolated from other children and supervised until his parents arrive. Be sure to ask to see this space, which is likely to be in the director's office or the staff room. He should *not* be on a mat in the middle of the playroom floor, where he'll find it hard to rest, be more contagious to the other children and monopolize the teacher's attention.

If a great many children are absent—half, for example—this center's health policy probably needs overhauling. (See chapter 17.)

Bathroom

The bathroom should be as clean as a whistle—not crying out, "Scrub me with Javex!" as you open the door. It's all right if someone misses the wastebasket once in a while, but the floor, slippery when wet, should be clean and dry. You wouldn't want to sit on a toilet seat covered with urine, and neither would your child. The toilets should always be flushed. Sinks should be clean, too.

Some daycare centers have large bathrooms used by all the children; some have a small bathroom with one or two toilets and sinks adjoining each room; some may have regular bathrooms like yours and mine. Some will have plenty of toilets and sinks; others will provide the minimum that provincial regulations demand.

Count the toilets. If the bathroom isn't part of the playroom and there aren't very many, the children may have a long wait for their turn.

It's better if the toilets are child-sized, but the center can make its regular toilets accessible by adding step stools.

You'll have to keep your eyes and ears peeled to observe the toileting routine at each place you visit—it's a key item, not to be missed. At some centers, where the bathroom is far away, the teacher will take the children in a group or one at a time, as necessary. In other centers, where the toilets are essentially part of the playroom equipment, the children use them as they need to, without fanfare.

Even in a lavatory equipped with urinals or doorless toilet stalls, the teachers should understand that each child has the right to his own private space and that entrance is by invitation only. On the other hand, the staff should be close enough to lend a hand if they're needed.

They should also supervise handwashing after the children have used the toilet. Faucets, soap dispensers and disposable paper towels should be at child level to encourage children to become competent and independent and to teach them good habits. (Of course, the bathroom sinks should be used just for handwashing.)

Regardless of age, bathroom accidents are a daycare inevitability. The staff should be gentle, helpful, unobtrusive and uncensorious. They should use disposable washcloths to clean the child and place his soiled clothes in a double layer of sealed plastic bags for his parents to deal with. (They should not rinse clothes in the toilet or wash them in the washing machine.) His parents should have supplied him with his own clean clothes to put on.

When the educator finishes cleaning up—and any time she helps a child go to the toilet—she should wash her hands well with warm running water and liquid soap, dry them and turn off the faucet with a disposable paper towel. Proper handwashing is critical and should *never* be neglected. It can cut daycare illness in half.[9]

Some parents and daycare centers like children to brush their teeth after every meal. Again, supervision is important. Toothbrushes must be labeled so that everyone uses his own; they must be stored so that they don't touch. Toothpaste, a natural spreader of germs unless each child has his own, isn't strictly necessary, but if it's used, it should be labeled and stored individually.

Kitchen

It is perfectly reasonable to expect a daycare kitchen to gleam—even if the food is for children, the chef here should be as conscientious and meticulous as the chef in a three-star French restaurant. The kitchen needs its own sink, used exclusively to prepare food, and a dishwasher that heats the water temperature high enough to sterilize the dishes. Needless to say, a stove or microwave and refrigerator are required.

How is the food stored? Is the refrigerator clean and the food fresh? Are boxes and containers carefully closed and housed in plastic when necessary?

Sleep area

You probably won't be around at naptime, but you should ask to see the rooms where the children sleep. To prevent illness, each child should have his own labeled cot, with his own sheets and blanket kept separate from the others and washed every week. You should also see cuddly objects that make the children feel more comfortable and secure.

If you see the room set up for nap, notice whether the cots are at least three feet apart so that the children don't breathe and cough directly into each others' faces.

PEOPLE

Numbers aren't all that counts when it comes to staff. Now that you've ascertained that this environment is safe, healthy and user-friendly, it's important to find out what the teachers are like, because they are the daycare's heart and soul, responsible for creating the atmosphere, loving and respecting your child and seeing that he grows in the best way he possibly can.

Look from afar

To begin with, let us regard the teachers from a distance. How do they view their job? At least one clue—so self-evident that we usually overlook it—is their clothing. The teachers should be wearing clothes that enable them to do their work well—clothes they won't mind getting paint on—and shoes that allow them to move around quickly without tripping or impaling small hands or feet.

Where are they? At some daycares you don't see the teachers right away because they are so well integrated with the children. At others they stand outside the group.

The teachers should be with the children, sitting at their level, talking and listening, guiding them to deeper understanding and to more complex play. But there will also be moments when children are learning to share and to solve problems without adults, and she won't want to intervene. To assess how well she is doing, tune into the interactions of the children. If the noise and activity level are lively but controlled, she is managing well.

What is not acceptable is a teacher standing at the wall with her hands in her hip pockets while children argue or do nothing. Another bad sign is a clump of teachers chatting together, clearly more interested in one another's weekends than they are in the children.

Close-up of a teacher

A teacher has the responsibility of fostering all aspects of a child's development—social, emotional, cognitive and physical. What qualities enable her to do her job well? How do you know a good teacher when you see one?

Let's scrutinize her at close range. This won't be easy—it takes patience and concentration to sit and watch carefully. But it's worthwhile to make the effort. In time you'll see how she deals with the children and how they respond to her. Trust your own gut feelings as you evaluate her.

First, a teacher should be warm and responsive, respecting the children as individuals and giving them lots of positive support.

Long before they can talk, children understand body language very well indeed. They know when a person means what she says. A teacher who is honest and spontaneous will make eye contact when she is with the children, and her facial expression will match the words that she says. She will squat or sit at children's level, and she will smile a smile from the heart—a sure sign that she enjoys being with them.

This ability to express her feelings and to really engage with the children—the ability to convey that she truly cares about each of them as an individual person—is called "affect." It is an essential characteristic in a first-class teacher. Usually when it occurs in a teacher it also occurs in the children around her. They seem especially involved in what they're doing and keen to express themselves.

It takes a certain awareness on your part to notice affect—to know you're with living, thinking human beings. Look and listen carefully. Does the teacher really smile, and are the children really happy, or are they just going through the motions?

Although some children like to be hugged, others need personal space. The teacher must be sensitive to the needs of individual children, allowing them to be comfortable with the relationship. Interestingly, research shows that high-quality caregivers don't smother the children with physical affection. Teaching and playing, giving verbal encouragement and offering specific suggestions are more important. [10]

Is there a sense of mutual respect? The teacher should talk and listen to the children as individuals. If she recognizes that they are at different stages in their development, and that they have different interests, abilities and learning styles, she will help them with different things and encourage them in different directions. A good educator will set up a variety of activities because she does not expect all the children to want to do the same thing at the same time.

She should manage to be with them one at a time, answering each child's questions promptly and asking him open-ended questions that allow him to respond honestly and thoughtfully. Rather than cutting him off, she will give him a chance to share his feelings and thoughts.

She fosters self-esteem, independence and feelings of competence in the children by encouraging them to do as much as they can for themselves, like dressing, washing their hands and putting the toys away. She also allows them time and space to explore and choose their own friends, materials and activities and to solve problems on their own. She does not direct, criticize or restrict them.

In any group of children, no matter how happy they are and how well they're cared for, sooner or later a child is going to cry—life is not a bed of roses, and conflict, frustration, confusion and skinned knees are inevitable. A teacher should immediately notice a child alone, crying or just looking sad. If she doesn't, or if she makes no attempt to discover what's wrong, you do not want your child in this daycare center. A crying child should always be comforted and a fearful child reassured. The teacher should come close and talk to the child at his level, listening and helping him to find a solution to his problem without telling him what to do. She should stay with him until he is ready to participate with a smile.

Discipline

Discipline is rather a dirty word among daycare directors and teachers. They much prefer more positive terms, like *guidance* or *behavior management*. In fact, discipline is really a matter of helping a child to develop self control. When a teacher asks a child to do something, she should be positive and clear ("It's time to put the blocks away, Jill"). Rather than demanding, threatening or punishing, she should encourage and praise ("The room looks lovely when you tidy it so well"). If a child doesn't want to comply with her request, she ought to resolve the conflict by offering choices and using logical consequences. Giving him the choice of doing a job alone or with the teacher, she asks, "Do you want to put the blocks away, or should we go put this puzzle back on the shelf together?"

A good teacher gives the children many chances to cooperate, negotiate and talk together, helping them to develop skills to solve their own problems. When Joey and Oliver both want the fire engine, she helps them to talk about it ("Have you asked Oliver to give you a turn when he's done?") and suggests tactics for sharing ("Let's look at the clock, and there will be two minutes for you and two minutes for Oliver"). She sets clear limits and heads off trouble by redirecting children to an acceptable activity ("Would you like a book to look at?") or offering them a chance to take a break ("Before you hurt yourself or someone else, let's sit down together for a minute").

What if a child misbehaves—tries to take a toy from another child or throws a block? A good teacher handles wrongdoing in a positive way. She must make an angry face and explain that what the child did was wrong, but she must never yell or call him bad. Instead, she should make a clear distinction between the child and the act. If teachers don't make this distinction, the children think of themselves as bad, a serious blow to their self-esteem.

To be fair, a good teacher differentiates between types of crimes. Sometimes she can handle the situation by helping the victim and ignoring the perpetrator, who then realizes he won't get attention by misbehaving. But sometimes the victim's sense of justice demands a consequence for his assailant. If Willy bops Nicholas over the head with a block, a teacher might put Willy on a chair away from the activity (but still in the room) while she attends to Nicholas. This strategy, which is very useful with two-and-a-half- to five-year-olds, is called "time out," and just one minute for each year of the child's age is both effective and appropriate.

Hang around to see what happens. After the teacher talks with the aggressor about his act, he should be able to return to the group and play properly without hitting Nicholas again three minutes later. If you see children on chairs in four corners of the room or children sitting outside of the group for 15 minutes, you'll know that the teacher does not know how to deal with the children appropriately.

PHYSICAL SPACE

If the caregivers seem to be doing a good job, take a closer look at the daycare's space. The way it's allocated, the way it's laid out, the way it's decorated, the way it's used all reflect a philosophy and a program. You ought to like it if you choose this center.

How does it look?

The ambience won't be sterile or institutional if the rooms are filled with plants and fish, books and toys, and colorful furniture and cushions. They should be bright and cheerful, with lots of windows, and kept at a comfortable temperature.

Look at the walls. There should be recent paintings, drawings, collages and sculptures displayed everywhere, especially at children's eye level. Children who are proud of their creations like to be surrounded by them—it makes them feel good when people say, "Annie, what a beautiful collage you made." A child's name should be on his work.

Experts believe that children learn more, express themselves more fully and have more fun when the teacher pays more attention to the process of creation than to the concrete results. The goal is to allow the children to explore and manipulate different media. Does the artwork on the walls use many different materials? Did each child use the materials in his own way?

Every group should have its own room, and the room should be big enough for the whole group—the children shouldn't bash into each other as they go about their business, and each child should have enough personal space.

If the area is well organized, the children will be able to work individually, in small groups and in a large group; and there will be spots for different kinds of play—quiet and active, messy and neat—though not necessarily in the same room. The furniture should be child sized and the toys and equipment set out at the children's level so that they can see and reach things without always having to ask an adult. Studies show that children develop better intellectual skills and get along better with their peers when the daycare has arranged its materials in an orderly manner.[11] Are they invitingly displayed at this center?

Choices

It is important for the children to have lots of stimulating choices and enough equipment so that they don't have to fight or wait too long for a turn. Look for big blocks, table-top games like puzzles, simple construction toys, markers, crayons and paper, and a book corner with a listening center where the children can listen to taped stories and music. Check the materials—the puzzles should have all their pieces, and the markers should actually write. Books should be attractive and well written and have all their pages.

Are there sand and water tables and play dough? Young children need tactile experiences, which are both fun and therapeutic.

Notice the opportunities for dramatic play, which teaches the children to talk and listen and to express their feelings. Is there a welcoming housekeeping corner with stove, sink, dishes, pots, pans and play food? Is there a dress-up space with plenty of clothes for make-believe? Are there dolls and puppets?

All of these things probably won't be out at the same time. Although a daycare should have a variety of toys, it must control the number that are in use. If there are too many, the children become overstimulated and confused; if there are too few, they will fight over them.

With so many people around all the time, it's important to find privacy once in a while. Every child needs a refuge where he can curl up with a book or listen to music. Make sure the daycare has a quiet space—a warm, pleasant, comfortable reading corner with pillows or soft chairs where a child can sit alone without being overwhelmed by the center's activity. Children need to know that an option is there.

Indoor gym
Given the Canadian climate, every daycare needs an indoor play space—a large room, a gym, a basement—that can be used for noisy free play, otherwise known as gross motor activity. As well as being fun and releasing pent-up energy, running, skipping, jumping, tumbling and climbing are vital to a child's development. As Penelope Leach puts it, "Doing helps [children] think, thinking makes them do. Doing helps them to understand what they feel and to stand the strength of their feelings, so feeling also makes them do.... As they rush around they are learning. Physical activities are just as important to a child's development and intelligence as other kinds of play."[12]

The room should be large and the slide and climbing apparatus should be sturdy, surrounded by gym mats and closely supervised. You should also see riding toys, pull toys and pounding toys, as well as a block area with several types of blocks and a carpet to reduce the noise when they fall.

Noise level
It's impossible to ignore the noise when you walk into a roomful of

children. If it's extremely quiet it will be a surprise, but if it's very noisy, it can be unbearable. Because there is a limit to a person's ability to hold himself together in a noisy environment, the noise level may be the key to whether your child will be happy in a particular daycare center. If there are children and teachers screaming in every room, he may dissolve into a puddle by the end of the afternoon. Where the noise level can't be controlled, the quality of care may actually suffer. You can safely assume that it will be constant. If it's acceptable now, it will almost always be acceptable; if it's intolerable, it probably won't improve.

If you are pregnant with your first child and you've been living in an adult world for a long time, any daycare is bound to sound deafening to you. You will probably have to adjust to reality. Children do make noise, and there's nothing wrong with a normal happy level of it.

There are four variables in assessing noise. The first is your child. To a certain extent, noise level is a matter of personal preference. Some people can happily tolerate a great deal of noise. If a teacher doesn't notice the rising decibel level, she won't make an effort to lower it. If this level is unacceptable to you, and you believe it would be unacceptable to your child, you have seen enough of this daycare. Thank the director politely and leave.

The second factor is the room itself. High ceilings, soundproofing, curtains, area rugs and soft cushions all make a difference in the character of the noise in the room. When a large number of children gathers in a cavernous space, even if they are relatively calm, the result may be ear shattering.

Another consideration is the type of activity going on at the moment. If the children are listening to a story, the room should be quiet; if they're playing the drums and ringing the triangles in a music lesson, it's bound to be noisy.

The last factor in the calculation is the teacher's control of the group. The noise you hear may be the sound of happily occupied children—or the result of chaos. Is the teacher screaming because everything has gotten out of hand? Yelling at a child is humiliating, ineffective and dangerous. He is much more likely to respond when a teacher explains the problem directly, personally and at close range. There are times when a teacher must scream—for example, to prevent a child from heaving a block across the room—but if she always screams, she will become like the boy who cried wolf, and no one will listen when it's important.

If it is too quiet, however, that may be cause for concern. If the teacher wields excessive power over the children, the atmosphere will be repressive, and they will be afraid to speak. The mouths of happy, comfortable, growing children never stay still for long—they talk, sing, giggle and whisper, no matter what they're doing. During the pre-school years, a lot of the magic lies in a child's language, says Penelope Leach.[13] Once he starts to talk, it's hard to curb a child's appetite for conversation, and who would want to? He needs to talk—and to be answered—in order to grow.

Language learning goes on all the time, in all routines and activities, big and small, as children and teachers spend time together. At daycare, as at home, adults are the role model for language development. Talking to pre-schoolers, daycare educators encourage them to use new words, to begin to identify first letter sounds or words that rhyme, to express themselves more freely and completely. You want your child to be where lots of talking is going on!

PROGRAM

Now we come to the question of program—what do the children do all day? How do they spend their time at daycare?

Schedule

Every moment requires thought and planning. If the director didn't give you a copy of the weekly or monthly schedule, see if you can find one posted.

It should include a mixture of activities: indoor and outdoor; quiet and active; individual, small group and large group; play that develops small and large muscles (fine and gross motor activities). A daycare should have art, circle and outdoor play every day.

In general terms, each of these activities can appear in one of three guises—as free play, as a semi-structured activity or as a structured activity—and good daycare usually offers some of each. Studies show that children learn more when there is a mix of structured and unstructured activities—some that the teachers initiate, some that the children initiate.[14] Are the children following the schedule?

What is free play and why is it important?

Many parents underestimate the value of free play because it seems so amorphous. Don't be deceived—free play is extremely important.

Regardless of their age, children do most of their learning when they are playing. It gives them an opportunity to experience the environment on their own personal level.

Without pressure, a child can do something active or passive, challenging or relaxing. He can deal with the world at any pace that suits his mood that day, following his own interests and making discoveries for himself. As he chooses among activities and playmates, he develops physical, verbal, cognitive and social skills and practices decision making. All of this builds his self-esteem.

In a good free-play environment, the children are all busy doing different things, either alone or in small groups. (This implies that there is enough for them to do.) They should be talking, laughing and sharing. It may be noisy, as long as the noise is controlled and no one's screaming to be heard. The caregivers are involved with the children and strategically placed to keep them safe.

What is a semi-structured activity?

A semi-structured activity encourages children to widen their horizons by exposing them to materials they wouldn't ordinarily choose. There is choice but not as much as in free play. A semi-structured activity is what educators call "teacher-selected but not teacher-directed"— meaning the caregiver chooses materials that teach skills that are appropriate for the children in the group, but she expects no particular outcome. She may assemble three different activities, but eight children will no doubt have eight different experiences.

There should be a variety of stimulating materials—books, puzzles, Lego, playdough, clay, markers, lotto, letter-recognition cards, bead patterns. As in free play, the teacher should make suggestions, explain and support as she is needed. When she sees what a child understands, she can challenge him to think further by adding more complex materials or ideas.

What is a structured activity?

Whether it be music, math, science, gym, art, story or circle, a structured activity is the teacher's show—she decides what the children will do. She is trying to develop a specific skill, and the younger the child, the simpler and more focused the skill should be. A two-and-a-half-year-old who is learning to cut, paste and color needs an art activity that allows him to concentrate on just one of those skills at a time. A five-year-old needs an art activity that challenges him to organize cutting, pasting and coloring at once.

Since different children have different learning styles, a lesson that provides a variety of opportunities to learn in different ways helps to ensure that each child will benefit from the experience.

Whether it's an art activity where everyone is cutting away, a gross motor activity where everyone is hopping on his left foot, or a teacher-directed science lesson where everyone is listening intently, you can tell whether it's good or bad by the children's level of involvement. Involved children are happy children, and involved children are learning. If they greet the teacher with blank faces, one has to wonder: Is the question or task too difficult? Are the children afraid to try? Are they totally uninterested? Most children love to participate. A fidgety group indicates that they are bored, which often leads straight to trouble. If two or three children are sitting outside of the group being punished, that's a danger sign, too.

Check the schedule for circle, a structured activity for a small group or the whole center, which should be a regular part of the daycare day. Make a point of watching it if you possibly can. Singing songs and playing games together gives everyone a nice sense of belonging and gives children a chance to bring the daycare world home—to sing daycare songs in the bathtub and teach them to the rest of the family.

With trained professionals in charge, there are so many great things to do that no child needs to watch television. Even "Sesame Street" should not be a scheduled part of the routine. But a half hour of it shown late on a particularly miserable winter afternoon can give everyone needed relief. An alternative should be available—some children are easily frightened by television or movies, and others can't sit long or just aren't interested.

Children should always be able to leave the group if they wish. Some never get immersed in an activity, no matter how skillful the teacher. What's important is how she handles the situation. Usually the less fuss she makes, the more willing the child is to participate. He should never be singled out and embarrassed, and there should be a quiet activity for him to do alone. Watch to see if the teacher encourages him to join in later.

Snack and lunchtime
No matter when you're at a daycare center, you'll probably see chil-

dren eating. Early in the morning there's breakfast. Then they have snack, and by 11:30 A.M. or noon, lunch is on the table. And each time both staff and children should wash their hands thoroughly before they handle the food. (Notice, too, if they washed the glue off the table before they set it!)

All provinces require daycare centers to serve adequate and nutritious food—utterly essential to children's health and growth. In addition, a daycare center should provide a model for good dietary habits. Take home a copy of the daycare's menu and decide whether it fits your idea of what children should be eating, but look now to see whether they're actually following it.

Eating away from home feels unnatural to many children. Ask yourself if you would be able to eat in this atmosphere. Is it inviting, or is it too chaotic and noisy for your child?

Mealtime is very care intensive, and all hands should be on deck. Once everyone has been served, the teachers should be eating with the children and engaging them in lively conversation. Mealtime is a natural social and learning time.

At the same time, the staff should be encouraging good eating habits. The children should be eating their dessert last, using spoons to eat their yoghurt and asking politely for more milk. The teachers, too, should be using polite language.

A two- or three-year-old may still be designing experiments to test the law of gravity, but for a four- or five-year-old, a spill is an accident. If Tami spills her milk, the teacher should help her to get a clean, dry shirt and set her up to finish eating. The teacher's attitude is more important than what she actually does—she should handle the situation with warmth and humor and spare the child as much embarrassment as possible.

Daycare centers have different rules about a child's leaving the table when he has finished eating. At some centers he may play or look at books in another section of the room, tempting others to join him even if they're not finished with their lunch. Think about your own child. Would he finish eating, or would he go hungry all afternoon because he couldn't resist the urge to play? At other daycare centers, the rules require him to stay at the table until everyone has finished. Again, consider your own child. Will he be able to wait quietly or will he discover new and interesting ways to twist in his chair and annoy his neighbors?

Although they're not allowed in the kitchen, older children should help clean up as much as possible. Doing their part will give them a sense of satisfaction and independence.

Cloakroom and outside play

Even if you're not around when the children are preparing to go out, amble into the cloakroom. When you're part of a large group, you need a spot to call your very own, and the cloakroom cubbyhole and/or hook definitely qualify. This is the place your child will leave his wet snowsuit and boots to dry, the place he'll keep his spare clothes, a safe haven for a cherished bear or rabbit.

Notice if each child has his own hook or cubby. It's all right for part-timers to share a hook or cubby if they're at the center at different times, but every full-timer should have his own. Picture in your mind's eye all those children trying to put their snowsuits on at one time. Is the space big enough? Does each group have its own area?

The weather doesn't always cooperate, but unless there's an Arctic chill or pouring rain, children should have fresh air and a chance to let loose and express themselves loudly and freely at least once every day. If the daycare schedule says it's time for outdoor play and no one is getting ready, ask why. Is it too cold, or would the children enjoy the snow? If the center is missing a staff member, why hasn't the director hired a substitute? And what has happened to the staff-child ratio?

If the children are going out, watch them in the cloakroom. Putting on a snowsuit can be fun and satisfying when you do it yourself. Without hovering or helping unnecessarily, the teachers should encourage the children to put on their jackets and boots by themselves. A slow dresser may need a game to hurry him along a bit ("I'm closing my eyes and when I open them Jeremy will have both feet in his snowpants"). Rather than sweating while they wait, the swifter dressers may be allowed to go outside with a teacher.

Once the children are all dressed, check them out. Their attire should be appropriate for the weather: hats must cover ears, snow pants must go into boots and both hands must have mittens. Seeing to details is essential in a daycare.

Watch how the children make the trek outside. In some daycares they just tumble out the door into the fenced yard; in others they have to navigate corridors, doors and stairs. Though they don't have to line up for a long march, they should follow an established routine, using a system for holding onto banisters and keeping doors open.

Although provincial regulations may accept the same ratio outside as inside, it is our belief that outside the daycare— whether in the play yard, the park or on a field trip—there must always be at least two adults, regardless of the size of the group. Then if a child takes a fall or needs to use the toilet, the teacher won't have to leave the rest of the group alone.

Rules for the outdoor equipment should be clearly understood and consistently enforced. Staff must ensure that the children take turns and hold on with both hands—and be close by to kiss a skinned knee.

Transitions

Now let's notice the bits of tissue that bind the activities together, the famous *transition.* You should certainly see at least one or two at every daycare you visit.

You'll notice transitions more when they don't work than when they do, but the truth is that the transition from one activity to the next is the hardest part of the daily routine. When you observe happy, cooperative children putting away toys, washing their hands, going to snack and getting ready to go outside, you don't stop to think about how difficult it actually is to move 16 four- and five-year-olds from point A to point B.

A good transition is quick and natural, allowing the children to move through the day without really being aware of any dramatic change. A first-rate teacher uses transitional tools with ease, in a twinkling of an eye transforming a collection of hungry pre-schoolers into a squadron of airplanes flying down the hall to snack.

When children spend endless minutes lining up like soldiers, you realize what to avoid. Standing around indoors fully dressed for outdoor play can be extremely uncomfortable, not to mention unhealthy, and children who are just hanging out waiting have a tendency to become bored and mischievous. This may mean that the teacher is meting out a lot of unnecessary punishment.

Because it is so avoidable, a rough transition is a signal that the teacher is using inappropriate means to control the children. You will probably observe her struggling with them throughout the day.

Once again, whenever children are moving around, the systems for getting them to their destination must be safe.

Entries

If you're at the daycare when the children are arriving for the day, you'll see another type of transition, from home to daycare. It, too, takes sensitivity and skill. While parent and child are getting ready, the teacher should greet the child warmly and help him to feel part of the environment right away. Does she know him as an individual with decided preferences about entering the scene? Do parent and teacher greet one another and exchange a few words about the child's night before they go their separate ways? The routine should be comfortable to everyone involved—child, parent, and teacher.

Exits

At the end of the day there's a reverse transition. If you have no choice but to observe the daycare on your way home from work, you can't expect it to be in mint, 9 A.M. condition. Though it will need a sweep and a scrub, staff and children should still be involved in whatever they're doing. Are teachers helping children to get ready to go home? Are parents sitting around chatting? Is there a relaxed ambience?

Now that you've been here for a while, how do you think *you* would feel about spending up to 50 hours a week here?

III. *TAKING THE TOUR AND USING THE CHECKLISTS*

Now you're ready to take the tour—go "on the floor," as the daycare educators say. But before you go, we offer some advice.

You are almost certain to find this whole affair intimidating, to say the least. Even a seasoned daycare director, venturing into a strange daycare for the first time, is temporarily dazed and dismayed. You have a lot to see and a lot of questions to answer, and you won't know where to look first or how you'll even find the question that's appropriate to what you're seeing. Do not panic. Go on the tour with the director, letting her lead and talk. Don't even try to use the checklist while you're with her—you'll be moving much too quickly.

As you go, notice how she and the children and staff behave towards one another. You will probably see her deal with several problems along your route. Do you like her solutions and her style of dealing with people? How do the children greet her? Wild enthusiasm may mean that the children love her—or that they see her very rarely. If the director spends a lot of time with them—if she works on the floor as well as in the office—they may take her presence very much for granted and greet her in an ordinary way.

Be sure to look at all the rooms. Maybe right now you're interested in babies, but soon you'll need to know if there will be space for your child in the toddler room. Maybe you're thinking of your two-year-old today, but in a year you may be looking for daycare for a new addition to the family. And in three years you'll wonder what the older children are up to. Looking all around gives you a sense of the daycare's philosophy, its community, the consistency of its teamwork. You'll get a sense of whether you'll be happy there for four or five years—or more if you have two children.

After this once-over-lightly, thank the director for her help and ask her permission to stay and watch on your own for a while. If she has nothing to hide, she should be pleased to allow you to linger for as long as you like and offer to answer your questions later. Then choose a group—preferably the group your child will be in if he attends this daycare—reintroduce yourself to the caregivers and settle in for a long careful look, this time with your papers. Wander around as you need to, and go through the checklist, question by question. If you have time left over, you can watch a second group. Try the one your child will be in next. You will want to observe several different caregivers so that you don't base your judgment of this center on a single teacher who might leave next year.

What you see will depend on how long you can stay and the daycare's routine. Don't worry about what you don't see—just pay close attention to what's going on in front of you *now*, whether it's the 8:30 A.M. drop-off or lunch at 11 A.M. If you don't see something that's on the checklist, don't make up an answer. Leave a blank and note the time—that way you can catch up on what you missed if you return.

If you're watching the infants, do be sure to see how the caregivers hold, change, feed and put the babies down to nap, how they attend to a child who cries, how they play with the children and how they handle a problem between two children. Notice, too, how they move from one activity to another. With pre-schoolers, ideally you should see a meal or snack, a bathroom trip, free play, a structured activity and a transition from one activity to another.

If you see something puzzling that isn't on the checklist, jot it down to ask the director about later. Or better still, ask a caregiver.

In fact, if you have any questions, ask a caregiver. Knowing that parents whose children are just entering daycare are real worrywarts, she should do her best to respond to your concerns. She might also ask you questions about your child, a good sign.

As you talk, try to confirm what the director told you. Ask the teacher, for example, about how often the babies go outside. Whether the answers sound like a canned text or the real thing, you'll learn something about the daycare. You can even ask philosophical questions, like what she considers important in group care. Then watch to see if she does what she believes in.

Remember, though, that she is working. She won't have much time to chat because child care is very labor intensive, and she's supposed to be with the children, not with you. If she's very busy and you can't talk to her without being rude or overwhelming, ask if you can come back at naptime or when she finishes her shift. Besides, if she's talking to you the whole time you're there, you won't have a chance to see how she relates to the children. Try to strike a happy medium between inquisition and observation.

As you observe, use your ears as well as your eyes. When you're in the room, the caregivers are always conscious of your presence and will be on their best behavior. When you're out of sight, they're more likely to revert to normal behavior. Listen for the sound of the water running when a teacher is changing a baby in the bathroom and you're in the playroom. Listen for the sound of her voice. Does she talk to the babies when she thinks you're out of earshot? Listening is also important because babies learn more than language when people talk to them—they learn about their place in the world as well. A caregiver who says, "Let's check your diaper. Are you wet? Let's go get you a clean diaper," sends a totally different message from one who scoops up a baby and plops him onto a changing table without a word.

In the course of all this observation, you are bound to meet a child or two. Sometimes they approach and want to know your name and what you're doing there. By all means, tell them—even though they're children, they are people who deserve an answer to their questions. They are simply showing healthy, friendly curiosity, and they should soon return to their play. But if you meet a child who wants to read you a story, talk to you, sit on your lap and who won't go away, that's another matter altogether. This child is probably quite unable to get the attention he needs from the caregivers here, and he is seeking it from you, a perfect stranger. When you look carefully at this center, you're likely to notice other evidence of poor-quality care. (In a daycare where we encountered a particularly tenacious child, we also saw the caregiver twice leave a roomful of children without supervision and then watched her change six diapers in a row without washing her hands.)

You must demand high quality, but no daycare is perfect. Keep your child's needs in mind as you look. Try to think, will this place be good for him? If you're pregnant, you couldn't possibly know how your child would cope with this particular daycare center. But you will know whether the children who are there now are coping with it. If they're miserable and depressed, your child will find it just as painful; if they are happy, your child probably will be, too. And that is the bottom line.

Following are questions that will help you to record and evaluate what you see at each center. Because you can't possibly answer them all, mark those that you really care about before you visit. Then you won't inadvertently omit them.

Remember that every daycare center is laid out differently, and this list of questions will apply to each center in a different way. As you enter a room, find out how old the children are and what they are doing.

Again, we've given you no scale for scoring. Instead the questions should act as a kind of shopping list—to jog your memory of the constituents of high-quality care. Answer them in a way that suits you—with checks, numbers or comments ("too noisy," "teacher never smiles," "beautiful room"). As soon as you leave the center, find a comfortable spot to sit down (in your car, at a bus stop, in a nearby park or coffee shop), and capture your immediate impressions on paper. Because you know what you're entitled to and what you consider important, your feelings will probably count heavily when you are making your final decision.

After you've visited several centers, you'll feel much more self-confident. At this point it becomes tempting to do the tour without your trusty checklist, which, after all, is a bit cumbersome. We strongly advise you to resist this temptation. It is no easy trick to remember several daycare centers with clarity if you never write anything down, and it becomes harder with each passing day. Six months from now you may need to base a decision on what you saw. Use the checklist, and keep all your notes for future reference.

INFANT CHECKLIST

Name of daycare: _____

Address: _____

Date: _____ Time: _____

PARENT INVOLVEMENT

1. Is there a workable, written system for relaying information about daily events (meals, naps, etc.)? _____

2. Are the comments on the daily sheets or in the book or chart written in an open, positive way? _____

3. Are there other signs of the children's connection to home—cuddly objects, photos, notices of parent meetings, etc.? _____

4. Are other parents present? _____

   What are they doing? _____

NUMBERS

1. How many babies are there? Check the sleep room to be sure you've seen them all. _____

   How many staff are there? _____

   Does the staff-child ratio fulfill provincial norms for infants under 18 months? _____

   How close is it to the recommended ratio of 1:3? _____

2. Is the size of the group in accordance with provincial standards for infants? _____

   How closely does it approach the recommended maximum of six to nine babies under 18 months of age? _____

3. Did the director give you the correct information about ratios and group size at this center? _____

PHYSICAL SPACE

1. Do infants have a space of their own that is separated from the rest of the daycare? _____

2. Are there separate rooms or areas for sleeping, diapering, eating and play? _____

3. Are the rooms clean, warm, light, spacious and uncluttered? _____

4. Are they well ventilated? _____
   Do they smell fresh? _____

5. Is the furniture sturdy? _____
   Is it made of a variety of materials (hard, soft)? _____

6. Are there several rocking chairs placed where babies cannot crawl behind them? _____

7. Are there low, safe tables for doing puzzles, table-top games and art activities? _____

8. Is there one playpen or none at all? _____
   Is it used sparingly? _____

9. Are there pictures of familiar objects at children's eye level and mobiles where they can be seen but not touched? _____

10. Are there unbreakable mirrors where babies can see themselves (next to changing tables, at floor level)? _____

11. Is there a reward for standing—a picture or mirror to look at when they're on their feet? _____

12. Is the floor surface clean and safe? _____

13. Are toys washable and unbreakable with no hard corners, splinters or small pieces? _____

14. Is there a wide assortment of toys, ranging from the simple to the complex, to be used alone and with assistance? _____

15. Are there enough toys to go around? _____

16. Are there plastic and cardboard books with bright pictures? _____

17. Are some toys and books on low shelves, accessible so that the children can make their own choices? _____

18. Are there safe steps, low climbing apparatus, barrels, boxes, tubes and riding toys for gross motor play? _____

    Is the climbing equipment surrounded by mats? _____

19. Is the number of toys controlled? _____

20. Is the noise at a tolerable level? _____

21. Are there places where a baby can be alone yet visible to the staff? ___

22. How would you feel about being here 50 hours a week? _____

SAFETY

1. Is every section of the room visible? _____

2. Are children always closely supervised? _____

3. Are cleaning materials and medicines kept in locked cabinets? _____

4. Are electrical outlets, heating grates, air-conditioning vents, fireplaces, stairways and the kitchen blocked off? _____

5. Are countertops and table edges at a safe height? _____

6. Is there a first aid kit? _____

7. Are emergency telephone numbers next to the phone? _____

8. Is a fire-exit plan posted? _____

9. Are there smoke alarms, sprinkler systems, emergency lights? _____

10. No caregivers are smoking or drinking hot tea or coffee. _____

HEALTH AND HYGIENE

Playroom

1. Is there a container to put toys in for washing after a child puts them in his mouth? _____

2. Does the teacher throw away the tissue and wash her hands every time she wipes a child's nose? _____

3. Are the children healthy enough to be there? _____

4. There are no sick children on mats or cots in the playroom. _____

Diapering area

1. Does the room look clean and smell fresh? _____

2. Does the diaper area have its own sink with running water? _____

3. Do changing tables have a strap or belt and high sides? _____
   Are supplies all within easy reach? _____

4. Are babies free of diaper rash? _____

5. Are disposable wipes used to clean babies' bottoms? _____

6. Are dirty diapers kept in lined, covered pails? _____

7. Are changing tables disinfected after every diaper change? _____

8. Does the caregiver wash her hands with hot running water and liquid soap, dry them with disposable paper towels and turn off the faucet with a paper towel every time she changes a diaper? _____

SLEEPING AREA AND NAPTIME

1. Are cribs and cots at least three feet apart? _____

2. Does each child have his own crib, sheets, blanket and cuddly object?
   _____   _____

3. Are linens dry and clean? _____

4. Do cribs meet provincial safety standards? _____

5. Does each crib have a clear aisle to the door? _____

6. Does each baby sleep on his own schedule? _____

7. If there are any crying babies, do the caregivers hear them and respond promptly? _____

FOOD AREA

1. Is the kitchen clean? _____

2. Does it have its own sink, used just for food preparation? _____

3. Does it have a dishwasher that sterilizes the dishes? _____

4. Docs it have a refrigerator and a stove or microwave? _____

5. Is the food properly stored? _____

6. Does the caregiver wash her hands with hot running water and liquid soap and dry them with disposable paper towels every time she prepares food or feeds a baby? _____

7. Do teachers take advantage of normal daily events to talk with and teach the children? _____

8. At mealtime does the teacher hold a baby for his bottle? _____

9. Does each baby eat on his own schedule? _____

10. Does she sit with the older babies to help them to eat? _____

11. Do they eat finger foods? _____

12. Are the teachers calm and good natured? _____

13. Are high-chair trays and tables disinfected after each use? _____

OUTDOORS

1. Is there a separate infant cloakroom equipped with safe changing tables and storage space? _____

2. Does each child have his own labeled cubbyhole or hook? _____

3. Do the infants go outside? _____

4. Are there multi-seated strollers ready for daily use? _____

WHAT SHOULD THE TEACHERS BE LIKE?

1. Are the caregivers warm, patient and gentle? _____

2. Do the caregivers seem to know each child as an individual with a distinct style, preference and rhythm? _____

3. Do the caregivers enjoy and appreciate the children—that is, do they have affect? _____

4. Do the children have affect? _____

Do they appear happy and involved? _____

5. Do the caregivers spend a lot of time in face-to-face interactions? ____

6. Do they smile, look into the baby's eyes, talk to him and echo his sounds?

_____

7. Do the caregivers hold the babies a lot? _____

8. When a baby cries, do they come at once to comfort him? _____

9. Does the teacher allow the baby to be in charge of his own play but stay around to help and stimulate him? _____

10. Does she gently stimulate him by bringing him toys and taking him to different spots in the center during the course of the day? _____

11. Does she talk, sing and read to him? _____

12. Does the teacher let a child solve problems on his own but prevent total frustration? _____

13. Does she encourage his efforts with guidance and praise? _____

Discipline

1. Does the teacher cope patiently and positively without saying no? ____

2. Does the teacher prevent situations which might end in conflict, violence or danger? _____ ____

3. Does she use positive methods to guide behavior? _____

4. Does she explain when a child has done something wrong but let him know that she still loves him? _____

5. Does she redirect him to another activity? _____

6. Does she refrain from using punishment? _____

7. Do teachers react to crises with calm humor and patience? _____

8. Do they act as models for peaceful, helping, sharing behavior? _____

Important feelings, reactions and observations, both positive and negative:

_____

_____

_____

_____

_____

TODDLER CHECKLIST

Name of daycare: _____

Address: _____

Date:_____ Time: _____

PARENT INVOLVEMENT

1. Is there a workable, written system for relaying information about daily events (meals, naps, etc.)? _____

2. Are the comments on the daily sheets or in the book or chart written in an open, positive way? _____

3. Are there other signs of the children's connection to home—cuddly objects, photos, notices of parent meetings, etc.? _____

4. Are other parents present? _____
   What are they doing? _____

   _____

NUMBERS

1. How many toddlers are in the room? _____
   How many adults are there? _____

Does this adult-child ratio meet provincial standards? _____

How close does it come to the acceptable ratio of between 1:3 and 1:5 for toddlers under two and between 1:4 and 1:6 for two-year-olds? _____

2. Does the size of the group meet provincial norms? _____

    How does it compare to the suggested maximum of ten for toddlers under two and 12 for two-year-olds?_____

3. Did the director give you the correct information about ratios and group size at this center? _____

4. Are there enough teachers so that they have time to care for the children's needs and help them to develop their skills? _____

5. How well will my child manage this ratio and group size? _____

PHYSICAL SPACE

1. Does the toddler group have a space of its own? _____

2. Is it clean, warm, light, spacious and uncluttered? _____

3. Is it well ventilated? _____

4. Is the furniture sturdy and child sized? _____

5. Are there pictures of familiar objects at the children's eye level? _____

6. Are the walls covered with the children's recent, signed artwork displayed at their eye level? _____

    Are many different materials being used?_____   _____

    Is each child's work unique, or does it all look alike? _____

7. Are toys and equipment made of non-breakable materials with no hard corners, splinters or small pieces? _____

8. Is there a wide assortment of toys, ranging from the simple to the complex, to be used alone and with assistance? _____

9. Are there lots of books with colorful pictures in good repair? _____

10. Are sand and water play available? _____

11. Is there enough equipment so that the children don't have to fight or wait too long and so that they can play together? _____

12. Are books and toys invitingly displayed on low shelves that the children can reach by themselves? _____

13. Are there areas for quiet (fine motor) and active (gross motor) play? (Instead of areas within a room, there may be whole rooms, like a gym, designated either for quiet or active play.)_____

14. Is the large gross-motor space well equipped with safe steps, sturdy low climbing apparatus, riding toys, blocks and dramatic play materials?

    _____

15. Is the number of toys controlled? _____

16. Is the noise the sound of happily occupied children? _____

17. Can my child tolerate this level of noise? _____

18. Is there a comfortable spot where a child can sit quietly and look at a book or listen to music and have some privacy? _____

19. How would you feel about being here 50 hours a week? _____

SAFETY

1. Is every section of the room visible? _____

2. Are children always closely supervised? _____

3. Are cleaning materials and medicines kept in locked cabinets? _____

4. Are electrical outlets, heating grates, air conditioning vents, fireplaces, stairways and the kitchen blocked off? _____

5. Are sharp implements, paint, glue, etc., safely out of reach? _____

6. Are countertops and table edges well finished and at a safe height for toddlers? _____

7. Is there a first aid kit? _____

8. Are emergency telephone numbers next to the phone? _____

9. Is a fire-exit plan posted? _____

10. Are there smoke alarms, sprinkler systems, emergency lights? _____

11. Are there safe systems set up; for example, for going outside, going to the gym, going to the bathroom? _____

12. Do the children understand and follow the safety rules, and do the teachers enforce them? _____

13. No caregivers are smoking or drinking hot tea or coffee. _____

HEALTH AND HYGIENE

Playroom

1. Are dress-up clothes, dolls and toys clean? _____

2. Is there a container to hold the toys that the children have put in their mouths so that they can be washed before they're returned to the shelves?

   _____

3. Does the teacher throw away the tissue and wash her hands every time she wipes a child's nose? _____

4. Does the teacher encourage children to cover their mouths when they cough or sneeze? _____

5. Are all the children healthy enough to be there? _____

6. There are no sick children on mats or cots in the playroom. _____

7. Are just a few children absent because of illness? _____

Diapering area and bathroom

1. Do the bathroom and changing area look and smell clean (including toilets, sinks and floors)? _____

2. Does the diaper area have its own sink with running water (that is, a sink that isn't used for anything else)? _____

3. Do changing tables have high sides? _____

4. Are supplies all within easy reach so that the caregiver doesn't have to leave the child alone? _____

5. Are disposable wipes used to clean bottoms? _____

6. Are dirty diapers kept in lined, covered pails? _____

7. Are changing tables disinfected after every diaper change? _____

8. Are there inviting small toilets or toilets with step stools in private spaces?

_____

   If there are potties, does each child have his own? _____

9. Does staff supervise closely yet allow children their privacy? _____

10. Are there enough toilets and sinks for all the children? _____

11. After they've used the toilet, do children wash their own hands? _____

12. Are faucets, liquid soap and disposable paper towels at their level? ___

13. Does the staff handle toilet accidents gently and without humiliation?

_____

14. Do they use disposable washcloths for cleanups and store soiled clothes

   in a sealed bag? _____

15. Does the caregiver wash her hands with hot running water and liquid

   soap, dry them with disposable paper towels and turn off the faucet with

   a paper towel every time she changes a diaper or helps a child go to the

   toilet? _____

NAPTIME

The director will have to answer most of your questions about nap, but
you should ask where the toddlers sleep. Since the center probably
uses these rooms for other activities during the day, you may not be
able to tell how they look at naptime.

1. If cots are set up, is there enough space between them (three feet) so that

   children aren't breathing and coughing on one another? _____

2. Are cots, blankets and sheets for each child labeled? _____

3. Are they arranged to enable children to reach the door safely and easily

   in case of an emergency? _____

FOOD AREA

1. Is the kitchen clean? _____

2. Does it have a sink of its own that is used only for food? _____

3. Are the dishes and flatware washed in a sterilizing dishwasher? _____

4. Is food stored properly in the refrigerator and cupboards? _____

5. Do staff and children wash their hands thoroughly before they handle food and eat? _____

6. Do teachers sit with the toddlers during meals, encouraging them to eat independently with finger foods and to use cups, bowls and spoons when they're ready? _____

7. Do the teachers promote good eating habits, politeness and lively conversation? _____

8. Do they use snack and mealtime as natural learning opportunities? ___

9. Are spills handled with humor, warmth and a minimum of fuss and embarrassment for the child? _____

10. Is the food healthy? _____

11. Is the menu being followed? (Ask for a copy and have a closer look at it when you get home.) _____

12. Are high-chair trays and tables disinfected after each use? _____

OUTDOORS

1. Is there a separate toddler cloakroom? _____

2. Does each child have his own labeled cubbyhole or hook? _____

3. Is there enough space for all the children to sit down and get dressed at the same time? _____

4. Do the children go outside everyday? _____
   If they aren't going today, does the director's explanation make sense to you? _____

5. Do teachers encourage the children to dress themselves? _____

6. Are the children dressed appropriately for the weather, with all details like hats, mitts and boots properly attended to? _____

7. Is there a system in use for getting the children outside in a safe and playful way? _____

8. Do the toddlers have their own safe, fenced, outdoor area equipped with low slides and climbing apparatus in good repair? _____

9. Is the surface a safe, soft material? _____

10. Is it large and well kept with both sunny and shady areas? _____

11. Are there activities for all seasons? _____

12. Do the children understand the rules of safe play? _____

13. Does the staff supervise closely? _____

WHAT ARE THE TEACHERS LIKE?

1. Are the teachers dressed appropriately for their jobs? _____

2. Are the teachers sprinkled around the room, engaged in activities with the children and working at their level (as opposed to standing in groups talking to one another or standing with their hands in their pockets)?

    _____

3. Is the teacher warm, responsive and patient? _____

4. Does she seem to know each child as an individual with a distinct style, preference and rhythm? _____

5. Is she smiling in a way that shows she enjoys and appreciates the children, that is, does she have affect? _____

    Does her facial expression support what she is saying? _____

6. Do the toddlers have affect? _____

    Are the children involved and happy? _____

7. Does she squat or sit at the children's level and look them in the eyes when she interacts with them? _____

8. Does she wait patiently for them to speak and amplify their comments to extend their vocabulary? _____

9. Does she answer their questions promptly? _____

10. Does she ask them open-ended questions? _____

11. Does she allow them to share their thoughts and feelings? _____

12. Do the children seem comfortable with the kind and amount of physical affection she shows them? _____

13. If a child is crying, does a teacher come immediately to soothe and comfort him? _____

    Is the communication warm and close? _____

14. Does she allow the children to make choices about their own play?

    _____

15. Does she let a child solve problems on his own but prevent total frustration? _____

16. Does she encourage his efforts with guidance and praise, increasing the range and complexity of his thinking? _____

17. Does she allow him to take responsibility? _____

18. Does she play with and read to the toddlers individually and in small groups? _____

19. Are structured activities planned? _____

20. Do the children have a good time participating? _____

21. If a child is not participating, does he have a quiet activity to do on his own? _____

22. Does the activity seem worthwhile to you? _____

23. Is the process of exploration and manipulation more important than the final result? _____

24. Does the teacher have control of the group? _____

DISCIPLINE

1. Does the teacher cope patiently and positively without saying no? _____

2. Does the teacher prevent situations which might end in conflict, violence or danger? _____

3. Does she use positive methods to guide behavior? _____

4. Does she explain when a child has done something wrong but let him know that she still loves him? _____

5. Does she redirect him to another activity? _____

6. Does she refrain from using punishment? _____

7. Does she react to crises with humor and patience? _____

8. Does she act as a model for peaceful, helping, sharing behavior? _____

Important feelings, reactions and observations, both positive and negative, should also be noted for further reference:

_____

_____

_____

_____

_____

_____

_____

PRE-SCHOOL-AGE PROGRAM CHECKLIST

Name of daycare: _____

Address: _____

Date: _____Time: _____

PARENT INVOLVEMENT

1. Is there a workable, written system for relaying information about daily events (meals, naps, who will pick up tonight, etc.)? _____

2. Are the comments written in an open, positive way? _____

3. Is there a parent bulletin board with information about child development, scheduled trips, interesting events, minutes of board meetings, etc.?

   _____

4. Are other parents present, and what are they doing? _____

5. Does this environment feel user-friendly? _____

NUMBERS

1. How many children are in the room? _____

   How many adults are in the room? _____

   Does this adult-child ratio meet provincial standards? _____

   How close does it come to the acceptable ratio of 1:3 to 1:5 for two-year-olds; between 1:5 and 1:8 for three-year-olds; from 1:8 to 1:10 for four-year-olds; and from 1:8 to 1:12 for five-year-olds? _____

   _____

2. Does this group size meet provincial standards? _____

   How does it compare to the recommended maximum of six to ten for two-year-olds; and ten to 16 for three-, four- and five-year-olds? _____

   _____

3. Did the director give you the correct information about ratio and group size at this center? _____

4. If the teacher is working alone with a small group of eight children or less, does she have everything she needs so that she does not have to leave the children? _____

5. Are the ratio and group size appropriate for the activity? _____

6. How well will my child manage this ratio and group size? _____

SAFETY

Indoors

1. Are cleaning materials and medicines kept in locked cabinets? _____

2. Are electrical outlets, heating grates, air conditioning vents, fireplaces, stairways and the kitchen blocked off? _____

3. Is there a first aid kit? _____

4. Are emergency telephone numbers next to the phone? _____

5. Is a fire-exit plan posted? _____

6. Are there smoke alarms, sprinkler systems, emergency lights? _____

7. Are toys and equipment made of non-breakable materials and kept in good condition? _____

8. Are the furniture and climbing apparatus sturdy and in good repair?

_____

9. Are countertops and edges rounded and well finished? _____

10. Are paint and glue non-toxic and kept safely out of reach, along with scissors and knives? _____

11. Is every section of the room visible? _____

12. Are children always closely supervised? _____

13. Do the children understand and follow the safety rules, and do the teachers enforce them? _____

14. If the cots are set up for nap, are they arranged to enable children to reach the door safely and easily in case of an emergency? _____

15. No caregivers are smoking or drinking hot tea or coffee. _____

Outdoors

Be sure to take a look at the outdoor play area, even if you're not there when the children go outside. _____

1. Do the children have a safe, fenced outdoor area? _____

2. Is it large enough for the children to run around, and does it have sunny and shady areas? _____

3. Is the surface a safe, soft material like sand? _____

4. Is it equipped with slides and climbing apparatus in good repair? _____

HEALTH AND HYGIENE

Playroom

1. Does the room look and smell clean? _____

2. Are there any windows open? _____

3. Are dress-up clothes, dolls and toys clean? _____

4. Does the teacher encourage children to cover their mouths when they cough or sneeze? _____

5. Does the teacher throw away the paper tissue and wash her hands every time she wipes a runny nose? _____

6. If children put toys in their mouths, are they put aside for washing before they're returned to the shelves? _____

7. Are all the children healthy enough to be there? _____

8. There are no sick children on mats or cots in the playroom. _____

9. Are just a few children absent because of illness? _____

Bathroom

1. Does the bathroom look and smell clean (including toilets, sinks, and floor)? _____

2. Are there enough toilets for all the children? _____

3. Are the toilets child sized and/or easily accessible to the children? ____

4. Does staff supervise closely yet allow children their privacy? _____

5. Does the bathroom have its own sinks not used for any other purpose?

_____

6. After they've used the toilet, do children wash their hands? _____

7. Are faucets, liquid soap and disposable paper towels at their level? ___

8. Does the staff handle toileting accidents gently and without humiliation?

_____

9. Do they use disposable washcloths for cleanups and store soiled clothes

in a double layer of sealed bags? _____

10. Does the staff wash their hands with hot running water and liquid soap,

dry them with disposable paper towels and turn off the faucet with a paper

towel every time they help a child go to the toilet? _____

11. Are toothbrushes and toothpaste labeled and stored separately? _____

Kitchen

1. Is the kitchen clean? _____

2. Does it have a sink of its own, used only for food? _____

3. Are the dishes and flatware washed in a sterilizing dishwasher? _____

4. Does it have a refrigerator and a stove? _____

5. Is food stored properly in the refrigerator and cupboards? _____

Sleep area

The director will have to answer most of your questions about nap,
but you should ask to see the rooms where the children sleep. Since
the center probably uses them for other activities during the day, you
may not be able to tell how they look at naptime.

1. Are cots, blankets and sheets for each child labeled? _____

2. If cots are set up, is there enough space between them (three feet) so that

children aren't breathing and coughing on one another? _____

PEOPLE

Look from afar

1. Are the teachers dressed appropriately for their jobs? _____

2. Are the teachers engaged in activities with the children and working at their level (as opposed to standing in groups talking to one another or standing with their hands in their pockets)? _____

Close-up of a teacher

1. Is she warm and responsive? _____

2. Does she look the children in the eyes when she interacts with them?

   _____

3. Does her facial expression support what she is saying? _____

4. Does she squat or sit at the children's level? _____

5. Is she smiling in a way that shows she enjoys the children? _____

6. Does the teacher have affect? _____

7. Do the children seem involved and happy? _____

8. Do the children seem comfortable with the kind and amount of physical affection she shows them? _____

9. Does she listen and respond to the children as individuals? _____

10. Does she manage to be with them one at a time? _____

11. Does she answer their questions promptly? _____

12. Does she ask them open-ended questions? _____

13. Does she allow them to share their thoughts and feelings? _____

14. Does she encourage them to do as much as possible for themselves?

    _____

15. Does she allow the children to make choices about their own play without directing, criticizing or restricting them? _____

16. If a child is crying, does she come immediately to soothe and comfort him?

    _____

Is the communication warm and close? _____

Does she succeed in bringing him back to the group with a smile? ____

Discipline

1. Is she positive and clear when she asks a child to do something? _____

2. Does she encourage and praise, rather than demand, threaten or punish?

   _____

3. When a child doesn't want to do as she asks, does she offer choices and use logical consequences? _____

4. Does she help the children to develop skills to solve their own problems?

   _____

5. Does the teacher head off trouble by redirecting the children to another activity? _____

6. Does she handle wrongdoing positively? _____
   Does she let the child know that she still loves him, condemning the act and not the person? _____

7. Is she fair? _____

8. Does she use time-out appropriately? _____

PHYSICAL SPACE

1. Is the room light, bright and cheerful, with a comfortable temperature and humidity? _____

2. Are the walls covered with the children's recent, signed artwork displayed at their eye level? _____
   Are many different materials being used? _____
   Does all the work look alike or is the process of exploring the materials more important than the finished product? _____

3. Does each age group have a room of its own? _____

4. Is there enough space? _____

5. Is the space organized so that children can work individually, in small groups and in a large group? _____

6. Are there areas for quiet and active play? (Instead of areas within a room, there may be whole rooms designated either for quiet or active play.)

   _____

7. Are books and toys invitingly displayed on low shelves that the children can reach by themselves? _____

8. Are there enough stimulating materials for the children to choose from and enough equipment so that they don't have to fight or wait too long?

   _____

9. Is the room equipped with table-top games, art materials, a book corner and sand and water tables? _____

10. Is it equipped with opportunities for dramatic play (housekeeping corner, puppets, dolls, dress-up clothes)? _____

11. Is the number of toys controlled? _____

12. Is there a space where a child can sit by himself and look at a book or listen to music without being overwhelmed by the activity around him?

    _____

13. Is there a large indoor space for gross motor activity? _____

14. Are climbing equipment and riding toys safe and closely supervised?

    _____

Noise level

1. Can my child tolerate this level of noise? _____

2. Is the room soundproofed enough? _____

3. Is the noise appropriate for what the children are doing? _____

4. Is the noise the sound of happily occupied children? _____

5. Is there a lot of talking going on? _____

PROGRAM

Schedule

1. Does the schedule include art, circle, outdoor play, structured activities and unstructured activities? _____

2. Are the children following the schedule? (If not, ask why.) _____

   _____

Free play

1. Are children absorbed in what they're doing? _____

2. Are they talking, laughing and sharing? _____

3. Are teachers sprinkled around the room, guiding, supporting and helping without telling the children what to do? _____

Semi-structured activity

1. Does the teacher allow children the freedom to define what they want to do themselves? _____

2. Is there a variety of stimulating materials available? _____

3. Does the teacher guide and support the children, thereby increasing the range and complexity of their thinking? _____

4. Are the children happily engaged in their work? _____

Structured activity

1. Are the children enjoying themselves? _____

2. Do they participate energetically, each in his own way? _____

3. Does the teacher have control of the group (or are several children being punished)? _____

4. Is there a circle activity? _____

   Are the children having fun? _____

5. Are the television and VCR used sparingly, on special occasions, to show special programs?

6. If a child is not participating in the group activity, does he have a quiet

activity to do on his own? _____

Snack and mealtime

1. Do staff and children wash their hands before they handle food and eat?

   _____

2. Are the tables clean? _____

3. Is the food healthy? _____

4. Is the menu being followed? (Ask for a copy and have a closer look at it when you get home.) _____

5. Is the atmosphere in the eating area inviting and calm? _____

6. Do teachers sit with the children, encouraging good eating habits, politeness and lively conversation? _____

7. Are spills handled with humor, warmth and a minimum of fuss and embarrassment for the child? _____

8. When the children finish eating, do they wait at the table, or do they get up and play quietly, allowing the slow eaters to finish? _____

   Will my child be able to manage the system at this daycare? _____

9. Do children help clean up? _____

Cloakroom and outside play

1. Does each child have his own labeled cubbyhole and hook? _____

2. Is there enough space for all the children to sit down and get dressed at the same time? _____

3. Is there a separate cloakroom for each age group? _____

4. While you are there, are the children going outside? _____

5. Do teachers encourage the children to dress themselves? _____

6. Are the children dressed appropriately for the weather, with all details like hats, mitts and boots properly attended to? _____

7. Is there a system in use for getting the children outside in a safe and orderly way? _____

Are there at least two caregivers outside with the group? _____

8. Do the children understand the rules of safe play? _____

9. Does the staff supervise closely? _____

Transitions

1. Are transitions quick and natural, allowing the children to move through the day without being aware of dramatic change? _____

2. Is getting there half the fun? _____

3. Are there safe systems set up, for example, for going outside, going to the gym, going to the bathroom? _____

Entries

1. Does the teacher greet each child warmly and help him to enter the daycare environment easily? _____

2. Do parents and teachers have a comfortable relationship? _____

Exits

1. At the end of the day, are children still involved in their play? _____

2. Are teachers helping children get ready to leave? _____

3. Is everyone, including parents, relaxed? _____

Is the ambience pleasant? _____

How would you feel about being here 50 hours a week? _____

Don't forget to write down your overall impressions:

_____

_____

_____

_____

_____

_____

"Mirror, Mirror, here I stand,
Who is the fairest in the land?"
"SNOW WHITE"

CHAPTER 12

Ranking the Centers

Now you have, let us say, five sets of completed checklists from five different daycare centers—your interviews with the director and notes from your tours of infant-toddler and pre-school programs—plus the questions that you asked on the phone when you first started. What do you do with these gigantic stacks of paper? How will they tell you which daycare center to choose?

Get yourself a cup of coffee, a pad of paper, a pencil and a comfortable chair. This will probably take some time.

The "no" pile
Some answers eliminate a center right away:

1. *The adult-child ratio and group size must always meet the provincial requirements.* If there are not enough teachers, the children will not receive high-quality care.
2. *The teachers must be trained.* If there are no trained teachers, the quality of the center will be lower.

3. *Infants must have a space of their own.* If they mingle with the older children during much of the day, they will get sick often, and they will not grow and flourish as they should.

4. *The answers to the questions in the safety section should never indicate a potential hazard to your child's well-being.* For example, a teacher who is smoking or drinking coffee near the children is violating one of the first principles of child care.

5. *A dirty center is unacceptable.* If caregivers aren't disinfecting changing tables and toys or if they aren't washing their hands properly, this center is not appropriate for your child.

   A dirty bathroom, with urine on the toilet seats, scum around the toilet and grimy faucets, also indicates an environment unfit for a child.

   A dirty kitchen should rule out a center, too. Dishes stacked in the sink while teachers eat with the children aren't serious, but if you saw cockroaches or accumulated filth in the corners, if the fridge or the cupboards stank of spoiled food, this center does not merit consideration.

6. *If the daycare center has a closed-door policy and doesn't admit parents beyond a certain point, you don't want to enroll your child there.*

7. *Teachers must be with the children.* If they stand in groups talking to one another in every room, they are not providing appropriate care.

8. *If you see a teacher physically discipline a child by slapping, shaking, pulling or pushing him, do not send your child to this center under any circumstances.*

The rest is harder

The next step is far less obvious. It is probably easiest to evaluate the centers by looking at the questions a section at a time. Read over all your notes on the first section, parent involvement, paying special attention to any questions you starred and comparing the centers on each point. Then try to summarize and make notes for yourself. On the whole, how good is the parent involvement in each center? Now rank them. Which daycare seems best? Which seem second and third best? Which is worst? Why?

When you've finished, move on to the next section, numbers. Read over all your notes, and repeat the process, ranking the daycares in order, just as you did with parent involvement. Go through the whole checklist, ranking the daycares by section. Don't forget to rank the director's questions, too.

Your notes will look something like this:

Parent involvement

1. University Daycare—really detailed comments on the daily sheets by both parents and staff. Seems very important.
2. Main Street—very open to parents; lots of them around.
3. Blue Bell—brief comments; bulletin board really boring.
4. Parents' Co-op—parents actually working in the classroom. I'm not ready for that!
5. Mountain—had the feeling they didn't want me there. Maybe they thought I was an inspector!

Numbers

1. University—great! Lots of staff plus students. Especially good with infants.
2. Main Street—small, well-supervised groups.
3. Blue Bell—too many in the pre-school group for my taste, but the other groups looked okay.
4. Parents' Co-op—parents working confused me. The teachers seemed to leave them too much to do and didn't do any teaching themselves.
5. Mountain—100 noisy kids! How do they keep track of them? How do they keep them in control? Definitely not for my shy child.

For all categories, look particularly closely at the items you starred. If one daycare emerges as strongest in those areas, you may have found your number-one choice.

Then look at your general impressions. Which center did you like best? Do your impressions correspond with the information on the checklist? Don't be fooled by attempts to dazzle. If you liked the open, spacious quality of one center, but its staff-child ratio is lower than that of another center, think carefully. What were you responding to? Which is more important? If necessary, adjust your rankings to take your impressions into account.

Is there more?

Now think back to your own philosophy. Which centers approach the world the way you do? Where did you feel really comfortable? If you choose a center with gorgeous equipment and impeccable safety and hygiene, but you don't feel good about the way the staff relates to the children and the general noise level of each room, neither you nor your child will be happy.

Consider your child's personality. Although any good center will treat each child as an individual, some caregivers seem more tuned in to the needs of a shy or awkward child, and others seem to respond best to extroverts. Where do you think your child will feel most at ease?

Now add location to the equation. Do you have a distinct preference for either community or work-place daycare? If you prefer community daycare but your work-place center has a much better infant-toddler program, consider using the work-place center for your child now and moving him when he's older, or think of other ways for your child to participate in the life of your community. If you prefer work-place daycare because you want to be close to your child, but your community center has an irresistible program of skating, cross-country skiing and swimming, you must think hard about your own priorities.

Which center is the most convenient? A few extra minutes of travel time may raise the stress level beyond endurance for some people, but for others the knowledge that their child is in a better situation lowers stress, even if it squeezes their time. Again, you must think about what is best for you.

Now is the time to take your feelings about profit and non-profit daycare into consideration. If you are weighing two equally good centers, one profit and one non-profit, we strongly recommend the non-profit daycare where you will have more say in policy over the years. (Don't forget that if the owner sells a for-profit center, drastic changes may occur in a matter of weeks.)

The crunch

Do you remember how you decided to get married? Was it a rational decision? How did you decide which apartment to rent, which high school or university to attend or which job to take? Use whatever techniques work for you—list the pros and cons, sleep on it, meditate, assign numbers. Talk about what you've seen and what you feel with your partner, your mother, your sister, your friend. Do anything that will help to clarify your opinions.

If you're still wavering, plan to visit a daycare or two again. Go at a different time of day, or take along your partner or a friend. Phone the parent whose number you got from the director, and without questioning her judgment ask her open-ended questions about the areas that bother you. For example, if the children didn't go outside on the day you visited, ask, "How often do the children go out?" Then she can reply, "Oh, they never go out when it's cold—it's too hard to put their snowsuits on," or, "They go out almost every day. Your child really needs to be healthy enough to stand it!"

Keep rereading the lists and the notes of your impressions. Eventually a pattern and a final ranking will evolve: "This is the best, this is the second best, this is my very last choice."

Since you've already applied to all of these daycare centers, the next step is wait for acceptances. In the meantime, file your papers carefully away in case you need them again.

We are happy to inform you....

One day you will receive a letter that says something like, "We are happy to inform you that your child has been accepted." If this letter comes from the daycare center that tops your list, you are all set—you and your child are on the way to a successful daycare experience. It's time to celebrate.

Unfortunately, not all of us are that lucky.

The daycare that is third on your list may well write you before you hear from your favorite. You would prefer to send your child to the one you like best, but you don't want to refuse this space because you really need it. What do you do?

Each daycare has its own timetable for admission. Call your first choice and explain your dilemma. If they have already begun the process of acceptance, they may be willing to tell you where you stand. If they're planning to accept you, they probably won't balk at sending you an early formal-acceptance letter so that you can safely reject your third choice.

If you discover that you're on the waiting list for your first choice with no assurance that you'll get in, try phoning your second choice to find out your status there.

Once it becomes clear that your third choice is your only option, accept the place they've offered and pay the 25 to 100 dollars non-refundable deposit or registration fee required to secure it. But be sure that you can live comfortably with it. You must *like* the daycare you accept, not view it with suspicion and dread. It will help you to visit again. You shouldn't feel as if you're being rescued from a burning building if your first choice offers you a place the week before school begins.

Even though they discouraged you when you phoned, you may hear from your first or second choice after you accept a place at your third-ranked daycare. If your first or second choice is significantly better, by all means take the place at the daycare you like best, even if you'll lose your deposit. You'll have to live with this choice for years.

We regret to inform you....

Despite this incredible effort, your worst fears may be realized—it's possible that you won't find an acceptable center or that you won't get into a daycare you like.

Does this mean that you won't be able to go back to work after all? What do you do?

One solution is to go back to the drawing board—your original list—and second-guess yourself. Did you rule out any daycare centers because they were too far away? Now perhaps you ought to reconsider them. Can you juggle your schedule to fit in an extra 15 or 20 minutes of travel in the morning and at night? Can your husband take over either the delivery or the collection? Can you arrange for a babysitter to pick up your child from time to time? Can a neighbor or friend help you in the morning or evening? If the center serves breakfast, that may give you a few extra minutes.

Think about a more expensive daycare. How flexible is your budget? Although high-quality care costs more, it's a bargain in terms of your child's happiness and development, your peace of mind and your increased productivity at work. Remember, too, the advantages at tax time.

Do not compromise. If your heart sinks every time you set foot in the daycare center, you have not succeeded in finding high-quality care. Once your child is settled, it will be difficult to withdraw him and make another arrangement. Having a child in daycare of dubious quality induces enormous guilt, which sometimes blinds us to obvious flaws. Besides, it seems to be human nature to grow accustomed to things that were once intolerable. Your child will make friends, and you could become complacent. Bound by the pressure of work, you may not be able to afford to see the truth. Putting your child into a daycare center that you don't feel good about is, therefore, an extremely dangerous course.

It makes more sense to find a babysitter or another form of child care until a space becomes available in the center of your choice. With a sitter in your own home, you're more likely to remember that the arrangement is temporary. You won't be able to put the two halves of your life into separate boxes, leaving the nasty situation behind you as you walk out the daycare door. In your own nice, clean home you will notice if the care is second-rate. You'll see that your two-year-old is bouncing off the walls because he watched television all afternoon and that the sitter hasn't changed the baby's diaper. And because the responsibility for this situation is so clearly yours, not the daycare director's, it will be easier for you to act.

After this frustrating and fruitless quest, you probably won't feel like embarking on another exhausting search, but, of course, you'll have to approach the alternatives just as carefully as you've approached the daycare centers. Fortunately, you have given yourself an excellent education in how to go about it, whether you prefer licensed family home care or a sitter or nanny in your own home. See chapters 4 and 5 for some hints.

In the meantime, keep phoning your favorite daycare center to check on the status of your application. Remind the director that you haven't found an alternative and that you are serious about wanting the place. We live in a transient society—spaces do come up. Eventually your time should come.

Simon says....
CHILDREN'S GAME

CHAPTER 13

Registration

When you register your child at the daycare center or family daycare, you'll know that your decision is final because you will be putting your money where your mouth is.

Even more important, you will finally bring your child fully into the picture.

If he can talk and understand, you've probably told him that you're going back to work. You have shown him around your work place, introduced him to your colleagues and explained to him that this is where you spent your days before he was born. He might have seen his dad's office, too. People going to work is an ordinary, natural part of his life.

You probably also told him—more than once—what would happen to him when you returned to work: "Someone very nice will take care of you, and you'll have friends to play with." Maybe he even knew that you were looking for a place he'd like, and you probably told him when you found one. Now it's time for him to see that his daycare really exists.

Tell him about it before you go, remembering as many details as you can—the playroom, the indoor climbing apparatus, the gym that the kids use on rainy days, the back yard with the tire swing, the blond caregiver named Lynn who looks like Alice in Wonderland. But don't overdo it. Children are very wise—if you come up with too many reasons for him to love it, he'll know you're trying to convince yourself.

If your partner hasn't yet seen the center or met the family caregiver, encourage him to join you. It is important for him to form his own impressions and feel part of this decision. He can also lend a hand. While one of you talks with the director or family caregiver and fills out forms, the other can help your child tour his new daycare environment.

Arrange a convenient time to get together, and before you go, make a list of the questions you had when you visited or thought of in the meantime. In a daycare center you will certainly want to ask the name of your child's teacher and find out when he can meet her and visit again before daycare starts.

You may also have information about your child that you'd like to pass along. It's nice to say something about your child in his presence to help integrate his interests into the daycare: "Annie loves books. Can she bring a book from home for you to read at storytime?" Saying good things about your child makes everyone feel good. "Ian is a really nice guy," Ian's mother said. "Everyone likes him—children in the playground, my adult friends. It's really a joy to have such a friendly, lovely child to bring."

Don't discuss your worries ("Claire is very shy and finds it hard to adjust to a new situation") in front of your child. In fact, it's probably better to keep them to yourself. Though Claire was shy in the past, she may not be at all timid at daycare. Don't create a persona for her and her caregivers to step into—let your child's character unfold by itself.

Since you visited before, the family is counting on you to know your way around. When you introduce your child, the director or family caregiver should address him by name and offer him something to play with (Duplo blocks are a favorite with toddlers and pre-schoolers). Don't be surprised if your child crumbles, grabs onto you and hides his head in your lap. This situation scares many children—they have no idea of what they're getting into, and they desperately don't want

to meet this strange person in this strange place. Given such an un-
welcome reception, the director or caregiver should demonstrate a
sensitivity to your child's feelings and back off.

Red tape

You won't have to worry about whether you'll get the classes you want,
but registration at a daycare center—and even at a licensed family
daycare—has its share of bureaucracy. Be prepared for this adult
business. Bring along your child's medicare card, birth certificate and
record of immunizations; and tuck your checkbook into your purse,
along with your address book containing the phone numbers of your
pediatrician, your mother-in-law and your best friend.

You can expect to fill out several forms. Read everything carefully
before you sign it.

Handbook

Every daycare center should have a handbook outlining its policies and
procedures. A home daycare might have a written policy with lists of
things to bring and rules to follow. If you didn't receive a copy on your
first visit, ask for one now. It will explain holidays, health policies, rules
about toys from home, emergency procedures and lots besides. Glance
at it quickly to be sure no great shock awaits you, and look it over
carefully at home.

Family and personal information forms

Besides your name, address and phone number at home and your
child's name and birth date, the daycare will want to know your
marital status, the language you speak at home and the names and
ages of your child's siblings. They must also know the kind of work
you do and the work addresses and telephone numbers of both parents
so that they can reach you in an emergency.

Unlike with an older child, the more you can tell the caregiver or
center about your infant the better. You will answer questions about
the kind and amount of food he eats, his eating and sleeping patterns,
his bowel movements, his developmental stage (does he crawl or roll
over? what words does he use?) and his special likes and dislikes ("he
hates being on his tummy; he goes to sleep most easily if you sing to
him"). If the caregiver or center doesn't have forms, write this information down and give it to them anyway—to provide high-quality care,
they must get to know your baby as quickly and as well as possible.

The forms will probably ask about your toddler's or pre-schooler's previous daycare experience, nap routines, favorite foods and fears ("Abby is afraid of the dark; she shouldn't nap in a dark room"). If they want to know about your child's personality, tell them in general terms without typecasting him—to reiterate, let your child have a fresh start. Behavior at home can be very different from behavior at the center. Joe was a terror at home, a stubborn child who had terrible temper tantrums. But in a parent-teacher conference, his mother learned to her amazement that at daycare he always smiled, participated and enjoyed every activity, engaged in any form of play with either boys or girls, behaved in a totally non-violent way and was a joy to talk to. In fact, his teacher said, "If only we had 50 Joes!"

Contract

You and the daycare center or family caregiver are entering into a legal agreement, with obligations on both sides. The contract spells them out. It will include the name of the child, the names of both parents, the dates and hours the child will attend (for example, full-time, Monday through Friday, 8 A.M. to 5:30 P.M.; or part-time, Monday, Wednesday, Friday, 8:30 A.M. to 5:30 P.M.).

It will clearly describe the fees and method of payment. The daycare may charge by the week or the month. Many daycare centers expect payment on the first of the month and require post-dated checks for the entire year or a deposit of the last month's payment in full. If you paid a registration fee, it probably won't apply to your fees.

The contract should also say that you agree to pay any additional fees for field trips and transportation. If the contract doesn't mention these charges, ask about them. Hidden costs are more likely to crop up in a profit center or unregulated family daycare.

The contract will also specify the procedure for withdrawing your child. Parents are usually asked to give one month's notice in writing as a courtesy.

Subsidy forms

If you need help paying your fees, be sure to discuss the procedure for securing a subsidy with the director, the family daycare agency or the caregiver herself. Depending on where you live, she will help you to fill out subsidy forms to send to the appropriate office. (In some provinces you'll have to make your application at the provincial or area daycare office.)

Medical forms

To give your child the best possible care, as well as for insurance purposes, the daycare or caregiver must have your doctor's assurance that your child is healthy enough to participate in all facets of the program. The forms your doctor fills out ask about your child's medical history: what major diseases and operations he's had, when he had the required immunizations, whether he has allergies or chronic health problems like asthma, whether he's prone to ear infections or wears glasses. They'll want your pediatrician's phone number, too.

Emergency consent forms

Emergencies demand immediate action. That means the daycare or caregiver can't wait until you return from lunch—it must have all the information required for a hospital to administer emergency treatment *now*, along with your permission to do it. This form asks for your child's name, date of birth, medicare number and children's hospital number, if he has one. It also asks the maiden name of his mother, the full name of his father, his doctor's name and phone number, and the names and telephone numbers of people to contact if you can't be reached. (Don't forget to ask your best friend if she's willing to shoulder this responsibility before you put her name down!)

Authorization to pick up your child

Inevitably you'll have the flu, you'll be out of town on business or your car will break down. Who else has the right to collect your child? You can designate a grandparent, a sister, a babysitter, a neighbor or a friend to do this important job, but you must give your official consent in writing before the daycare will hand over your child. (A parent, including your former spouse, can always pick up his child unless there is a court order forbidding it.) This system is for your child's protection.

Permission for field trips

The center or family caregiver may ask you to give blanket permission for your child to go to places within walking distance—the library, skating rink and playground. This request should state the number of adults who will be present and limit the destinations to those reachable on foot. Any special trip—to the aquarium, the zoo, the museum—that utilizes hired buses, cars or public transportation should require a separate permission slip, distributed several days in advance, detailing when and where the group will go and how they'll get there.

Research

Sometimes scholars in early childhood education or child development wish to study a group of children like those at a daycare center. No one can study or evaluate your child without your written permission. Ask for a complete description of the intended research, and read it carefully before you sign. If you have any reservations about the methods or the goals, feel free to say no.

Parent list

Because your child's name, address and telephone number are confidential, the center or caregiver needs your permission to put this information into a directory that circulates to other parents. (It is also courteous to ask.) Of course, you have the right to refuse if you wish to keep your phone number private.

What if the center or caregiver doesn't have a contract?

A family daycare agency will certainly ask you to sign a contract and medical authorization forms, and virtually all daycare centers have them. But sometimes small or new centers and caregivers who work on their own—even when they're regulated—have not reached this degree of organization or don't consider them necessary. We do.

Written agreements make many people uneasy. They feel as if they're not showing trust in their caregiver (or nanny or sitter) if they write something down and ask her to sign it. In fact, however, contracts protect everyone. For one thing, having one impels you to clarify issues in your own mind. For another, when both you and your caregiver know what you expect and what is expected of you, you have a fighting chance to head off trouble before it starts. A contract is a concrete reminder that this is a business relationship, with obligations and rights for both parties.

We strongly recommend that you write one yourself in the form of a letter. Include the information mentioned above: your child's name; both parents' names; the name, address and phone number of the provider; the hours; days; fees; and method of payment (including whether you will pay on holidays, vacations and when your child doesn't come). Note that she will provide tax receipts, too. The agreement should also say how you can withdraw your child from care.

The letter should outline the health policy—the caregiver will probably ask you to keep your child at home (or to pick him up if he falls ill during the day) when he has a fever, vomiting, diarrhea or an infectious disease. She may ask you to supply a doctor's letter with the dates of your child's immunizations, and you should definitely authorize her to get medical care for your child in an emergency. (Don't forget to give her your child's medicare number and the name and phone number of your emergency contact.)

The caregiver shouldn't give your child medicine without your consent either, but rather than giving her permission to do this at any time, it's better to wait until he actually needs it and then give specific instructions. The same holds true of field trips. You might allow your child to walk around in the neighborhood but agree that she will let you know a few days before a major excursion.

You'll want to mention that the caregiver will provide a safe, healthy, stimulating environment for your child and that she will give him a nutritious lunch and two nutritious snacks every day. You can include information about the daily schedule and about discipline, too—that she will take your child outside every day, that she will not use corporal punishment, etc.

Make two copies of your letter, one for you and one for your caregiver or daycare center. Both of you should sign each copy. For a sample, see appendix D.

"Mother," he said, said he,
"You must never go down to the end of the town
If you don't go down with me."

A. A. MILNE

CHAPTER 14

Integrating Your Family into the Brave New World of Daycare

Congratulations! You've done it! You've made a daycare arrangement that suits you and your child, and together you are about to embark on a new and important phase of family life. Your daycare center or family daycare home seemed wonderful when you visited: happy children were engrossed in a cornucopia of creative activities with the assistance of warm and competent caregivers, and you felt that your child was ready to join them.

But now that the time has come, you're getting the jitters. Questions keep popping into your mind. Will my child be happy there? What if he cries? What do I do if he doesn't want me to leave? Should I stay at home one more month? Maybe he's ready, but I'm not!

For some parents, putting a child into daycare for the first time is an ordinary event that barely makes a ripple in their lives. But for most of us, this move evokes incredibly strong and complex feelings. On the one hand, you feel intense pride that your child is growing up (and pride in yourself for having found such a satisfactory daycare arrangement); on the other, you feel sad that you and your child are parting and jealous of the person who seems to be taking your place, even if you know full well that no one can really take your place. (Research shows that children by far prefer their mothers to their caregivers.) Some parents worry that their child is not yet ready for so much independence and they're demanding too much of him. And because society often tells us that it's better for the child to be at home, guilt gnaws at us all. Both those who are eager to return to work and those who have no choice about it sometimes hear a tiny voice deep down inside saying, "Don't go, don't go. He's too young to leave."

Your child is going to feel frightened and lost and very scared that you won't come back for him, especially if he's very small. Although an older child, three and a half or more, who has been to Grandma's and friends' houses and stayed with a babysitter, will be excited and curious about making new friends, he, too, will be nervous. Your child is extremely sensitive to your feelings, and he will know that you have doubts, whether you express them directly or not—if you grip his hand too tightly, he'll find it hard to let go. For his sake and for yours, it is important that you believe in what you're doing and do your best to resolve your own feelings before you start out.

It's a little like getting married. You must decide if your reservations are the ordinary ones that everyone has before taking such a big step or if they are special and real. This is probably one of the first big decisions you've made as a parent, and you may be setting a pattern for how you will respond to other crises in your child's life. Are you going to say, yes, the water's cold but I'm going in anyway? Or will you spread your towel on the beach and wait for a warmer day? How many of your doubts are real and how many are just part of the process? If they are real, how serious and important are they? Can you cope with them and compensate for them by spending special time with your child at home?

If this daycare arrangement is your first choice, your doubts are probably small ones. The difficulty arises if you have had to settle for a center or a family daycare that was way down on your list. If this step feels all wrong to you, if you really don't think that you can be a convincingly positive parent, perhaps you ought to wait. Consider getting an interim babysitter and keeping in touch with the daycare centers or family daycare homes you preferred so they know you're really interested. But if you believe that this solution is best for the family, you may decide to go ahead. Sometimes doubting Thomases, inching carefully forward, turn out to be supportive and happy parents of contented, well-cared-for children.

There are ways that you can ease the stress for both you and your child and at the same time come to terms with your feelings and reassure yourself about the course that you are taking. Putting your child into daycare does not mean that you have suddenly lost all control of his life. A successful integration can be the key to a positive daycare experience.

INTEGRATING INFANTS

Parents of infants probably feel most anxious about leaving their child in the care of others. Having a child is new; seeking care is new. Parents of babies inevitably ask themselves, "Am I doing the right thing by leaving my child in daycare?" "Is this a good daycare?" and "Is my child going to be happy here?" A parent wants to walk away from his child in the morning feeling, "Yes, this is a good place. These people will take good care of my child."

Go to visit

Before you leave your child there, a visit or two will help. You'll have an opportunity to ask questions and see how the routines work. Depending on his age, your baby may or may not feel more comfortable after getting a closer look at his home away from home, but it's certain that his parent will.

While you're there, the daycare or family caregiver will probably ask you to fill out long forms full of details about your baby's schedules and habits. This is an important step in ensuring individualized care because each body has its own rhythm, established early in life, and it's essential to keep that rhythm. If no one asks you to fill out a special questionnaire, you can still write down when and how long your baby usually naps, when and what he eats and what pleases him—that he likes to sleep on his right side, that he wants to hold your finger when he has his bottle, that he loves listening to music and looking in the mirror. It's a good idea to make a copy for yourself so that you'll know exactly what you've told the caregiver or center and what new information would be useful.

If you're breast-feeding, tell the caregiver when you'll be able to come to feed your baby, and ask her to phone you if he wakes up early.

(If you're just a few minutes away, she can hold him off until you arrive.)

Stick around

If you haven't yet returned to work, you'll find it easy to do what many caregivers and directors recommend: make yourself available to stay at the daycare with your child for a few days. If you're already back at your desk, do arrange to take some time off—this first week of daycare is usually much less stressful if you decide beforehand to put your job on the back burner temporarily. In the long run, having your child content at daycare will make you a more valuable and productive employee. Talk to your boss and see if you can arrange your schedule to give your child as much time as he needs. If necessary, take some vacation days or trade shifts with a colleague. If your job makes it absolutely impossible for you to be free during the first few days, ask your partner, your mother, your father-in-law, your babysitter—someone your child knows well—to be with him at the daycare center or family daycare home. Try not to start a new job at the same time that your child starts at a new daycare.

Daycares that run on a school calendar and admit all their new children in September may hold an orientation day for the parents, but they should ask the infants to come a few at a time in the beginning to minimize confusion and give everyone a better chance to get acquainted.

In a center or family daycare that accepts newcomers all year round, integration may be much easier because the others already know the ropes, leaving the caregivers freer to focus on your baby. Mothers who are old hands will also try to make you and your child feel welcome.

When you arrive together, show your baby around as you put away his things. Even a baby likes knowing where his special spots are—his cubbyhole for his jacket and boots, the shelf for his diapers, the corner in the fridge for his baby food and bottles and his very own daycare crib with his own blanket and his own cuddly toy. Some caregivers recommend that you buy a duplicate set of very precious items—discovering that you've left Teddy at daycare on Friday night is a storm to avoid if possible.

Show the caregiver how your baby likes to be held, and give her a chance to try it herself. Demonstrate, too, tricks you use to change your baby's diaper, to feed him, to extract that difficult burp and to put him to sleep. You've been paying close attention to how this baby behaves for at least three or four months; you must expect someone else (even a baby expert) to take a little time to figure out how to give him what he needs. Let her make as much physical contact as possible with the baby while you're there. She will feel more secure about her ability to handle him, you will feel good about her efforts, and your baby will benefit from making her acquaintance. Eventually he'll know her touch and smell and smile.

How long should you stick around? That depends on you and your baby. Some babies (and parents) feel at ease by the second or third day, while others need a couple of weeks to make the break. Whether your child is entering a daycare center or a family daycare, it is best to go slowly while you feel out the situation. On the first day, come for an hour or so while he imbibes the sights and sounds and smells of the daycare, suggests Kelly Schmidt, supervisor of the Queen Street Childcare Centre in Toronto. Then take him home. The next day you might stay for several hours, including a feeding, before you leave together. On the third day try hanging around for some feedings and a nap. (If it's quiet enough, take this opportunity to talk to the caregiver. But don't count on it—the babies seldom sleep at the same time.) By the fourth day, you might feel secure enough to step out for a while, leaving your baby in the care of those loving, competent caregivers. You may go for just an hour or two initially, but gradually increase the amount of time that you're away over the next few days. The caregivers will help your child to deal with your departure.

Saying goodbye

When you're ready to leave, look for an educator whom your child seems to like. Ellen Unkrig, director of the Royal Victoria Hospital Day Care Centre in Montreal, says, "When the parent gives the child to the educator (rather than the educator taking the child from the parent), this tells the child that his parent is giving him to a person she trusts." Unkrig adds that it's a good idea to put the message in words, too: "I'm giving you to Toby. She'll take good care of you." This advice applies whenever you're leaving an infant in the care of another, whether it be in a center, family daycare or with a babysitter.

Saying goodbye is a crucial part of the ritual. If you sneak out one day, your child won't trust you out of his sight after that. He needs to know that you're going and that you'll be back.

As soon as you say you're going, go. Otherwise he'll pick up on your hesitation and hang on for dear life. Marilyn Neuman, director of the McGill Daycare Centres, counsels: "If you're insecure when you leave, you're giving the child the message that there's something dangerous in this environment. You have to give him the reassurance that this is a safe place, and you have to have confidence in your child. The only way to do that is to say, 'See you later,' and go with a cheery face. Then you can go home and cry."

If you're really worried about how he's doing, phone as soon as you get to work. The caregivers and director understand your concern and will give you a full and truthful account of how he's doing.

What is the key?

Becoming attached to a particular caregiver is usually the key to an infant's successful adjustment. You can tell by his body language—he doesn't fidget or go rigid or make strange faces when she approaches. He'll eat when she feeds him and seek out her cuddles when he's tired or sad. In a daycare center, the baby usually chooses this person himself. (No one knows for sure whether it's because she's the first one he meets or the one with glasses like his mommy.) But older babies also get attached to their peers and look forward to coming to daycare to see a particular friend.

It takes anywhere from a few days to a month or two for an infant to become truly settled. Sometimes, after two or three weeks of seemingly perfect adjustment, he suddenly realizes that he's really going to daycare and begins to wail inconsolably. But this quickly passes, and, more often than not, when you enter the daycare together he'll kick his legs and wave his arms with joyous anticipation.

INTEGRATING TODDLERS AND PRE-SCHOOLERS

On your mark

When you registered at the family daycare or daycare center, you brought your child with you to see what it was like. But before your child's first day, it is a good idea to visit again—two or three times if you can squeeze it in. Most caregivers will welcome you and help you and your child to get to know the environment better.

Plan to go just a month or so in advance so that what your child sees will remain fresh in his mind. Call first to find out the best time of day to come and whether there is a limit to how long you should stay. If you're going to a daycare center, ask if your child's teacher will be around. Although meeting her is one of the goals of this visit, luck may not be on your side. She will be working and may not have much time to spend with an extra child or she may be on vacation. And it is an unfortunate fact of daycare life that staff does change—the freckle-faced redhead whom you meet in July may no longer be around when your child arrives for real in September.

Because your child is not currently attending the daycare, he is not covered by its insurance policy. This means that you must stay with him while he's on the premises. Take the grand tour again—mosey through all the rooms, looking at books, dress-up clothes, blocks, gerbils, dolls. He can play with the toys and join in the activities as long as he abides by the rules, which is sometimes surprisingly difficult. He may still be too young to understand he can't bring a toy up the slide because it's dangerous. Don't forget the bathroom. And show him the hook or special cubby where he'll hang his coat and keep his own things. In a family daycare, you can even introduce him to his future playmates.

The warm hugs and gentle reassurances that you see will help you to feel better about your decision. As you watch the children negotiating for the biggest dumptruck, designing the latest Lego space ship, and creating egg-crate masterpieces, you will realize how well they know each other, and you will be able to imagine how your own sweet darling will fit in. The transition will start to feel more natural.

While you are there, confirm what you were told about the routine with the caregivers and share it with your child—how nap follows storytime, how dark the room is, how books are allowed if he reads quietly to himself.

As you go home from this visit and during the weeks that follow, talk about the center or family daycare with your child, remembering what he's seen and done there. Take it casually—you don't want to frighten him by making this all sound too grand and important—and be sure to mention that, of course, he'll be eating dinner at home with you and sleeping in his own bed at night.

Involve the whole family. Going to daycare becomes more real to your child when all the important people in his life share in the new experience. Grandma would probably love to drive over and peek at it.

Allow your child to master his own feelings around separation by playing some of his favorite games of coming and going, of being lost and being found, like peekaboo and hide and seek. They will remind him that you always reappear. Maybe the dolls go to daycare as well.

The first day

What will he need for the first day? Show him the extra clothes—all labeled with his own name—that he will put in his cubby in case he spills apple juice on his shirt or gets his socks wet playing in the snow. Since they'll certainly be used—accidents happen all too frequently in the beginning—make sure to include a complete set, from hat and mitts down to socks and shoes (or slippers). Children are remarkably aware of which clothes are whose, and they always prefer to wear their own.

If the daycare center or family daycare doesn't serve lunch, a lunch box is in order. Let him pick it out himself—he'll be delighted to take one in a favorite color, decorated with a superhero or comic character he adores. Tuck a special note or a photo of the family inside.

Another way to make that important connection with home is to give him something of yours—wearing Mommy's scarf or Daddy's tie will help him to feel safe. A favorite blanket or cuddly toy to hug at naptime is invaluable. But during the rest of the day it is better if he leaves it in his cubby, where it won't isolate him from the group or give him something extra to worry about. In that safe place it will not get lost or stolen or mislaid.

Get set

Now that you're all ready, take the next step to helping your child adjust to daycare: be there for him. If this is his first experience away from home, he has few tools or mechanisms for coping. Although the caregivers will help, your child is relying on you, first and foremost, to give him clues about how to handle this new world. If you are around, he'll feel secure enough to explore the terrain without being overwhelmed by it. As he feels more at ease, he will need you less and realize that other people can meet his needs, too.

As we suggested earlier, take some time off (or if necessary recruit a trusted surrogate) to be with him during his first few days at daycare. Time invested now will pay off handsomely later. Your objective should be to reduce the time it takes you to leave and increase the time before you return each day, taking advantage of natural intervals like snack, circle, outside play, lunch and nap.

Orientation

Many daycare centers set aside a special time to introduce new children to their new home away from home. Don't miss this initiation period. Although it may last just an hour, it is very helpful to parents and children alike. You will have a chance to meet other new parents (who may well become part of your support system), and your child will acquire a sense of his place in the new world. Now it will be very clear that he belongs: a cubby will bear his name; he'll appear on a list of the children in his group; his birthday may be posted; and a warm and friendly person—his very own teacher—will be there to take care of him. Complete with name tag and class list, she'll be waiting for you, so identify yourself and your child to her as soon as possible. And be sure to remember her name!

The orientation day is usually a mini-version of the daycare's regular program. Parents and children may stay together during a short circle time, while everyone sings old favorites and the teachers and children get acquainted. Because eating away from home is sometimes difficult (new food, new tables and chairs, new table mates and much too much noise), the daycare often serves a small snack to accustom the children to the experience.

Besides your child's teacher's name, make an effort to tuck a few key details about the center into your memory. Which toy did your child play with first? Was there an indoor climbing apparatus that looked exciting? Were the rooms painted a special color? Did you notice a favorite book? Talking about the daycare in very specific terms will help your child to remember it and give him something to look forward to.

If the new daycare year begins without an initiation period, and old-timers and greenhorns arrive at the center all at once, integration may take a little longer, but don't let that throw you. By all means, plan to go with your child and create your own orientation. Again, identify yourself and your child to the teacher immediately, and as you spend the morning going through the daycare routine, try to remember special elements to talk about after you leave together.

During the first few days, when you are staying at the daycare longer than usual to help your child to integrate, it is difficult to know what to do. It's very crowded because so many parents are present, and more children are crying than will ever be crying again. You have to find your own way in this mess. Some parents prefer to explore with their child without the caregiver; others, who are even less comfortable in this foreign country than their child, need a teacher's assistance; and still others want to sit on the sidelines while their child does the exploring. Remember that the goal is to help your child to feel comfortable in this setting. Be there when he needs you, but let him lead the way.

When too many adults cluster around him, a child can become confused and nervous—convinced that there's more to this daycare stuff than meets the eye. For many good caregivers, a parent's presence is sufficient, and they won't intervene unless you make it clear that you need some guidance. So don't wait for the teacher to bounce up to your child and say, "Hi, I'm Beth. Let's go read a story together." If you want her, it's up to you to let her know—her antenna will be up and tuned to your frequency.

If your child is starting in the middle of the year, there is much less need for an orientation. In fact, coming after the screaming meemies are over and everyone knows where he's going isn't so bad—all the attention can be focused on your child. You might want to stay until you are both comfortable, but unlike during the first days of a new year, you will probably be the only parent present. Don't let this intimidate you. Again, there is no formula. Open communication with the teacher on the first day, and take your cues from her and your child.

Go

How do you know when to go? How do you say goodbye? What a puzzlement!

How long you stay is much less important than how you leave. In the beginning, a graceful, untraumatic exit seems absolutely beyond reach, but believe it or not, over time you will develop all the skill you need. For a start, you want your child to be comfortable. Bring him into his room, guide him to a particular person, activity or toy, and stay until he is settled (or until you absolutely have to go to work).

Roger's father discovered that a red fire engine had caught Roger's eye. Together they drove it across the table, extinguished numerous fires, rang bells and climbed ladders. Roger was so involved in playing with the ladder on the red fire engine that he hardly noticed when his dad said goodbye. Every morning Roger went straight to the fire engine. The other children miraculously understood that it made Roger feel better, and they readily acknowledged his claim to it.

Enlist the support of a caregiver. Even if everything seems calm, there's no guarantee that your child will simply say goodbye when you go out the door. He is more likely to be upset, desperate and frightened. But if you tell the caregiver you'll be leaving in five minutes, she can position herself to take over. Because she's made your child's acquaintance very recently, she will be depending on you to let her know whether the art table or the housekeeping corner will best ease the tension, but she will quickly pick up the cues and help your child through your departure.

The cardinal and unbreakable rule of leave-taking is this: always say goodbye. Even if your child is riveted to the blocks, even if he hasn't deigned to notice you for the last ten minutes, *do not sneak out.* Though your intentions are honorable, he will inevitably see your departure as a betrayal, and he will be especially wary at the daycare. (He may never quite trust you the same way again.) Instead, be clear and warm and loving and to the point. Tell your child that you have to go to work and when you will be coming back. Use terms that he'll understand—after lunch, after story, after nap—so he knows that you won't be gone forever.

Once you've begun to leave, get on with it. Do not linger, even if your child starts to cry. The biggest mistake you can make is to chicken out. If you appear uncertain, your child will no longer know what's expected of him, and you'll never find a time to go.

If you feel awful, there's no point in torturing yourself—phone as soon as you get to work. Phone as many times as you want to during the day. The daycare should always be open to your queries.

This is the first of many times that you'll have to leave your child, and if you do it well, you'll make all the inevitable future separations that much easier—you will both learn to cope.

Coming back

Do, please, pick up your child at the time you promised. Your child is counting on you, and until you actually turn up he may be worried that you aren't coming back. But being eager for your return doesn't mean he'll greet you with joy. Don't expect him to drop everything and run to you—re-entry is often as difficult and delicate as separation. Yes, he is happy to see you, but he is also very tired and very confused—angry that you left him, relieved that you've come back, happy to have had a wonderful time, frustrated at not being able to tell you what went on while you were gone. He may burst into tears. He may hit you. He may ignore you. Or he may greet you with a hug and a smile.

When you arrive, do not overwhelm him, and do not panic. Give him time and space and a hug. If he is happy playing with his new friends and toys, observe from a distance. Wait until he sees you, or approach him slowly and join in his game. You absolutely have to admire his creations, and you might want a word with the caregiver. If you notice that he hasn't eaten his lunch, ask her why and what he choked down between sobs. In ten or 15 minutes, he will probably be happy to leave—at least for the first few days. After he realizes that his major fear—the fear of desertion—is unfounded, you'll have to solve a whole new problem: how to extricate him.

How long, oh Lord?

How long should it take for your child to be happy? On average, perhaps a month will elapse before you can rely on him to wave you a cheerful goodbye. A toddler who is intensely attached to his mommy may take as long as two months. But every child is different, and there is no formula that will guarantee an easy time. Some children walk in the first day and never look back. Others consider it their birthright to launch a national protest.

A second child, who has been at the daycare a zillion times with his older sibling, usually feels right at home when he enters daycare himself. He knows how it all works and has probably met the caregiver, too. But even if the whole family is much more relaxed about daycare life, don't take it for granted that your younger child can make the transition entirely on his own—he, too, will probably need a little help from you.

Don't worry if your child cries—it is perfectly normal to want to stay with the one you love. After he sheds a few tears to let you know that you're really important to him, he'll probably be into the Lego.

It will be smooth sailing after he makes a friend or develops a special relationship with a caregiver—or a toy, as Roger did. There is usually a steady daily improvement. When her mother left her the first time, Megan cried her heart out and refused to allow anyone to help her with her misery. Three days later, she cried for approximately one minute before reaching for the magic markers.

Wednesday's child

There is always at least one child who has a truly difficult time getting used to the idea of leaving home or spending the day away from Mommy or Daddy. A month of adjustment can seem interminable when your child clasps your leg as you turn to go each morning, comes home with the contents of his lunchbox intact and bursts into tears at every change of activity.

If this child happens to be yours, you will no doubt feel as awful as he does. But don't helplessly shred yourself into a million pieces. It is important to do all that you can to reduce the anxiety. Talk to the teachers, the director or family caregiver—they will appreciate sharing your concern. A distraught child is a problem for them, too. Tears are contagious, and when one child in the group needs extra attention it is difficult to care for the other children. Try to take the staff's advice— years of experience and expertise stand behind it. Although they listen closely to the children and will slide a cassette into the tape recorder if your child says, "I want to sing," it helps if you supply the concrete information that he likes Raffi's peanut-butter song and never cries when he sits on someone's lap.

Try to figure out why this is happening. Is it a reflection of your doubts? If one parent has more trouble parting than the other, make a switch—it might do the trick if Dad takes him to daycare instead of Mom. Or for a three- or four-year-old, invite one of your child's daycare friends to visit on the weekend. With this extra boost, he may make that all-important first friend.

Do not hesitate to phone during the day to see how he is. But even if he seems to be doing better, it might be a good idea to adjust your schedule to stay with him longer and pick him up earlier for a while.

14-day-itis
Sometimes a child is so stimulated by his playmates and the new environment that he does not think about what it means. About two weeks later, the truth dawns on him: this is serious business. He has no choice; he will have to come to daycare every single day, and maybe not all of it will be quite as exciting as he first thought. He suddenly doesn't want to go; he looks frightened, clings, cries, doesn't want you to leave. He isn't going to let you off the hook totally guilt free—he wants to make sure that you know he loves you, and now he feels absolutely comfortable telling you so.

We call this phenomenon 14-day-itis. In some ways, it can be more stressful than first-week blues. You have already gone through the cycle of anxiety and relief. Believing the evidence of your eyes and ears, you thought that you had made a good choice for your child. He certainly *seemed* happy. You inevitably feel disappointed. Now you can't help wondering if this is the wrong daycare for him or if he is ready for daycare at all. The cure for this disease is a few days of patience and reassurance (saying "I love you, and I know you love me" over and over), coupled with several really good nights of sleep.

Blue Monday

Blue Monday is another familiar syndrome. Even if your child has been asking to go to daycare on Saturday and Sunday, after spending the weekend with you some children have almost forgotten daycare and re-enter reluctantly. If you can, plan to stay a little longer and go in to work late. Then your child should be at ease and the rest of the week should be fine.

Mondays and days following long weekends like Thanksgiving may continue to be difficult for several months.

Behavior changes

Children often react to daycare by changing their behavior at home. Using all their energy to cope with the daycare day, they seem fine there, but the stress is taking its toll, and they save their explosion for you, the people they trust most. Sometimes they become as sticky as your shadow; sometimes they are wildly aggressive; sometimes their sleep pattern turns upside down. This is not a time to make other big changes or increase the pressure in your child's life.

Before panicking, remember that changes in behavior at home may also have physiological origins—a result of the physical demands of daycare. Your child is expending more energy, and if he was used to watching "Sesame Street" in the afternoon with milk and cookies and is now getting celery and cheese for snack instead, his sugar intake is down. He may be really hungry when he gets home because daycare snack finishes at 3:15 and he never really let his stomach get empty before. He may be overtired and desperately crave an earlier bedtime. It is all right for him to be hungry and tired. Try to be sensitive to his needs—give him something to eat and a place to relax, and ten minutes later he'll probably be perfectly happy. (Maita, who threw herself on the floor and kicked and screamed when she came home from daycare, was her cheerful self once she'd eaten.) With time, he should revert to his former self.

If the problems persist after a month of rearranging schedules and accommodating his new needs, form a mini-support group for yourself—discuss the matter with your partner and with friends who've had children in daycare or were supportive when you made your choice. Or ask the daycare to put you in touch with a parent who survived this ordeal last year (bearing in mind that people tend to forget the hard times, your friends included).

But if the situation seems to be going from bad to worse, if he is regressing, if a toilet-trained child has frequent accidents, if he is withholding bowel movements or having nightmares, then it may be a more serious matter, and you may have to reconsider your options. See chapter 20, "Switching Daycare."

The more we get together, together, together,
The more we get together, the happier we'll be.
TRADITIONAL SONG

CHAPTER 15

The Parents' Role in Ensuring a Positive Experience

The first stressful weeks of child care are over. Your child is happy as a clam most of the time, you're back at work, and the family has settled into a routine. With a successful adjustment under your belt, it's tempting to put the daycare or the sitter into a slot in your mind along with the laundry and the meals—yes, you take care of them, but not with your best energy or your whole brain. You naturally assume that your child will continue to be happy and that life at daycare or with the sitter will take care of itself.

False.

You have now stepped into a major supporting role—that of Child Care Parent—and it's a surprisingly difficult one to play. Your appearances on stage will probably be brief, but they will require enormous subtlety and sensitivity to your child's needs.

YOUR RELATIONSHIP WITH YOUR CHILD'S CAREGIVERS

Let's talk for a moment about your collaborators in this production, the people who make it all possible: the caregivers.

Every parent, like every child, has a different relationship with his child's caregivers. The character of these relationships depends entirely upon the personalities of the people involved, but caregivers tend to take their cues from you. If you are willing to listen, they will probably share both the good and the bad with you on a regular basis. If you always rush in and out, they might feel uncomfortable slowing you down long enough to say that Debbie made a new friend today.

It is best for everyone if the interactions between parents and caregivers are frequent, informal and governed by a sense of mutual respect. Be polite and friendly, but don't feel that you have to make the caregiver love you. A professional, caring daycare educator gives her best to all the children, whether she likes their parents or not. So does an appropriate sitter.

Just like you and me

Being human, caregivers also appreciate a little thanks, praise and recognition from adults now and then. If you notice that your child's teacher has set up a particularly exciting learning center, tell her. If Alexandra has been talking non-stop about dinosaurs since she heard about them at the daycare center, tell her. If Carl's skating has improved dramatically under the caregiver's tutelage, tell her. If Sebastien gets ready for family daycare on Saturday mornings and cries when he hears he isn't going, tell her. You'll make her day.

Although you can ask a sitter to babysit in the evening or to stay for supper, you would be imposing if you asked your child's daycare teacher. If she visited only one or two children at home, she would be playing favorites, and it would be virtually impossible for her to visit them all. Inviting her to David's birthday party is a kind gesture, but bringing her a piece of cake the next day would be much more suitable.

If you want to involve her in your life at home, introduce her to your ethnic culture and language. Tell her about special holidays and bring some materials and food into the daycare so that your child can share his heritage with his classmates. For Chinese New Year, one family at the McGill Community Family Center prepared a snack of golden dumplings (symbolizing the wish for a prosperous year), while another brought sparklers (substituting for the traditional noisy firecrackers) so that their four-year-olds and their friends could celebrate the arrival of the New Year together.

Keeping in touch

Talk to the caregiver for a minute or two every day just to say hello and exchange basic information. This prevents her from feeling like a piece of furniture. But once a week or so, set aside a little extra time for a chat—to tell the teacher about changes at home ("Liane has been dry for two nights in a row"), to get caught up on what's been happening at daycare and to find out about new skills your child is acquiring. If the group is learning to cut, it's time to buy a pair of blunt scissors for Stephanie to use at home. But it's also time to watch her carefully—that blissful silence may be the sound of a self-styled haircut in progress.

Promptly inform the caregivers about important events in your child's life, good and bad. Moving to a new home can be very exciting for you, but seeing his worldly possessions disappear into cardboard boxes may create intense anxiety for your child. If you are going away for two nights and leaving your spouse in charge, your child will probably worry about where you are and when you'll be back. If he spent the weekend having a wonderful, exhausting time at his father's house, he may be very overtired. These occurrences will certainly affect your child's behavior during the day, and letting the caregiver know about them will help her to help your child to cope. If you don't want your child to hear the discussion, phone the daycare as soon as you get to work.

It's up to you to decide how much to say in front of your own child. Sometimes it's important for him to be there. In Lea's presence—but not in the presence of the other children—you might want to tell the teacher, "Lea's grandmother died yesterday, and we're going to Toronto for the funeral tomorrow. But we talked about it and Lea said that she'd like to come to daycare. I wanted you to know that she might be feeling sad."

Keep in mind that even when she's talking with you, the caregiver's primary responsibility is the children. When you need to have a serious discussion touching on delicate personal matters like a marital separation, an abusive partner, financial difficulties or a problem with a teacher, you might prefer to make an appointment to talk with either the caregiver or the director in the privacy of the director's office. Away from the children and other parents and in the presence of a mature and experienced adult, you'll feel more at ease talking about your troubles and crying if you want to. The director will treat anything you say in confidence, but if it is affecting your child's behavior, she will have to tell the caregivers to enable them to do their job properly.

To talk about serious and personal matters with your sitter, nanny or family caregiver, again try to arrange a private time away from the children. This may be extremely difficult, because children sense when an important conference is going on without them and immediately claim your attention, but don't give up. Talk on the phone if you feel comfortable, ask your partner to come home early, or set up a special evening date.

At more formal parent-teacher conferences, held several times a year in a good daycare center, you will have the opportunity to pursue your questions about your child's development and about the daycare program. Even if you talk to the caregiver every day, it's a good idea to reserve a time slot. This meeting may provide an opportunity to talk on a different level. It also demonstrates your respect for the teachers as professionals.

Sometimes I love you, sometimes I hate you

A little ambivalence in your relationship with your child's caregiver is normal. She is so competent and relaxed that it's hard not to feel a bit jealous—and somewhere deep down inside, you wonder, Does Tommy prefer her to me? He doesn't. Researchers say that children whose mothers work outside the home are just as attached to their mothers as children whose mothers stay at home full-time.[1]

It's also normal to feel occasionally that the caregiver is judging your competence as a parent. Sandra's mother, who has a Ph.D., feels very frazzled and inept when she picks Sandra up at the end of the day. Sandra never wants to leave, and she cries and runs down the hall without her boots just as her teacher says, "She's been so cooperative all day." When the teacher intervenes—and succeeds in getting her fully dressed and out the door in two minutes flat—her gesture may feel to you like a slap in the face, but she isn't silently criticizing you. It's just that she plays a different role in your child's life—she's not her mother, and the stakes aren't as high. Try to roll with the punches.

Remember that sometimes the shoe is on the other foot: because you have put so much love, time and effort into raising your child, you may find fault with the caregiver. In fact, you're certain to find fault—no one will ever do everything exactly as you would, including your dear partner. But you've chosen your child's caregiver with great care. Now you have to have faith that she will do the job well, and you have to have faith that your child will manage nicely—and grow and learn—even if her way is slightly different from yours. Children and caregivers need the opportunity to work things out between them. The ability to resolve problems with his peers and with adults is one of the most important skills your child can acquire.

Listen to your child, but keep a level head. When Lori says, "Mommy, I don't like Pat. She yelled at me," ask her why, but don't leap into their dispute. The next day Lori will probably love Pat again. But if she doesn't, or if things go from bad to worse, talk with Pat and include Lori in the discussion. Lori will realize that you take her seriously; she will have a chance to present her point of view, and she will see how things look from Pat's perspective.

When you're talking to the teacher about a problem, be as polite and tactful as you can. Two prickly, oversensitive adults can all too easily alienate one another. Choose a private time and place—away from other children, parents and teachers—and keep the communication channels open by staying calm and bringing your ego involvement under control. You might not solve the problem, but chances are everyone will feel better about it.

STARTING THE DAY WITH PATIENCE

Almost all of your contact with your caregiver will take place in the mornings and in the evenings. Squeezed between home and work, both of these encounters probably feel more like intermissions than full scenes in the play. However, unlike intermissions, transition times are full of tension—you're worrying about the traffic, about getting to work on time, about meeting the deadline for your presentation. And you may be feeling guilty because you were too tired last night to read to your daughter. It's hard to focus on this tiny fragment of your life. But a transition sets the tone for all that follows. Like a star's cameo appearance, it is well worth the time and effort required to do it well.

Take it easy
Get up earlier if you have to, but *slow down*. A hurried, stressful

morning will produce immediate unpleasant results—your child will cling when it's time to leave, and he may have trouble joining in the fun.

Ask your sitter to come a few minutes before you have to leave for work. That way you'll have time to tell her all about what's happened since she left the night before. You'll both feel more in control of the situation, and if you're not waiting for her with your coat and boots on, your child will feel much less like a package being handed over for delivery.

When you're taking your child to daycare, plan to spend ten to 15 minutes there with him each morning. This is a chance to have a few minutes of intimacy. Getting his boots and snowsuit off and his running shoes on in a relaxed way will make both of you feel better. It doesn't matter what you talk about or even how much you say, as long as it's calm, loving and unhurried. It makes a big difference if the day begins with a smile.

If you are leaving an infant, the problem is not the child's separation anxiety but your own. Give yourself enough time to feel that he is comfortable. Take off his snowsuit, change his diaper, take a walk around the center, and find a toy he likes. If you fed him when he first woke several hours ago, you might want to include a few moments of nursing or feeding time in your schedule. Wait until a caregiver is free so that you can leave your baby in familiar arms, and tell her about his night and morning so far. Even though you write your news on the daily sheets or in the daycare ledger, making the informal chat a habit each day will create a bond between you and the caregiver and enable you to speak frankly and work together closely when the situation demands it.

A toddler is unpredictable. His behavior depends on how much sleep he had, the mood you're both in, who is dropping him off and which children and caregivers greet him when he arrives. Leaving him with the same person every morning helps him to feel secure, and the caregiver will know exactly whether a cuddle, a puzzle or a picture book will make him feel more at home.

Though your pre-schooler can probably find his own way from the cloakroom to the playroom, you should escort him into the daycare and make sure that he finds a friend or something to do. Even if your whole message is, "Hi, Scott is here," touch base with his caregiver. She must know that your child is present. For some children, taking those first two steps in the morning is like climbing a mountain. If your child seems clingy and you have time, stay to do a picture or puzzle with him, then bring him to a caregiver, tell him when you'll be back in terms he understands (after nap, when it gets dark), give him a hug and say goodbye. The caregiver will take over.

But he cries

When 16-month-old Kevin comes to daycare with his mother, he hangs on tight, reluctant to let her go. But when his father takes him, he runs right in and begins to play with the big blocks without stopping to look back. He barely finds time to kiss his dad goodbye. Like Kevin, many children separate more easily from one parent than from the other; and many parents, like Kevin's, solve this problem in a simple way: they structure their day so that Dad delivers him to daycare as often as possible, assigning Mom to collect him instead.

Rachel, who's four, has been coming to daycare for three years. Although she has friends, loves her teachers and thoroughly enjoys her days at the center, she has never said goodbye happily and gone off to play while her parents were still in the room. What is going on here? Why is parting such sweet sorrow?

Some children excel at making their parents feel bad when they leave them at daycare. Their way of saying they love you is to produce tears and beg for hugs. This behavior can become persistent and painful. To discover exactly how much substance underlies the dramatic display, call the daycare when you arrive at work. The director will probably reassure you that the storm has passed and your child is fine. You could also wait in the corridor just outside the classroom door where he can't see you—and hear for yourself exactly how long he cries.

If he really is inconsolable, talk to the caregivers and arrange to spend some time at the daycare. Consider inviting a daycare friend to the house to help him feel more at ease.

ENDING THE DAY

Picking up your child at the end of the day carries its own portfolio of stress. You have spent an entire day apart. Maybe you were particularly busy at work, and to top it off, you had an argument with your boss. You know that your own day is far from over. You still have that whole second job to do—cooking dinner, cleaning up, giving your child a bath, reading him a story, throwing a load of wash into the machine and squeezing in a few minutes with your partner sometime before the 11 o'clock news.

Somehow, somewhere, you have to pull yourself together before you meet your child. Although he is undoubtedly happy to see you, he has just spent eight or ten hours in a world miles from yours, and he might not be able to shift gears instantly. As Jason, five, so aptly put it one evening as his mother tried unsuccessfully to rush him out of the daycare center, "I haven't been with you all day, and it's hard to make the change."

Save yourself for your child

T. Berry Brazelton advises, "Save some of yourself for the end of the day with your child."[2] First of all, regardless of your child's age, we recommend that you schedule a minimum of ten minutes to make the transition at the end of the day, just as you scheduled time for the transition in. Even when you're returning home to the sitter, it takes time for everyone to modulate.

Secondly, be on time. Your child is counting on you, and you'll be letting him down if you're late. Be on time for your sitter, too. Your child will notice her anxiety and anger if you make her wait, and if she's standing at the door with her coat on, it's a clear statement that she doesn't want to be there. Because this is a two-person transition—just you and the sitter—you can set the tone and make it whatever you choose. You might plan to have a cup of tea together while you hash over the day's events.

Third, take a deep breath and focus on the positive. Noticing the purple paint on his shirt instead of the masterpiece he painted will not create a joyous reunion. A child may respond to your reappearance in dozens of different ways, but if you are calm, relaxed and looking forward to seeing him, it will only be a matter of minutes before everyone is collected and on the right track.

Researchers at the Child Development Unit of Boston Children's Hospital found that babies functioned at a low key all day—not excited or fussy—until their parents arrived. Then they let themselves go, crying loudly and angrily, having stored up their strong emotions for the people they really cared about.[3] Quietly holding or nursing your infant is a good way to feel close again, and changing his diaper before you leave is a practical act as well as a step towards getting back into the home routine.

Like the infant, the toddler is overjoyed to see you, but his behavior may surprise you. Although he cannot tell time, he knows that he can expect you when the other parents begin to arrive. When you do appear, he is filled with relief and happiness. But he may also be slightly confused. Who's in charge now, he wonders, my dad or the teacher? Sometimes he will fly into your arms, ready to go at once; at other times he'll burst into tears, hit you or ignore you altogether.

Entering his territory

With both toddlers and pre-school-age children, it is a good idea to wait until your child puts the finishing touches on his art project or the last piece into the puzzle. Sit beside him and help, talk to the director or your child's caregiver (if she is not too busy) or chat with other parents. Let your child show you his work and introduce you to a friend. This is a good opportunity for you to see him in relation to his peers, to understand his world and to show your respect for it. After all, you are not rescuing him when you come to get him; you are visiting his territory. Brazelton points out that "children who feel this interest [from their parents] have more confidence in themselves. They have an important audience to show off for and live up to. They can bring home their feelings and frustrations because they know you are interested and involved."[4]

You should feel welcome when you linger—not like a patron nursing a cup of coffee in a crowded restaurant. But do try to arrive about 15 minutes before closing. Most children don't like to be the last to leave, and worrying that you'll be late may make your child averse to going in the morning.

Before you leave, don't forget to ask for your child's artwork. His creations are valuable experiments that he is proud to show you. Hang the most precious pictures on the door to your child's room or the kitchen cupboard, bring a few to your office, and send some to the grandparents. Too many parents collect their child's work at the end of the day, drop it in the nearest garbage can, and wonder why he doesn't like art.

If the teacher hasn't seen you and your child is ready to go in a flash, don't forget to say goodbye. Otherwise she'll think that she's lost him!

Changes in routine

A change in your routine may create unanticipated problems. When you have the afternoon off unexpectedly and you'd like to spend it with your child, he may greet you with tears. Older children who have to leave earlier than usual become angry about missing an activity that they enjoy. What should you do? Some parents leave and come back later; some hang around with their child until they can make a smooth exit; and others drag a screaming child into the cloakroom and out the door. We certainly do not recommend the latter, but if he has a dental appointment or you have to pick up Uncle Zach at the airport, you don't have much choice. Although your child might not want to admit it, there is definitely life outside of daycare.

What additional tips can we offer you? At night, as in the morning, time is key. Try to avoid rushing. Count on your child to be hungry and thirsty and come equipped with an extra juice, an apple, some bread sticks. It doesn't hurt to give him something to look forward to on the way home—a visit with the neighbor's dog, a new book to read on the bus, a favorite tape to sing along with in the car. Let him know what you'll be doing: "We're going to drive home and then you can help me to make chicken-noodle soup for dinner. If we hurry we'll be able to watch 'The Polka Dot Door.'" But don't promise him junk food or presents. Although they may assuage your guilt, in the end your child will sense your uncertainty, catch some of it and demand more and more. You can't build a relationship on bribery.

Give your child a chance to share his day with you if he likes, and tell him about yours. But some children really don't want to talk— they'd rather just go on with life. Knowing your child as a person, you can best gauge how to feel close again as you wind down into dinner, playtime, bath, story and bed.

DAYCARE FRIENDS

Even very young children who see each other day in and day out at daycare form strong bonds. Infants find one another fascinating. They pat and lick each other as if they were puppies, imitate each other and play simple games.[5] An eight- or nine-month-old baby kicks and wiggles with delight as soon as he sees children he knows. But he is far more interested in adults than he is in other babies, and it is his relationship with the adults that makes him feel at home in daycare, not his relationships with friends.

By 12 months a child knows the names of the children in his group and will choose a particular child to play near. Toddlers sometimes even cooperate, but they usually play alongside—rather than with—their playmate, building two block towers or digging two holes in the sand, not one. Seeing the same teachers and children in the same setting every day enables them to be happy and comfortable away from home, and an important element of that stability is the anticipation of playing with a special friend. (In the playground, where a child sees new children every day, the interaction is quite different.)

At 18 months, children choose playmates who enjoy the same activities that they do. When toddlers and pre-schoolers make friends, they really look forward to getting together each morning. With a friend, a child discovers how to care, share and work out differences, to lead, discuss, negotiate, compromise—in short, he learns social skills that are important in adult life. He also begins to define himself by comparing himself with other children. Sometimes they intimidate him, but when he realizes Jacob can skip, it may spur him to think, That doesn't look so hard. Maybe he can show me how to skip, too. He explores the environment more imaginatively when he's with friends. He becomes a member of a group apart from his family, gaining support for his burgeoning independence. "Friends make a child feel special—someone who is liked and accepted, whose absence is missed and whose presence brings joy," say Ellen Galinsky and Judy David of the Work and Family Life Studies Project of New York.[6]

For some children making a friend is especially important because it helps them to participate. A shy child like Melissa often attaches herself to an outgoing one like Bethany, whose presence gives her the courage to explore the world. When she enters the daycare center in the morning, Melissa is extremely shy, and she isn't quite sure of who she is and who she wants to be. The moment she spots Bethany, her whole body changes. She straightens up, smiles and heads right to her friend. With Bethany's help, she can manage the day just fine.

"You're not my friend!"

Although their feelings are intense, pre-schoolers are still too young to deal gracefully with all the intricacies of a grown-up relationship. Acutely aware of others' possessions and fickle to boot, they describe a friend as someone they're playing with now or someone who owns a particular toy or wears certain clothes or someone who does what they want him to do. "You're not my friend," Erin says when Melanie declines to relinquish a play chicken leg. Emma, who never cares about what she wears, suddenly refuses to go to school in sweat pants because she wants to wear dresses like Amy. Pre-schoolers don't yet understand that people can have different points of view, and they do hurt each other's feelings. But given time, space and reasonable boundaries, they will learn. When your child says, "I don't like it when Jamie comes to play," listen and be there for him. Try to see his problem at his level.

As your child becomes a social animal, he may depend too heavily on one friend (or a friend may rely too much on him), or you may not like the friend he insists on asking to your house. The solution to both problems is the same: expand his horizons by inviting other children. He's too young to understand why you want him to play with different people, but as he enlarges his circle of friends he will become less dependent and more open.

But before you replace his friend with one you've selected, look closely at this friendship. What is your child getting from it? Melissa is certainly getting self-esteem from her friendship with Bethany, and soon she will be able to apply the skills she is learning to her relationships with other children. If your four-year-old befriends a three-year-old and seems to be regressing (a common event in both family care and daycare centers), your first reaction might be to substitute a child of his own age. But as he shares his knowledge and expertise with someone who looks up to him and respects him, your child may be gaining a sense of self-confidence that he can't get from his peers. His three-year-old friend is his way of solving a problem. When he is ready, he will play with children his own age.

Sometimes, however, parental values override other considerations. When Sybil, three, boasted that she owned ten Pretty Ponies and wanted to know how many Marika had, Marika's mother decided to discourage the friendship: she did not want her daughter to measure her friends by their possessions.

Reinforcing friendships
Even though the caregivers encourage friendships every day, it helps if parents reinforce them. A Sunday afternoon visit can be a tremendous boost for a shy child—and a lot of fun. You may want to call the parents of someone whom your child talks about or whom you've seen with him at the end of the day. Many daycare centers distribute class

lists with addresses and telephone numbers. (Being in a community center or daycare home in the neighborhood will simplify this undertaking, but if you can face the long trek to the home of someone your child has befriended at your work-place center, it will be worth the trouble.) The older your child, the more time he'll want to spend with friends. But even parents of infants find relaxation and delight in hashing over the problems of balancing parenthood and career with other parents. Getting the children together provides a superb excuse for creating your own support system.

HAND IN HAND

Some issues absolutely require your collaboration with your child's caregiver. When you act in concert, you make your child's life much easier. Breast-feeding, weaning from the bottle to the cup and toilet training clearly demand joint planning and consultation. This double-barreled attack also works well with behavior problems like biting.

The nursing mom
If you are nursing your baby, you must be sure that everyone knows and respects your schedule. It's no fun to arrive breathless, having dashed down corridors and up stairs, to find your baby contentedly burping after a bottle. And it's even less fun to return to your office with engorged, dripping breasts and a wet blouse. For the occasions when you can't feed him yourself, express breast milk to keep in the daycare freezer.

Weaning
You don't need your caregiver's help to switch from the breast to a bottle, but do let your caregiver know. On the other hand, the change from a bottle to a cup requires some cooperation. Don't let your caregiver pressure you into making the move too soon. If your child still finds the bottle comforting and doesn't depend on it to soothe him every time he gets upset, he probably isn't ready to give it up. If you still love to hold him on your lap to feed him, *you* may not be ready, Ellen Galinsky and Judy David point out.[7] When the time comes, work out a plan to wean him gradually, giving up some bottles and keeping others. If you and the caregiver choose the same style cup, he'll quickly get the hang of it and feel very satisfied with himself.

Bottles and baby food

If you're bringing the bottles and baby food, be sure you have enough for the day and that everything that you put into the daycare fridge is labeled with your child's name and the date.

Tell the caregiver when you introduce new foods, and pass along information about likes, dislikes and sensitivities that you discover.

Toilet training

You can't go it alone when it comes to toilet training either. How can your child decide whether to use the toilet (never mind *how* to use it) if you talk about pee and the caregiver takes the children to urinate or if you drag him into the supermarket just when he says he has to go and the daycare center takes him to the bathroom every two hours on the dot?

First of all, either you or the caregiver will notice that your child seems ready to try. Sometime between 18 months and three years, he'll have enough muscle control to stay dry for several hours, know when he's wetting or soiling, undress himself without too much trouble, sit and stand easily, say enough words so that you know quite clearly what he means and show you that he's interested. Furthermore—and this is very important indeed—he won't automatically say no to everything you suggest.

This is the time to talk with the caregiver. Go over the signs together. Do you agree that he's ready? If the daycare or sitter wants to start and you don't, listen carefully to her reasoning. The teachers have trained a lot more children than you have and may be more alert to the signals of readiness.

But you don't have to agree if they simply say, "That's our policy," or "I always train my babies at two." You can refuse if you don't think your child is ready. Your child will sense your ambivalence and play on it for all it's worth, and you'll be no further ahead.

It's rare for the caregiver to be the reluctant party, but it can happen. Again, she may know more than you do about training, and parents do sometimes insist the time is right when it clearly isn't. After changing a wet child from head to toe four or five times a day for a week, the caregivers may rebel and explain that you'll have to wait.

But it's also possible that they just haven't noticed your child growing and changing. If he is dry all weekend and the daycare says he's not ready, something is wrong—they're probably not paying enough attention to the obvious signs. Plan to spend some time observing, talking to the caregivers and the director and looking carefully at other parts of the program. This refusal may be just one symptom of a larger problem. If that is so, consider making a change in your child care arrangements.

Once you and the caregivers agree, work out a plan. Does the center use the toilet or potty chairs? Do they take the children at regular intervals or watch closely and take them as needed? Do they always wash hands afterwards?

Which words do you want your child to use: pee, urinate or number one; poo, B.M., bowel movement or number two? Which words do you want to use yourself?

How much praise is appropriate? Do you believe in gold stars? Does the center approve of Smarties as a motivating force? (Criticism and punishment for failures and accidents are *never* acceptable.)

Does the center recommend diapers or training pants? Which clothes work best? (Don't send your child to school in overalls that Houdini couldn't undo, and be sure to send a large supply of extra everything to prepare for the inevitable.) Should you take your child to buy beautiful flowered panties or big-boy underpants with a fly, or will that put him under too much pressure?

What will the center do at naptime, and what should you do at night?

Report on your progress. If you find that your child can stay dry all morning and use the bathroom on the weekend, tell your caregiver. If the daycare finds that he is waking up dry after nap, they in turn must let you know.

Don't be surprised if you find the going rougher than your caregiver does. Watching friends in the act can be very persuasive. Besides, he's safe with you. He knows you'll love him even if he doesn't pee in the pot. Be patient.

Managing behavior problems

Consistency is important in dealing with behavior problems, too. A child has to know that the two halves of his world are really one whole world and that everyone in it agrees. A child who misbehaves by hiding, running away, hitting, biting or throwing things does not have a problem if he does these things just once. They become a serious concern when they recur, and the family and caregiver must work out a plan to deal with them together.

Diane loved to play hide and seek at home, and whenever it was time for the children in her family daycare to go to the park, she disappeared. When Susan, her daycare provider, talked to her parents about it, they agreed to help. "Hiding is not a game unless everyone knows you're playing," her mother told Diane. "Susan gets very worried when she can't find you." If you know that your child likes to run away, be sure to tell his caregiver. She can be his partner on outings until he learns the importance of sticking with the group.

A child often bites because he's been told not to hit, and when Roger takes a toy from him, George thinks that biting may be a socially acceptable way to get it back. Again, clear explanations that biting hurts and isn't allowed either at home or at daycare will break this habit eventually.

BLANKETS, BUNNIES AND LUNCH BOXES

Some times of the day are harder than others. Even though they get easier as the routine becomes familiar, naptime, snack and mealtime and outdoor playtime make many children anxious. They're especially difficult if your child is coming down with a cold or if he's had a bad night or a rushed morning.

Just like Linus
The familiar smell and touch of his own fuzzy white rabbit or his own yellow blanket with the silky edge to rub against his cheek will help make a child feel secure and facilitate the transition from home to school and any transitions in the day. The caregiver may try to wean him from it during playtime ("Let's put Peanut on the counter while you play with the blocks"), but it should continue to be available at nap. If you can manage to create acceptable substitutes for these precious objects (by buying doubles or snipping off an edge, perhaps), leave extras in his cubby or bag while you bring others home to wash on the weekend.

Naptime
Children of all ages find sleeping away from home difficult. Pre-schoolers worry that they won't be able to fall asleep, that they won't be able to lie down quietly for long enough or that they'll be afraid of the dark. Like infants, toddlers and pre-schoolers love to cuddle up with their own favorite furry animal or soft blanket. A scarf or one of

your gloves—something that clearly belongs to you—can also help your child to feel safe. A book might work, too. If your child still seems nervous about nap, talk to him about it and relay his concerns to the caregiver.

However, you can't solve this problem by suggesting that your child give up nap entirely, even if he never naps at home and has trouble falling asleep at night. Children who spend a full, active day at daycare get very cranky and overstimulated if they don't rest. They *need* some down time. The length of the nap might be a problem, especially for older children, who should be allowed to read or play quietly in another room. But bear in mind that the staff must have a lunch hour, too. For most daycares, meeting everyone's needs at this time of day requires a real juggling act, but the children shouldn't be the ones to suffer.

Lunchtime

Because children almost always eat at home with their families, eating away from home is hard, too. For some it's a treat; but others find the noise distracting, and anyone who wants to play and eat and talk all at once gets very confused and frustrated. Although daycares try to make nutritious food geared to children's tastes (macaroni, spaghetti, fish fingers), to some children it is truly alien.

When the daycare serves meals, it's hard to know how much your child eats each day. Because he'll probably come home ravenous even if he's eaten well, his hunger is not an index of whether he's had lunch. He may not be able to tell you much himself, and the caregiver may not keep close tabs on the eating habits of the older children. If he doesn't yet talk or if you're concerned about what he's eating, ask the teacher to monitor his meals. If your child seems well—if he has good color, lots of energy and is behaving and developing normally—he's probably getting what he needs.

Active children should be hungry. Whether it's the cause or the effect of his troubles, the fact that he doesn't eat bears investigation. If he seems tired, listless, complains about the food at the daycare and has little appetite at home, it may be cause for concern. Pack yourself a lunch and make a surprise lunchtime visit or two. Maybe you'll find the food the daycare dishes out as unappetizing as he does. Daycares that serve meals don't usually allow you to bring your own (except for health or religious reasons), so you'll have to approach the problem from another angle. If the food is really so disgusting, go to the director and insist on changes for the sake of all the children. Call the parents together if need be. Maybe the rushed, noisy atmosphere is more of a problem than the food. If your child is feeling neglected or freaked out, see what the caregiver suggests. Maybe she'll sit beside him and make it more fun to eat.

If your child's daycare doesn't serve hot meals, you're facing a different set of problems. You've already taken him to buy his very own lunch box; now you have to fill it with interesting and nutritious meals that he'll actually eat. Soup in a thermos is usually a big hit. Try putting a happy face of raisins on an open-faced peanut-butter sandwich or use cookie cutters to make sandwiches into circles or stars. Pack lots of little things—some strawberries, some crackers, a couple of pieces of cheese—if your child won't eat a sandwich. Cookies that you made together over the weekend say I love you. So does a funny picture or photo. (*The Lunchbox Book* by Patricia D. Exter [McBooks Press] is crammed with helpful suggestions. So is *The Nutritious Lunchbox Cookbook*, compiled and distributed by the McGill Community Family Center in Montreal.) Many daycares send home the uneaten food—when you unpack his lunch box you'll know which of your creations hit the spot.

Many centers have rules about the food that children can bring. Gum and candy are almost universally outlawed, and some daycares don't permit cookies either.

Birthdays

They'll probably break their sweets rules for a birthday party, though. Some centers have one big party for all the children born each month and ask parents to contribute something—a cake, decorations, balloons. Some daycares ask the child to give a book or a tape to the center in honor of his birthday. Find out your daycare's birthday policy and try to do your part. If you can actually be there to join in the fun, your child will be thrilled.

Clothes and equipment

Babies need a constantly replenished supply of diapers, and all the other children at a daycare center or family daycare home (including the babies) need an extra set of practical clothes, fully labeled, at all times.

If your child gets wet, either outside or in, and wears his spare clothes home, replace them the next day. If by some lucky chance the extra clothes are languishing unused, check them periodically. Your child won't want to wear shorts in December or corduroys in July. Besides, they may no longer fit.

Don't forget to bring shoes or leave a pair at the daycare for the days when your child wears boots. His own blue running shoes with the Velcro straps are much more comfortable and practical than boots or bare feet.

In the summer going out is a breeze, but getting dressed for winter taxes everyone's patience and ingenuity. Your child needs the full complement of winter gear: snowsuit, hat, scarf, mittens, boots. Make sure that everything is comfortable. Boots that are too big or heavy, a snowsuit that's too big or too small, a hat that covers his eyes as well as his ears, and mittens that aren't waterproof will limit his ability to move around and enjoy himself outside.

If the children go skating, be sure he has his skates and helmet on the right day. And don't forget his swimsuit, cap and towel on swim days.

A special toy

One day your child refuses to budge from the kitchen floor unless he can bring his favorite fire truck to school with him. What should you do? If the daycare forbids toys from home, it has good reason: unless it's a cuddly animal or blanket for naptime, toys at the center are supposed to be shared. He may not want to share it, and it may get broken or mislaid. In other words, once at the daycare his toy from home will probably make him feel worse, not better. Let your child know that he can bring it on the bus or in the car but that it can't go into daycare with him.

Show and tell

He'll have to wait until show-and-tell day, when the goal is to share something special with your friends. Giving each child a chance to talk, show and tell also presents a good learning opportunity for the whole group when the teacher asks, "What color is your fire truck?" "What is it used for?" "Who drives it?" It is also a natural occasion to integrate home and school.

Mind you, if the daycare has show and tell every week, you might find it tedious, and your child may find it stressful. If he can't decide what to bring, the teacher can offer suggestions, but the rule of thumb is to avoid fragile or expensive items. It's fun to coordinate with the daycare themes, and using them gives the whole affair a much less commercial character—bring in a beautiful leaf for fall week and a photo of your dog or cat for pet week. Most important, send your child with something. Select it together the night before, and write yourself a note so you'll remember it in the morning.

Read your mail

Daycare centers communicate officially with parents in several ways. There are personal messages on daily sheets, announcements of meetings and other events on bulletin boards, and sometimes there are letters or newsletters to keep you posted about whatever is happening at the moment—a case of scarlet fever, the theme of the month, an upcoming guest speaker, a university research project in the works. Daycares can't afford to send these missives by Canada Post, so they usually arrive via child courier. Keep an eye out for them in your child's cubby or lunch box. You're bound to find out something interesting.

The wheels of the bus

You may find out about a trip. Apart from regular outings to the skating rink and pool, the library and playground, daycares occasionally take the children on grander expeditions—to the post office, the fire station, the aquarium. You should be informed and give written permission at least a week before each of these trips. What arrangements has the daycare made? Will there be enough adults to handle the children in a strange place? You would delight your child and his teacher by volunteering to go along. Do volunteers and extra staff know the rules? What about name tags and first aid kits? Will anyone visit the site ahead of time? Does the bus have seat belts?

In your opinion is the destination appropriate? Or is this trip designed to please the parents? If you think a visit to Santa Claus is too commercial, or the zoo is too crowded and dirty, you always have the option of keeping your child at home that day. You can also speak up— tell your child's teacher and the supervisor what you feel about their choice, and suggest some other possibilities.

At some daycares trips cost extra. If you can't afford to send your child, does the center assist you? Or will your child be left out? If you and your child find yourselves in this awkward position, don't take it silently. Go to the director and the board and let them know just what lessons they are teaching your child about the world.

STAYING ATTUNED

When you hang around the daycare center or chat with your caregiver in the morning and evening, when you drop in at lunch or telephone during the day, you are doing two vital jobs at once: you are helping your child to feel comfortable in his environment, and at the same time you are monitoring the quality of his care.

Observe

Being there with your child gives you a natural opportunity to keep an eye on things. You can see exactly how the caregiver welcomes the children and makes them feel at home, whether she washes her hands after wiping their noses, whether the toilet is clean, how many teachers and children are in the room, what they are eating for lunch.

Ask

When you don't like or don't understand what you see, you have a perfect right to ask about it. (We might even say you have an obligation.) Remember that you can talk to the director, the board and other parents, as well as the caregiver herself. The answers you receive ought to make sense to you and jibe with what you know about high-quality care.

Supervise

With a sitter or nanny, you have the sole responsibility for overseeing your child's care. That calls for more contact than just a casual hello or goodbye as you pass in the front hall. When she first starts coming to look after your child, stay home and work alongside her for a day or two. After you return to work, check in often. Phone at different times and listen for crying and the sound of the television in the background. (On a beautiful sunny day, no one should be home.) Drop in from time to time. If you can't manage to get away from the office, recruit your partner, your mother-in-law or your neighbor to find an excuse to come by. Rushing home to collect some books, Claire found her two-year-old daughter and her sitter on the front steps eating chocolate and drinking Coca Cola. "Oh, we do this every day," he explained. Claire's visit ended the trips to the corner store, but not her child's junk-food habit.

Ask your sitter or nanny to keep a diary or scrapbook of daily events, and make it a nightly ritual to go over it with her in detail. Once a week, schedule a longer session so you can share experiences and air gripes from the last week and plan activities for the next. You'll know exactly what your child is up to and have a wonderful record of his development, your sitter or nanny will feel that you appreciate her work, and your child will have better and more consistent care because you're communicating and coordinating so well.

No matter what kind of child care you are using, research shows that parent participation is important to high quality.[8]

What does your child say?

It is also essential to pay close attention to your child. His reaction to his experience will give you even more crucial information about what's going on.

Daycare sometimes transforms children. Sabrina now puts away her toys when she finishes playing, sings French songs in the bathtub and takes turns with her older sister. She can use the toilet successfully, dress herself in the morning and flip her jacket over her head to put it on alone. She even says please and thank you.

Jenny, on the other hand, talks back, uses language that shocks her mother and stubbornly refuses to do anything she's asked. To top it all off, she has started drawing on the walls.

Some children, attracted to the negative behaviors of others, can't resist testing your response to their new-found skills. Others use so much self-control at daycare that they desperately need to let go when they get home, and they condense their uncivilized impulses into the few waking hours you have together because they know you'll love them anyway. Many children just need to lie around and not do much of anything, while others, overstimulated by the day, end up flying around the ceiling before they crash land into bed.

Normal behavior

For most children, these behavior patterns are absolutely normal. In fact, many of them would occur even if you didn't go to work—sometimes we forget that our children are growing, developing people and put all the blame on the daycare or the sitter. When we're at work all day, we tend to have idealistic expectations. We think that when we're reunited we'll have "quality time," cuddling and exchanging important thoughts and feelings. Instead we pick up a kid who won't sit still, makes rude noises, throws supper on the floor and floods the bathroom. It's a real shock.

All of this is very trying. An exhausted, overworked parent doesn't relish coming home to a stubborn, aggressive child. And bad tends to escalate into worse. Although he's just asking for a little of your time, his obnoxious behavior makes you less—not more—inclined to give it.

Normal guilt

Et voilà! The situation has magically resurrected your nagging guilt about leaving your child in the care of another and its companion fear that maybe you didn't pick the best daycare after all. These feelings, which are perfectly natural, come with the territory and are virtually inevitable.

What to do

How can you make everyone feel better? Working and parenting put a lot of demands on everyone. Are your expectations unrealistic? Would your child calm down if you sat together to read a story when you got home or bathed him or fed him earlier or put him to bed earlier? Urge your partner to pitch in. Two people doing the work lightens the load—to the whole family's benefit.

Again, talk with your child's caregiver or the director. She can offer useful hints for coping with your trials and tribulations. Talk to other parents—they may be experiencing the same traumas, whether or not their child is in daycare. Then at least you'll know whether you're dealing with a daycare-induced problem or one that's basically developmental.

Ellen Galinsky and Judy David interviewed parents who gave this advice: "...I just try to avoid a war with my child. Maybe we'll have a minor skirmish but not a war."

"If I can, I keep a sense of humor and remember that tomorrow's a new day."[9]

This is not to say that you should accept all kinds of behavior as normal—or strong feelings of guilt, for that matter. Far from it. If either the behavior or the guilt persists and intensifies, that may indicate serious problems. We will tell you what to look out for in chapter 20, "Switching Daycare."

This is the way the teacher stands
Fold your arms and clap your hands.
CLAPPING GAME

CHAPTER 16

Red Tape – Respecting Daycare Rules

When you enroll your child in a daycare center or family daycare, it is not just your child who's involved.

No, my friend, daycare is a tandem bicycle.

Whether or not you sign a contract or a letter of agreement that spells them out, a daycare parent assumes certain obligations. Just as the center or family daycare provider agrees to care for your child, you agree to abide by their rules and regulations. In a daycare center, the people in charge have probably spent a lot of time and energy hammering them out, and they are part and parcel of the care. A family daycare agency will draw up rules for its providers, and an independent family caregiver may very well have painstakingly developed some on her own. (If she hasn't, the two of you should sit down and work some out right now. Chapter 13, "Registration," contains some pointers.)

Rules and regulations are essential to the smooth functioning of any organization, daycares included. Everyone should know exactly

what to do and what the penalties are for failing to hold up his end
of the bargain. Some rules may seem to concern very mundane
matters, hardly worth bothering about. But their application prevents
molehills from turning into mountains. Policies and regulations are
intended to prevent that.

What are the unbreakable rules?

Pay your fees on time

In a small organization with a chronically tight budget, late or unpaid
fees take a big bite out of the monthly income. If you are two or three
months behind, your daycare center or family daycare might have no
choice but to ask you to withdraw your child and replace him with one
whose family pays on time. Although this policy is a matter of survival
for some centers, the person who suffers will be your child, who has
to start all over again in a new place. Daycare directors and family
caregivers are human beings, so if you're having financial problems,
talk to them and see if you can work out a plan that suits everyone.
(The advantage of a small organization is that they'll bend over
backwards to understand and accommodate you if possible.)

For family caregivers a parent who doesn't pay is an especially
awkward problem. Money for the apple juice your child drinks and
the markers he draws with at her kitchen table comes directly from
her pocket. But because she needs your good will as much as she needs
the revenue you bring, it's hard for her to play the role of bill collector.
With the unpaid bill at the back of her mind, she'll feel uncomfortable.
If you don't talk about the money with her, she could get the idea that
you don't appreciate or respect what she's doing, and she'll almost
unconsciously hold back in discussions of your child. Again, if you have
a financial problem, it's important to discuss it openly.

Be on time

Respect for the daycare's hours is basic, too. An educator's work is very
demanding, very intense—and grossly underpaid. To deal with the
stress, she needs her time off with her own family and friends to
prepare, relax and recharge. If she appears at the center before it
opens, she plans to arrange the day's materials and savor a peaceful
cup of coffee before the children arrive (remember, she can't have it
at her desk the way an office worker can). Don't expect her to be
available to care for your child before opening time.

Closing time is equally sacred, and centers usually charge very stiff fines to emphasize this point. If you know you're going to be late, it is imperative to phone for your child's sake. The caregiver can then say with conviction, "Don't worry. Mommy phoned, and she'll be here in ten minutes." If you're 15 minutes late and haven't informed the center, even the caregiver starts to worry. It is extremely hard on your child to be the last one collected.

A family caregiver, whose private space is invaded daily and who already works a ten- to 12-hour day, desperately needs your respect of her hours (they're probably more flexible than a daycare center's in any case). You must be very careful not to take advantage of her. If you are always late and it is impinging on her private life too much, she may ask you to go elsewhere. A good family caregiver is in great demand and can pick her clients in the same way that you may have chosen her.

What is an acceptable reason for being late?

If you phone to say you'll be late because your car broke down, the bus never came, or you couldn't leave a meeting that ended later than you had anticipated, the teacher or family caregiver will sympathize and show your child a nice time. But if this scene repeats itself, she may be less favorably inclined. It is not acceptable to be late because you lost track of the time. It makes everyone furious if you call and say, "I just looked at my watch and it's ten to six. I'm putting everything away and I'll be there in twenty minutes."

Sometimes an honest mistake causes an unacceptable situation— as in a divorced family with imperfect communication. Allison's mother and father each believed that the other would pick Allison up at the daycare on Friday night. When neither parent had appeared by 6:15 P.M., the daycare director tried to phone them, but neither was home. Eventually the director reached Allison's emergency contact, her aunt. Although her aunt was extremely loving and gracious with her niece when she arrived at 7 P.M., Allison inevitably felt very sad, unloved and unwanted. Because we live in such a fast-moving society, this happens much more often than you might think. When parents don't get their acts together, their child pays a heavy price.

Follow identification procedure

It is also extremely important to follow the correct procedure when you send a different person to collect your child. The daycare or family caregiver has to enforce the rules strictly to protect you and your child:

the consequences of a false move in this area are far too grave. Whoever picks up your child should expect to show identification, even if you have telephoned or given the daycare or the family caregiver written instructions. You want to avoid embarrassment for everyone—the child, the adult and the caregiver.

Keeping up to date

The daycare will assume that the information on your registration form is correct unless you tell them otherwise. If you move or change jobs, marital status or emergency telephone numbers, immediately notify the center in writing. If you and your partner will not be at your usual places during the day, be sure to give the caregiver a telephone number where one of you can be reached. If you know that you are going to be unreachable by phone, check with your emergency number to be sure she will be available. It will not be a joke if your child needs stitches after a fall in the playground and no one can reach you.

Health

Your obligations here are extensive and complicated. They include keeping a sick child home, informing the daycare about contagious diseases and following proper procedures for medication. We will explain all this and more in the next chapter.

Ring-a-ring of rosies
A pocket full of posies,
A tishoo! A tishoo!
We all fall down.
MOTHER GOOSE

CHAPTER 17

Daycare and Your Child's Health

Bright and bilingual, two-and-a-half-year-old Andrew seemed more than ready to leave his grandmother's care and tackle the wider horizons of the daycare world.

When he started in September, the youngest in his group, he adjusted well to the routine and started to make friends. Then he got sick. Colds metamorphosed into ear infections and croups. He was allergic to antibiotics, and the doctors discovered he had asthma. Each time he returned to the center, he caught another cold and spent two weeks at home. Because he was so seldom around, he had to make new friends whenever he reappeared.

His parents wondered if they should withdraw him. Perhaps he'd fare better next year, when he was older. It was painful seeing him so sick, and his mother, who nursed him when her own mother couldn't come to look after him, was losing far too many days at work.

But Andrew liked going to the daycare most of the time, and they kept thinking he would build up his resistance. The winter would soon be over, and, for now, the price seemed worth it. They decided to stick it out.

This is the down side of daycare.

You ache when your child is sick. He seems so small and so vulnerable, and there seems to be so little that you can do to help him.

What's worse, you may not have the chance. Even though he needs a few days of chicken soup, stories and cuddles at home with mommy, you probably have to go to work as usual. That is the unfair, frustrating reality.

I. HEALTH

It is a sad fact of daycare-center life that your child is going to be sick three to four times more often than a child who stays at home with a babysitter. Dr. Julio C. Soto, public health advisor to 56 Montreal daycare centers, points out that on average an older child will come down with two new respiratory infections and one case of diarrhea a year, while the members of the under-two set will contract double that number.

One of the ways that young children explore their world is by touching it—with their hands, their bodies, their mouths. (They put their hands to their mouths once every one to three minutes.)[1] As they touch objects and exchange hugs and kisses with their teachers and each other, they also touch, breathe and swallow germs. With germs come disease, some in benign form, like colds, chicken pox and lice (yes, lice!), others in more dangerous guise, like pneumonia, hepatitis and meningitis.

When children aren't toilet trained, the possibilities multiply. There is 3.6 times more diarrhea in centers that accept diaper-wearing children under the age of two. Large centers, with more children, more contact and more chances to spread germs, have more disease as well. When there aren't enough teachers for the number of children, the teachers don't have time to wash their hands and follow other rules of hygiene, so a low staff-child ratio also increases the risk. So does a staff that isn't properly trained in disease prevention—particularly in handwashing, the best defense against infectious disease.[2] And children in profit daycares face greater risk than children in non-profit centers.[3]

You looked at these factors when you were choosing a daycare. But even a center that adheres to the rules religiously will have its share of sick children. It is simply inevitable. Yours will no doubt be among them, especially the first year.

HEALTH POLICIES

When you registered your child, you probably received a copy of your daycare center's health policies. If they are well drawn and intelligently followed, these dull pages represent your child's passport to a healthy and safe voyage through his daycare years. Life will be much easier if you make it your business to read and understand them.

Health form

The center's first step will be to put together a health file for your child. To begin with, he needs his doctor's approval to follow the program the daycare offers, especially if he has allergies, asthma or any other health problem. This means a visit to the doctor just before he starts. The center will supply a special form for the doctor to fill out, describing your child's health history.

Immunizations

With exposure to infection (and with age), children do eventually acquire immunity. But there are some diseases that you just don't want your child to get. Vaccination is a much safer way to shore up his defenses. Before he sets foot inside, daycare centers may require your child to have all of those which are appropriate for his age: diphtheria, tetanus and pertussis (the DTP shots which normally begin when he's very young); poliomyelitis (given orally at the same time as the DTP); and measles, mumps and rubella (done in one shot at about 15 months).

Many health authorities now strongly recommend one additional vaccination—against *Haemophilus influenza* type b illness, otherwise known as Hib. Primarily attacking children under five, Hib is a bacteria that can cause serious, sometimes fatal illnesses like pneumonia and meningitis. Children under two and those in a daycare setting are particularly at risk. If your doctor doesn't suggest it, ask him about the new vaccine, which can be given at 18 months. Because it takes several weeks to become effective, it is better to give it before your child is exposed—in other words, for a child 18 months or older, before he enters daycare.[4] But because Hib's period of risk after a case appears is almost two months, a vaccination at the time of exposure may protect him.[5]

It is important to keep your child's immunizations up to date. In 1989, 10,000 Quebeckers, including almost 2,000 children under the age of six, both in and out of daycare centers, came down with measles. Five people died.[6] Vaccinations are a crucial part of keeping everyone healthy at daycare, and unprotected children should not attend.

Exclusion

The daycare center has the right—and the responsibility—to exclude children who are ill. It is an extremely difficult and controversial responsibility to exercise sensibly and fairly, one that all too often lands them in hot water.

The center's mandate is to care for children so that their parents can work. In many cases, children who are ill have exposed all the others to their germs before they showed any symptoms, so a strict exclusion policy doesn't really affect the incidence of infectious diseases in the daycare center.[7] If a child is functioning normally, he won't interfere with the group's activities.

On the other hand, no parent wants his child in close contact with a pal who has untreated strep throat or galloping diarrhea. If a child has a fever that's turning him into a whiny monster and he wants to sit on the teacher's lap all day, he shouldn't be at daycare.

As the daycare staff make decisions to admit and exclude, they must look at the whole picture and act as reasonably and flexibly as possible.

Children have different levels of strength and immunity. Some rarely get sick; others catch—and can't shake—anything that comes their way. Although it doesn't seem fair for the child like Andrew, who has just had a cold, bronchitis and an ear infection, to be sneezed on as he walks through the daycare door, the director cannot turn away a child with a mild cold just because Andrew is there for the first time in three weeks. But she and the staff can be aware of every sneeze and cough in the room and do their best to protect him by airing the room well and reminding the others to cover their mouths and wash their hands correctly.

If you're not sure about whether to send your child to daycare, call the director. Getting turned away at the daycare door—or getting called back two hours after you arrive at work—is no picnic.

Most daycares do not allow children to attend when they act sick, which usually means they have:

- a fever of 38.5 degrees centigrade (100 degrees Fahrenheit)
- diarrhea (meaning liquid stools or several stools in one day) or vomiting within the last 24 hours
- pain, as in an earache
- chicken pox
- an undiagnosed rash
- a serious illness like infectious hepatitis or meningitis

Many centers tolerate the coughs and dripping noses of the common cold because all of the children come into contact with the germs anyway. Ear infections, a painful complication of the common cold, aren't contagious.

Following the rules

No one objects to excluding a child when he is very sick, with a high fever or lots of vomiting, for example. It is perfectly clear that he needs a trip to the pediatrician or family physician, rest, special foods and fluids and lots of extra attention. In his condition, he couldn't conceivably handle a long, active daycare day.

The trouble usually crops up when a child is not too sick, at the very beginning of an illness when no one knows quite how serious it is or at the end when he's recovering. He may seem reasonably fine to you, especially in comparison to the way he dragged himself around the day before, and if you'll pay heavily for yet another missed day at work, you may be tempted to stuff him with Tempra and send him off to daycare.

Before you do, consider the situation carefully.

When the effects of the Tempra wear off and his fever and listlessness return, will he be well enough to participate fully in the program? He'll have to go outside with his group whether he has the stamina to manage it or not. He may be bouncing off the walls at home, but the constant noise and activity of the center may make him droop long before your customary arrival time.

Does the daycare have enough staff to give an ailing child the attention he needs? The whole staff-child ratio gets thrown out of whack when a teacher has to devote all her time to just one child.

How necessary is it for you to go to work? How many days have you missed? Can you work from home? If you absolutely have to send your child to daycare, can you pick him up early?

If you don't want another child spraying a known case of flu into your child's face, you have to do your best to prevent your child from spraying a known case of flu into his. In daycare, staff and parents have to work as a team in order to protect everyone's children.

A course of treatment

Some illnesses are no longer contagious once you've begun treatment. After 24 hours on medication, a child with strep throat can return to daycare if he feels well enough. (But if he's still quite lethargic and you think an extra day at home is in order, trust your own instincts, even if the doctor has given you the green light to send him back.)

Sufferers with conjunctivitis, impetigo, ear infections, ringworm and parasites who've been treated and who are feeling fine can also go back. Children with head lice can return after their hair has been treated and all the nits removed. (You'll have to wash all their clothes and bedding and spray your furniture as well.)

If your child has to take medication for several days, your daycare will have strict rules for its administration. A doctor must prescribe the medicine (even Tylenol and aspirin—but aspirin is not recommended for daycare children because of the risk of Reye's syndrome, a rare but dangerous disease),[8] and it must be in the original pharmacy bottle labeled with directions for its use. When you get the prescription filled, ask the pharmacist for an extra labeled bottle to bring to the daycare. The daycare must also have your written authorization to give the medicine to your child.

Don't pack it in your child's lunch box—its pretty pink color and sweet taste may entice him (or another child, who might be allergic) to drink it down like juice. Give any medication directly to your child's teacher. She will put it in a locked box in the refrigerator (or out of the refrigerator, as required). Be sure to tell her in writing exactly how to store and administer it—for example, with a full glass of water, a half hour before eating or with lunch. The daycare should keep a written record of the time and date that he took the medicine and the name of the teacher who gave it to him. Even daycare teachers can turn into absent-minded professors—and a two-year-old isn't likely to mention that he already had his lunchtime dose.

Inform the daycare

Of course, whenever your child is sick and won't be coming—whether because of a nuisance like head lice, a minor cold or a major disease like meningitis—you must tell the daycare. The director can then take appropriate steps to contain the illness, inform other parents and staff and consult the daycare's health specialist and local health authority. Dr. Soto advises parents to tell their doctor that their child goes to daycare. This information will help him to diagnose and treat the child's illness correctly. Parents should ask for the diagnosis, Dr. Soto says. Then they can give this important information to the director to pass along to the community public-health officers if necessary.

(In the past some doctors have disapproved of daycare and be-littled or dismissed any illness in a daycare child as inevitable. Although these attitudes are on the way out, you might consider changing doctors if yours persists in denigrating daycare.)

Check the bulletin board or daily message center and your child's cubby to find out what's going around, and notify the center, too, if any family member comes down with hepatitis. Although children don't usually get sick with this serious liver ailment, they may carry the hepatitis virus, especially when they aren't toilet trained. Research shows that there is a risk of hepatitis among adults in contact with diapered children who attend daycare.[9] Those who've been exposed may need a shot of immunoglobulin.

Hib also spreads to families of daycare children. So does cyto-megalovirus (CMV), which, like hepatitis, children carry without symptoms. Because it poses a danger to a fetus, especially in the first two trimesters, pregnant mothers of daycare children should consider asking their doctor for a test to find out if they are at risk.[10]

There have been very few cases of AIDS (acquired immunodeficiency syndrome) among children in Canada. Because the risk of person-to-person transmission of AIDS or HIV (human immunodeficiency virus, its precursor) in daycare settings seems to be extremely low, this illness doesn't represent a problem at this time. Decisions about a child with AIDS or HIV should be made by the chief of the department of community or public health in collaboration with the child's doctor and the parents.[11] Whatever the illness, it is important to cooperate fully with the public health authorities—their measures don't work unless everyone complies.

A SICK CHILD AT HOME

"This is the daycare calling"

When your child gets sick during the day at daycare, the family caregiver, teacher or director will telephone and ask you to collect him. While he waits, he'll rest or play quietly on a cot or mat away from the other children, where someone can keep an eye on him and give him a drink and his blanket.

As a parent you have three responsibilities in this situation.

The first is to be sure that the daycare can reach you or your emergency contact at any time, on any day. Simultaneously ask your work place to inform you promptly as soon as the daycare phones, and tell your emergency pick-up people—your partner, your neighbor, your mother-in-law—what they're expected to do if the daycare calls when you're unreachable.

Your second responsibility is to come as quickly as you possibly can. It's no fun being sick and harder being sick away from home. Besides, the daycare isn't set up to provide long-term sick care.

Thirdly, because you weren't around to watch your child becoming ill, try to find out exactly what is going on. What time did he first throw up? How many times has he thrown up since? How high is his fever? How many times has he had diarrhea? Has he been sleeping? Did he have anything to eat or drink? Sometimes parents who didn't see the initial symptoms don't realize just how sick their child is. If the caretaker indicates that he's had a tough time, it's a good idea to give him at least a whole day off. He probably needs it.

Who will look after your child?

Now that he's at home, you have come face to face with the hardest problem of daycare. What do you do when your child is sick? Who will look after him?

In the beginning you can put your head in the sand and act as if this problem doesn't exist. You can probably improvise successfully for a while, but eventually you'll have to think about how you'll manage. This problem is so knotty that you may not find a perfect—or permanent—answer, even with lots of thought, research and ingenuity.

Staying home

Probably the best solution is to stay home yourself. It's hard to concentrate at work when you're worrying about your child, and he will feel more comfortable with his mom or his dad around to take care of him. No one who's under the weather is really up for an adventure in babysitting.

Some parents—the fortunate few—belong to labor unions that have negotiated family leave in their collective agreements. Those who belong to the Canadian Auto Workers, for example, can take three days of paid leave a year for family reasons, and members of the Canadian Union of Public Employees who work for Metro Toronto can use their own sick leave to care for their ill children.[12]

Even if you have no official family leave, you can save your own sick days to use when your child is ill. In principle, we advocate telling your boss the truth—that you're staying home to care for your child—so that employers will eventually understand the very real need for family leave. But what sounds good in theory may not work in practice; and if you'll face disciplinary action or lose a day's pay, you'll have to call in sick yourself.

In any case, find out about your company's policy—and the policy of your partner's employer. Perhaps his boss will have a more enlightened attitude. Then discuss the matter thoroughly between you. If he refuses to stay home, it doesn't matter what the company's policy is.

Sitters

For many parents, staying at home for very long is totally unrealistic. One alternative is to find a babysitter. Sometimes Grandma or Aunt Sue is available, but these days they're probably working, too. If you are lucky enough to have a friend, relative or neighbor willing to pitch in occasionally, you must be prepared to return the favor, if not exactly in kind, at least in spirit. Otherwise your relationship won't survive your child's first year at daycare.

Does the daycare maintain a list of sitters? Investigate community facilities. Maybe a local senior-citizens' group has a granny to spare. Perhaps a student at the nursing school, local college or university has a free day or two in her schedule. Your clergyman may know someone who can use occasional work. As you collect names, ask for references and check them out. Then interview your candidates and let your child get to know them—again, staying with a stranger when you're sick is very unappealing. (For more information on sitters, see chapter 4, pages 28-50.)

A few community child care agencies, like Family Day Care Services in Toronto and Andrew Fleck Day Care Centre in Ottawa, which operate large family daycare programs, can—for a hefty fee—provide caregivers to their own families who need care for a sick child at home. Sometimes, too, the agency sends its clients with mildly ill children to family daycare providers who have special training, extra help and a small number of children to care for.[13]

In some cities you can pay a fee to join an agency which will provide a sitter on 24 hours' notice. Although agencies are listed under "Babysitters" or "Home Health Services" in the Yellow Pages, word of mouth is probably a better source. Ask friends with children and aging parents if they've ever used an agency. Then check them out by calling the Better Business Bureau and your local referral center. You can find the number in the front of the white pages in the emergency listings. Be sure to ask whether the agency has checked the references of its sitters, whether they're bonded and insured and whether they will give you the phone numbers of other clients who've used their services. Even if you succeed in getting a qualified sitter, this solution is far from foolproof. Agency care tends to be very expensive, and you may get a different person every time you call, even if you request a proven family favorite.

Chicken soup daycares

In the United States, a new type of sick-child care is springing up—group centers. Sometimes a special "get-well" room at the child's own daycare center, sometimes a separate sick-child's daycare with different rooms for chicken pox, stomach upsets and respiratory illness, these controversial programs are attracting Canadians' interest, but they haven't made much headway here yet. In 1987, Manitoba health authorities refused to allow a center for mildly ill children to open in Portage la Prairie, despite the fact that a registered nurse was slated to supervise it.

Other kinds of daycare

With babysitters and family caregivers, the problem is slightly different. First, children alone or in very small groups probably won't get sick so often. Second, because they care for fewer children and are more flexible, these caregivers may agree to look after a mildly ill child, a distinct plus for the child, who'll stay on his own turf with his own familiar caregiver.

But opposite these pros stand some cons: when the caregiver gets sick (or when the child is very sick or contagious), there is no daycare director to find a substitute. In agency-sponsored family daycare, the agency may find another caregiver, and family caregivers who belong to a network may keep a substitute list or help each other out in an emergency. But on occasion most parents using sitters and family daycare find themselves in exactly the same spot as families who use daycare centers. They, too, must plan for the day when the phone rings at 7 A.M. and they discover they have no child care.

Be sure to tell your caregiver—whoever he or she may be—all about your child's illness and any special treatment he requires.

PREVENTION OF ILLNESS

When he's sick all the time

If your child is frequently sick and epidemics seem to decimate the daycare regularly, the center may be handling health and hygiene matters inadequately.

When you're in the daycare, make a point of looking around carefully. Notice particularly when and how the staff and children wash their hands. It seems very boring, and sometimes it feels as if they spend half their time in the bathroom, but as we've said before, proper handwashing is absolutely crucial to daycare health.

You looked at hygiene practices and the arrangement of children and space when you were choosing a daycare. Now look at them closely again. Babies need a space of their own. All food preparation, including snacks, must be done in a different area (with a separate sink) from diaper changing and bathroom hand washing. The same staff people should not handle food and change diapers. Good staff-child ratio and small groups are imperative. Children should go outside every day. Drop in at 2:30 or 3 P.M. as nap is ending. Is your child in the right cot? Is it labeled? Does it have a clean sheet? Are the cots at least three feet apart? Are the windows open? Does the daycare actually use the office to isolate sick children, or do staff plunk them down to sleep in the middle of the playroom?

If you see that the daycare is slacking off in any of these areas, discuss the problem with the director. Perhaps a nudge from the parents will help her to tighten up the policies. The local health authorities or consultant pediatrician may welcome the opportunity to review handwashing techniques and other health practices with the staff—and even with parents, if you ask. If the director is unsympathetic, tell your parent board about your concerns.

If the problems seem unfixable—if, for example, the teacher can't wash her hands because she has too many children to care for, and the director refuses to consider augmenting the staff—find alternative care for your child immediately.

II. *ACCIDENTS AND INJURIES*

No matter what form of care you've chosen, no matter how carefully one anticipates, no matter how safe the environment, children are bound to get hurt in daycare, just as they sometimes do at home. They need to take risks and test their abilities, and the real risk-takers (and the very clumsy) seem particularly accident-prone. But safe equipment and carefully designed rules and procedures will minimize the danger for everyone.

The daycare should tell you promptly about every injury, no matter how small. No bruise, cut or bump on the head should ever come as a surprise at bath time. In the case of a very slight injury, the daycare might choose to inform you about it when you pick up your child rather than phoning you at work, but it is important for an adult to tell you exactly what happened and how. The staff should also let you know about serious accidents that befall other children. Your child may be frightened and want to discuss it with you.

RECEIVING UNWELCOME NEWS

Your heart will probably leap into your mouth any time the daycare calls. The news that your child has had an accident is especially frightening. Somehow the fantasy is always worse than the reality, and all normal concerns get thrust to the back of your mind.

As you race to your child's side, pull yourself together. It will not help him if you arrive at the daycare or hospital in a hysterical flap or a furious rage. Remember that you are going to soothe, comfort and support him, and that you may need to make tough decisions quickly. Take some deep breaths and strive for self-control.

Christine, three and a half, caught her fingers in her classroom door at the daycare center. Even with ice compresses, they began to swell and turn blue, and the director phoned her parents to explain what had happened and suggest an X ray. She offered to meet them at the hospital, but they preferred to come to the center. When Christine's father arrived, she was sitting on the director's lap with an ice pack and listening to a story. Without asking a single question, he grabbed her from the director's arms. Christine, who had finally calmed down, began to cry as soon as she saw her father's angry face. By the time they reached the outside door she was hysterical. The X ray showed a fractured finger.

It is easy to identify with this father. Frightened and concerned, he turned his anger on the daycare staff. But parents must realize that this behavior affects their child, who will take his cue directly from his parent. It also hurts the caregivers who have been doing their best to comfort and care for the child.

When you arrive, appraise the situation carefully. Professional daycare educators should provide both basic first aid and tender, loving care. Find out what happened, when and how, so that you can tell the doctor or hospital. In order to make a proper diagnosis, they need to know what happened and what has been done to control the pain, bleeding or swelling.

In case the daycare can't reach you or you can't get to the hospital as soon as you'd like, it's important to have a signed consent form that permits the hospital to begin treatment without you. At registration every daycare should ask you to sign a form containing all the information that the hospital needs.

THE OTHER CHILDREN

Bear in mind that the children who witness an accident react to it, too. Again, your behavior can frighten them to death—or help them to deal with the situation successfully.

Gregory, four, was playing on a climbing apparatus at a nearby park when he took a wrong step and fell, hitting his forehead on an iron bar on his way to the ground. To the relief of the caregivers, who were already worrying that he had knocked himself out, he began to cry immediately. Joanie, the teacher, quickly whipped out the daycare's emergency kit—mandatory equipment on all expeditions—and with an instant ice pack applied pressure to the cut to stop the bleeding. A city parapoliceman, at the site by chance, called an ambulance, and the attendants put Gregory onto a board and lifted him in. Joanie got in with him.

Scalp wounds are very dramatic; they bleed copiously. The ambulance and the board, normal procedure for head, neck and back injuries, were alarming, too. Concerned about how the other children would react, the three educators in the park explained everything step by step. The children asked a lot of questions, but because Gregory was conscious and comfortable and the bleeding had stopped, they focused on the excitement of it all—the ambulance, the sirens, the flashing lights.

Still, it seemed likely that some of them would be scared at the end of the day, when they'd had a chance to think. They would wonder, What will happen to Gregory? Will that happen to me?

Summoned to the hospital by a phone call from the daycare, Gregory's mother realized what the children might be going through. On the way home, she brought Gregory to the daycare to reassure them. He proudly showed his friends his seven stitches and told them about the ride in the ambulance. Although the caregivers discussed the incident with the children and the daycare sent the parents a short note, Gregory's mother made all the difference in their feelings about it. If your child is ever concerned about a particular child, pick up the phone and let the children talk if they'd like. Caring about others is a wonderful quality for a child to learn at daycare.

REVIEW THE EVENTS

After your child has been treated following an accident, it is important for your own peace of mind—and for the well-being of all the children in the center—to review the events surrounding it as objectively as possible. Be sure to get a written accident report. Then ask yourself why the accident occurred. Could it have been prevented? Was it a result of staff negligence or poorly maintained equipment? Was the situation handled calmly or did everyone panic? Was correct treatment administered immediately? Did the caregiver apply pressure to stop the bleeding or ice to reduce the swelling? Did she stay with your child until you arrived? Was the caregiver relaxed and able to provide the warmth and comfort that your child needed? Was your child calm and secure, despite his injury? If your child required emergency treatment at a hospital, did the daycare react quickly? Did they immediately inform you? Can the caregiver clearly explain the events that led up to the accident?

If this is not an isolated event and the daycare always seems to be rushing children to the hospital for stitches or X rays, you should investigate further. Sometimes incidents where no one is hurt bear investigation, too—for instance, when a child has been forgotten in the park. Talk to the director to find out exactly what happened (don't rely on gossip) and what is being done to eliminate hazards or reduce the frequency of incidents. If your child tells you that another child was rushed to the hospital after falling off the same slide that he did, maybe there is a problem with supervision or the actual safety of the apparatus. Again, don't hesitate to phone the child's family in order to compare situations.

Keep an eye on the proceedings at the daycare. Good supervision—meaning a good staff-child ratio and attentive caregivers—is essential at all times. Teachers have to know the children well—know their developmental stage and individual capacities. They have to teach rules for safe conduct and enforce them rigorously. The physical environment must be safe, the equipment sturdy and well maintained.

A two-year-old narrowly escaped death in July 1988 when the slide in his Mississauga daycare center fell on him; and in December 1988 a three-year-old in Dryden, Ontario, was strangled when her head got caught between the narrow bars of the climbing equipment in her daycare's play yard. If you discover that insufficient staff, inadequate supervision or poorly maintained apparatus caused the accidents at your center, act at once. Withdraw your child, but at the same time phone other parents and contact the provincial daycare office to request an inspection. Do not allow your child to return until you are certain that both premises and practices are safe. When your child's safety is at stake, you can't leave the responsibility to anyone else.

"Here! You may nurse it a bit, if you like!"
the Duchess said to Alice, flinging the baby
at her as she spoke.
LEWIS CARROLL
ALICE'S ADVENTURES IN WONDERLAND

CHAPTER 18

Parent Committees and Boards of Directors

Your daycare needs you! Like the armed forces, daycares are always recruiting volunteers. Even centers that aren't parent cooperatives believe that parents can make a vital contribution, and the experts support that view.

There are lots of good reasons to get involved in your child's daycare center, but they all have the same bottom line: your child.

The first reason is that he'll benefit directly if you're around from time to time. When you take part in his daycare life—even briefly and infrequently—his self-esteem seems to soar, says parent involvement expert Polly Greenberg. Children whose families are involved often have more motivation, aspiration and self-discipline.[1]

The second beneficiary of your participation will be the daycare (to repeat, your child). Although there is no direct research on this subject, many experts believe that involved parents make daycare better. In fact, parental involvement is one of seven key elements of high-quality daycare identified by the Task Force on Child Care.[2] The more parent involvement there is, the more accountability there is to parents, the more care conforms to parents' values and the higher its quality. A study of 431 daycare centers in Metropolitan Toronto found that those operated by parent boards were much more likely to meet government standards.[3] Belief in this connection is so strong that many provinces have written it into their daycare policy, often making it a condition for licensing or funding.

You, too, will reap rewards from participating in your child's daycare (and again, you will help your child). You will have some say over the care your child receives when you aren't there, which will give you confidence and peace of mind. You will become part of a community and make the friendships that that implies. You will have a chance to do something worth doing. And if you join the board of directors you will have a real voice—a rare opportunity for most of us, but especially for women and young people. In short, you'll garner satisfaction, support and empowerment.

We advise you to jump at the chance. It will be much harder to make yourself heard when you're face to face with the huge, entrenched bureaucracy that rules most schools.

So roll up your sleeves and dig in.

I. *WHAT CAN YOU DO?*

The list is long, and it ranges from the most basic to the extremely skilled. What you choose depends on your time, energy, interest and expertise. Remember that spending ten minutes at the daycare with your child in the morning and at night and paying close attention to his needs, reactions and development are extremely important contributions.[4] Everything we suggest here is a supplement to that—not a substitute for it!

HELP OUT AT THE DAYCARE

One possibility is to work in the daycare, either on a regular basis or when you have a spare minute. Read a story to the group when you come to eat lunch with your child. Bake bread with the children. Go with them on a field trip to the fire station. Paint a bookcase.

HELPING IN THE DAYCARE

Here are some things to do at the daycare center if you have time:

- Read to the children
- Help write stories to go with paintings
- Work with special skills, e.g., art, sewing, dance
- Bake with the children
- Help with gym equipment
- Drive on trips
- Help on trips
- Clean paint easels and tables
- Wash and scrape glue
- Tidy book shelves and take out books needing repair
- Sort blocks, puzzles
- Check dress-up clothes for tears, dirt
- Mix paint
- Wash window sills, sand toys and table tops
- Participate in special clean-up days at the center by scrubbing, painting and repairing equipment, walls, etc.

HELP FROM HOME

If your job doesn't allow you to participate so directly, you can do it from home. Take care of the guinea pig over a long weekend. Tape records, type notices, wash the sheets, make curtains.

HELPING FROM HOME

These are things that you can do from home or work:

- Act as a resource person for special projects
- Clip topical newspaper and magazine stories
- Tape records
- Tape stories
- Type notices
- Collect scrap wood
- Collect useful garbage for crafts—newspapers, toilet-paper rolls, yoghurt containers, egg cartons, shoe boxes, fabric scraps, buttons, etc.
- Contribute useful scraps from your work place (ends of paper rolls from

a printer, cardboard from a picture framer, pieces of carpet, computer paper, etc.)
- Send in plastic shopping bags
- Bake for holiday celebrations and bake sales
- Help with fund raising
- Sew doll clothes
- Mend toys, furniture, puzzles, books
- Wash paint smocks and sheets
- Photocopy notices
- Volunteer for the phone chain
- Invite a group of children to visit your work place or home
- Help to organize an out-of-daycare-hours party for children, parents and staff

IN OR OUT OF THE DAYCARE

- Share your talents, expertise and cultural celebrations by arranging special visits, bringing in special program materials and sharing ideas with your child's teacher
- Make a video of a special or an ordinary event (children love to see themselves on television)

These suggestions were made by Umbrella Central Day Care Services, Toronto, and the McGill Community Family Center, Montreal.

II. *TAKE UP THE CHALLENGE*

Or you can get involved in the actual running of the daycare center.

In a for-profit daycare, the owner holds all the decision-making power. He sets policy, and although he may invite parents to sit on a parent committee, he will always have the last word. He is accountable only to himself. In fact, parents may know very little about what goes on. One former staff member in a commercial center told us that her employer warned her never to say anything negative to a parent—not about a child, not about the program. Her job was to keep parents—the customers—happy. But even with its limitations, a parent advisory committee in a commercial center serves an important function: your involvement benefits your child.

Non-profit centers are different. Each has its own structure and its own procedures for making decisions, but the board of directors has the ultimate responsibility.

Daycares operated by a large organization like the YMCA or a community college are usually run by the organization's board of directors with the help of administrators and a parent advisory committee. These parent committees rarely handle money or do hiring and firing, but they can still deal with real concerns and bring issues to the board if they aren't satisfied.

In many non-profit centers, the board is composed of parents—either exclusively or in combination with staff and members of the community.

At first glance, sitting on a daycare board or committee may look like a piece of cake (a lot easier than getting 16 pre-schoolers on and off a city bus, for instance). The director or supervisor does all the work anyway, you think. You attend an evening meeting for a couple of hours once a month, make a few phone calls now and again, and reward yourself by feeling self-righteous.

Let us set the record straight. Sitting on a daycare board is *hard work*. But don't let that put you off. As the Michelin guide says about Mont-St-Michel, *il vaut le voyage.* In fact, sitting on a daycare board is as challenging, stimulating, frustrating and exciting a job as you'll ever find for yourself.

WHY?

The responsibility

First, being a member of the board is not an honorary position. It is an immense responsibility. The board of directors is legally charged with the management and control of the daycare center. The daycare director or supervisor handles the day-to-day operation; but she reports to the board, and the board creates the policy that she executes. It must keep communication with her open and honest, have confidence in her (as she must have in the board) and provide her with the support she needs to run the center. It is the board's responsibility to make sure that the daycare center functions as it's supposed to.

Paul Schrodt, who has been working with non-profit boards for 22 years, describes how he first came to understand this as a new member of a daycare board: "At the third meeting, when we were talking about carrying a deficit into the next year, when we were looking at laying off a staff member who'd been involved in a difficult personal incident, when we were looking at an unsuccessful fund-raising campaign meaning possible lay-offs, I suddenly realized that I was responsible for a lot."

There's a staggering amount to know and we know very little of it

Although many daycares are still friendly, little shoestring operations with just a few employees in a church hall, others are sophisticated, complex organizations with half-a-million-dollar budgets. Small centers may be easier to run than large ones, but neither kind is a picnic for amateurs, which is what youth and inexperience make most parents of young children. (Many boards include more experienced community members for exactly this reason.)

What don't we know about?

1. *Money.* The first (and second and third and...) problem most boards face is money. Daycares receive revenue not only from parental fees and their own fund-raising efforts but also from several levels of government, school boards, charitable organizations, churches, colleges and universities, hospitals and corporations. Still, most of them suffer from perpetual underfunding, turning daycare life into a constant struggle to hold body and soul together.

   In this world, people with bookkeeping, accounting and financial-management skills are as valuable as diamonds, and, sad to say, they're just as rare. All too frequently novices end up keeping track of the money, developing budgets (the key instrument of daycare policy) and planning for the future—difficult work to do competently and creatively when you don't know the basics.

2. *Personnel.* The board is an employer who first hires a director and then oversees the selection and performance of all its staff. It has responsibility for establishing and reviewing personnel policies and procedures—figuring out everything from hiring and firing to salaries, benefits and working conditions—and then seeing that they're properly carried out. Because daycare work is very demanding and very underpaid, daycare workers can be a hard group to manage—a devilishly difficult assignment for people

whose only experience with personnel matters comes from having a job themselves.

3. *The law.* There are lots of legal problems to grapple with, too: incorporation, fulfilling all the requirements of the laws that affect the daycare license, insurance, rental agreements and so on and so forth.

4. *Program.* Last, but certainly not least, the board of directors needs to know about daycare itself—which is to say, about the program, or how the children spend their days. Unfortunately, the board has so many other things to do that the program often doesn't even get onto the agenda. Janet Davis, a child care program advisor for the Toronto Board of Education who goes to dozens of daycare board meetings, says, "The percentage of time that's being spent on program-related matters is minimal."

How much confidence should parents have in their own views of what's important for children? Although they may join the board so that they can influence what goes on in the playroom, they are not experts in daycare. They probably didn't go to daycare themselves, so they have no experience to fall back on, and spending a total of 20 minutes a day dropping off and picking up a child will not turn them into authorities overnight. The director and the staff are the experts. And yet if the daycare is to meet the parents' needs, it must listen to their voices.

Emotion

This whole setup is often fraught with more emotion than logic. Because your child is so precious to you—and because you probably have strong feelings about not being with your child, about using alternate care, about wanting the best for your child—your investment in the daycare is bound to be enormous. The director and staff probably have an equally high investment. They usually choose this work because of their strong commitment to children, and they virtually subsidize the daycare's existence by accepting wages that do not remotely reflect the extent of their training and experience or the difficulty of the job.

As parents of children in daycare, you are consumers of daycare services who depend on directors and teachers to provide your children with the best possible care. As daycare board members, you are employers who set conditions of work for those same directors and teachers. If you offer them a raise that you know they deserve, you may have to increase fees—which may shred your personal budget. If you refuse to give them a raise because the parents can't afford a fee hike, they may have no choice but to hand in their notices. When the daycare director and/or staff are also board members (and they should be because they provide valuable information and insight), these conflicts of interest intensify.

With politics running rampant, a daycare center needs clear policies and procedures for resolving conflicts and dealing with complaints and grievances. It needs agreement about objectives and agreement about roles. Job descriptions are just as important for board members as they are for the director or supervisor and the staff. Again, level-headed, detached community members can help. If people use these tools, good discussions will lead to thoughtful, creative decisions, and the center will be stronger.

Turnover

To compound these problems, a daycare board member can serve only for a limited time—either the daycare bylaws or the irrepressible tendency of children to grow up will bring your term to a close just as you're finally getting the hang of it. Or—equally frustrating—you may elect to stick around for a second or third term, but newcomers join, giving the old soldiers the impression that they're reinventing the wheel. New boards, with different points of view, may attempt to throw out tried-and-true procedures or rewrite philosophies. Orienting new members and staying on track take planning and time as well as a concise handbook and minutes of the previous year's meetings.

JOIN THE BOARD AND SEE THE WORLD

Now that you know what you're getting yourself into, we urge you to take on this mission. Even in a profit center or in a non-profit organization where parents "advise" the owner or the board and don't have much power, it will be good for your child, good for the daycare and good for you. It will probably also be fun, if you can believe that!

What qualities do you need to be a good board member?

1. *Time.* It helps to have some time—a commodity that full-time working parents of young children just don't have. How much time is hard to pinpoint. At a bare minimum, you'll have to attend

monthly meetings, but various projects will doubtless crop up along the way. If you become a board officer, you'll have extra responsibilities, of course. Think in terms of staying at least two years so that you'll know what you're doing by the time you leave. If you're already involved in other organizations outside of work, forget it.

2. *Expertise.* Of course it's great if you have expertise in one of the areas we mentioned earlier: finance, law, personnel or education. If you do, your daycare definitely needs you. But anyone can become more knowledgeable in at least one area—daycare itself.

To a degree, every parent is a monitor of the daycare almost automatically, but a board member has to bring this reflexive action into the realm of the conscious. It is part of the commitment of being a board member.

Talk to the director and the teachers—the professionals who really *are* experts. Ask them questions about their work. Do some research on your own—read books and articles about child development and daycare and share them with your fellow board members. Review the checklist questionnaires (pages 182-206) from time to time—those questions are always applicable and provide good guidelines to high-quality daycare. Keep an eye on things when you come in the morning and evening. If a doctor's appointment brings you to the center at an unusual hour, have a look around. Is the staff who greeted your child so warmly in the morning still treating the children with care and patience?

As you read, listen and watch, you will understand more about what is supposed to take place in a first-rate daycare, and you will gain confidence in your own judgment. You will also gain the respect of the professionals whose world you are entering. Then when you see things that make you uncomfortable—caregivers standing in a clump in the playground; children being punished because they have nothing to do but find ways to get into trouble—you will speak from knowledge, and your views will carry more weight. Taking the responsibility along with the job will enable you to make informed decisions.

3. *Reliability.* A board member should be reliable—a person who always comes to meetings and phones the people she promises to phone. Paul Schrodt calls this "everyday heroics...a person who can make things happen in the way that organizations get things done, which is bit by bit."

4. *Enthusiasm.* Being enthusiastic is equally essential. Says Schrodt, "You can't live in these organizations without enthusiasm." New parents in the daycare and parents of infants and toddlers—who are always very interested in everything that goes on at the daycare—are, therefore, prime board material.

5. *Diversity.* A board needs as much diversity as it can muster. It should have parents from each group of children, parents from single- and two-parent families, members of different ethnic, religious and economic groups, people from different neighborhoods and people from different departments in a work-place center.

6. *The ability to see the whole picture.* But once you join the board, you have to put your special interest aside and look at the interests of the organization as a whole. What you think is good for your child may not necessarily be right for the rest of the daycare. If the supervisor wants to switch your child's favorite teacher to another group, can you listen to her arguments with an open mind and base your judgment on the welfare of all the children? Can you make a decision that will be best for the daycare at large and believe, therefore, that it will be best for your child? A person who can see the right and fair thing for everyone makes an invaluable contribution.

7. *Common sense.* Because the board has so much work to do and the possibility of conflagration is so great, you must be able to keep your feet on the ground, to think clearly and to deal honestly and openly with your fellow board members, the executive director and the staff. People on personal power trips can wreak havoc in a daycare center.

8. *Discretion.* Discretion is another important quality. As a member of the board, you will become privy to the daycare's problems, like a drop in staff morale or a desperate financial situation. Talking about them can start rumors, lead to a loss of confidence and make matters considerably worse. When you learn that your child's teacher will be going on maternity leave in three months, you cannot run home and tell your child in order to prepare her for this event. You must wait, like any other parent, for your child to learn the news in the way that the teacher and supervisor have planned.

9. *Appreciation.* Besides making a contribution yourself, it's great to be able to see other people's contributions and express your thanks and appreciation to them directly. When a board member brings

in a thorough and practical report on recycling at the center or the director handles a difficult personnel problem with great tact and diplomacy, tell her what a wonderful job she did. That builds relationships, increases communication and gives everyone a bit more courage to continue the fight.

HOW DOES THE BOARD WORK?

Every year, non-profit centers hold at least one meeting, called the annual general meeting or annual general assembly, for all the members of the organization—that is, the parents plus any other people the bylaws define as members. Electing the new board of directors is an important item on the agenda. In many daycares, a nominating committee presents candidates it has chosen for the membership's consideration or encourages people to nominate themselves; in others, parents volunteer or are nominated on the spot. (Either way, the candidates have presumably thought the matter over before declaring their intention to run.)

Ask the director how you can be a candidate. Nominees will probably introduce themselves and talk about what they have to offer the daycare board. Then the members vote, selecting as many board members as the bylaws specify. The board will elect its own officers and committee heads and hold orientation sessions for new members.

What happens at the regular meetings?

The board has an agenda, distributed ahead of time so that members know what they'll discuss. They approve minutes of the previous meeting (which should then be posted for everyone in the daycare to read), hear and approve reports from the director and their various committees (the finance committee will bring everyone up to date on the state of the treasury), discuss issues, make decisions and form policy based on their reports and discussion.

They will probably use a very relaxed form of parliamentary procedure, and they'll certainly try to maintain focus on the important matters, always keeping the philosophy and objectives of the daycare at the front of their minds. Hopefully everyone will have an equal chance to speak—the chairman may set time limits or allocate turns—and the process will be thoroughly democratic.

Committees

Committees do a lot of the board's work. Appointed by the board, they make recommendations to it, but they don't have any power of their own. Standing or permanent committees are in charge of one special area. Daycares commonly establish standing committees for finance, personnel, program, nominations, fund raising, advocacy, health and nutrition, public relations and environment. The board also creates ad hoc committees to deal with a specific task, like working out a policy on the use of videos at the center. Once an ad hoc committee presents its report to the board, its job is done, and the committee dissolves.

Joining a committee is an excellent way to get your feet wet. Committee members needn't be members of the board—you can volunteer your services for just a short time and see how it all works. A committee may allow you to make the best use of your talents; a nurse is an ideal member for a committee that's revising the center's health policies.

Having a say

What if you're not on the board and you want to make a suggestion or a complaint or express your views on an issue before the board? Understanding what a large commitment the board is, you might well choose not to be on it. But that doesn't mean that you can't have your say. Suppose the center is going on a field trip to a nearby farm, and the children will travel on a bus without seat belts. You are upset. You think that the daycare shouldn't go if the bus has no seat belts, and you take your concerns to the director. She believes that it's important for the children to have field trips, and in your community no bus is equipped with seat belts. Furthermore, the center has no seat-belt policy. But you are not convinced, and you think the issue is too important to drop.

No doubt your immediate instinct is to talk to the first parent you meet at the cubbies that night. While you're collecting sweaters and art work, you tell her what's happening and what you think about it. But you're not sure what to do next.

Every daycare should have a policy and a procedure (carefully described in the parent handbook) for dealing with these situations. A parent should have the right to go to the board, but he must use proper channels. Depending on the issue, it will probably entail talking first to the educator involved, then to the director and making a serious, honest attempt to work matters out. Some daycares have a parent liaison, usually the chattiest person in the center, whose job is to talk to parents regularly about their concerns and bring them to the board when necessary.

Going to the board is a last resort, to be used sparingly indeed, because it undermines the director's respect and authority, so crucial to her ability to run the center.

Although many boards hold open meetings that anyone can attend, don't just show up and expect to be heard. Speak to the chairman of the board about putting an item on the agenda. She might ask you to write a letter expressing your concerns. If you would like to be present during the board's discussion—a good idea if you want them to take you seriously—say so. The board will discuss the issue and eventually make a decision. In this case, they might postpone the trip, create an ad hoc committee to formulate a seat-belt policy and name you as chairperson! Of course, you have no vote. You will have to accept the board's decision, whether you agree with it or not.

Need some help?

Because each daycare is an independent institution that works in isolation, a board may find it hard to get help when it's having a problem or when it wants to know other ways to handle a particular issue. In some cities, the daycare information and referral center can suggest resources. The provincial daycare authority or your university's school of commerce or business administration may well know of management experts who are available as consultants. The Toronto Board of Education offers its daycare boards the services of a program advisor.

But for those who don't have access to these specialists, we heartily recommend the *Child Care Board of Directors' Handbook*, published by the Ontario Coalition for Better Child Care. You can order it from them at 297 St. George Street, Toronto, Ontario M5R 2P8, (416) 324-9080. It's free to members of the Coalition. For non-members the cost is approximately 50 dollars, well worth the price.

Umbrella Central Day Care Services, 361 Danforth Avenue, Toronto, Ontario M4K 1P2, (416) 461-0958, has also published a manual for daycare boards called *Umbrella Board Manual.*

She had two children that were like two
rose-bushes; one was called Snow-white and
the other Rose-red.
"SNOW-WHITE AND ROSE-RED"

CHAPTER 19

The Second Child

If you've gone through seven sitters and lost 38 days of work in your first two years of parenthood, you are probably not in the mood to add to your responsibilities at the moment.

On the other hand, if you're pleased with your daycare arrangement—whether center, sitter, nanny or family daycare—you may have the courage to think about having another baby.

Of course, wonderful daycare is not in itself a sufficient reason to have another child. But if the other factors point towards this decision (or if they don't but you find that another's on the way anyway), what does this mean? How in the world does a family manage daycare for two children?

GOING BACK TO SQUARE ONE

You are back at square one. Will you make all the same choices that you made the first time?

Money matters

Daycare for two children costs the moon. Infant care in a daycare center is even more expensive than care for toddlers or pre-schoolers. Some centers give a discount for the second child, some don't. Family care may be cheaper, but for two children the total is going to be sky high all the same. If your income is modest, now that you have a second child you may be able to get a subsidy for either center or agency-sponsored family care. Ironically, a sitter, a solution that seemed outrageously expensive for one child, looks like a bargain for two—provided you can find a Mary Poppins.

From a financial point of view, is it worthwhile for you to go back to work? How will you feel about putting a hefty chunk of your income into child care? Would it make more sense for you to stay home with the children yourself and manage on less money?

By all means go to your employer, your union and your local Employment and Immigration Canada office to check out the current maternity rules and benefits. New company policies, collective agreements and legislation may entitle you to more leave and/or more money than you collected last time.

But at the end of the day, most of us need whatever income we bring home to buy diapers and food or to pay off the mortgage and indulge ourselves with an occasional evening at the movies. The demands of the job or of the psyche may exert as much pressure as the demands of the pocketbook.

Therefore, when your maternity leave is over, or soon thereafter, you will probably be going back to work.

Who is this second child?

If you stayed at home for an extended period with your first child, you may feel that you must somehow do the same with your second—that you owe them the identical start in life.

This is an easy trap to fall into. Of course you want to give your second child the best possible beginning, just as you did your first, but it's impossible to replicate the experience. Both you and your partner are different people now than you were when you were brand-new parents—your own relationship has evolved, your attitudes towards child rearing have changed, and you're at different stages in your careers. Your only child is becoming an older sibling, altering the family chemistry with explosive force.

Furthermore, this child is a different person from the first. His behavior will be different, his needs and demands will be different, and your responses to him will be different, too. You will give him what *he* needs, not what some abstract "second child" requires. One corollary of this state of affairs is that what's good for Liz isn't necessarily good for Janice. If you can accept these facts at the outset and deal with this new baby as an individual, unique unto himself, you will save yourself a lot of trouble.

While you're pregnant, you'll probably have some hints about the newcomer's personality from his behavior *in utero*—from his constant somersaults or his peaceful response to Bach. Unfortunately, you have to make the crucial decisions about child care before you know him well. But we urge you to keep as many options open as long as you can to enable you to treat your child as an individual human being.

Some children, social beings from birth, thrive in groups at a very young age. Others, shy or wary of strangers, desperately crave the security of a single caregiver. Your child—and consequently everyone else in the family—will be much happier if you don't try to force a square peg into a round hole. If the option you've selected looks wrong, all wrong, for your child, be prepared to junk it and find a better one.

MAKING COMPROMISES

If you work in a place that has infant care or if your older child's daycare center has an infant program, sign the baby up right now, before you read another word. Every minute counts. Even though siblings usually have priority, a delay of a day or two at this stage can mean a wait of several months when both you and the baby are ready to go. If you think you'll need a subsidy, call the subsidy office. The lineup there never gets shorter.

But most people just aren't in a position to make any phone calls right away. If you have a babysitter who's great for a three-year-old but can't handle infants, if your two-and-a-half-year-old is supposed to start daycare in the fall, if your daycare center doesn't have infant care, you really have to sit down and think about the situation.

Welcome to Compromise City. Child care for more than one child involves compromises. It is practically impossible to hit upon a solution that doesn't sacrifice someone or something. The sacrifice may be large or small, and it's a good idea to know exactly what you're giving up and what you're getting in return.

Here the question of the adult's interest versus the child's interest rears its ugly head. With two children in the household, time becomes a scarce and precious commodity. A day can't possibly hold all that needs to be stuffed into it, and the mother is usually the one left holding the laundry bag, the shopping bag and the garbage bag.

Remember that your children aren't the only people in the family to consider. You have needs, too. If the choices that suit them are so inconvenient and exhausting for you that you'll have no energy left for job or family, the price isn't worth it. Do what works, and try not to feel guilty about it. Everyone will be better off in the end.

THE OLDER CHILD

Should your older child stay where he is?
It all depends. In theory, if your older child is happily ensconced in a daycare center or family daycare, it's probably a good idea to leave him where he is. Life is going to be pretty turbulent once this intruder comes to live in his house, and he will be much more cheerful if he can escape to the familiar, stable world of the daycare for part of the time. He can continue to get the stimulation of being with his peers and receiving care that is appropriate for his age. And if he doesn't spend all his waking hours with the baby, he may tolerate him much better when they're together at home.

Leaving him with the same sitter or nanny you have now
If he's been at home with a sitter or nanny, leaving him there and adding the baby to the equation is much trickier. In a daycare center or family daycare, he is used to sharing his caregivers. But at home, he has always had his sitter all to himself. Here he'll be forced to share what he considers his very own.

Children respond to this challenge in different ways. Some are proud, some are overprotective, some look for opportunities to commit murder. Because the sitter doesn't nurse the baby and isn't his mother, he may accept the baby's presence relatively calmly—until he starts crawling and butting in. (He probably won't want to wait until his brother is napping to play with his tiny Lego pieces.) To make this arrangement work, your sitter or nanny must be a very special person who really understands what's happening and won't use the baby as an excuse—someone who's willing to let the baby nap in the stroller and thereby give up the only peaceful time in her day in order to take the older child to the playground.

Should you change your older child's daycare arrangements?

A change of any kind—to be at home with a sitter, nanny or grand-mother or to go to a family daycare or a daycare center that will accept both children—will add stress to your older child's life at a time when he already has his fair share. It is very hard to manage so many changes at once, and he may blame the baby for the switch.

Moving him to be with the baby and a sitter at home will give him an immersion course in dealing with the newcomer. His emotions won't be so diluted, and he may come to terms with them (and the baby) more quickly if he doesn't kill him first—and if the sitter handles the situation well. He may resent his changed circumstances and miss his friends, teachers and activities at the daycare center or family daycare home, especially if the sitter can't take him out "because the baby is sleeping" or "the baby is hungry." Although he'll pitch in and help if he's given half a chance, he'll find life relatively boring. A baby just can't *do* very much.

On the other hand, if he's been at home with grandma or a sitter but is reaching the age when he will benefit from contact with other children, it may be time for a change. If the baby weren't on its way, you might have decided to send him to daycare or pre-school. If you can manage it, we'd advise you to go ahead as you'd planned, with one proviso: beware of your timing. To keep him from feeling displaced by the baby, make sure he starts at least a couple of months before the baby's due date. This is also a period in which you may have the time to settle him in nicely.

THE YOUNGER CHILD

When your first child was born, you no doubt thought long and hard about infant care. Your daycare experiences may have changed your ideas, but this problem—and its solutions—are old friends. Your baby's emerging personality may alter the picture slightly, but you probably know exactly what you'd do if you could afford it, and you know what feels comfortable and what works for you. It's important to hold onto this picture as you enter the next round of the search for daycare. Then you will know which compromises you can live with. If you haven't found child care that pleases you, use this opportunity to think about what's wrong and try to fix it.

THE SOLUTIONS

We've talked about the older and the younger child. There are so many possibilities—so many combinations and permutations. What are the advantages and disadvantages of each? Which one will work best for the whole family?

Two children in a daycare center

Your older child is blissfully happy in a daycare center that also accepts infants. What are the advantages of putting your little one there, too?

First, you know the center well, and you know that it is a good one. Since you chose it, you probably agree with the philosophy and the way it's implemented. You're familiar with the routine, and you know the director and the teachers. If your older child went there as an infant, the same infant caregivers may still be there. If your child began as a toddler or a pre-schooler, try to get to know the infant-room staff a little during your pregnancy. If you like what you're seeing, you will have confidence that this center can give your baby good care.

Second, if your older child loves his daycare, he can stay where he is content. Although there is turmoil all around him at home, this part of his life will be an oasis where he does not have to compete with his baby. Each of your two children will have his own space, teachers and friends.

Because they will be at the same center, they will have the possibility of seeing each other from time to time. At Gare de Rires, the daycare center attached to CN in Montreal, some infants go outside to play with the toddlers while others sleep. At the Queen Street Childcare Centre in Toronto, open visiting between the rooms allows Carol to keep an eye on her little sister Allegra and to comfort her when she's sad. A younger sibling who regularly goes with you to deliver and collect his brother or sister feels comfortable in the center before he begins himself.

There are practical advantages, too. Usually the second child doesn't have to go to the end of a very long waiting list at his sibling's daycare—he can skip almost to the top and get a place months (or even years) earlier than a non-sibling who signs up on the same day.

Having both children in the same center simplifies life and cuts travel time and pressure, freeing several hours in the week for the family to spend together. It also means that both children spend about the same amount of time away from their parents. Because geography compels Renée to pick up two-year-old Michael first, four-month-old Derek spends ten hours a day with the family caregiver. Renée dreams of the day when Derek attends Michael's daycare and both boys stay just eight and a half hours. Then she can avoid rush-hour traffic on the expressway by spending half an hour with them in a downtown park before trekking home.

What are the disadvantages of sending the second child to the first one's daycare? As we've already mentioned, having two children in a daycare center can bankrupt just about any family, especially if you fall into the category that just misses being eligible for financial assistance.

With two children at the center, you'll have double the logistical problems. There will be two sets of caregivers to talk to and two daily sheets or logbooks to check. Whom do you dress first? Does the toddler sweat in his snowsuit while you get the baby bundled, or does the baby develop a heat rash while the toddler struggles to dress himself? If you're nursing and the baby is hungry, what do you do with your exhausted pre-schooler? (Come equipped with carrots, juice, etc., for the older one.)

How will your older child feel about sharing his daycare with his little brother or sister? He'll probably be immensely proud—though he may worry about his baby and do his best to protect him from everyone and everything in sight. Even if he resents this invasion of his territory, he will react with less intensity than he would at home. He is merely sharing his roof, not his caregiver or his friends.

Two children with a babysitter

Many Canadians with two small children have a babysitter. In fact, the Task Force on Child Care reported that parents make more effort to arrange for child care by a non-relative in the family home if they have two or more young children needing care.[1]

Whether you already have a gem of a sitter or you're going out to look for one now, this arrangement offers some very practical pluses.

As we mentioned earlier, a sitter for two children suddenly looks economical, especially if the person can do some light housekeeping and laundry or prepare the evening meal. A sitter saves time and effort—you need not dress, transport and undress two offspring every morning and every evening. The chances are that one child is now verbal enough to tell you what happens when you aren't there, allowing you to supervise more closely. And although two children double the frequency of colds, ear infections and flu (and they never seem to be sick at the same time), with a sitter you'll have built-in backup care.

What problems will a sitter have with two children? We have already hinted at some of them. You know all too well how hard it is to stretch yourself in two directions and care for two people with totally different needs. Your sitter has to be game enough to make this effort in your stead. Can a grandmotherly type who loves babies cope with the endless questions and rocketing energy of a three-year-old? Caregivers who adore babies may park an older child in front of the television. Will she provide him with educational activities, take him to the park and bring him together with other children his own age on a regular basis? Being at home with a sitter can be a total disaster for an older child and a painful letdown for one who's accustomed to the daily stimulation of a top-quality daycare center. On the other hand, a sitter who really enjoys pre-schoolers may lose patience with the baby and let him stay in his crib too long and too often.

You will also want your sitter to deal with your two children the same way you do. If you encourage them to settle their own disputes, you won't want your sitter to resolve the problem by taking away the dump truck or insisting that your four-year-old kiss the 18-month-old brother who just tore up his painting. And, of course, you won't want her to compare them and tell two-year-old Joanna to finish her lunch as nicely as her older sister did. Will your sitter be able to treat them as individuals, each with his own infuriating and endearing characteristics?

And sitters quit far too often. A special person who can understand and respond to the individual needs of an infant and toddler or pre-schooler is hard to find even once. Twice is almost impossible. How flexible is your job? With one child you can call a friend or grandma to stand in for a few days until you find a new sitter, but when two children are involved, these understudies mysteriously disappear.

You'll find more about sitters in chapter 4.

Two children in family daycare

Family daycare for both children is a kind of hybrid of sitter and daycare-center care, with the assets and liabilities of both. (For a fuller rundown of these, please see chapter 5.) Though she may be more expensive than a sitter because you pay per child, a family daycare provider may charge less than a daycare center, and she may offer a discount for two children. If your older child is there already, he can stay where he's comfortable, and because the daycare provider knows you, she will probably make an effort to find a space for your baby as soon as possible. Then there is the distinct convenience of having both children in the same place.

Again, you'll need a caregiver who can cater to several ages and personalities at once and who will deal with your two different children your way. In a family daycare, your older child will probably have friends and peers; and he'll have his younger brother or sister, too, meaning he'll have his own little competitor—pest and worshipper at once—to haunt and hug him 24 hours a day.

Combinations

Another possibility is a combination of different kinds of care, like leaving your older child in daycare and finding a babysitter or family daycare home for the baby. Although this is an expensive solution, it is practical if your child's daycare does not have an infant program or if you prefer to keep your baby in a home-like setting for the first 12 to 24 months. The older child can enjoy his playmates while the baby gets his own special caregiver. A sitter can also care for the older child when he is too sick to go to daycare, an important point if your boss doesn't approve of sick days for child care. Either a sitter or a family daycare provider can provide a safe haven for a school-age child to return to after the school bell rings. From a secure base in his own neighborhood, he can do his homework, go to the playground or hockey rink and visit his friends.

You might arrange for your older child to attend a half-day preschool program and spend the rest of the day with the baby and the sitter or family daycare provider. This solution has the same advantages as the previous combination and it is less expensive, but it has some drawbacks, too. Although your children will have a chance to be together, again babysitters who are brilliant with infants are not necessarily interested in providing exciting activities for a toddler or pre-schooler. (When you're looking for family care, notice whether the provider seems equally interested in children of all ages.) If the pre-school isn't within easy walking distance, you'll have to depend on a car pool, school bus or taxi service to take your child back and forth—always a slightly unreliable and sometimes expensive arrangement. And of course, if your older child is in a new setting, he'll have to settle into a different routine and find new friends.

If your firstborn is attending a daycare near your home, but there is a daycare center with excellent infant care at your work place, you may decide to leave the older one where he is and bring the infant to your work-place center so that you can continue to breast-feed, spend extra time with him during your lunch break and pick him up early. The major objection to this scheme is cost.

Twins

Child care for twins or triplets is even harder to find than child care for ordinary siblings. A sitter is far and away the thriftiest solution, but caregivers who'll treat your two children as individuals are hard to find. If that's important to you—and if you can afford it—daycare is probably your best option. In a group they will be just two children among many, each child an individual, and they can forget they're twins for a while. Two different daycares present terrible logistical hassles, so look into the possibility of a daycare with multi-aged groupings or two groups the same age so that each child can have his own teacher and friends. Another solution is a daycare that allows great freedom of choice and movement so that the two of them can select their own activities and friends and separate during the day if they want to.

SELECTING A DAYCARE CENTER FOR YOUR SECOND CHILD

If your older child has graduated from daycare and you haven't visited his center for a while, or if your younger child will be starting daycare much earlier than your first one did, be prepared to expend as much effort and care in the search as you did the first time around. Your previous experience in making the right choice will help, but life is a dynamic process, and your needs and values might have changed in the meantime. The center may have changed, too, especially if it has a new director.

Even if you already know and love a center, reread the infant section of chapter 11 (pages 140-157) and visit the daycare's infant rooms with the checklist in hand. Some centers provide superb infant-toddler care and only mediocre pre-school care; others have first-rate three- to five-year-old programs and unacceptable infant rooms.

You'll want to ask the director or supervisor how much your two children will see one another. Being in the same building doesn't guarantee they'll be together. What is the center's philosophy about siblings? Do they actively encourage them to have a special relationship? Do they deliberately separate them? Which do you prefer? Are the older ones allowed to visit the infant room? Under what circumstances?

SETTLING INTO DAYCARE FOR TWO

When should you tell your older child's teachers about your pregnancy?

Once you tell your child about the baby, the whole daycare center will know: the next day he'll run in shouting, "I'm going to have a baby!" At the first opportunity, be sure to tell the director and caregivers about the pregnancy yourself—let them know when the baby is due and how the older one is taking the news. Outwardly he'll be thrilled about 90 percent of the time—having a baby is almost as exciting as getting a puppy. But inside he may be feeling uncertain, and as the day of arrival draws closer he won't know quite what he's feeling. He may not share the way he used to, and he may burst into tears at the drop of a hat. The daycare staff will be able to help him through the next few months by watching for changes in behavior and giving him extra loving attention.

When you're at home on maternity leave, should your older child go to daycare or stay at home?

At first glance, you could construe this as a parenting question, but in fact it is strategic. A space in a high-quality daycare center or family daycare home is worth its weight in gold, and if your child is happily established in one, you must guard it with your life. Daycare centers usually do not give maternity leave to children—they can't spare 15 weeks of revenue (let alone 25), and it's not in anyone's best interest to put a substitute child in that spot until your child returns. There-fore, if you want your child to stay at his center or family daycare home, you will probably have to continue to pay for his space, even if he will be at home once the baby arrives.

The alternative is to talk to your director or caregiver as soon as you're pregnant. Ask her what will happen if you withdraw your child during your maternity leave. If you put him on the waiting list now, will there be a space when you're ready to return to work? Will he have priority? The director will advise you according to the admissions policy and the state of the waiting list. By using this tactic, you will save some money, but there is no guarantee that there will be room for your child when your leave is up, and you may find yourself relying on ingenuity for a few months. (Of course, the arrangements you make for your baby will figure prominently in this decision. With a sitter or nanny at home you'll have more flexibility.)

If you're receiving a subsidy, call your subsidy office to find out what happens to your financial assistance while you're off work. In some provinces—Ontario, for example—your subsidy stops when you go on maternity leave, and you'll have to reapply for both a subsidy and daycare. With this unpleasant fact in mind, put your name back on the lists the minute you get the results of your pregnancy test. Again, hopefully you'll have some priority. In other provinces, like Quebec, maternity leave doesn't affect your subsidy at all.

Once you've dealt with the logistics, you can focus on parenting matters. If it's important to you to create a sense of family warmth and unity, you might want to keep your older one at home with you for some or all of your leave. If the baby cries all night and you desperately need to sleep, you might want to send your older child to daycare.

In general, however, extremes bring problems. If your child stays at home too long, he may have difficulty separating from you when he goes back. If he knows that you're at home with the baby all day and he's never allowed to join you, he may feel very angry, jealous and left out. Try to compensate in some way. Make his day at the center shorter, and do something special with him when he comes home so that he isn't just fitting into the baby's routines.

Take your cue from your child if you can. When Gabrielle's mother came home from the hospital with Gabrielle's baby sister, she thought Gabrielle would stay at home with them for a few days. But at 6 A.M. the next day, the three-year-old was up, dressed and ready to go to daycare, eager to show all her friends the baby's hospital photo. Because she wanted to go so much, her parents acquiesced.

Bringing the baby to daycare

Children love it when their parents come to pick them up with their baby in tow. Anthony got angry if his mom came to get him without his baby brother, who, as a result, practically grew up in the daycare center. (The babies love coming, by the way—if they're awake, they find the children and the activity all very exciting.) Unless your older child requests otherwise, make the effort to bring the baby, even when it's very cold. Because a baby's needs are so much greater than a toddler's or a pre-schooler's, home is an environment where your older child always has to bend over backwards for the baby. When you bring the baby to daycare, you're doing the reverse—fitting the baby into the older one's life. It's the same idea as your sitting in the daycare at the end of the day and giving him a chance to show off his world—his friends, his achievements.

Will the older child feel dethroned by the baby? Not likely. In fact, he will probably end up on a bigger throne because his baby is there. Having a little brother or sister is a very common experience for children of this age—many of them have a baby in the family, and your child wants one, too. He also longs to display him proudly to his friends the same way his friends displayed their babies. The other children will be interested, but only for a limited time. The teachers, who are trained professionals, should know how to give attention to the baby through the older child. Comments like, "What a beautiful baby you have," "Does he cry a lot at home?" "I bet the first person he smiles at is you," and "Do you help Mommy take care of him?" all make the child feel prouder.

Even daycares in schools, churches and office buildings strive to create a homelike atmosphere for the children in their care, and that means that the whole family is part of the daycare experience. Everyone should be welcome, including the baby. He is part of life, not an embarrassment or a disruption.

Incidentally, younger siblings are just as proud of their big brothers and sisters. They talk about them at daycare all the time. During an art activity, Donald brags that his older brother can draw beautiful circles with his eyes closed; when Joelle sees Sam wearing a baseball cap, she pipes up, "My brother plays baseball." It's important for them, too, to share their families with everyone in the daycare, and they're thrilled beyond belief on those rare occasions when the older one appears in person.

Preparing to go to daycare together

If you always bring the baby with you when you deliver and collect your older child, they will be ready to go together to the daycare center or the family daycare when the time comes. It will be an organic process—the little one will already know the place, and the older one will be used to having the little one there.

Tell the older child about your plans as soon as you make your decision: "Charlie will come to daycare with you when he's old enough to use a bottle" (or "...to hold up his head," or "...after Christmas"— choose a concrete event that makes sense in child's time, rather than an abstract concept like a month).

Integrate the older one into the little one's world. Perhaps you can take him to visit the infant room, and together you can see what the babies do all day—where they sleep, how they eat, which toys they play with. Ask him about his baby: "Which toy do you think he'll like?" If he was an infant there himself, ask him about the toys he liked best. He won't remember, but he'll be sure to pick out something to show you. Maybe he can meet the infants' teachers "so that they'll know who you are when you visit Charlie."

The more natural things are, the easier the transition will be. If you have conflicting feelings about sending him, the older one might have conflicting feelings; if you're comfortable about bringing your younger one there, your older one will be comfortable, too.

What about you in all this?

Because two children create far more work than one, life will be harder and much more hectic—the enlarged family will require everyone to readjust. Each of us is different, and we all have different feelings. You might feel guilty about your older child; you might feel guilty about your younger one. You might even feel guilty about them both. Relax and ride with it if you can.

Amazingly enough, some people find it easier than they did with their first to let go of the baby and get back to work— somehow they've learned to live with their situation. Says Renée, "I've learned to accept that I have to go to work. I didn't marry a millionaire, and there isn't enough money to go around if I don't work." But along with this acceptance comes an enhanced sense of freedom. As Renée puts it, "I was stuck inside all winter with two kids who were on opposite schedules. I really enjoy them, but I love going to work and meeting adults. Right now the only time I have to myself is my lunch hour, and I love it."

But many people aren't so serene. They feel just as protective about the second child as they did about the first. Part of the difference lies in the baby himself—some babies are going to walk away from you no matter how hard you hold on, and others beg you to cuddle them forever. Your relationship with your partner and your relationship with your older child influence these feelings, too. But by now you know yourself better as a parent, and you have more confidence in your own ability to function in this important role. You know more of what's important to you, what works for you and how to go about getting it. Though you and your children will continue to change and grow, you've come a long way down the working-parent road.

"Dear, dear! How queer everything is today!
And yesterday things went on just as usual.
I wonder if I've been changed in the night?"
LEWIS CARROLL
ALICE'S ADVENTURES IN WONDERLAND

CHAPTER 20

Switching Daycare

Once you've settled your child into daycare, you'd like to think he'll stay there forever—or at least until kindergarten.

Believe it or not, this is rarely the case. Among them, our four children had a grand total of 16 different child care arrangements in their first five years: seven sitters, three pre-schools, one family daycare home and five daycare centers, an average of four per child. Studies that have followed children over a period of time have found that about half of them changed to a new care arrangement within one year, and 30 percent changed within six months.[1]

At some time in your child's daycare career, you, too, will probably contemplate a switch. You may embrace it willingly or have it foisted upon you, but change you will.

LETTING GO

It is very difficult to reach this point. You selected your daycare arrangement, usually after careful thinking and searching. You have a lot of your own ego in it—after all, you're an adult capable of making sound judgments, and you tend to think of yourself as an exemplary parent. Lulling yourself into believing that everything is satisfactory is much easier than shedding illusions. Admitting that your daycare isn't perfect is a little step; admitting that it isn't working for your child is a giant one. It requires great courage and open-mindedness to let go.

Is change traumatic?

You also worry that changing daycare will harm your child. You picture him totally upset and disrupted, and you know it will take weeks of effort to get him resettled. The result is that you play head games with yourself trying to figure out which is worse, the daycare arrangement or the change.

It's a little like deciding to buy a car. You know your old car well. You recognize its every knock and jiggle, and you have complete confidence in your ability to assess its mechanical strength, even if you're not sure whether it'll get you from A to B. But behind the wheel of another car, you're driving a total stranger. You don't know what its glitches are. Before you take it for a long drive, you don't know whether to check the water in the radiator or the connections to the battery. You're on the road without a map. Even though the old car was in far worse condition, there was comfort in knowing its problems.

What do the experts say?

This is a terrible dilemma, and the child development experts don't help much. Research on the topic has produced some very fuzzy answers.[2] On the one hand, some studies say that forming a secure attachment is a most important task for a young child[3] and that children learn better from a person they love.[4] Loss of a caregiver is very painful,[5] and having too many caregivers creates stress, puts children at risk for social and emotional problems, and in general leads them to distrust human contact.[6] Fredelle Maynard sums up this point of view, "Changing a daycare arrangement is so stressful for the child that you should explore all possibilities for improvement before deciding that this one won't work."[7]

Other experts regard children as more resilient and change as normal and inevitable.[8] They conclude that there is no relationship between change and social competence, that children have the ability to attach to more than one person and that change "can have

positive benefits by providing variety and enrichment...."[9] Daycare
expert Alison Clarke-Stewart says, "Staying with a poor caregiver is
undoubtedly worse for the child than changing to a good one."[10]

In the face of these monumental contradictions, how is a mere
parent to make up his or her mind?

Because fooling yourself is so easy, you have to look at the situation very carefully and very hard. Of course you're going to be nervous.
Constant change *isn't* good, but constant personal compromise is
worse. It hurts the soul—both yours and your child's.

Is it worth it?

But, you say to yourself with despair, I don't want to go through that
whole exhausting, time-consuming process of looking for daycare all
over again. I'm working full-time and how can I possibly fit it in?
Besides, in the end I probably won't find anything better, so why
bother?

If you sense this nihilistic thinking creeping in, take a deep breath
and try to throw it off. "You're never completely locked in," says one
mother who placed her child in three different daycares trying to find one
that met his needs. "Your options might not be exactly what you want,
but you're never, ever stuck." It may be hard work to find a better alternative, but when you see the change in your child, it will be worth it.

I. *NON-URGENT CHANGE*

The reasons for changing daycare are legion, but in general they fall
into two categories: non-urgent and urgent. Later in this chapter we
will help you to recognize and handle an emergency. But first, let's
consider garden-variety change—the kind most of us encounter.

WHEN DO WE THINK OF CHANGE?

Sometimes we're the victims of circumstance. Your sitter or nanny
quits without notice; you're offered a job you can't refuse in another
city; you or your husband gets laid off, rendering your daycare and
your budget incompatible; you and your partner separate, and you
need a subsidized daycare space to survive on a single income.

You may also change daycares or sitters for reasons of convenience. Someone who is marvelous with the children may prove to be
totally unreliable about time, making a hash of your own workday. A

space may open up in a daycare center much nearer your work or home. You may have so much trouble getting backup care when your child is sick that you decide a sitter at home will work much better than a daycare center.

At other times your child's development may prod you to make a move. Perhaps your child is outgrowing his current caregiver and a change seems a natural evolution. Paula, age 14 months, had a doting sitter who had been with her since birth. But there were no children or parks within easy walking distance of the family's small apartment, and every day Paula's demands for activity and other children grew more insistent. Her parents decided it was time to try the new daycare center at the hospital where they both worked. After Christmas, Paula, then 18 months, joined the toddler group, where she had friends to play with and a playground to run in.

Or you may feel that your child isn't getting enough stimulation. Emily, born with a smile on her face, loved her family home caregiver and loved being with the other children, who were like her family. It was Pete, her father, who was unhappy. He knew the caregiver was very loving, but as Emily grew older, he worried more and more about the amount of television she watched, the lack of value placed on books and verbal skills, the caregiver's imperfect grammar. He felt his daughter needed more structure and more stimulation. "It sounds terribly snobby," says Cathy, her mother, "but you react to these things on an intuitive level."

Sometimes you and your caregiver or daycare center don't seem to be on quite the same wavelength, and you have nagging doubts. The paintings your child is bringing home from daycare are just like everyone else's and not at all like his previous work. The wheels on the stroller look as if they've never left your front hallway, despite your instructions to take your child to the park every day. If the guilt you felt when he first started daycare hasn't subsided, that may be a sign that this is the wrong daycare for him, Ellen Galinsky and William H. Hooks suggest in *The New Extended Family*.[11]

WHAT DO YOU DO?

In all of these situations, changing daycare is certainly one solution, but it may not be the only one. When you look closely, in most cases you won't find anything terrible. But you have a responsibility to your child to investigate.

Watch the daycare

Spend more time at the center or family provider's home in the morning and at night and drop in on your caregiver unexpectedly. You may discover that the activities are boring and your child is being punished because he wanders away or interrupts. His caregiver might have favorites and he is not among them, she may yell at him, or another child might be picking on him.

Talk to the caregiver

How well does the caregiver know your child? Does she know what kind of a day he had? Maybe the problem is a failure of communication. A good talk with her or with the daycare director and a little more attention on your part may do wonders. But if she doesn't understand your expectations or respond to your concerns, change should remain on your agenda.

Talk with other families

The parents at Emily's family daycare pooled their information and realized that their children were watching television almost all day long. "I picked my daughter up at ten to take her to the doctor, and the TV was on," one reported.

"It was on when I came for Tom at three," another chipped in.

Seeing this broad picture clarifies the situation.

Family council

Talk to your partner. For months Emily's parents kept up a running dialogue about Emily's daycare provider, with Pete pushing hard for more stimulation and Cathy arguing for stability. "Look, she's happy where she is," she said. "Is this change for change's sake? What are we doing to her?" Through these discussions, Cathy eventually came round to Pete's point of view.

Heed your child

Keep a close eye on your child: his behavior will probably be your best guide.

Like adults, children frequently have more than one persona—they are one person at home and someone quite different at daycare. Most of the time this is normal behavior. In fact, it's an important life skill to acquire. But their behavior must be appropriate for their surroundings. If a rambunctious child is quiet at daycare but still rambunctious at home, that's fine—unless he's twice as obnoxious as usual.

When a normally excited, happy little girl stops talking at home or talks like a steamroller over everyone else, that's a problem.

In other words, if the behavior carries over from one setting to another in an inappropriate way, if your child's behavior at home changes as a result of the behavior required of him at daycare—especially over a period of time—that's an indication that things are out of kilter. The daycare is demanding something that he finds too difficult to give. The result is that he acts out his real feelings in the one place he feels safe and loved, his home.

Weigh the risks and benefits carefully

"With every situation there are pluses and minuses," says Cathy. Consider your child as a person. What is the present arrangement doing to him? Is it grinding him down, or does he float above it and cope? What price is he paying in order to fit in? Are you willing to see him give up his originality and creativity? Is your shy child being totally ignored? Has your curious child stopped asking questions? How does he deal with change? How hard is it for him to make friends? "You have to keep measuring and balancing," says Cathy. "How grave are your reservations? What are the alternatives?"

FINDING NEW CARE

This experience will certainly color your views about what you *don't* want in daycare. Now that you know you can't tolerate a sitter who leaves a mess behind or a daycare teacher who always greets you with bad news or a center where the children don't go out at least once a day, any daycare arrangement that sports these features will automatically eliminate itself.

But be careful not to throw the baby out with the bath water. There are no doubt plenty of wonderful aspects to your daycare setup that are very important to your child. Try to unravel them from the bundle of feelings you have and remember them as you look around for something new. Bear in mind, too, that no arrangement is perfect—try to find what's most important to you, with drawbacks you can live with.[12] (See chapters 8–11 to refresh your memory.)

Look at the options

Seeing other daycare options may inspire you to make up your mind. This is an important step in the process of changing daycare. Because spaces in good centers aren't just sitting around empty, you'll have to make calls and visits and put your name on lists once again. Then you'll have to wait your turn—perhaps for several months. It therefore makes sense to start your search as soon as the idea of change occurs to you.

If a place materializes, you don't have to accept it, of course, but it's nice to have the choice. When Emily's name came to the top of the waiting list at Pete's work-place daycare center, the three of them rushed over for another look. They were impressed with the lovely outdoor playground, the exciting toys and equipment and the loving teachers. They decided to take the gamble.

The time element

While you're deciding or waiting for a spot in a daycare center, watch your child closely. Is the situation improving, holding steady or deteriorating? Being on a daycare waiting list is a little like being on a list for elective surgery: if you wait too long, what was once an elective procedure can become an emergency.

PARTING WAYS

Eventually you and your caregiver will go your separate ways. How should you manage the transition?

Giving notice

In a non-urgent situation, it is courteous, fair and businesslike to give your sitter, nanny, family caregiver or daycare center notice that you intend to make a change. Since you don't want your child to convey the news to your caregiver, tell her yourself first.

A sitter, nanny or family caregiver will need two weeks' notice. You may worry that she will take her anger out on your child, but it's more likely that a sitter or nanny will look for another job and leave you in the lurch as soon as she finds one. If you can afford it, consider paying both your sitter and your new caregiver for a short period. While the child gets used to the new arrangement, the sitter or nanny can look for work.

A family caregiver might feel less committed to your child and take less interest in him during this lame-duck time.

A daycare center needs a month's notice to fill the place you're vacating, but there should be no repercussions for your child.

What should you tell your child?

Before you say anything, talk with your partner and your caregiver about the best way to present the news to your child. Chances are he will know that something is in the air: children always do. Their antennae pick up our stress and distress signals with astonishing sensitivity. It is wise, therefore, to inform your child promptly and thoughtfully.

Try to explain the change in terms that he will understand and accept, keeping his self-esteem in the front of your mind. Be sure that you feel comfortable with what you say and that you understand its implications. (Don't tell your child that his caregiver is leaving town if he will run into her in the park with another child in a week or two. He will know you lied, and you will lose his trust.) It's important, too,

---

WHEN YOUR CHILD'S TEACHER LEAVES

These days it is hard to find a daycare center where there is no staff turnover at all. Salaries and working conditions for daycare teachers are so abysmal that educators often change jobs or drop out of the profession altogether. A recent U.S. study showed a 41 percent turnover in teaching staff (higher in for-profit centers), compared to 15 percent a decade ago.[1] The turnover rate among home-based caregivers is a staggering 60 percent.[2]

Sooner or later, almost every child will face the loss of a beloved teacher or caregiver. What should you do when you find out that your child's teacher is leaving the daycare to go back to school (or have a baby or work in the textile business)?

A high-quality daycare center will tell parents when and why a teacher is leaving.

With your child, you can decide whether to give her a card, a picture, a small gift, a kiss. Don't forget that even in a daycare setting you will have to deal with your child's sense of loss at being deserted by someone he loves, his sadness, his anger and his fear of what comes next. Encourage him to talk about his feelings, reassure him that her departure is not his fault, and remind him that he is strong enough to handle the situation.

If the daycare does nothing to mark the occasion, you as a parent have a right to ask why the caregiver has gone and why you weren't informed.

to continue a sense of trust between the caregiver and the child for as long as your child will be with her.

Be positive. Ask your child what new things he'd like to do and learn, and talk about the adventure that lies ahead. If you approach the switch as an opportunity for growth and a positive new experience, he'll see it in that light, too.

This is a relatively easy task when you're changing from one type of care to another. When a child leaves a sitter or family daycare to go to a daycare center, he is growing up. He's ready for the fun and excitement of new equipment and new friends his own age. When Emily asked, "Why can't I go to Wendy's any more?" Pete and Cathy explained that she would go to "school" like her older brother and sister. Emily, the third child in the family, was thrilled. Television watching was never mentioned.

But when a loved and trusted caregiver leaves, explanations don't roll off the tongue quite so readily. Even if her departure clearly has nothing to do with your child—if, for instance, she is moving to Vancouver to get married—your child will probably take it personally. On some level, he will think to himself, "She wouldn't leave if she really loved me." As far as he's concerned, she is deserting him. Of course each child is different, and each situation is different, but in a basic sense there is no way for you to coat this loss with sugar and make it palatable. It is very sad and very difficult. Someone that he loves is leaving him, and you really can't shield him from that reality.

Getting through it

Each of us has our own way of dealing with these issues. Not all of us are ready at the same time to understand that we can't make life perfect for our children; not all of us recognize at the same time that they are separate people from us. We evolve as parents at different rates. The departure of a loved one presents a major problem for a child. Though we can't make it go away, we can help him to get through it. If you are there for him, and you help him to have confidence in himself, he will deal with this loss successfully.

Let him know that this change is not his fault. Changing daycare is like getting a divorce: it's a grown-up decision. The child has done nothing wrong, but for various reasons the situation must change.

Every change carries with it a period of mourning. He may miss his friends and caregivers. Let him share his feelings of loss and sadness and anger. Those people are gone from his life forever, and tears are certainly acceptable.

He will probably be fearful, too. Listen to what he says, and don't try to talk him out of his feelings. But let him know that you believe in his ability to handle the new situation.

Make a plan for you and your child to say goodbye. Goodbyes recognize the fact that a part of your child's life is finishing, that he is completing a cycle. It's very comforting to have something concrete to do. A simple hug or handshake will suffice. Your child might want to give the caregiver a small gift or take some photos of her or give her a photo of him. Later, if the child wants to, he might write her a letter, send her a picture he drew or write a story about the good times they had together or what he's doing now. He could invite her to tea on Sunday, or phone her once in a while. Retired 65-year-old Lydia, who raised Heather and Sean, still comes to take care of them whenever they're sick. Having a tie with the past helps to deal with it.

STARTING A NEW DAYCARE ARRANGEMENT

When you talk to your new caregiver or interview the director of your new daycare center, tell her about your child's previous daycare experience. Be honest about the reasons for the change, your concerns and your expectations. This is, after all, the beginning of an open, caring relationship.

Bring your child to visit. Katy's parents drove by her new daycare center on weekends to show her the outside play area; and to help her to make new friends, the family spent several Sunday afternoons in the neighborhood playground. When she came to visit, Katy saw where she would hang her coat, met her teacher and accepted an invitation to stay for snack. Since she was familiar with both the environment and the children, she adjusted easily when she actually began daycare three weeks later.

It's probably wise to assign the parent who's more enthusiastic about the change to do the integration. Pete, sensing his responsibility, brought Emily on the first day. Cathy says, "I didn't want her to pick up on my hesitation."

Plan to stay with your child for the first few days, or take him home after half a day, just as you did when he started the first time. Each child will of course have different needs, but one who has already been to daycare knows the routine much better than any parent and may well send you packing. Emily's good experience at the family daycare had given her the tools she needed to enter this new situation with confidence, and she walked right in and spent a full day as if she had been going there forever.

A child who is slow to warm up in a new situation will take longer, but he will adjust just as well in the end if you stay calm and let him express his fears. Remind him that he made friends before and that he'll do it again. Work out some strategies together (after a week or so, invite a likely playmate to spend Sunday afternoon at your house). If you're confident that he'll be fine, he will be.

Depending on the circumstances, his personality, and his coping style, your child may feel the effects of the move for quite a while. He may be sad; he may cling; he may withdraw; he may become aggressive. This is perfectly normal behavior, but it should not last longer than two or three weeks. Encourage him to talk about what he feels and what he misses, and let him be sad if he wants to be. It's okay for you to feel sad and say so, too. ("I know what you mean; I miss Danny's mommy.") Again, he can write a letter or draw a picture or make a phone call.

Remember that it takes a long time to get used to a new place and that both you and your child have to work to establish solid relationships with the new caregivers. It may be months before they know your child really well and months before you both feel truly comfortable with them.

II. URGENT CHANGE

An urgent situation is one in which the child's daycare arrangements must change immediately in order to protect his well-being. Luckily, a crisis of this magnitude is rather rare—most parents never face one.

Sometimes your child's behavior seems odd to you, and you just have a gut feeling that things aren't quite right. Because you know your child best, you will know better than anyone else if something is seriously amiss.

Sometimes something in the environment gives you an unpleasant nudge. You don't really trust your sitter or family caregiver the way you'd like to. When she told you she doesn't smoke and you smell smoke as you enter the house, when your baby's diapers are always so wet they're practically falling off, when there are almost always too

many kids and too few teachers in the playroom, you're bound to have
. doubts.

Some urgent situations are very hard to face and deal with, and
your reaction to them may be disbelief and shock. We don't want to
sweet-talk you into thinking it's easy or burden you with guilt if you're
moving slowly, but you must remember that ultimately you have both
the responsibility and the power to care for your child. You are not a
helpless bystander. There may be times when you *must* act—not
necessarily today, but quickly nonetheless.

WHICH IS WHICH?

What distinguishes an urgent case from a non-urgent one?

Sometimes it's easy: when you find your child tied up in his stroller,
crying, and the caregiver washing dishes on another floor, that's urgent. But often it's hard to tell. Here are some clues.

In an urgent case, the child will probably disturb the whole family. He will bring his troubles home from the office and spread them
all over your floor. He won't act like himself. He won't eat or sleep
normally. He will not want to go to daycare. (A child who plays with
his siblings as usual, eats his dinner and sleeps through the night is
almost certainly all right, even if he cries when he hits the daycare
door.)

Trust your instincts and your knowledge of your own child. When
asked, a caregiver or director may admit that a child is unhappy, but
if she (or someone else at the daycare) is the cause of the problem, she
may not be a particularly reliable source of information. It is far better to rely on your own feelings.

Finally, and most important, red lights should flash when the
symptoms we are about to describe come in clumps—that instantly
turns them into danger signs.

DANGER SIGNS

These are the telltale signals that every parent must watch for:

Physical signs
If your child is injured, the caregiver should tell you immediately—
without your having to ask. If you notice any unexplained cuts, bruises
or scrapes on any part of your child's body when you bathe him, ask

about them the next day. The caregiver or director will probably explain the incident to your satisfaction ("He fell, and we put ice on it, and he seemed just fine. I'm very sorry that I forgot to mention it"). But if it happens again, or if other children seem to be having accidents, too, pay attention. This is not a safe environment for your child.

There is no such thing as an acceptable explanation for burns or for fingerprints on an arm.

Behavior patterns
Everyone has a bad day once in a while, and many children pick up unpleasant habits from their friends. We're not talking about that here. We're talking about a pattern where you see several disturbing and lasting changes in behavior that can show up in children of any age.

Signs in babies
Even a baby has ways to tell you something is wrong. His behavior can change—and astonishingly rapidly. He may cry much more than usual or much less. If your infant who cooed, kicked and giggled incessantly suddenly seems indifferent to your words and smiles, if ordinary sights and sounds make him agitated and jumpy, he may actually be depressed.

These are serious signs, demanding immediate intervention. Your baby may be spending his days alone in a crib—literally without enough human affection and attention to keep him alive. Even though he eats normally, a severely depressed infant can lose the ability to process his food, which in time will affect his immune system and make him prone to infection. Together these symptoms make up what doctors call "failure to thrive" syndrome, first observed in orphanages where no one talked to the babies.[13] A baby doesn't have many ways to call for help. If crying brings no response, he may simply give up.

Signs in older children
Toddlers and pre-schoolers have a larger repertoire of behavior to convey their feelings. If your child doesn't want to go to daycare every once in a while, it may mean that he's getting a cold or that his favorite jeans are in the laundry. But if he never wants to go; if he starts to panic at the mention of daycare; if he doesn't want you to leave when the sitter comes; if he can't sleep at night or has nightmares; if he stops eating; if he's wetting the bed or having accidents during the day when he used to be dry; if he's holding his bowel movements; if he cries and

clings (or avoids you); if he seems more fearful or anxious than usual; if he is very quiet or very aggressive; if he stops caring whether he's getting praise or reprimands; if he's feeling negative about himself; if a generally happy child becomes a generally unhappy child—the situation is serious. We repeat: if you see several of these changes in him, you'd better have a good look at what's going on, and fast.

WHAT CAN YOU DO?

First, don't panic. People operating under stress tend to make lousy decisions. But don't let the fear of finding something awful prevent you from looking under the rug.

Investigate

If your baby doesn't seem normal for any reason, take him for a checkup. The doctor may discover that he's ill or find evidence of depression. If so, for the sake of the other babies in the daycare, phone their parents and tell them what has happened. Are their babies ill or depressed, too?

What exactly is the ratio of caregivers to babies? Are the caregivers so overwhelmed by the work that they are suffering from depression themselves? Is the babysitter drunk or so tired that she sleeps all day?

Talk to the director, family caregiver, nanny or sitter, and listen hard to what she says. Someone who knows that she is providing less than adequate care will reply very cautiously indeed.

Danger signs in a toddler or pre-schooler point straight to a conversation with your child's caregiver and/or daycare director. Take a morning off and spend it at the daycare, either with your child or out of sight but close enough to see how he is doing. You may discover that the educator is calling your son names when he doesn't sit still. There might be a lack of supervision that creates a frightening environment. Your child who's afraid of the dark may be napping in a pitch-black room.

It's possible that you won't notice anything particularly frightening or difficult in the situation, and it's unlikely that you'll witness any physical abuse—because your presence will prevent it. But remember that you probably aren't seeing all there is to see. Put yourself in your child's shoes. If he is being terrorized, you must take it seriously. (We will deal with sexual abuse later.)

What recourse do you have?

In a daycare center or regulated daycare home, one possibility is to try to alter the caregiver's behavior. Another is to get rid of her altogether. These are both jobs for the daycare director or family daycare supervisor.

But before you approach her, phone other parents—their children may be having problems, too. If you meet with her as a group, your arguments will carry more weight.

The director or supervisor must observe the caregiver for herself and review the legal position of the center or agency—she will not terminate a contract on the basis of your word alone. You may be wrong, and she should have other methods for correcting the situation. But in the next day or two, depending on the severity of the problem, you can expect her to schedule a meeting to outline her plans to solve the problem.

If you can't live with the solution she suggests—if your child is really suffering—you have a third option: remove him, even if you have no firm plans. An interim solution may be preferable to leaving him where he is. To manage this, you need all hands on deck: one adult to take care of your child and another to look for daycare. Perhaps you and/or your spouse can take time off work or work at home or work half-days for a while. If you have a friend, neighbor or relative with small children, perhaps she or her sitter would help out for a week or two. Maybe Grandma would fly in from Winnipeg to hold the fort. Try the people you've called when your child was sick—agencies, students. Does your local Y or drop-in center have any babysitting services?

Jed, who moved to the city from the country when he was three and a half, hated his daycare. He felt cooped up in the tiny rooms and the cement front yard, and in four months he never made any friends. When his mother Martha came to get him, she sometimes found him hiding under a table. Though she had been actively searching for another daycare from the second week, one day she just couldn't take it any more. "I had to have a strong reaction at some point," she says, "seeing what I was doing to him each day taking him there." Though the available alternatives didn't suit Jed exactly, they were a vast improvement—and well worth the disruption of the change, she decided, even if they didn't meet all his needs.

With a babysitter or nanny, it is harder to figure out what is happening. Drop in unexpectedly and phone at odd times of the day to observe the lay of the land. If you have reservations about what you see but the offenses seem minor and repairable, discuss your complaints with the nanny or sitter and make a plan to fix them. But if her crimes seem major or you're still feeling uncertain about her even though you don't know exactly why, it's probably best to end the relationship.

Making a change

Under these conditions, you won't give notice—you'll simply withdraw your child or dismiss your sitter or nanny as soon as possible. If you've made a temporary child care plan and you don't yet know what comes next, tell your child the truth—that Grandma will look after him for a couple of weeks, and that you are looking for someone very special to take care of him when she leaves. Emphasize that you have the situation in hand and that you will make sure that he is all right.

Even when your child is unhappy, it's hard to explain a switch. What's important is to let him know that it is not his fault—that he is not responsible either for the change or for any of the bad things that happened to him.

Saying goodbye

Should you say goodbye even if you want to get away as quickly as possible? Yes. When he grows up, all that your child may remember of this episode in his life is that he was whisked away, and he may wonder what he did to bring this about. Saying goodbye helps to close that door. It gives him a sense that there is no shame attached to his departure, that he is leaving because it's good for him to leave. You can say, "We are saying goodbye because this is not a good place for you. People are doing things they shouldn't." If your child never wants to see your caregiver or put foot inside the daycare again, don't insist. But be sure he understands that he is all right, that he has the power to make the decision and that he has nothing to be ashamed of.

Does a bad experience with a sitter or daycare damage a child forever?

Our children are so precious that we often focus on their vulnerability. But they are tough and resilient at the same time. How resilient are they? How hard is it to recover from a bad daycare experience?

Research on the effects of poor daycare is still in its infancy. Although some limited studies indicate that a child's social behavior in elementary school reflects the quality of the daycare he attended three or four years earlier, his ability to bounce back depends a great deal on his family background.[14]

When they move to a new daycare, children who've had bad experiences react in many different ways. One child may observe rather than participate until he feels that he understands and trusts the group dynamics. Martin sat back and watched for several weeks before announcing to his new teacher, "I love you. You never hit anyone, and there are so many wonderful toys to play with." And then he mucked right in.

Jed, who had been so unhappy at his daycare and was facing major problems at home, lived through several rough months in his new regulated family daycare. Though he never complained about going, he behaved badly there, hitting the other children and deliberately soiling the house. It was as if he were at last able to express his rage about the previous four months when he'd felt so helpless. The supervisor helped the caregiver to deal with his anger, and gradually it ran its course and his behavior began to improve.

When he finally got into a daycare center that really met his needs—providing children his own age, as much space and physical activity as he had had in the country and teachers who paid close attention to him as an individual—he began to flourish at last. His mother still watches him every day, but now he goes off to play with his friends and babbles happily about his day on the way home in the car, and she knows that basically he's okay. "That was a horrible experience, and he had a strong reaction to it, but he can talk about it, and he's let it go. He feels good about himself and about his environment."

A formal complaint

If the gravity of the situation forces you to withdraw your child from a daycare center or a regulated family daycare home, you have an obligation to file a complaint with your provincial child care authority (listed in the appendix). The idea of reporting someone is very disturbing, but as the Child Care Board of Prince Edward Island puts it, "This action could very well be the key factor in recognizing a child who is in danger." The daycare authorities will investigate and give the daycare a deadline for rectifying the problem. Although they have the power to revoke the license, in practice they rarely shut a daycare down.

Your name will be kept confidential, but, of course, if your child is the only one involved, and if the case ever reaches a hearing or trial, your identity will eventually come out.

Follow up to find out what happened.

Poor daycare centers and family daycare homes continue to operate partly because working parents don't dare to complain: they are afraid they will lose their child care. But the cost of silence is much too high—we are putting our children at risk.

III. *SEXUAL ABUSE*

We have left for last one situation where changing daycare is vital. That is sexual abuse. In fact, many of the same guidelines that apply in other urgent situations also apply here, but our feelings about sexual abuse are much stronger and much harder to control, rendering us more helpless. Where sexual abuse is involved, we need special help.

The vast majority of people who choose to look after children are responsible, loving adults who would not dream of hurting a child. But in the mid-1980s, reports of sexual abuse in daycares in Canada and the United States shocked parents across North America. How could those who are entrusted with the care of innocent children possibly betray them in this way?

Now we know that no child is immune from sexual abuse. It cuts across all religious, cultural and socio-economic boundaries and mostly takes place at the hands of relatives or friends—people the child knows. But we still find it hard to accept. We don't want to believe that it could happen to us, and it takes special effort to see the signs. Although far less child abuse takes place in daycare centers than at home,[15] parents cannot afford to close their eyes and ears.

A SAFER DAYCARE CENTER

A daycare center's best defense against sexual abuse is an open-door policy. Parents should be permitted (and encouraged) to visit at any time of the day, without notice. If the daycare center locks its doors to keep out intruders, as many urban centers do, parents should have keys or know the combination of the lock. No daycare should become a fortress.

Having two adults with the children at all times also greatly reduces the risk of sexual abuse—and of physical and emotional abuse as well. Bathroom routines should emphasize privacy, and an adult must never be alone with a child in a locked room. The supervisor and/or the board of directors should routinely check the backgrounds of all employees, including the janitor and the kitchen staff.

SIGNS OF SEXUAL ABUSE

How will you know if your child is being abused? Abuse doesn't often show on a child's body. You must be on the alert for changes in behavior. There will probably be several at once. A child in a long-term relationship with an abuser will develop a pattern of abnormal behavior—he will be extremely withdrawn, overly aggressive, very seductive or emotionally needy. The behavior may be so consistent that the parent almost forgets what the child used to be like.

In contrast, after a recent assault behavior changes suddenly and radically. A child who's been quiet may become very aggressive; one who's been aggressive may withdraw totally. A usually affectionate child may pull away and resist hugs and kisses. Often an abused child will become overly aware or protective of his genitals or pay unusual attention to cleanliness. He may not eat or sleep; he may have nightmares or develop nervous mannerisms. He may cry more than usual and become very fearful. He may refuse to go to daycare or stay with his sitter or nanny.

LISTEN

Such a child is giving a signal that something is very wrong in his life. Don't jump to the conclusion that it's sexual abuse—it could be many other things—but try to find out what's bothering him without giving him the third degree. If you've already set up an open and comfortable environment and he knows you're behind him, he'll feel more free to talk.

If you suspect that the daycare is the source of the problem, it's better not to send him. Your trust in the caregivers has been shattered, and, even more important, if you force a gravely unhappy child to attend, he'll feel that he has no say in what he does. You may be creating a pattern of powerlessness that sets him up for abuse later in his life. Although looking for another daycare or sitter is an unappealing prospect, it is advisable if you can manage it.

A pre-schooler who's been assaulted probably won't tell you his story in a straight line, all at once. Listen carefully and patiently to what he has to say without trying to interpret it. Because the reality is so hard to accept, he may fill his tale with fantasy—monsters, animals and other non-human characters—to explain what is happening.

The Child Assault Prevention Centre in Montreal advises, "Let your child know he is believed, cared about, whole, and protected." Stay calm. Your response to an assault will determine how your child feels about it. If you get very upset and angry in his presence, he will feel worse.

Assure him that the assault was not his fault. Let him know how glad you are that he told you, and tell him that you can get help for him. But don't make promises you can't keep.

PEOPLE TO CONTACT

Your local Youth Protection office or children's hospital will refer you to a trained counselor who can help you decide what to do and give you emotional support. If necessary, they will direct you to a doctor who knows how to look for signs of sexual abuse. Your family doctor or pediatrician probably won't have this expertise, and a specialist will also know how to collect evidence for a criminal proceeding.

Since abusers often assault more than one child, you might want to talk to other parents. But be selective—if you call everyone at the daycare, you'll end up in the middle of a hysterical mob. Instead contact one or two parents you trust to approach the situation calmly. They might help you to get more information.

There is no point in approaching the daycare teacher, director or babysitter concerned, says David Singleton, coordinator of the Child Assault Prevention Centre. Confronting an abuser is rarely successful. Because abusers deny so convincingly, it could undermine your faith in your own child. Let Youth Protection or the police deal with them.

The Youth Protection Act obliges you to report suspected child sexual abuse, even if you have no proof. Although you can call anonymously, giving your name will lend credibility to your case. The office will keep the source of the information confidential. David Singleton warns that entering into an investigation won't be easy—officials may put both you and your child on the defensive.

The Quimbys paid Howie's grandmother
to look after Ramona until one of her parents
could come for her after work. Mrs. Quimby said
she could not hold a job unless she knew where
Ramona was. Every single minute.

BEVERLY CLEARY

RAMONA AND HER MOTHER

CHAPTER 21

Where Do We Go from Here?
School-Age Child Care

Not very long ago, when we were turning four or five or six and it was finally time to start kindergarten or grade one, our parents walked a few blocks to the neighborhood school and signed us up. If we were Catholic, we went to the nearest separate school. It wasn't much of a decision: proximity was everything.

Location is still important in the choice of a school, and many cities induce parents to make decisions by setting uncrossable geographical boundaries. But these days, even for families who prefer their children to attend the neighborhood school, location is just one of several factors to consider.

There is, of course, the education itself. Present-day schools—both public and private—are trying to find distinctive characters for themselves. You may choose a private school (if you can afford it) that offers a strict, traditional approach or a public school that regards the fine arts as the basis for a good education. What kind of learning experience do you want for your child?

Religion still weighs heavily, and language has become a crucial element, too. All over Canada parents stand in line to enroll their children in French-immersion schools, though some parents prefer programs that teach Cree or Chinese or German.

Although kindergarten isn't compulsory, schools in almost every province and territory offer it, and it is popular everywhere. Even here some families have choices. Would you like your child to begin junior or pre-kindergarten at age four, or would you rather he start at five? Would you prefer a half-day or a full-day program?

But what about child care?

There is one more factor that may in the end eclipse all the others: child care. Children do not magically stop needing child care when they leave daycare and enter kindergarten or grade one. Selecting a school because there's a school-age child care center in it is neither unique nor stupid. In fact, people will lie about where they live in order to qualify for a school with a first-class after-school and after-kindergarten program. The reason for this is simple. They are few and far between.

In 1990 the majority of Canadian women with school-age children were in the labor force.[1] These mothers probably weren't around to welcome their children home from school. But there were only 75,000 licensed school-age child care spaces, concentrated in a few provinces, in the whole country—enough to look after just 4.46 percent of those children.[2]

In some very real ways, finding high-quality school-age care is much more difficult than finding high-quality pre-school-age care. In the last 20 years, the energy of educators and parents has gone into creating care for the little ones for whom no other care existed. School-age children, including kindergartners, who after all had school to fill part of their day, seemed much less needy. Now our neglect is catching up with us. The pre-schoolers with working parents have grown into school-age children with working parents, and they still need care desperately. Yet very few among us—educators, parents, schools, school boards, communities, employers, governments—have given the matter much thought.

It's a shock, isn't it, especially if you struggled through the trying early years thinking, "It will be easier once they're in school." Welcome to the next stage in the real world. Child care doesn't get easier.

What are the alternatives?

Some of the alternatives are familiar—a school-age child care program (which usually encompasses before- or after-kindergarten care), a sitter in your home, a family or home caregiver.

There are two other choices that parents sometimes make. One is patchwork care, where the child goes to recreation programs, the library, Brownies or music lessons after school. Different adults supervise him at each activity, but he is usually responsible for getting from one place to the other.

The last possibility is latchkey care, sometimes called self-care. With the key to his house around his neck, the child is in charge of himself.

Let's look more closely at these alternatives.

I. SCHOOL-AGE CHILD CARE PROGRAMS

School-age daycare and its little sister, before- and after-kindergarten care, are really the stepchildren of the child care field. Latecomers that didn't get underway in Canada until the end of the 1970s, they are still all too often under regulated and under monitored, run and staffed by part-timers with little or no training in child development, early childhood education, or other fields related to school-age child care. The adult-child ratios are sometimes absurd, the safety precautions sometimes non-existent. One program we heard of, for example, operates with one classroom, 20 children, one untrained adult and no telephone.[3] Though the caregiver may be a wonderful, warm person, the children in her care are very much at risk. Sadly, in school-age child care this may not be an isolated incident.

Don't misunderstand. There are some truly marvelous school-age child care programs in Canada. Let's hope that you'll be lucky enough to find one in *your* neighborhood.

If you chose a daycare center for your pre-schooler, you'll probably be inclined to choose a group program for your school-age child, too.[4] Although your child won't be so vulnerable because he's older and more resilient and because he'll spend less time there, selecting and living with a school-age child care center will still call for all the skills you honed as a daycare parent. You'll have to look at the program closely before you enroll your child and from that moment on keep an eagle eye on the proceedings. Though parents of the school-age set often seem less interested in child care than parents of younger children ("We're used to entrusting our children to others," one parent admits),[5] being a school-age child care parent may turn you into a daycare advocate despite yourself!

LOOKING FOR A SCHOOL-AGE CHILD CARE PROGRAM

Is school-age child care licensed and regulated?

How could such a simple question require such a complicated answer? Well, once again the federal government has passed the responsibility to the provinces, but this time some of the provinces haven't quite made up their minds about whether to accept it. In Ontario and Manitoba, for example, the matter is relatively clear: the buck stops with the province, which licenses school-age child care centers like other daycare centers and expects them to follow regulations regarding safety, health, ratio, space, training of staff and so forth. But even in those provinces many recreational programs that don't have to adhere to those standards are also providing school-age child care. In Alberta, the province licenses buildings for school-age daycare, but the municipalities regulate the programs themselves—if they choose to. In Quebec, the provincial daycare office, the Ministry of Education and the school boards all have their fingers in the pie, but they've set very few norms for operating their centers. In British Columbia, buildings are well regulated, but programs aren't.

Write or phone your local daycare office (see the appendix or check the blue government pages of your telephone book under the social or community services department) to ask about the regulations in your province. The appendix has a list of the required staff-child ratios for each province.

How do I find a school-age child care center?

Some provincial and local child care offices and municipal information centers furnish names of school-age child care programs, and many pre-school-age daycare centers accept school-age children, too. But schools are the most obvious place to try when you start your search.

While you're phoning for information about the school, ask whether there is a school-age program attached to it and get the director's name and phone number. The school administration probably won't have all the crucial details. You'll have to call the program itself to learn all you need to know.

Then, if you're considering this school seriously, go to visit both it and the child care center.

Here are the questions to ask. If you're a daycare veteran, you may find them quite horrifying—like a glimpse of the Dark Ages.

We will begin at the very beginning, with general information. Then we will tell you about who should staff a school-age center, what the program should be like for kindergartners, and what the program should be like for the older children.

GENERAL INFORMATION

Who runs the school-age child care program? Is it profit or non-profit?

You may naively assume that your school or your school board runs it. You will be wrong, wrong, wrong (or the exception that proves the rule). Your school or school board is more likely to be its landlord. Like pre-school-age daycare centers, school-age child care centers can be organized and administered by all kinds of groups, some non-profit, some profit. You may encounter centers run by parents, pre-school daycare centers, large non-profit organizations like the YMCA or the Boys and Girls Clubs, parent-teacher associations, local governments and for-profit companies. It is important to know who is running your center because that information will give you a clue about its quality, tell you how much influence you're likely to have and indicate where to direct your questions, suggestions and complaints. (See chapter 8, pages 98-100, on the importance of profit and non-profit centers.)

What are the hours?

Your work day is probably longer than your child's school day, especially if your child is kindergarten age, and your child care will have to cover whichever hours are left over. They may be before school, after school, lunchtime, pedagogical or professional days (when teachers learn special skills and children don't attend classes), school holidays, Christmas break, spring break and summer. Do not assume that your school's child care program will operate during all of these times. Do not even assume that it will operate during most of them. Some school daycares are open on school days only. Some don't have any before-school care. Many are open only until 5:30 P.M. Some after-kindergarten care ends at 2:30 P.M. Be prepared for the worst. Ask.

Where does the program take place? Is it in the school?
Many programs are in school buildings—but not all. Some move children to the Y on foot, some bus them to another school, some take place in shopping malls.[6] Again, ask.

Who can attend? How old are the children at the center?
Some pre-school-age daycare programs add on or include school-agers. Depending on how it's done, this may be very hard on the older children.

Sometimes a school will offer an extended kindergarten program that ends at the last school bell and makes no provision after that.

Sometimes a school that says it offers after-school care really offers only extended-kindergarten care and has no program for first- to sixth-graders.

At many schools, after-school care peters out at about grade three. This may not concern you when you're registering a kindergarten child, but we can assure you that it will loom considerably larger when you have a nine-year-old with no place to go.

What are the fees?
Most school-age child care centers are very reasonably priced (we've heard of programs ranging from 145 to 300 dollars a month), but, of course, kindergartners who stay a longer day have to pay more. The program will charge extra on pedagogical days and during school breaks, and if it runs a summer program the fees may be competitive with the local day camps. You may have to pay extra to have your child bused from one location to another.

Provincial subsidies may be available for eligible families, but the same bureaucratic rules apply. Get your request in early because there aren't nearly enough subsidies to go around.

Those child care receipts come in handy at tax time, when you can claim up to 4,000 dollars for a five- or six-year-old and up to 2,000 dollars for a child from seven to 14 years.

What is the emergency policy?
Emergencies do happen, and every program needs to prepare itself to handle them. Certain elements are essential.

All of the staff should be trained in first aid and CPR.

There must be at least two staff present at all times. One adult simply cannot cope with 20 (or even ten) children in an emergency.

Who will take a child to the hospital? Who will stay with the other children? In many schools, principals, secretaries and even janitors all leave the building before the child care center closes. Who will cope with a burst pipe? It's better if some school staff is on the premises.

The program also needs basic information like both parents' telephone numbers at work, the child's medicare number and your written permission to obtain medical treatment for him if necessary. (It goes without saying that the staff must have access to this information.)

There must be a phone and a list of emergency numbers— hospitals, poison control, ambulance, fire, police, etc. A phone also allows the program to receive calls from parents who are delayed or who want to inform the staff that someone else is picking up their child. If no staff is available to receive the calls, there should be an answering machine which is regularly checked for incoming messages.

No parent should ever entrust his child to a daycare center that doesn't provide these basic safety measures.

How do the children get to the after-school program?
This is another basic safety issue. A staff member should collect the younger children from their classes or at the bus stop and deliver them to the program. If they arrive by themselves or from a different school, how do they check in? Does the program know if they don't turn up as expected? How does it trace their whereabouts? Every morning at General Wolfe School in Vancouver, Spare Time Club House director Pam Perry takes calls from parents and makes sure that all the children who come to the school-age child care program are safe and accounted for. Parents should be especially wary of programs that accept children on a part-time and drop-in basis. These safety mechanisms are very tricky to institute when different children show up every day.

With the older children, who need some independence, more complicated questions arise. If they go to other parts of the school during the course of the program, how are they supervised? A staff member need not accompany them, but someone must know where they are. Do they sign in and out? Do they need a pass? The program should always be accountable for their safety and well-being.

Some programs allow the older children to go home alone, but under what conditions? They cannot guarantee that the walk home will be safe, and they may refuse to let a child leave unless the parent is already at home to receive him. Parents should give written permission for these arrangements.

Do you have a health policy?

Even if a child has been sick in school all day, the child care program should be able to isolate him, allow him to rest and contact his parents to take him home. Is there a suitable place like the director's office for him to stay with an adult while he waits?

The daycare should maintain a level of hygiene and cleanliness that does not put your child's health at risk. Some children find school bathrooms so disgusting that they manage not to use them all day, and they are definitely in need by the time they reach the child care program. Are the bathrooms clean? Does the program allow the children to use them whenever they want to? They may have avoided sinks all day, too, and they should always wash their hands before they eat.

Do you serve meals or snacks?

School-age children are always hungry. Milk, juice or water should be available throughout the day, and there should be copious supplies of healthy snacks with limited sugar content. Kindergarten and pedagogical-day lunches (if the program serves them) should be well balanced and nutritious. Ask for a menu.

The kitchen, too, should be clean and the food properly stored in the refrigerator and cupboards.

What is the nature of the relationship between the child care program and the school?

A school-age child care center fits logically into a school building, with its special facilities and equipment, and no one needs to worry about busing the children there. But a good relationship between a school and a school-age child care program means sharing more than libraries, computers and gyms. It means that people have to talk to one another. Regular communication lets both teachers and child care workers know what the other is doing, which in turn helps the child. It also helps to dispel the stigma that sometimes adheres to daycare children at school.

Ask whether the child care staff and the teachers are in the building at the same time. Does this center have any mechanisms for getting them together periodically? Do their programs overlap or contradict one another, or do they complement and extend one another's work? Do they ever discuss the children and hammer out a common strategy for dealing with a problem child? At Clinton School in Toronto, staff from the School-Age Day Care Centre attend school staff meetings; and whenever a team is formed to help a child in jeopardy, the child care staff is naturally included.

When a program is located away from the school, it's obviously much harder for the child care staff to have contact with the teachers.

STAFF

What is the staff-child ratio? How large are the groups?

You remember, of course, that quality is closely linked to the size of the group and the number of children per teacher. The Wellesley College School-Age Day Care Project, which has been studying school-age daycare since 1979, recommends a group size of 16 to 24 children ("small enough for each child to receive some individual attention and big enough to get a softball game going") and a staff-child ratio of 1:10 ("there is no one who could give more than ten children what they need in terms of individualized attention").[7]

Most Canadian regulations, however, require a ratio of only 1:15 or even 1:20, except for kindergarten children.[8] Often the groups are even larger, because several ages occupy one large room. Smaller groups and better ratios usually make for better care—care that will help the child to grow. You have the right to expect this as a bare minimum.

Who is the staff?

The school-age daycare team needs a combination of qualities, with each member contributing different strengths. Once the children hit school we tend to focus all our attention on their intellectual side, but they are never really too old to nurture. There should be at least one staff person with a strong parental streak who will give them hugs from time to time and make sure they dress themselves properly when they go outside to play.

The staff should be sensitive to the complex needs of this age— to the desire to be part of the group yet an autonomous individual who makes his own choices. Caregivers need excellent communication skills, too—it is no easy task to get a child who says he has no homework to bring his knapsack and get out his books without embarrassing him.

The ability to control a group is also vital in working with elementary school children. When the teacher plays British bulldog alongside them, they have a great time; if he walks away or talks to another staff member, they find the game hard to sustain. They are just too tired, too close to the brink of conflict and total disintegration at the end of the day.

Staff training sharpens all of these skills.

A surprising number of centers don't employ any professionals at all because very few jurisdictions require it. Ask about the director's training and experience. A trained, full-time administrator is much more likely to run a high-quality program.

The staff in a child care program for kindergartners, who spend nearly six and a half hours a day with the children, should be qualified teachers or early childhood educators. But it is hard for extended kindergarten programs to have the money to pay qualified staff and even more difficult to find trained personnel for after-school hours for children in grades one through six. Still, there is no question that training in early childhood education, child development, elementary education, recreation and special skills like dance, drama, karate, art, gymnastics, team sports or ecology is all relevant and useful. Involved, qualified staff will develop an environment the children can learn from and enjoy. Ask about each teacher's background.

How long have the staff members been with the program? Because the work is part-time, there tends to be a lot of turnover, but in school-age child care, just as in pre-school-age daycare, children do better when the staff sticks around for several years.

KINDERGARTEN

From daycare to kindergarten and back

The life of a kindergartner is full of change. Even though they're old hands in a group situation, daycare graduates will find plenty at kindergarten to challenge them. They will be the youngest in their school, no longer the big fish in a small pond. There will be new children to make friends with—more than before because kindergarten groups are usually larger than daycare groups. Because she teaches up to 20 children, the teacher may use more discipline and control than they've been used to—and she may speak to them in a different language.

And there will be a whole new child care situation.

Kindergarten often lasts for less than three hours. Even a so-called "full-day" program may end by 2:30 or 3 P.M. There are hours and hours in the day when your child is not in school and you are still at work. All this is a lot for a young child to handle, and his new child care should help him to cope with it.

One program or two?

Although it is best for kindergarten-aged children to have the same child care staff all day long, unfortunately many programs don't work this way.

Some schools arrange afternoon kindergarten for the children who need child care. Although this allows them to enter the school-age child care program (joining children aged six to 12) in the afternoon, it ignores the problem of before-school care entirely.

Some schools provide morning kindergarten, followed by an "extended-kindergarten" program until early afternoon and a school-age child care program (again with the older children) for the balance of the day.

A new teacher comes on the scene with every switch, and the room and the children may change each time, too.

To us the most sensible plan is to send your child to a school where he can go to kindergarten in the morning and to a single daycare program in the afternoon. That way he can have continuity in his day, the same familiar caregivers to give him lunch, read him a story and organize nap and afternoon play.

This set-up works much better than sending him to afternoon kindergarten, which requires him to eat lunch at 11 A.M. and prevents him from having a rest in the afternoon. Even if he is with the same caregivers and children before and after kindergarten, the day may be too long and too tiring. However, this arrangement is better than going to three different programs—kindergarten, extended kindergarten and school-age child care.

If you have another child at home with a sitter and you think your child can handle more than just two and a half hours of kindergarten, you might want to send him to full-day kindergarten or to the morning kindergarten-extended kindergarten combination. Then he could get on the school bus and spend the balance of the day at home.

Space

If possible, the kindergarten group should have a space of its own. Even grade ones and twos tower over them, and they are easily intimidated. However, if the older children do join them later, the staff should integrate them without uprooting the little ones and backing them into the wall. Is the space large enough for everyone? Is the environment set up so that the age groups have separate areas?

Program

Kindergartners need a balanced and stimulating curriculum that is both structured and flexible and will respond to each child's level of readiness and interest. They still need a rest, and they still like to dress up, paint, play with large blocks, puzzles and playdough, but they should have some activities that they haven't been doing in daycare for the past two or three years. Although they're ready for cooperative games and taking turns, they also need a chance to let off steam in the park, playground or gym without competition or organized games.

They can handle more complex instructions, group projects and discussions; they are learning how to share their thoughts and feelings and how to listen to others. They like computers and enjoy books being read to them a chapter at a time. Though they are still very attached to adults, they need less direction than younger children. They're looking for warmth, a sympathetic ear, an opportunity to choose some of their own activities, a chance to be alone, a hug.

THE SIX- TO 12-YEAR-OLDS

School-age children are growing by leaps and bounds. They are hungry, big, noisy and they never sit still. They find themselves and their peers the most fascinating part of life, and they're exquisitely sensitive to criticism. They want to learn new skills, plan and execute vast projects, visit places they've never been. Above all, they want to be independent, responsible, autonomous people living in the real world. They've created quite an agenda for themselves.

Space

First, a school-age program needs space—lots of space—so that these huge creatures who've been sitting and concentrating most of the day can expend some of their boundless energy without tripping all over each other. Of course schools have gyms and playgrounds, but you'll want to know whether the child care program has access to them and whether the staff organizes and supervises them properly. Do they take the kids to the local arena to skate? Can they join in the community recreation department's soccer program, or will the rec department help run a soccer program for the child care?

Does the program have a large indoor space of its own? Though a creative director and staff can do wonders with a lunchroom and movable storage cupboards, everyone certainly feels more comfortable in a permanent, "dedicated" space.

Older and younger children need spaces of their own or rooms that can be divided so that they at least feel separate. Six to 12 is an enormous span of time in terms of development. Six- to eight-year-olds still need nurturing and guidance, and their child care space should give them a sense of coming home to a warm hug. Nine- to 12-year-olds, on the other hand, want to let loose. They've been feeling cooped up and fenced in, and they need a place to express themselves, to turn up the ghetto blaster and dance. Privacy and pride of ownership are particularly important to them. At home they're starting to close the door of their room, and at the school-age program they also like to mark their territory by putting posters on the walls and leaving a chess game out to finish tomorrow.

The space should be arranged and the equipment and materials accessible for several different kinds of activities during unstructured time—games, art supplies, crossword puzzles and mazes, cassette player and tapes, chess. There should be private nooks and crannies with pillows and soft furniture for a good read, a quiet conversation, some extra time to do homework.

Homework

Homework is a very dicey issue. Some parents want their children to do their homework at home so that they know what's going on at school. Others say, "By the time we get home and eat dinner, my child is too tired to do his homework, and it's almost bedtime. I want his homework done at the child care center." Perhaps, too, they'd like to relax with their child rather than squeezing homework into an already hectic evening.

But where, when and how should it be done? Some child cares handle homework in a study-hall setting. A teacher sits at the front of a classroom while the children sit at desks, working independently. When they have completed their homework, they are permitted to play in another room.

At the other extreme, students with homework sit at a table in the playroom with their friends playing all around them. The environment is noisy and distracting, but if the child's parent wants the homework done, the child must stay put until he's finished.

A better alternative is a separate, quiet homework area and a staff member who circulates among the students, checking to see who needs help. Children often say, "I don't have any homework" when they do. If it is important to you to have your child do homework during the after-school program, ask the monitor to double check. A sensitive caregiver will not mortify your child by searching through his school bag but with a bit of encouragement and a sense of humor will help him to remember that he really does have a math assignment to complete. Children in the same class might find it fun and useful to do their homework together.

The timing is also problematic and depends on when school ends, what time you collect your child, how much work he has and what other activities are going on. When school lets out at 2 P.M., it may be easiest to do homework right after snack and have activities later. When school finishes at three o'clock, a program might find it easier to schedule homework for 5 P.M., when it's quieter and the children feel as if they're missing less. Clinton School-Age Day Care in Toronto offers the children some flexibility. They know that if they need help from the staff, the best time to do their homework is at homework time. But they can choose instead to do it during playtime, to go to the school library or to consult their classroom teacher, who often remains in his room until 4 or 4:30 P.M.

As a parent, you have to look closely at the program's homework policy and working conditions, consider your child's personality, learning style, work load and energy level (as well as your own) and figure out what to do together. Once you've made your decision, make it known to the people running the program and be sure your child understands what you expect and why.

Choice
It's hard to learn autonomy, independence and responsibility when someone is telling you what to do all the time. For that reason, choice

is a crucial part of a school-age child care program. At the Spare Time Challenge Club at Kingsford-Smith School in Vancouver, children sign themselves in when they arrive, help themselves to a snack from a trolley, and at about 3:30 P.M. decide what they'd like to do that day. Some will go to the gym with the dance teacher; others will go outside with the outdoor supervisor; some will start an art activity. Different days bring different options, but the children aren't locked into their choice; and if they change their minds, they are free to do something else. Staff are responsible for areas, not for specific children, and act as facilitators, not as directors of activities.

This is particularly important with the nine- to 12-year-olds, who may rebel against the idea of child care altogether unless they make decisions and feel as free as their friends on the outside. The seven Vancouver Spare Time Clubs, which all successfully woo a large nine- to 12-year-old population, use a club concept. The older children are members of the Leaders' Club; and there are games, activities and privileges for them alone. At one program the leaders set the rules for the use of the Nintendo. At another, one leader handles the entire school breakfast program, making porridge and pancakes and seeing that everyone eats who is supposed to. The leaders think up and implement their own projects from start to finish, and they spend a lot of time out in the community. These popular programs have very few discipline problems, and no one teases these kids about going to daycare!

The Westmount Park School-Age Daycare Program in Montreal believes in flexibility within structure. Exhausted by their school day, the children find it easier to make choices when the staff sets the outer limits. Besides snack and homework time, the program has a free time when the children can choose indoor or outdoor play, organized or unorganized games, a private talk in a corner for two or a game of dodge ball for ten. During the structured part of the day, the staff sets up activities according to age, offering gym, computers, arts and crafts, cooking, skating, drama, etc., on different days. A child who doesn't want to participate in one can select another. At the end of the day the children can choose to play in their group rooms, in the gym or in the computer room.

However, choice for the children does not mean that the staff abdicates. Some degree of organization and supervision is always called for.

Parent involvement

As our children become more capable, we have to let go and allow them to manage more of their own lives. It is true that they will get along without us. But that does not imply that we are of no further use. Take a look at your child's school-age center. Chances are it's calling out for your help.

At one Toronto school, parents who were listening to their children realized that they didn't want to go to their school-age center, where there was too much disruptive behavior and too little interesting activity. After discussion with the staff, they came to an important decision: they would hire another full-time person and raise fees to balance the budget. With the help of a consultant from the Toronto Board of Education, they began lobbying the school for a second classroom and applied for an equipment grant. Thanks to the parents' efforts, a program that was on its last legs is now going full steam ahead.

Not every program requires such drastic intervention, and not every parent group can afford the expensive solution that this group found. But there are many ways to contribute to high-quality school-age child care. Talk to your child. Find out what is going on and what he feels about being there. Go in and see for yourself. Talk to other parents, the director of the program, the members of the center's board of directors or parent committee, your child's teachers and principal at school and your child's teachers at child care. Join the child care center's board or parent steering committee. School-age child care needs parents who know what good quality is. You can make a difference.

You can also make a difference in a more mundane but equally important way. Let your child know that he attends the child care center not because you regard him as incompetent but because you love him and worry about his well-being. If you make sure he has everything he needs to participate, visit with his teachers, meet his friends and look at the work he's doing there, you will show him that you care, and he will feel better about going.

II. *SITTERS AND NANNIES*

If you have had a sitter or nanny that your child loves and you trust, think seriously about asking her to stay. If you have a younger child, this decision should be relatively easy. But if you don't, you will need to become a silver-tongued orator to persuade her. The biggest problem, of course, is that once your child goes to school, he needs much less care, and your sitter or nanny can't earn a living wage working part-time. Perhaps she would be willing to make dinner and take over the family laundry? Could you afford to pay her at a slightly higher rate for the hours that she works? Could you scout out another family who needs her in the mornings?

You might also consider hiring a college student (or a mature teenager who's still at high school). They are often looking for part-time work, and they bring a refreshing interest and energy to the job.

Chapter 4 gives a full explanation of the pros and cons of sitters, but here are some of the factors you should weigh for school-age children:

Home free
If he attends a neighborhood school, your child can easily get there and back on foot or by bus, alone or with his friends, and a reliable person will be at home to keep track of whether he's arrived safely. Siblings can be together to have a real sibling relationship, and because they're supervised they presumably won't tear each other apart. But the best part of being at home is that your child *is* at home, to relax and be himself. He can eat the snack of his choice, watch television for half an hour, do his homework with the radio on full blast, get together with a friend, go to soccer practice, be part of the neighborhood network.

A special person
Though the school-age child is rapidly growing away from home, increasingly independent and responsible, he still likes to feel special—more so now that he's one of 20, 25 or 30 children in a classroom. He definitely enjoys one-on-one contact with someone who cares about him—someone who understands how he feels about the friend who didn't wait to walk home with him or the teacher who picked on him during math. He likes having someone to share his enthusiasm for collecting hockey cards or playing Monopoly, to teach him to make pizza, to help with his French homework, to let him go to the corner store for some junk food once in a while.

But because there is just one adult around, she had better be good. If she isn't interested in your child, if she spends all her time with your younger children, if she doesn't understand what school-age kids need and what activities they like, if she's too lax or too strict and controlling, your child will be bored, lonely, unhappy, neglected.

Parent control

With a sitter, you as a parent can make some decisions about what will go on after school—in consultation, of course. What food will be available for snacks? How much time can your child spend on the phone and watching television? You must give a fair amount of leeway to the sitter—who has to enforce your rules—and to the child—who needs freedom in order to grow. But you can talk with the sitter and your child every day and keep tabs on events.

The trouble here, of course, is that this care is unregulated. Although your child is old enough to tell you what's going on, he may choose to hold his tongue (because he's by nature uncommunicative or because he's spending all his time watching television) or he may be afraid to speak out (if he's being abused). You will have to keep a clear eye on his behavior at all times, because you are totally responsible for monitoring his care. No one but you will check references, drop in unexpectedly, phone periodically.

Cost

Now that you need her only for after-school hours and occasional full days, a sitter will be much more economical, especially if she's looking after a younger child as well. However, she'll still cost more than either family daycare or a school-age child care program, and the government won't give you a subsidy to help pay her salary. Ask her for receipts so that at tax time you can claim up to 4,000 dollars a year for your five- or six-year-old and up to 2,000 dollars a year for your seven-to 14-year-old. (For more details about taxes, insurance and registering as an employer with Revenue Canada, see chapter 3.)

Hours

A parent who works early, late or odd hours needs child care at those hours, too. A sitter is likely to be more flexible than either a family caregiver or a school-age child care program, but it may be hard to find someone whose schedule dovetails with yours and your child's. You may cover the after-school hours successfully, only to find that the sitter can't come in the mornings on pedagogical days or during spring or Christmas break. Summer is also a problem, which many families solve with camp.

With luck, or if you pay her a retainer, you may get your sitter to come full days when your child is sick, a considerable advantage for both you and your child, who'll have a friend around when he's feeling low.

Backup

Because your sitter will no doubt be sick herself from time to time (or have to study for exams—or worse but more likely, quit without notice), you'll need a backup system. Can your child go to a friend, neighbor or relative in an emergency?

III. *FAMILY OR HOME DAYCARE*

If your child attended a family daycare as a toddler or a pre-schooler, and you believe that your caregiver knows how to handle older children, this may be a particularly attractive possibility. (To refresh your memory of family daycare, see chapter 5.)

Understudy Mom and home

A trained and supervised family daycare provider knows what a child needs when he comes home from school: a nutritious snack, a chance to cut loose, someone to appreciate his troubles and/or triumphs, some interesting activities to choose from. A caregiver who has school-age or teenage children of her own may be especially tuned in.

Being at family daycare can be a lot like being at home. If the conditions are right, your child can relax, be alone, play with the younger children (including his own brothers and sisters), take his time figuring out what he'd like to do. There's relatively little pressure.

Your caregiver can collect your child from school or meet his school bus. If he's old enough, and parents, caregiver and family daycare supervisor agree, the child can have the pleasure of walking home with his friends—and of going by himself to softball or choir practice in the neighborhood.

Regulation

If you succeed in finding regulated and sponsored family daycare, you can feel more comfortable about the safety, health and general well-being of your child. But if you have an unlicensed, unregulated caregiver, you may know very little about her, about how many children there are or what the care is actually like. It is up to you as a parent to monitor it closely yourself—to pay attention to what your child says and how he behaves at home and at school, to talk frequently with the caregiver herself, to keep in touch with the other parents at the family daycare, to phone and drop in from time to time. (See chapter 5 to learn more about licensing and sponsorship.)

The quality of care depends largely on the quality of the caregiver herself. If she's trained, and if she's warm, sensitive, creative and energetic, there will be time for talk, privacy, interesting activities. If she's preoccupied with the younger children in her care or she doesn't know much about the development and interests of school-age children or her beliefs are different from yours, she may leave your child on his own for hours or give him far too much direction. Supervision is perhaps the most important area to discuss with her. Your child needs to learn new skills and make decisions for himself. How much scope will there be for taking initiative and responsibility? What limits should be set? If you and your caregiver agree, life will be much easier for your child.

Ratio

Some children just can't handle a crowd after being in a big group at school, and they prefer the intimacy of family daycare. The provinces control the total number of children allowed in a regulated family daycare home, including the number of school-age children.

Sometimes a caregiver will make a specialty of elementary school children, but it is more likely that a five- to 12-year-old will join a maximum of four or five younger children. Unless the caregiver is very skillful, this grouping presents real problems. Very young children severely restrict the group's activity, and an older child really needs company his own age. At least one other school-age child should be included, though you never know whether that child will turn into a really close friend, a hated enemy or someone whose presence your child merely tolerates. (He can't invite anyone else over because it will exceed the ratio.)

Space

A school-age child needs space—physical and mental—after a long sedentary day at school. He needs a place to be noisy—with his friends and in active, outdoor play—and a place to be quiet—to be alone, to do homework, to listen to music, to play a game. A family daycare home may be just too small and too geared to the younger children to give your school-age child the space, quiet and privacy he craves.

Hours

A caregiver who sees herself as a professional will provide family daycare all year around (except for her own vacation time, which she should clear with you). She will certainly be prepared to care for your child on pedagogical days and during breaks; and although she may be willing to have him over the summer, he is probably better off in camp.

If your job requires you to work late or on different shifts, perhaps she can accommodate you, though this is a matter of luck.

On the other hand, an unlicensed, unregulated caregiver may not be nearly so reliable.

Cost

Family daycare will cost less than a sitter but may charge more than a group program. Ask to be sure.

In a regulated private home daycare, both subsidies and receipts should be available.

IV. LATCHKEY AND PATCHWORK CARE

A great many Canadian families—no one knows exactly how many—haven't succeeded in finding any care for their school-age children. They've probably tried sitters and family daycare, and they've found them to be more trouble than they were worth. In these families' experience, sitters didn't turn up when they were supposed to, quit without notice and didn't do what the job required. Parents might have tried school-age child care programs, too, but perhaps the centers didn't provide care for youngsters beyond grade two or three; and at a certain point their children no doubt put forward a very strong argument for staying home alone. Frustrated by the absence of alternatives and worn out by years in the daycare wars, parents often capitulate, launching yet another Canadian latchkey child into the world. [9]

ALONE

Latchkey children, who range in age from five to 12, wear their keys around their necks (or put them in their pockets, purses or school bags), well hidden from public view, because they don't want anyone to guess that they're going home alone to an empty house. They come from all socio-economic groups,[10] and in the last two decades, as their mothers joined the labor force in increasing numbers, there have been more and more of them—probably hundreds of thousands, though reliable data is impossible to collect.[11]

What are the effects of latchkey care? Is it harmful?

So far, there are no definitive answers to this huge and complicated question.

Some researchers believe that for older children (older meaning from age nine and up), latchkey care has no adverse effects. In fact it may help them to develop self-help and problem-solving skills and to assume more responsibility. But, they caution, all this is more likely to happen if they get along well with their parents and brothers and sisters and if they live in a safe neighborhood with friends they can turn to in times of trouble.[12]

Other experts vigorously denounce this view. Even the term "self-care," meaning the absence of an adult, legitimizes neglect in their opinion. They have found that latchkey children, whether six or 12, suffer from heightened fear and stilted social development. Too much responsibility too soon creates enormous stress and anxiety, leading to social and emotional problems in later life.[13] Calling unsupervised care "unsafe, illegal, and unfair," American school-age child care specialists state this position clearly: "Parents must not be lulled into believing that it is all right for their children not to have adult guidance, protection, and supervision."[14]

What dangers do latchkey children face?

In fact, some research has found that 8 percent of latchkey children have to deal with a serious emergency.[15] Here are some of the very real problems that they can face alone:

1. *Fear.* Parents of latchkey children suffer from something called the "three o'clock syndrome." Until their child phones their work place to announce his safe arrival at home, they don't get much work done.[16] Kids suffer from it, too. Every day they worry about whether they'll make it home in one piece. And they wonder whether everything will be in its usual place when they open the door.

   Latchkey children also fear what might happen once they're

inside. They worry about fires, about accidents and injuries, about break-ins, assaults and kidnapping.

If an older brother or sister looks after them—a solution many families use, though the sibling usually isn't old enough or mature enough to take on this heavy commission—they often fear being alone with him because he picks fights and sometimes even abuses them.

Let us reiterate—these are real fears. These events actually happen to children who are home alone.

2. *Loneliness*. Once he has locked himself inside, the child at home without an adult is almost totally isolated. If his parents allow it, he can talk to his friends on the phone, but he can't invite them over because there is no grown-up to supervise. He probably isn't allowed to go out, because his parents think that it is safer for him, once home, to stay home, where they know his whereabouts. He isn't supposed to answer the door under any circumstances, and he has to be careful about what he says on the phone, concealing the fact that no adult is present. He has no one to confide his troubles to or to help him with his math homework. At this very social age, he feels rejected and lonely, deprived of both adult support and leisure with his peers, which is so necessary to making special friends.

3. *Bored*. His closest companion is probably his television set. Research shows that latchkey children watch an average of four or five hours a day.[17] His body craves physical exercise and his brain cries out for intellectual stimulation. But without any grown-up to guide him or friends to share his interests—and with the tempting boob tube at his fingertips—it's hard to figure out something new and exciting to do.

PATCHWORK CARE AND OTHER VARIATIONS ON THE LATCHKEY THEME

Patchwork is a sub-category of latchkey care. The difference is that instead of going home, patchwork kids have activities after school. They go to jazz ballet, hockey practice, Brownies, band practice, the orthodontist. Sometimes the activities take place in the school building, but the children often manage the walk, bike ride or bus by themselves, and they know the adults who are in charge (even if you don't).

But in some respects, patchwork care is just like latchkey. After his activities are over, the child still returns to an empty house. He just isn't there as long. On the days with no scheduled activities, he may be a latchkey kid like any other.

Leaving your child at home alone is potentially hazardous, whether for four hours or for one. We always think it can't happen here; it won't be us. But it can. It takes only one crazy stranger, one careless moment at a stove, one awkward movement with a knife.

Five conditions are absolutely essential before you can even ponder patchwork care as a possibility for your child:

Is the neighborhood safe?

First, your neighborhood must be safe for the child to move around in. He must be able to deal with the traffic, the geography and the darkness in the winter (remember how early it falls in December and January). And both you and he must have confidence that he has acquired enough street smarts to deal with the unexpected. Perhaps he'll go to the activity by himself and you'll pick him up there, especially if he's alone.

What is there to do?

Next, lots of activities must be available. If you live in a bedroom suburb where the only recreational facility is the mall, there just won't be enough for a child to do. A community with an active recreation department, a library, an arena, a Y, a swimming pool, a youth band, a choir, Cub Scouts and Brownies offers a venue a parent can seriously consider.

However, you have to look at the activities first. They are probably exempt from licensing. Are they taught by professionals or by high school students with no training and little experience? What is the ratio of staff to children? Sometimes recreation programs require only one teacher with 30 or 35 children or have no ratio rules at all.

Equally important, is your child interested in this activity? Whose idea was it for him to learn to play the piano? Are you signing him up for jewelry making because it's the only course given on Mondays? Or is he choosing it for himself?

Adult contact

Your child should always have a person to call in an emergency. In these days of push-button phones, he can be in touch with his emergency contact with one fingerstroke. It is important, too, for him to have someone to call when he's sad, lonely or worried.

Not too often or too long
Fourth, your child must not be left alone too often or for long stretches of time. Handling a little time on your own is quite different from consistently having the full responsibility.

Is your child ready?
Last, your child must be ready, willing and able to undertake this project. This seldom happens before the age of 12 and often not until later.[18] For a parent, making this judgment is agonizingly difficult, and it should always be left open to revision. You have to be willing to admit you've made a mistake: the hazards are just too great.

Kids often bite off more than they can chew, wanting to please you, help you, show you. How do you reassure them that they can handle it, yet let them know it's all right to be afraid?

Present it as an experiment to begin with. Tell your child ahead of time that this will be hard for both of you, and that no one will be failing if it doesn't work out. You can try again next year if you feel like it.

If you come home and discover a frightened, crying child, you'll know you have to make a change. But many children hide their fear behind a swagger or an angry outburst. Don't wait until dinnertime or bedtime to speak with your child. As soon as you get home, ask, "How are you? How did it go today?" Then listen, really listen to the answer and keep watching how your child behaves. Is he himself?

Eventually, if not this year or next, he'll really be old enough to come home alone, get himself a snack, do his homework, get together with a friend.

And they lived happily ever after.

FAIRY TALE

CHAPTER 22

Conclusion

This book has given you the tools to find high-quality daycare for your child. But unlike fairy tales, this story's happy ending doesn't occur by magic. It is the result of your own effort and research. When you are a knowledgeable consumer, you will buy a better product.

All daycares and caregivers are not alike. Once you've actually spent some time looking around—whether at sitters, nannies, daycare centers, family daycare homes or after-school programs—you will know all too well how rare high-quality daycare is and how important it is for your child to have it. If you don't demand it and recognize it, you probably won't find it.

But what about the others?
Even if you find good care for your own child, there are many other children in Canada who are still in need. How will they get what every Canadian child should be entitled to?

We can help. If the parents of young children don't care about young children, who will? Who's going to show others what really counts?

We are squandering a precious national resource. Our children belong to us all, and child care is everyone's responsibility, not just the responsibility of parents. Now that an entire generation is involved, no one among us can afford to look the other way. Grandparents and grandparents-to-be who stayed at home to raise their children must understand that daycare is an inevitability for their grandchildren. Communities and schools must open their facilities and their resources to deal with the children who need them. Employers must realize that benefits like liberal maternity leave, flexible work schedules, parental leave days to look after sick children, on-site child care and child care information and referral are in the best interests of our children and our country—as well as in the best interests of their employees and their businesses.

Bankrupt and burned out

Talking about quality is almost irrelevant unless there is money to pay for it. Daycare fees probably strain your household budget to its limits right now, but daycare doesn't seem to be very high on the government's wish list. As a result, your daycare center or family caregiver is still struggling from crisis to crisis, unable to find the funds to tackle the problems.

Perhaps the most serious crisis involves the daycare workers themselves. They are the cornerstone of good daycare, the ones who deal directly with the children. Without enough trained, caring staff, the system just doesn't work very well. Notoriously underpaid, workers have always subsidized daycare through their low salaries. Though many of them are qualified, they earn barely enough to live on, and the community at large doesn't give them the status or recognition they deserve.

As a result, the child care profession has trouble recruiting and holding onto talented and interested young people. Because we need so many qualified daycare teachers compared to the number who are available, training programs must settle for candidates whose only qualification is that they have applied. The dedicated few, willing to give up fame and fortune for a dream, tend to regard daycare as a jumping-off point, not a career for life. They burn out, or they move on to more prestigious, better paying positions in other fields.

The research is very clear about this. High-quality daycare depends on trained teachers, a high staff-child ratio, small groups and low staff turnover. Unqualified teachers, not enough teachers, too many children and high turnover mean bad daycare and suffering children.

Government must lead

Ultimately government must take the lead and make a national commitment to daycare. No matter how energetic and devoted they are, parents cannot solve problems of this magnitude alone. Concerned, well-informed, responsible people must plan, set priorities and allocate funds to carry out policy, not just leave a hodgepodge to grow as best it can. At the moment vast differences exist between provinces, and the system is so complicated that almost no one knows where to go or how to make it work. Buck-passing is the primary modus operandi.

One thing governments could do is enforce their own rules. If elevators fail inspections, they're closed for repairs. But if daycare isn't safe—if the staff-child ratio isn't up to par, if equipment is broken and dangerous—no one tells the parents, and the center continues to operate. Although the government attempts to make the offending daycare follow the rules, it worries that if it shuts a center down, the parents who send their children there will lose time from work. It seems to forget that violating licensing standards is hazardous to children's health. In the end, daycare quality must be more important than quantity.

In many European countries, daycare is a right, not a privilege. First-class care is accessible to every child because the government plans it, licenses it, subsidizes it and makes it a national goal for its children to develop and thrive. The money that it spends on good-quality child care today is money that it saves later—in schools, social services and in the criminal justice system.

As parents and citizens, we must continue to believe in and fight for high-quality daycare, even when our own children have outgrown it. We must support daycare-advocacy groups in our community, talk to friends and neighbors, write letters to newspapers and to our politicians on every level—federal, provincial, municipal, school board—telling them what we want and voting accordingly.

Today's children are Canada's future. They deserve a chance. Every child in Canada should be able to attend a high-quality daycare program.

Where to Find Out about Daycare Regulations and Daycare Centers in Your Province

BRITISH COLUMBIA

> Community Care Facilities Branch
> Ministry of Health
> 7th floor, 1515 Blanshard Street
> Victoria, British Columbia
> V8W 3C8
> 604-387-2659

Contact the community care facilities office of your local health unit or health department—whose number is in the blue government pages of the phone book under Ministry of Health—to get a list of licensed daycares, family daycare homes, nursery schools and out-of-school care programs in your area. The ministry also publishes a booklet about selecting and monitoring licensed daycare and a booklet about selecting and monitoring unlicensed care.

In the Vancouver area, call:

Information Daycare
3998 Main Street
Vancouver, British Columbia
V5V 3P2
604-875-6451

For information about daycare anywhere in B.C., get in touch with:

Corporate ShareCare
Suite 202, 1318 56th Street
South Delta, British Columbia
V4L 2A4
604-943-4867 or 943-4873

Copies of the "Community Care Facilities Act, 1979," and the "Provincial Child Care Facilities Regulations, 1981," may be obtained for a small fee from:

Crown Publications
546 Yates Street
Victoria, British Columbia
V8W 1K8
604-386-4636

ALBERTA

Day Care Programs
Department of Family and Social Services
11th floor, 7th Street Plaza
10030 – 107th Street
Edmonton, Alberta
T5J 3E4
403-427-4477

The provincial office can supply the address and phone number of your regional office, or you can find it in the blue pages of the telephone book under Provincial Government, Child Care Branch. The regional office can give you a listing of daycare centers and homes, the daycare regulations, information about subsidies and useful booklets about choosing a daycare center and family day home. The social services office also takes complaints.

School-age programs are the responsibility of the municipalities. Some municipalities provide information to parents through the social services department.

SASKATCHEWAN

> Day Care Branch
> Saskatchewan Social Services
> 1920 Broad Street
> Regina, Saskatchewan
> S4P 3V6
> 306-787-7467
> Toll free: 1-800-667-7155

The central office will direct you to one of three regional offices, which will supply listings of licensed daycare centers and approved family daycare homes in your area. They also have information about selecting a caregiver, information about subsidies and copies of the "Day Care Regulations." Subsidy applications are available at licensed centers or approved daycare homes.

MANITOBA

> Manitoba Child Day Care
> Department of Community Services
> 114 Garry Street, 2nd floor
> Winnipeg, Manitoba
> R3C 1G1
> 204-945-2197 (Winnipeg)
> Toll free: 1-800-282-8069

Manitoba doesn't send out its act and regulations, but they will send a useful little book called *Quality Child Care — A Parents' Guide.* To get a list of daycare centers, you must reach the daycare coordinator for your area, whose number can be obtained from the provincial office listed above. You can get subsidy forms and information from your area office or from an approved daycare center or family daycare home.

ONTARIO

> Child Care Branch
> Ministry of Community and Social Services
> 2 Bloor Street, 30th floor
> Toronto, Ontario
> M4W 3E2
> 416-327-4870

The Ontario government is completely decentralized. The number above is the provincial office, which can direct you to the regional office of the Ministry of Community and Social Services near you. Although they may not actually have a list of daycares in your neighborhood, they can refer you to resource centers that do. Your local Community Information Service will probably also be able to provide a list. If you're interested in a subsidy, ask them exactly where to apply. Subsidies are usually handled by the social services department in your local municipality.

For daycare in Metro Toronto, get in touch with the Metro Toronto Information Centre. They publish a directory of child care centers in Metro and can also deal with telephone inquiries:

> Metro Toronto Community Information Centre
> 590 Jarvis Street, 5th floor
> Toronto, Ontario
> M4Y 2J4
> 416-392-4575

You can get the "Day Nurseries Act" and regulations from:

> Publications Ontario
> 880 Bay Street, 5th floor
> Toronto, Ontario
> M7A 1N8
> 416-965-6015
> Toll free: 1-800-268-7540

QUEBEC

> Office des services de garde à l'enfance
> 100 rue Sherbrooke est

Montreal, Quebec
H2X 1C3
514-873-2323

L'Office publishes a list of all licensed daycare centers, family daycare agencies and after-school programs in the province, as well as several useful pamphlets. Subsidies are available through daycare centers or licensed family homes.

You can buy the daycare regulations from:

Publications du Québec
3, Complex Desjardins
Montreal, Quebec
H5B 1B8
514-873-6101

NEW BRUNSWICK

Provincial Coordinator, Early Childhood Services
Office for Childhood Services
Department of Health and Community Services
P.O. Box 5100
Fredericton, New Brunswick
E3B 5G8
506-453-2950

The Provincial Coordinator will provide a list of daycare centers and refer you to your regional coordinator for more specific information. The regional coordinator also knows about community daycare homes and is responsible for handling complaints. For a subsidy, parents must contact their regional office of the Department of Income Assistance.

NOVA SCOTIA

Day Care Services
Family and Children's Services Division
Department of Social Services
P.O. Box 696
Halifax, Nova Scotia
B3J 2T7
902-424-3200

As well as the "Day Care Act and Regulations," Nova Scotia publishes a daycare directory chock full of information—location, number of licensed spaces, age range, whether full- or part-time and whether subsidies are available.

PRINCE EDWARD ISLAND

> Coordinator for Early Childhood Services
> Department of Health and Social Services
> P.O. Box 2000
> Charlottetown, Prince Edward Island
> C1A 7N8
> 902-368-4957

The central office will provide a directory of licensed daycare centers, daycare homes and after-school programs, information about subsidies, as well as the booklet "A Parent's Guide to Early Childhood Programs," which summarizes the provincial regulations.

NEWFOUNDLAND

> Division of Day Care and Homemaker Services
> Department of Social Services
> Confederation Building
> P.O. Box 8700
> St. John's, Newfoundland
> A1B 4J6
> 709-576-3590

The Division of Day Care Services can tell you the address and phone number of your district office, which in turn will help you to find the daycare centers in your neighborhood. (You can also find the number of the district office by looking in the blue pages under Government of Newfoundland, Department of Social Services.) The daycare centers will supply subsidy application forms, which should be returned to the Department of Social Services.

NORTHWEST TERRITORIES

    Day Care Section
    Family and Children's Services
    Department of Social Services
    P.O. Box 1320
    Yellowknife, Northwest Territories
    X1A 2L9
    403-920-3314

This office will supply a list of licensed daycare centers, family homes, and after-school programs, a copy of the "Child Day Care Act" and "Child Day Care Standards Regulations, 1988," and information about how to obtain a subsidy. You can also apply for a subsidy at a child care center.

YUKON

    Child Care Services Unit
    Department of Health and Human Resources
    Government of Yukon
    P.O. Box 2703
    Whitehorse, Yukon
    Y1A 2C6
    403-667-3002
    Toll free: 1-800-661-0408

As well as supplying the names of licensed daycare centers and family day homes, the department publishes an excellent little book describing licensing standards for both daycare centers and family daycare homes. Intended primarily for those setting up a child care service, it is also very useful to parents seeking daycare for their children.

APPENDIX B

Where to Find Out about Family Daycare in Your Province

Research shows that family daycare providers who are supervised by an agency or who are members of an association usually give better care. It is a good sign when a caregiver belongs to one.

BRITISH COLUMBIA

In British Columbia, the Ministry of Health licenses family daycare directly and keeps listings of homes. (See appendix A.)

Daycare home associations
The Western Canada Family Day Care Association, listed below, is an umbrella group for all the daycare associations in the province. They can put you in touch with the association in your area. The Ministry of Health or your health unit can also give you the name of your local association.

> The Western Canada Family Day Care Association of B.C.
> c/o Westcoast Child Care Resource Centre

3998 Main Street
Vancouver, British Columbia
V5V 3P2
604-876-8440

Family Day Care Support Programs
The B.C. Day Care Support Programs monitor quality in family daycare
by making assessments and offering training, support and resources
to both regulated and unregulated providers. They also maintain
registries of homes and can assist parents in selecting an appropriate
caregiver. Information Daycare in Vancouver has a list of all the
support programs in the province. (See appendix A.)

ALBERTA

In Alberta family care is licensed through agencies, which can be either
profit or non-profit. They can also be operated by municipal governments. To find out about the approved agencies in your region,
get in touch with the Alberta Day Care Branch listed in appendix A.

SASKATCHEWAN

To find a licensed home, contact your regional Day Care Branch, which
approves individual family daycare homes. (See appendix A.)

Family daycare home associations
There are several associations in Saskatchewan that act as support
networks for providers and at the same time help parents to find family
daycare homes. The association in Saskatoon can direct you to the
homes and associations in your area:

Saskatoon Family Child Care Home Association
P.O. Box 8821
Saskatoon, Saskatchewan
S7K 3L7
306-374-7317

MANITOBA

In Manitoba family daycare is licensed directly by the government, which inspects and supports the homes.

Family Day Care Association
The Family Day Care Association of Manitoba, with 400 members, can tell you where to find private home daycare all over the province. They have support and services for providers, insurance, training, etc.:

> Family Day Care Association of Manitoba
> 203 – 942 St. Mary's Road
> Winnipeg, Manitoba
> R2H 1J2
> 204-254-5437

ONTARIO

In Ontario, private home daycare is regulated through agencies, some profit, some non-profit.

Daycare home associations
Ontario has several family home daycare associations. The Private Home Day Care Association of Ontario has a large education program for parents all over the province. It will send out an information kit and a list of the agencies in your area, as well as answer questions that come up in the course of your search:

> Private Home Day Care Association of Ontario
> 801 Eglinton Avenue West, Suite 302
> Toronto, Ontario
> M5N 1E3
> 416-783-1152

In the Ottawa-Carleton region, there are two providers' networks, which include both agency-sponsored and unsponsored caregivers. Both associations provide the caregivers with training, support and resources:

> Independent Child Caregivers Association
> 120 Holland Avenue, Suite 205
> Ottawa, Ontario

K1Y 0X6
613-729-9954

Ottawa-Carleton In-Home Child Care Providers Association
2527 Baseline Road, Room 204
Ottawa, Ontario
K2C 0E3
613-726-0838

Child Care Resource Centres
Ontario also has a loose network of government-funded Child Care
Resource Centres that provide toy libraries, caregiver registries,
workshops, drop-in programs and playgroups, etc., for both caregivers
and parents. Many of them list child care programs and some even
counsel parents about how to look for high-quality care. You can find
them through your local Child Care Branch or Community Information
Service (see appendix A).

QUEBEC

L'Office de service de garde à l'enfance, mentioned in appendix A, has
a list of all the agencies that take charge of regulated home daycare.
The agencies select and supervise the homes, as they do in Ontario
and Alberta, and they will help you to find a home in your area.

Family daycare association
The family daycare agencies also have an association.

Regroupement des agences de garde en milieu familial du Québec
100 A rue Gigiguère
Lac Etchemin, Québec
G0R 1S0
418-625-3853

NEW BRUNSWICK

New Brunswick has no licensed family home daycare, but has lots of
small daycare centers run out of homes. You can find these through
the provincial daycare office listed in appendix A.

NOVA SCOTIA

Three agencies screen and supervise family home daycare in Nova Scotia: one in Sackville, one in Guysborough and one in southern Nova Scotia. There are also five satellite family daycare homes attached to daycare centers. In addition, the province has many small licensed and inspected daycare centers in people's homes, where the provider is allowed to take up to seven children. You can find out about the programs near you by calling the provincial daycare office (see appendix A).

Family daycare association
Nova Scotia also has a family daycare association that is drawing up guidelines for family daycare in the province. They can direct parents to the agency nearest them:

> Nova Scotia Family Day Care Association
> 70 Memory Lane
> Lower Sackville, Nova Scotia
> B4C 2J3
> 902-865-8982

PRINCE EDWARD ISLAND

The Prince Edward Island Department of Health and Social Services licenses family daycare homes directly. They publish an annual "Directory of Licensed Child Care Programs" that includes daycare homes. Appendix A tells you how to get a copy.

NEWFOUNDLAND

Newfoundland is in the process of developing a policy for family daycare. At the moment there are no regulated homes.

NORTHWEST TERRITORIES

Information about licensed day homes in the Northwest Territories can be obtained from the Day Care Section of the Department of Social Services listed in appendix A.

YUKON

The Yukon licenses family daycare homes individually. The Child Care Services Unit keeps a listing. See appendix A.

Sample Letter of Agreement with a Nanny or Sitter

This is an example of a letter of agreement you might write to your nanny or sitter. Of course, you may arrange the terms to suit you and the caregiver you hire. You may want to indicate more or less television time, more or fewer chores (or none at all). Make and sign two copies, one for you and one for your nanny or sitter.

> 123 Your street
> Your town, Your province
> The date

Caregiver's name
Caregiver's address

Dear Caregiver:

    We are delighted that you will be looking after our children, _____, starting next week, _____.
    You will work from _____ A.M. to _____ P.M., Monday through Friday. Your salary will be $ _____ per week, payable by check every

Friday. I will sometimes work late on Wednesdays and Thursdays and I will let you know each Monday whether I will need your help in the evenings that week. When this occurs you will be available until _____ P.M. We will pay you overtime at a rate of $ _____ per hour.

We will be responsible for remitting CPP, UIC, and income taxes. You will sign receipts for the money you are paid.

If you are ill or must be absent for any reason, you will tell me in advance (the night before, if possible) so that I can make alternate arrangements for the children. We will pay you for _____ sick days a year and for the usual statutory holidays.

You will have _____ weeks of paid vacation, which is to be taken at the same time as we take our vacation. We agree to figure out dates that are acceptable to all of us.

The children will be your top priority at all times. A detailed job description is attached, but in general you will be responsible for seeing to all of their needs during the day, including nurturing, feeding, diapering and naps, as well as their social, intellectual and physical stimulation. Weather permitting, you will take them outside to play, read them stories and organize art activities daily, and take them swimming at the Y once a week.

When the children are awake, the television set is to be turned off, except when the children are watching "Sesame Street" once a day.

You will respect and try to follow our philosophy of child rearing and discipline, encouraging and praising the children rather than criticizing them. Physical punishment or humiliation is not allowed under any circumstances and will be considered grounds for immediate dismissal.

You will give the children a nutritious lunch and two nutritious snacks every day. No candy or gum is allowed unless arranged ahead of time.

In the event of an emergency, we have supplied our work phone numbers, the number of a friend in case we can't be reached and other emergency telephone numbers and medicare numbers. Unless the children are napping, you will use the phone only for emergencies or to arrange outings for the children.

Besides taking care of the children, you will be responsible for doing their laundry and for cleaning up after their meals and playtime. You will make a salad for the family dinner every evening.

You will be on probation for two months, during which time either you or we can end this arrangement by giving two weeks' notice. Once the probation period is over, you agree to stay for at least one year, at which time we will discuss renewing this contract. We will review your salary in six months.

We look forward to working with you, and I know the children will flourish under your care.

Please sign below to indicate that you agree with these terms of employment.

_____   _____
Signature of caregiver   Signature of parent

Date _____

A LIVE-IN CAREGIVER

If your caregiver will be living in, you may want to add another paragraph or append a list of your own house rules. What do you think is appropriate behavior for a self-sufficient young woman in your house? Remember to discuss the rules with her first, and don't make any you can't enforce.

In the beginning your nanny is a stranger, and this contract is intended to protect you and your lifestyle—you don't want her boy-friend raiding your fridge every night. After several months, when you've grown to know and like one another, you can always relax the rules.

SAMPLE PARAGRAPH

You will have a private room and bath, a television and use of the family phone. The children will not be allowed in your room without your express permission. Please feel free to use all of the family areas of the house, including the kitchen, and to join us for meals and when we're watching television. You may have visitors in your own room in the evenings and weekends only, and they are to leave by 11 p.m. on weeknights and by midnight on weekends.

Sample Letter of Agreement with a Family Home Daycare Provider

This is an example of a letter of agreement between you and your family home daycare provider. Regulated, licensed caregivers usually ask you to sign a letter of their own, and in provinces where family daycare homes are regulated through an agency, the agency provides a contract. But in case your caregiver doesn't have a letter of agreement, this sample will give you an idea of how to write one. Needless to say, the letter should set out whatever terms you negotiate when you are making the arrangement.

Prepare and sign two copies, one for you and one for your family caregiver.

> 123 Your street
> Your town, Your province
> The date

Caregiver's name
Caregiver's address

Dear Caregiver:

As we agreed, starting next week, you will care for our child, _____, in your home Monday through Friday, from _____ A.M. to _____ P.M.

We will pay you $ _____ per week by check every Friday. We understand that fees are payable on statutory holidays and on days when our child doesn't come to daycare. We also agree that if we are late in picking up our child, we will pay an overtime charge of $ _____ per hour. You will provide us with signed receipts for our fees.

We understand that you will take a three-week vacation in the month of July. We will not pay for that period. If we take our vacation at a different time, we will pay the usual fees.

If anyone else is going to pick our child up at your home, we will let you know.

We will not send our child to daycare if he is sick—for example, with fever, vomiting, diarrhea or an infectious disease—and we expect that other parents will follow the same rule. If our child becomes sick at daycare, you will phone us and we will come to get him as soon as possible.

We have given you our telephone numbers at work and the numbers of two friends to contact if we can't be reached in an emergency. We have also signed a medical authorization form which includes our child's medicare number and the name and number of his doctor.

If you are unable to provide care, you will give us 12 hours' notice, and we will be responsible for finding our own backup care.

As we discussed, you will serve our child a nutritious lunch and two nutritious snacks, which do not include sweets. He will nap every afternoon. (In the case of a baby, you might say: As we discussed, you will allow our infant to set his own schedule as much as possible, permitting him to sleep and eat when he needs to. You will hold him when giving him his bottle and take him outside every day.)

One reason that we have chosen you as our daycare provider is that you understand the importance of offering our child a stimulating environment that includes daily outdoor play, stories, and art activities. (For an infant you might write: muscle exercise and sensory stimulation.) We also very much approve of your loving, nurturing care and your method of disciplining the children by praise and encouragement, rather than by restricting and criticizing them. We support your policy of not allowing them to watch television, except for "Sesame Street" once a day.

We all consider physical punishment or humiliation grounds for immediate termination of this contract. Otherwise we agree that either of us can end our relationship by giving two weeks' notice.

By signing this letter, both you and we agree to abide by its terms.

We look forward to having you as our family daycare provider.

_____   _____
Signature of caregiver   Signature of parent

Date _____

APPENDIX E

Sample
Medical Authorization Form

This form assumes that your caregiver will phone you in case of a medical emergency and that you will be meeting your child at the hospital momentarily. If you are planning to be away overnight or for longer, the form should be properly witnessed so that your caregiver can sign hospital consent forms for anesthesia and surgery.

Child's name _____ Telephone _____

Child's date of birth_____

Child's medicare number _____

Does the child have a hospital card?_____

Name of hospital _____

Hospital card number _____

Mother's name _____ Work phone _____

Father's name _____ Work phone _____

Persons to call if parents cannot be contacted:

Name _____ Telephone _____

Name _____ Telephone _____

Child's physician _____ Telephone _____

I authorize my caregiver, (her name), to obtain any emergency medical treatment deemed necessary for my child in my absence. This includes taking him to the hospital and beginning treatment before I arrive.

Date_____ Parent's Signature _____

APPENDIX F

Staff-Child Ratios for School-Age Child Care

British Columbia   6–7 years = 1:10
                          7+ years = 1:15

Alberta   5–6 years = 1:10
                          Ratios for older children are
                          set by each municipality

Saskatchewan   6–12 years = 1:15

Manitoba   5–6 years = 1:10
                          6–12 years = 1:15

Ontario   5–6 years = 1:12
                          6–12 years = 1:15

Quebec	5 years = 1:15
	6–12 years = 1:20
New Brunswick	5 years = 1:12
	6–12 years = 1:15
Nova Scotia	5–12 years = 1:15
Prince Edward Island	5–7 years = 1:12
	7+ years = 1:15
Newfoundland	5–6 years = 1:8
	7-12 years = 1:15
Northwest Territories	5–10 years = 1:10
Yukon	5–6 years = 1:10
	6–12 years = 1:12

NOTES

Introduction
1. Margie I. Mayfield, *Work-Related Child Care in Canada* (Ottawa: Women's Bureau, Labour Canada, 1990) 2-3.
2. *The First Man* (New York: Time-Life Books, 1973) 15, 130.
3. Derek Freeman, *Margaret Mead and Samoa: The Making and Unmaking of an Anthropological Myth* (Cambridge, Mass.: Harvard University Press, 1983) 202-3.

Chapter 1 "How and When to Start Thinking about Daycare"

1. T. Berry Brazelton, *Working and Caring* (Reading, Mass.: Addison-Wesley Publishing Company, Inc., 1985) xix.
2. Nancy Miller Chenier, research by Hélène Blais Bates, "The Informal Child Care Market: Public Policy for Private Homes," *Background Papers for the Task Force on Child Care* (Ottawa: Status of Women Canada, 1986) 173.
3. National Child Care Information Centre, "Status of Day Care in Canada, 1989" (Ottawa: Health and Welfare, 1990) 6-7.
4. Carollee Howes, "Quality Indicators in Infant and Toddler Child Care: The Los Angeles Study," *Quality in Child Care: What Does Research Tell Us?* ed. Deborah A. Phillips (Washington D.C.: National Association for the Education of Young Children, 1987) 86; Hillel Goelman and Alan R. Pence,

"Effects of Child Care, Family, and Individual Characteristics on Children's Language Development: The Victoria Day Care Research Project," *Quality* 89.

Chapter 2 "What Is the Best Age to Start Daycare?"

1. Mayfield 3.
2. Sandra Scarr, *Mother Care/Other Care* (New York: Warner Books Inc., 1984) 92-105; Alison Clarke-Stewart, *Daycare* (Cambridge, Mass., Harvard University Press, 1982) 71-74.
3. National Center for Clinical Infant Programs, "Consensus on Infant/ Toddler Day Care Reached by Researchers at NCCIP Meeting" (Washington D.C.: 23 Oct. 1987).
4. Brazelton 21.
5. Scarr 152.
6. Clarke-Stewart 72.
7. Brazelton 60.
8. Frank Caplan, ed., *The First Twelve Months of Life: Your Baby's Growth Month by Month* (New York: Grosset & Dunlap, 1973) 176.
9. Brazelton 61.
10. Caplan 244.
11. Sally Provence, Audrey Naylor and June Patterson, *The Challenge of Daycare* (New Haven and London: Yale University Press, 1977) 64.
12. Scarr 160-61.
13. Ellen Galinsky and Judy David, *The Preschool Years* (New York: Times Books, 1988) 117.

Chapter 4 "One Alternative: Nannies and Sitters"

1. Deborah A. Phillips and Carollee Howes, "Indicators of Quality Child Care: Review of Research," *Quality* 3-5.
2. Clarke-Stewart 123.
3. Brazelton 115.

Chapter 5 "Another Choice: Family or Home Daycare"

1. *Who Cares... A Study of Home-Based Child Caregivers in Ontario*, Vol. 1 (Ottawa: Independent Child Caregivers Association, 1990) xiii, 96-97.
2. Katie Cooke, Jack London, Renée Edwards and Ruth Rose-Lizée, *Report of the Task Force on Child Care* (Ottawa: Status of Women Canada, 1986) 122.
3. Cooke et al. 154.
4. Hélène Blais Bates, "Day Care Standards in Canada," *Background Papers for the Task Force on Child Care* 27.
5. Cooke et al. 133.
6. Clarke-Stewart 92.
7. Chenier 173.

8. A. Pence and H. Goelman, "Parents of Children in Three Types of Day Care. The Victoria Day Care Research Project" (Ottawa: Social Sciences and Humanities Research Council of Canada, 1985).
9. *Who Cares* 41.
10. K. Strangert, "Respiratory Illness in Preschool Children with Different Forms of Day Care," *Pediatrics* 57 (1976): 191-195; M. Stahlberg, "The Influence of Form of Day Care on Occurrence of Acute Respiratory Tract Infections among Young Children," *Acta Paediatr Scan* Supp. 282 (1980): 1-87; A.V. Bartlett et al., "Diarrheal Illness among Infants and Toddlers in Day Care Centers. I. Epidemiology and pathogens," *Journal of Pediatrics* 107 (1985): 495-502.
11. *Who Cares* 78.
12. Pence and Goelman, "Parents."
13. Clarke-Stewart 93; Donna S. Lero and Irene Kyle, "Day Care Quality: Its Definition and Implementation," *Background Papers for the Task Force on Child Care* 105.
14. Clarke-Stewart 106.
15. *Who Cares* 150.
16. *Who Cares* 79.
17. *Who Cares* 83.
18. *Summary Report: A Survey of Private Home Day Care Services in Ontario, 1988* (Toronto: Ontario Ministry of Community and Social Services, 1989) 7.
19. *Who Cares* 50; *Summary Report* 24.
20. Clarke-Stewart 125.
21. *Who Cares* 54.
22. Clarke-Stewart 106-107; June Deller, *Family Daycare Internationally: A Literature Review* (Toronto: Ontario Ministry of Community and Social Services, 1988) 139; Lero and Kyle 105.
23. *Who Cares* 36-39.
24. Clarke-Stewart 93.
25. *Who Cares* 72.

Chapter 7 "The Daycare Center Option"

1. Cooke et al. 95-6; 100-101.
2. Pence and Goelman, "Parents."
3. Cooke et al. 194-98; Childcare Resource and Research Unit, *Information Sheets* (Toronto: Centre for Urban and Community Studies, 1988).
4. Cooke et al. 96.

Chapter 8 "How to Find a Daycare Center"

1. Lero and Kyle 100.
2. Clarke-Stewart 93.
3. Bates 16.
4. Lero and Kyle 98.

5. Cooke et al. 130.
6. Cooke et al. 131.
7. Phillips and Howes 7.
8. Clarke-Stewart 85.
9. Cooke et al. 132.
10. Marcy Whitebook, Carollee Howes and Deborah Phillips, *Who Cares? Child Care Teachers and the Quality of Care in America.* Executive Summary National Child Care Staffing Study (Oakland, Calif.: Child Care Employee Project, 1989) 16.
11. Whitebook, Howes and Phillips 4.
12. SPR Associates Inc., *An Exploratory Review of Selected Issues in For-Profit Versus Not-For-Profit Child Care,* Report to the House of Commons Special Committee on Child Care (Ottawa: 1986) 4.
13. Julio C. Soto, *Un modèle de surveillance épidémiologique pour le contrôle des maladies infectieuses en garderie,* thèse doctorale, Université de Montréal, 199; Larry L. Pickering et al., "Acute Infectious Diarrhea Among Children in Day Care: Epidemiology and Control," *Research in Infectious Diseases* 8 (1986): 539-547.
14. *The Day Care Book,* Vicki Breitbart, ed., quoted in Ellen Galinsky and William H. Hooks, *The New Extended Family* (Boston: Houghton Mifflin, 1977) 128.
15. Whitebook, Howes and Phillips 15.
16. Sharon M. West, "A Study on Compliance with the *Day Nurseries Act* at Full-Day Child Care Centres in Metropolitan Toronto" (Toronto: Ontario Ministry of Community and Social Services, 1988) 38; Sharon Lynn Kagan and James W. Newton, "For-Profit and Nonprofit Child Care: Similarities and Differences," *Young Children* Nov. 1989: 7-8; Martha Friendly, *Daycare for Profit: Where Does the Money Go?* Report to the Special Committee on Child Care, 1986: 18-19.
17. Whitebook, Howes, and Phillips 15; Friendly 16.
18. Avril Pike, personal communication, 18 Mar. 1991.
19. Kate Fillion, "The Daycare Decision," *Saturday Night* Jan. 1989: 24.
20. Pike, personal communication.
21. SPR Associates 21.
22. Andrew McIntosh and Ann Rauhala, "Who's Minding the Children?" Toronto: Series in *Globe and Mail*, 3-8 Feb. 1989.
23. West 24, 31, 38.
24. SPR Associates 21.
25. McIntosh and Rauhala, 3 Feb. 1989, A11.
26. SPR Associates 21.
27. Rothman Beach Associates, "A Study of Work-Related Daycare in Canada," *Background Papers for the Task Force on Child Care* 91.
28. Rothman Beach Associates 93.
29. Mayfield 5-6.
30. Rothman Beach Associates 74.
31. Rothman Beach Associates 93.

32. Rothman Beach Associates 77.
33. Rothman Beach Associates 90.
34. Mayfield 53-57.
35. Mayfield 82.
36. Mayfield 115.
37. Rothman Beach Associates 112.

Chapter 10 "Interviewing the Director"

1. Clarke-Stewart 93.
2. Cooke et al. 130; Clarke-Stewart 108.
3. Clarke-Stewart 107.
4. Marcy Whitebook, Carollee Howes, Deborah Phillips and Caro Pemberton, "Who Cares? Child Care Teachers and the Quality of Care in America," *Young Children* Nov. 1989: 45.
5. Monica Townson, "Care for Sick Children: The Issues, the Responsibilities,
   and the Cost," Presentation to Conference on Financing Sick Child Care,
   Waterloo Region Branch, Victorian Order of Nurses, 19 Feb. 1990: 7.
6. Brazelton 89.

Chapter 11 "How to Look at a Daycare Center"

1. T. Berry Brazelton, "Cementing Family Relationships," *Infants We Care
   For*, ed. Laura L. Dittmann (Washington D.C.: National Association for
   the Education of Young Children, 1973 and 1984) 4.
2. Hermine H. Marshall, "The Development of Self-Concept," *Young Children* July 1989: 47.
3. Marshall 47.
4. Robert E. Black et al., "Handwashing to Prevent Diarrhea in Day-Care
   Centers," *American Journal of Epidemiology* 113 (1981): 445-451.
5. Dr. Julio C. Soto, personal interview, 14 Feb. 1990.
6. Abby Shapiro Kendrick, Roxane Kaufmann and Katherine P. Messenger,
   eds., *Healthy Young Children* (Washington D.C.: National Association for
   the Education of Young Children, 1988) 25-28.
7. Burton L. White and Michael K. Meyerhoff, "What *Is* Best for the Baby?"
   Infants We Care For 28.
8. Soto, *Un modèle de surveillance épidémiologique*.
9. Black et al.
10. Clarke-Stewart 128.
11. Alison Clarke-Stewart, "Predicting Child Development from Child Care
    Forms and Features: The Chicago Study," *Quality* 37.
12. Penelope Leach, *Your Baby and Child From Birth to Age Five* (New York:
    Alfred A. Knopf, 1988) 406.
13. Leach 365.
14. Clarke-Stewart, *Daycare* 85.

Chapter 15 "The Parents' Role in Ensuring a Positive Experience"

1. Scarr 19.
2. Brazelton, *Working and Caring* 94.
3. Brazelton, *Working and Caring* 93.
4. Brazelton, *Working and Caring* 184.
5. Galinsky and David 117; Provence, Naylor and Patterson 97.
6. Galinsky and David 120.
7. Galinsky and David 203.
8. Cooke et al. 132.
9. Galinsky and David 385.

Chapter 17 "Daycare and Your Child's Health"

1. Ken Finkel et al., "Report of the Canadian Pediatric Society Task Force on Quality Out-of-home Child Care," *Canadian Children* 14 (1989): 9.
2. Finkel et al. 9.
3. Pickering et al. 539-547.
4. Kendrick, Kaufmann and Messenger 249, 251.
5. Soto, personal interview.
6. Julio C. Soto, "L'impact des maladies infectieuses en garderie pour l'enfant, la famille et la communauté" in *Cours d'education sanitaire pour le personnel des garderies* (Montreal: Département de santé communautaire Hôpital St-Luc, 1989) 14.
7. Soto, personal interview.
8. Soto, personal interview.
9. Finkel et al. 9; Kendrick, Kaufmann and Messenger 233, 240-243.
10. Kendrick, Kaufmann and Messenger 265.
11. Kendrick, Kaufmann and Messenger 234; Soto, personal interview.
12. Martha Friendly, Gordon Cleveland and Tricia Willis, "Flexible Child Care in Canada" (Toronto: The Childcare Resource and Research Unit, 1989) 15.
13. Friendly, Cleveland and Willis 10.

Chapter 18 "Parent Committees and Boards of Directors"

1. Polly Greenberg, "Parents as Partners in Young Children's Development and Education: A New American Fad? Why Does It Matter?" *Young Children* May 1989: 62.
2. Cooke et al. 129.
3. West 23-24.
4. Richard Cloutier, "Pourquoi des parents à la garderie?" *Petit à petit* 3(6), mars 1985: 22-24, quoted in Alma Estable, *Choosing with Care: Selected Literature on Some Aspects of Infant and Toddler Daycare Research* (Ottawa: Child Care Education Services, 1989) 80.

Chapter 19 "The Second Child"

1. Cooke et al. 58.

Chapter 20 "Switching Daycare"

1. Clarke-Stewart, *Daycare* 109.
2. Phillips and Howes 10; Clarke-Stewart, *Daycare* 109.
3. Phillips and Howes 10.
4. Fredelle Maynard, *The Child Care Crisis: The Thinking Parent's Guide to Daycare* (Markham, Ont.: Penguin Books, 1986) 114.
5. Phillips and Howes 10.
6. Howes 82.
7. Maynard 212.
8. Alan R. Pence and Hillel Goelman, *The Puzzle of Day-care: Choosing the Right Child Care Arrangement* (Toronto: University of Toronto Guidance Centre, 1986) 46; Clarke-Stewart, *Daycare* 109.
9. Clarke-Stewart 109-110.
10. Clarke-Stewart 110.
11. Galinsky and Hooks 249.
12. Galinsky and David 442.
13. Brazelton, *Working and Caring* 104.
14. E. Vandell, V. Henderson and K. Wilson, "A Longitudinal Study of Children with Day-Care Experience of Varying Quality," *Child Development* 59 (1988): 1286-1292; Carollee Howes, "Relations between Early Child Care and Schooling," *Developmental Psychology* 24 (1) (1988): 53-57.
15. David Finkelhor et al., "Sexual Abuse in Day Care: A National Study— Executive Summary" (Durham, N.H.: University of New Hampshire Family Research Laboratory, 1988), quoted in Estable 143.

Box "When Your Child's Teacher Leaves"

1. Whitebook, Howes, Phillips and Pemberton 44; Whitebook, Howes and Phillips 4.
2. Phillips and Howes 10.

Chapter 21 "Where Do We Go from Here? School-Age Child Care"

1. Mayfield 3.
2. National Child Care Information Centre 7.
3. This caregiver talked about her situation at "Grandir avec toi," Conference on School-Based Child Care, Montreal, 27-29 Oct. 1989.
4. Donna White, personal communication, 28 Sept. 1990.
5. Andrea Genser and Clifford Bedan, eds., *School-Age Child Care: Programs and Issues*, Papers from a June 1979 conference at Wheelock College (Urbana, Ill.: ERIC Clearinghouse on Elementary and Early Childhood Education, 1980) 63.

6. Jake Kuiken, "School-Aged Child Care Programs Outside Quebec," Round-table discussion at "Grandir avec toi."

7. Ruth Kramer Baden et al., *School-Age Child Care, An Action Manual* (Dover, Mass.: Auburn House Publishing Company, 1982) 65-66.

8. Cooke 130.

9. Donna S. Lero, "Balancing Work, Family and Child Care," Workshop at "Grandir avec toi."

10. Helen L. Swan and Victoria Houston, *Alone After School: A Self-Care Guide for Latchkey Children and Their Parents* (Englewood Cliffs, N.J.: Prentice-Hall, Inc., 1985) vii.

11. Jake Kuiken, *Latchkey Children*, Report to the House of Commons Special Committee on Child Care (Calgary: 1987) 9; Martha Friendly, personal communication, Nov. 1990.

12. Kuiken, *Latchkey Children* 26.

13. Nancy P. Alexander, "School-Age Child Care: Concerns and Challenges," *School-Age Child Care* (Washington D.C.: National Association for the Education of Young Children, [no date]) 14-15.

14. Judith Bender, Barbara Schuyler-Haas Elden and Charles H. Flatter, *Half a Childhood: Time for School-Age Child Care* (Nashville, Tenn.: School Age Notes, 1984) 12.

15. Swan and Houston 26.

16. Margie I. Mayfield, "School-aged Child Care Programs Outside Quebec," Round-table discussion at "Grandir avec toi."

17. Swan and Houston 17.

18. Kuiken, *Latchkey Children* 85; Alexander 14.

BIBLIOGRAPHY

Alexander, Nancy P. "School-Age Child Care: Concerns and Challenges."
School-Age Child Care. NAEYC Resource Guide. Washington D.C.: National
Association for the Education of Young Children, [no date].

Background Papers for the Task Force on Child Care. Ottawa: Status of
Women Canada, 1986.

Baden, Ruth Kramer, Andrea Genser, James A. Levine and Michelle Seligson.
School-Age Child Care, An Action Manual. Dover, Mass.: Auburn House
Publishing Company, 1982.

Bartlett, A.V. et al. "Diarrheal Illness among Infants and Toddlers in Day Care
Centers. I. Epidemiology and pathogens." *Journal of Pediatrics* 107
(1985): 495-502.

Belsky, Jay. "Infant Day Care: A Cause for Concern?" *Zero to Three*. Sept.
1986.

Bender, Judith, Barbara Schuyler-Haas Elden, and Charles H. Flatter. *Half a
Childhood: Time for School-Age Child Care.* Nashville, Tenn.: School Age
Notes, 1984.

Bertrand, Jane. *C-PET Key Informant Survey: A Survey of Key Informants
Involved with Parent/Community Boards of Directors for Non Profit Child*

Care Services in Ontario, 1989. Toronto: Ontario Coalition for Better Child Care, 1989.

Black, Robert E., et al. "Handwashing to Prevent Diarrhea in Day-Care Centers." *American Journal of Epidemiology* 113 (1981): 445-451.

Brazelton, T. Berry. *Working and Caring.* Reading, Mass.: Addison-Wesley Publishing Company, Inc., 1985.

Bredekamp, Sue, ed. *Developmentally Appropriate Practice in Early Childhood Programs Serving Children From Birth Through Age 8.* Expanded edition. Washington D.C.: National Association for the Education of Young Children, 1987.

Breese, Charlotte and Hilaire Gomer. *The Good Nanny Guide: The Complete Low-down on Nannies, Au Pairs and Mother's Helps.* London: Century, 1988.

Caplan, Frank, ed. *The First Twelve Months of Life: Your Baby's Growth Month by Month.* New York: Grosset & Dunlap, 1973.

Child Care Board of Directors' Handbook. Toronto: Ontario Coalition for Better Child Care, 1990.

Childcare Resource and Research Unit. *Information Sheets.* Toronto: Centre for Urban and Community Studies, 1988.

Childcare Resource and Research Unit and City of Toronto Planning and Development Department. *Children at Child Care, Parents at Work.* Toronto: Ontario Ministry of Community and Social Services and City of Toronto, [no date].

Clarke-Stewart, Alison. *Daycare.* The Developing Child Series. Cambridge, Mass.: Harvard University Press, 1982.

Cooke, Katie, Jack London, Renée Edwards and Ruth Rose-Lizée. *Report of the Task Force on Child Care.* Ottawa: Status of Women Canada, 1986.

Darragh, Colleen. *The Perfect Nanny.* Toronto: Window Editions, 1988.

Day Care and the Canadian School System: A CEA Survey of Child Care Services in Schools. Toronto: Canadian Education Association, 1983.

Deller, June. *Family Daycare Internationally: A Literature Review.* Toronto: Ontario Ministry of Community and Social Services, 1988.

Dittmann, Laura L., ed. *The Infants We Care For.* Revised edition. Washington D.C.: National Association for the Education of Young Children, 1973 and 1984.

Doxey, Isabel and Anne Ellison. *School-Based Childcare: Where Do We Stand?* Canadian School Trustees' Association, [1990].

"Employer-Supported Child Care." *Child Care Directions.* Toronto: Ontario Ministry of Community and Social Services, Oct. 1988.

Estable, Alma. *Choosing with Care: Selected Literature on Some Aspects of Infants and Toddler Daycare Research*. Ottawa: Child Care Education Services, 1989.

Fillion, Kate. "The Daycare Decision." *Saturday Night*. Jan. 1989.

Finkel, Ken, et al. "Report of the Canadian Pediatric Society Task Force on Quality Out-of-home Child Care." *Canadian Children* 14 (1989): 1-22.

The First Man. New York: Time-Life Books, 1973.

Fraiberg, Selma H. *The Magic Years: Understanding and Handling the Problems of Early Childhood*. New York: Charles Scribner's Sons, 1959.

Freeman, Derek. *Margaret Mead and Samoa: The Making and Unmaking of an Anthropological Myth*. Cambridge, Mass.: Harvard University Press, 1983.

Friendly, Martha. *Daycare for Profit: Where Does the Money Go?* Report to the House of Commons Special Committee on Child Care. Toronto: Childcare Resource and Research Unit, 1986.

Friendly, Martha, Gordon Cleveland and Tricia Willis. *Flexible Child Care in Canada*. Toronto: Childcare Resource and Research Unit, 1989.

Galinsky, Ellen. *The Six Stages of Parenthood*. Reading, Mass.: Addison-Wesley Publishing Company, Inc., 1987.

Galinsky, Ellen and Judy David. *The Preschool Years*. New York: Times Books, 1988.

Galinsky, Ellen and William H. Hooks. *The New Extended Family*. Boston: Houghton Mifflin, 1977.

Genser, Andrea and Clifford Bedan, eds. *School-Age Child Care: Programs and Issues*. Papers from a June 1979 conference at Wheelock College. Urbana, Ill.: ERIC Clearinghouse on Elementary and Early Childhood Education, 1980.

Godwin, Annabelle and Lorraine Schrag, eds. *Setting Up For Infant Care: Guidelines for Centers and Family Day Care Homes*. Washington D.C.: National Association for the Education of Young Children, 1988.

"Grandir avec toi." 4th Conference on School-Based Child Care. Montreal: 27-29 Oct. 1989.

Greenberg, Polly. "Parents as Partners in Young Children's Development and Education: A New American Fad? Why Does It Matter?" *Young Children*. May 1989.

Howes, C. "Relations between Early Child Care and Schooling." *Developmental Psychology* 24 (1988), 53-57.

Information Sheets. Toronto: Childcare Resource and Research Unit, 1988.

Johnson, Laura C. and Janice Dineen. *The Kin Trade: The Day Care Crisis in Canada*. Toronto: McGraw-Hill Ryerson Limited, 1981.

Kagan, Sharon Lynn, and James W. Newton. "For-Profit and Nonprofit Child

Care: Similarities and Differences." *Young Children*. Nov. 1989.

Kendrick, Abby Shapiro, Roxane Kaufmann and Katherine P. Messenger, eds. *Healthy Young Children*. Washington D.C.: National Association for the Education of Young Children, 1988.

Kuiken, Jake. *Latchkey Children*. Report to the House of Commons Special Committee on Child Care. Calgary: 1987.

——. *School-Age Child Care*. Ottawa: Health and Welfare Canada, 1985.

Leach, Penelope. *Your Baby and Child From Birth to Age Five*. New York: Alfred A. Knopf, 1988.

Marshall, Hermine H. "The Development of Self-Concept." *Young Children*. July 1989.

Mayfield, Margie I. *Employer-Supported Child Care in Canada*. Ottawa: Health and Welfare Canada, 1985.

——. *Work-Related Child Care in Canada*. Ottawa: Women's Bureau, Labour Canada, 1990.

Maynard, Fredelle. *The Child Care Crisis: The Thinking Parent's Guide to Daycare*. Markham, Ont.: Penguin Books, 1986.

McIntosh, Andrew and Ann Rauhala. "Who's Minding the Children?" Four-part series. *Globe and Mail*. 3-7 Feb. 1989.

National Child Care Information Centre. *Status of Day Care in Canada, 1989*. Ottawa: Health and Welfare, 1990.

National Center for Clinical Infant Programs. "Consensus on Infant/Toddler Day Care Reached by Researchers at NCCIP Meeting." Press release. Washington D.C.: 23 Oct. 1987.

"Parent/Community Boards." *Child Care Directions*, Toronto: Ontario Ministry of Community and Social Services, July 1988.

Pence, Alan R., and Hillel Goelman. "Parents of Children in Three Types of Day Care. The Victoria Day Care Research Project." Ottawa: Social Sciences and Humanities Research Council of Canada, 1985.

——. *The Puzzle of Day-care: Choosing the Right Child Care Arrangement*. Toronto: University of Toronto, Guidance Centre, 1986.

Phillips, Deborah A., ed. *Quality in Child Care: What Does Research Tell Us?* Washington D.C.: National Association for the Education of Young Children, 1987.

Phillips, Deborah, Kathleen McCartney, Sandra Scarr and Carollee Howes. "Selective Review of Infant Day Care Research: A Cause for Concern!" *Zero to Three*. Feb. 1987.

Pickering, Larry L., Alfred V. Bartlett and William E. Woodward. "Acute Infectious Diarrhea Among Children in Day Care: Epidemiology and Control." *Research in Infectious Diseases* 8 (1986): 539-547.

Provence, Sally, Audrey Naylor and June Patterson. *The Challenge of Daycare*. New Haven and London: Yale University Press, 1977.

Ross, Kathleen Gallagher. *A Parents' Guide to Day Care: Finding the Best Alternative for Your Child.* Vancouver: Self-Counsel Press Ltd., 1984.

———, ed. *Good Day Care: Fighting For It, Getting It, Keeping It.* Toronto: The Women's Press, 1978.

Scarr, Sandra. *Mother Care/Other Care.* New York: Warner Books Inc., 1984.

Secor, Christine Dimock, ed. *A Handbook for Day Care Board Members.* New York: Day Care Council of New York, Inc., 1984.

Soto, Julio C. "L'impact des maladies infectieuses en garderie pour l'enfant, la famille et la communauté." *Cours d'education sanitaire pour le personnel des garderies.* Montreal: Département de santé communautaire Hôpital Saint-Luc, 1989.

———.*Un modèle de surveillance épidémiologique pour le contrôle des maladies infectieuses en garderie.* Thèse doctorale. Université de Montréal, 1990.

———. Personal interview. 14 Feb. 1990.

———, ed. *La santé... ça se garde.* Un colloque sur la prévention des infections en garderie. Montreal: Département de santé communautaire de l'Hôpital Saint-Luc, [1988].

SPR Associates Inc. *An Exploratory Review of Selected Issues in For-Profit Versus Not for-Profit Child Care.* Report to the House of Commons Special Committee on Child Care. Toronto: 1986.

Stahlberg, M. "The Influence of Form of Day Care on Occurrence of Acute Respiratory Tract Infections among Young Children." *Acta Paediatr Scan* Supp. 282 (1980): 1-87.

Stanwick, Richard. "Safety in Day Care is no Accident." *Interaction.* Winter 1989.

Strangert, K. "Respiratory Illness in Preschool Children with Different Forms of Day Care." *Pediatrics* 57 (1976): 191-195.

Summary Report: A Survey of Private Home Day Care Services in Ontario, 1988. Toronto: Ontario Ministry of Community and Social Services, 1989.

Swan, Helen L. and Victoria Houston. *Alone After School: A Self-Care Guide for Latchkey Children and Their Parents.* Englewood Cliffs, N.J.: Prentice-Hall, Inc., 1985.

Townson, Monica. "Care for Sick Children: The Issues, the Responsibilities and the Cost." Presentation to Conference on Financing Sick Child Care, Waterloo Region Branch, Victorian Order of Nurses. 19 Feb. 1990.

Umbrella Board Manual. Toronto: Umbrella Central Day Care Services, 1990.

Vandell, E., V. Henderson and K. Wilson. "A Longitudinal Study of Children with Day-care Experience of Varying Quality." *Child Development* 59 (1988): 1286-1292.

Weissbourd, Bernice and Judith Musick, eds. *Infants: Their Social Envi-*

ronments. Washington D.C.: National Association for the Education of Young Children, 1981.

West, Sharon M. *A Study on Compliance with the Day Nurseries Act at Full-Day Child Care Centres in Metropolitan Toronto.* Toronto: Ontario Ministry of Community and Social Services, 1988.

White, Donna. Personal interview. 28 Sept. 1990.

Whitebook, Marcy, Carollee Howes and Deborah Phillips. *Who Cares? Child Care Teachers and the Quality of Care in America.* Executive Summary National Child Care Staffing Study. Oakland, Calif.: Child Care Employee Project, 1989.

Whitebook, Marcy, Carollee Howes, Deborah Phillips and Caro Pemberton. "Who Cares? Child Care Teachers and the Quality of Care in America." *Young Children.* Nov. 1989.

Who Cares... A Study of Home-Based Child Caregivers in Ontario. Vol. 1. Ottawa: Independent Child Caregivers Association, 1990.

INDEX

Printed in Canada